Jewish Women in Fin de Siècle Vienna

T0373070

Jewish History, Life, and Culture
Michael Neiditch, Series Editor

Alison Rose

*Jewish Women in
Fin de Siècle Vienna*

University of Texas Press Austin

The Jewish History, Life, and Culture Series is supported by the late Milton T. Smith and the Moshana Foundation, and the Tocker Foundation.

Requests for permission to reproduce material from this work should be sent to:
Permissions
University of Texas Press
P.O. Box 7819
Austin, TX 78713-7819
www.utexas.edu/utpress/about/bpermission.html

∞ The paper used in this book meets the minimum requirements of
ANSI/NISO Z39.48-1992 (R1997) (Permanence of Paper).

Library of Congress Cataloging-in-Publication Data

Rose, Alison.
  Jewish women in fin de siècle Vienna / Alison Rose.
      p.   cm. — (Jewish history, life, and culture)
  Includes bibliographical references and index.
  ISBN 13: 978-0-292-72159-3   ISBN 10: 0-292-72159-5
  1. Jews—Austria—Vienna—History—19th century.   2. Jews—Austria—Vienna—History—20th century.   3. Jewish women—Austria—Vienna—Social life
and customs—19th century.   4. Jewish women—Austria—Vienna—Social life
and customs—20th century.   5. Jewish women—Austria—Vienna—Social conditions—19th century.   6. Jewish women—Austria—Vienna—Social conditions—
20th century.   7. Jewish women—Austria—Vienna—Education.   8. Jews—
Austria—Vienna—Identity.   9. Vienna (Austria)—Ethnic relations.   I. Title.
  DS135.A9R595   2008
  305.48'892404361309034—dc22
                                                        2008011078

To Mitch, Ilan, and Keshet

Contents

Preface and Acknowledgments

During the course of my research and writing on Jewish women in fin de siècle Vienna, which began with the early stages of my dissertation research in 1989, I have come to feel quite close to the personalities I study, without of course having met any of them. Whenever I have found that one of these women met a tragic end I have felt an inevitable sadness and despair. While unfortunately many ended their lives in tragedy, I hope that my work will help them to be remembered for their caring and compassion for their fellow human beings, which guided them in their lives, as well as for their accomplishments, which are manifold. So many of the women in this study devoted themselves to bettering the world in which they lived, to improving the lives of the less fortunate, to contributing to progress in humanistic and scientific scholarship, to expanding the possibilities for education and freedom for youth. The tragedy that in many cases no one was there for them in their hour of need inspires me to see that I do all I can to prevent similar injustices from being perpetrated in the present. I hope that in some small way, telling the stories of these women, their struggles, their successes, and their inner strength, will inspire readers to think more about the way that they perceive and treat those who appear to be different or "other" in their world today.

I would like to express my deep appreciation to many individuals and institutions that have provided essential assistance and support for me during my research, which is now in its second decade! I apologize for any inevitable omissions as over the years I have crossed paths with so many, and I of course am solely responsible for all errors.

My parents, Myna and Terry, and my sister, Holly, have always been there for me, believed in me, and supported me in countless ways. I first learned my love of history from my history teacher at Aspen High School, George Burson, and I first learned that I cared about politics and was destined for a career involving public speaking from my speech and debate coach at Aspen High, Ken Lyon. These experiences and my desire to move further west led me to an incredible learning experience at Reed College, where I was constantly engaged and excited by many inspiring professors—especially Christine Mueller, who advised my senior thesis and ignited my interest in the Habsburg monarchy; Richard Wolin, who introduced me to intellectual history; and Leila Berner, who first taught me Jewish history. At the University of Washington in 1986 I benefited from several supportive professors, particularly Hillel Kieval, who advised me for my master's thesis on Arnold Schoenberg, and John Toews, who furthered my knowledge of European intellectual history, introducing me to the work of Carl Schorske.

My time at the Hebrew University of Jerusalem working on my Ph.D. was enriched by many professors, friends, and fellow graduate students. There is no way I can begin to express my gratitude to Robert Wistrich, who took me on as his graduate student and advised me in writing my dissertation. I learned so much from his wisdom and knowledge of Viennese Jewry, anti-Semitism, and Zionism. Without his support I am certain I would not have made it this far. As a recipient of a Wiener Library Fellowship in 1992 on the topic of women in European history, I pursued my research in the supportive environment of Tel Aviv University under the guidance of Shulamit Volkov and Billie Melman, who both provided direction and feedback on my work in progress. Participation in the University of Vienna Summer School in Ströbl helped me immeasurably with the German language, and there I formed connections with the Heine family in Mödling, the Rossbachers of Salzburg, and Ursula Reisenberger, all of whom supported me during my research. Also, the Liska and Moskovits families kindly hosted me for Shabbatot in Vienna.

During the writing of my dissertation and after, many have provided guidance and advice, lending their expertise to help me develop my ideas, pursue my research, and refine my arguments, and offering various sorts of assistance. Among those who have provided feedback and suggestions at various stages of my research and writing are Paula Hyman, Marion Kaplan, Susannah Heschel, Steven Aschheim, Sander Gilman, David Biale, Marsha Rozenblit, Ben Baader, Claudia Prestel, Keith Pickus, Alan Levinson, Jay Berkowitz, Howard Adelman, John Hewitt, Alan Zuckerman, Jay Harris, Mark Kaplowitz, Michael Silber, Lisa Pollard, Elisabeth Malleier, Klaus Hödl, Michael Satlow, and Harriet Freidenreich. Sometimes a simple word of encouragement or kindness was all I needed to regain my commitment and drive, and there was always someone there to provide it when it was most needed. All of my friends in Providence and beyond have been there for me at those times.

Several institutions have also provided support for my research over the years. These include the Inter-University Fellowship in Jewish Studies, the Tel Aviv University/Wiener Library Seminar, the Fritz Halbers Fellowship of the Leo Baeck Institute, the Research Center for Hungarian Jewry at the Hebrew University of Jerusalem, the Jewish Studies Institute, Hebrew University, and the Center for Jewish Studies at Harvard University. Librarians and archivists in many institutions have provided essential assistance, including the Central Archives for the History of the Jewish People, the Leo Baeck Institute, the Austrian National Library, the Wiener Stadt- und Landesarchiv, the Wiener Stadt- und Landesbibliothek, the Austrian Resistance Archives, the Widener Library, the Schlesinger Library, the Radcliffe Institute, the Austrian National Library, the Jewish National and University Library at Givat Ram, and the University of Rhode Island Library.

My students and colleagues in the History Department and at the College of Continuing Education at the University of Rhode Island have been a wonderful source of support and inspiration for me, and I have often gained new insights about European history from students in my European History courses.

At the Association for Jewish Studies conference of 2005, I had the pleasure of sharing a taxi to the airport with Jim Burr, who, as it turned out, was from the University of Texas Press, which was in the process of launching a new series in Jewish Studies. Jim has been a fantastic editor, and his enthusiasm for this project and his friendly and disarming manner have been much appreciated. I also thank manuscript editor Megan Giller for her enthusiasm for and dedication to this project.

When I got married, in 1990, I not only gained a husband, but I also gained a second set of parents. Liz and Ron Levine have been an immense source of support, and I feel truly honored to have them as my parents-in-law. And finally, I owe my biggest thanks to my lovely, warm, and entertaining family for being there for me and understanding when I am not there for them. I am so happy to be with them, and so I dedicate this work to Mitchell, Ilan, and Keshet.

Jewish Women in Fin de Siècle Vienna

Introduction

In fin de siècle Vienna, Jewish women figured prominently as heroines and victims in Jewish tales of the ghetto and as subjects of Freud's most famous case studies of hysteria. They attended the University of Vienna when it opened its doors to women, built new and progressive schools, organized more than a dozen charity societies, and joined political movements, contributing many important ideas. They became doctors, teachers, scientists, socialists, psychoanalysts, Zionists, and writers. However, a perusal of the literature on Vienna, both in Jewish and general history, gives the reader a very different impression. In fact, Jewish women are virtually absent from most works on fin de siècle Vienna and Viennese Jewry.[1] What accounts for this discrepancy?

Sexual instincts, human psychology, mass politics, and cultural modernism: these notions bring to mind the Austrian fin de siècle. Because of their enduring relevance, they also account for contemporary interest in the phenomenon which Carl Schorske coined *fin de siècle Vienna*.[2] The attempt to explain these enduring cultural and political developments occupies many works on fin de siècle Vienna, while works specifically on Viennese Jewry focus on the Jewish contribution to culture, assimilation, identity, and anti-Semitism.[3]

Pierre Loving wrote in 1916, "As long as men and women will continue to be intrigued by the elusive enigma of life, by subtle states of the soul, by problems of the subliminal self, so long, we may venture to predict, will the plays of Arthur Schnitzler compel attention from the truly great audiences of the world."[4] Schnitzler, alongside many of his Jewish contemporaries in Vienna such as Sigmund Freud, Theodor Herzl, Arthur Schoenberg, Karl Kraus, and Otto Weininger, occupies a central role in histories of fin de siècle Vienna, demonstrating on the one hand the importance of the Jewish element in the cultural and political milieu, and on the other hand, that those Jews remembered for their contributions to fin de siècle Vienna were primarily male. Schorske tends to downplay the Jewish role in Viennese culture in general, subsuming it into the bourgeoisie, writing that "the failure to acquire a monopoly of power left the bourgeois always something of an outsider, seeking integration with the aristocracy. The numerous and prosperous Jewish element in Vienna, with its strong assimilationist thrust, only strengthened this trend."[5] As a corrective, many have noted the importance of Jews in Viennese culture; however, usually the focus is on male Jews. For example, Marsha Rozenblit writes that Jews "played a central role in creating modern culture in Austria. Franz Kafka, Stefan Zweig, Arthur Schnitzler, Karl Kraus, Otto Weininger, Richard Beer-Hofmann, Sigmund Freud, Gustav Mahler and Arnold Schoenberg are just a few of many outstanding cultural figures of Jewish background in Austria."[6] Reading Schorske's work and many of the subsequent studies inspired by it begs the question: where were Jewish women in all this?[7]

The goal of this book is to reintegrate Jewish women into the history of turn of the century Vienna in order to demonstrate their importance as cultural creators. At the same time, it is the first work to focus on images and perceptions of Jewish women in Viennese Jewish sources. In both respects this reintegration of Jewish women into the study of the culture of fin de siècle Vienna necessitates a revision of the historical narrative. For example, images of Jewish women as well as their personal struggles and activities demonstrate that fin de siècle Vienna can no longer be thought of as a place where "any of the city's cultural leaders could make the acquaintance of any other without difficulty and many of them were in fact close friends despite working in quite distinct fields of art, thought and public affairs."[8] In fact, women in general and Jewish women in particular often were unable to find positions due to their gender, and faced more obstacles to successful careers than did Jewish men. Furthermore, Jewish women in Vienna became actively engaged in politics, calling into question the view of some historians that the culture was dominated by men who retreated into aesthetic culture when faced with the decline of liberalism.[9]

Jews and women of the Habsburg monarchy both underwent somewhat similar processes during the nineteenth century. Both experienced the fight for emancipation, being defined by the dominant culture as the "other," and the emergence (or re-emergence) of a group consciousness. Because of their status as "other," Jews and women in Viennese culture shared many similarities of image. Issues of gender and sexuality occupied a central role in cultural and political life. Responding to the emergence of a "feminist consciousness," the male-dominated society dedicated its efforts to defining the appropriate realms of activity for men and women.[10] In comparison with the status of Jews, emancipated in 1867, similar achievements for women lagged behind. Women lacked civil freedom, facing restrictive codes of dress and conduct, and limited educational opportunities.[11]

Jewish men's representations of Jewish women took place in the context of the gender question, the Jewish question, and their intersection in Viennese culture of the fin de siècle, a time of profound cultural, social, and political innovation and turmoil. As in all times of crisis and change, those invested in the traditional social order feared groups, such as Jews and women, who appeared to threaten the status quo. This widespread anxiety resulted in a dual crisis of masculinity and Jewish identity. The perceived Judaization and feminization of Viennese culture gave rise to hostility toward women and Jews.[12] The demonizing of women and Jews went hand in hand with the linking of these groups to one another. Having roots in earlier stereotypes, such as the medieval notion of the menstruating male Jew, the linking of the Jew and the woman resonated powerfully in turn of the century Vienna. The belief in the femininity of male Jews naturally led to a growing tendency from within the host culture to blame Jews for the so-called feminization of Viennese culture.

The dominant culture often portrayed the Jews as feminine, materialistic, and sexually deviant or aggressive, and questioned their loyalty to the state. These stereotypes in many respects mirror the fin de siècle images of women, which juxtaposed the ideal of the virtuous mother with the dangerous, seductive prostitute. This dual image of the woman rose to prominence in fin de siècle culture in general, while the linking of the Jew with femininity and sexuality arguably found its most fertile breeding ground in Vienna.

This cultural linking of Jews and women in the dominant culture influenced the lives of Jewish men and women as well as the frequency and nature of images of Jewish women created by Jewish men. For Viennese Jews, the woman seemed to embody their own sense of difference. The Viennese preoccupation with sexuality combined with the discourse about Jewish sexuality compelled many Viennese Jewish men and women to confront the question of Jewish women's otherness. As a result, Jewish men displaced anxieties of their own sexual difference onto women. The gender stereotypes created by Jewish men in their representations of women assisted them in negotiating their way through the changes and challenges of modernity. Each segment of the Jewish population created stereotypes of the Jewish woman in order to address its own dilemmas. Discussions and depictions of Jewish women can be found in the works of Viennese Jews of every conceivable political, intellectual, and religious orientation.

These circumstances contributed to the difficult, at times hostile, environment which confronted Viennese Jewish women. Jewish women's scope of involvement in society, culture, and politics remained circumscribed by the resulting stereotypes of them, but at the same time their activities allowed them an avenue by which to negotiate their way through the conflicting ideologies of their environment. Jewish women used their involvement in various movements in coming to terms with their dual identity as Jews and women. In social and political activism and creative output, Jewish women found ways to reconcile multiple loyalties and competing ideologies, such as femininity, feminism, traditional Judaism, religious reform, and assimilation. The experiences of Jewish women in fin de siècle Vienna represent an early attempt to forge a positive Jewish female identity amid a male-dominated non-Jewish host culture.

This study focuses primarily on two aspects of Viennese Jewish women's identity, as Jews and as women, but the context in which they negotiated these identities, in the capital of the multinational Habsburg monarchy, is important as well. Recently, Marsha Rozenblit put forward the tripartite identity thesis as a way of understanding Austrian Jewish identities, which she explains as follows:

> The very structure of the Habsburg Monarchy allowed Jews a great deal of latitude to adumbrate a Jewish ethnic identity, even as they adopted the culture of one or another group in whose midst they lived and articulated a staunch Austrian political loyalty. Jews in Habsburg Austria developed a tripartite identity in which they were Austrian by political loyalty, German (or Czech or Polish) by cultural affiliation, and Jewish in an ethnic sense.[13]

With this analysis, Rozenblit provides a useful tool for the understanding of the complex nature of Jewish identity in Austria. It was an identity with many interwoven strands and one which allowed Habsburg Jewry more room for their Jewishness, according to Rozenblit. For the Jewish women explored in this book, gender also played an important role in their identity. Perhaps by taking gender into account, Austrian Jewish women can be understood as having a quadripartite identity—Austrian loyalty, German (or other) culture, Jewish ethnicity, and female gender, which in itself could be manifested in feminism or in femininity or in some combination of the two. The female aspect of their identity affected and was affected by the other aspects of their identity. For example, it shaped how they saw themselves as Jews.

The following chapters aim to reinsert the Jewish woman into her proper place as a pivotal figure both in the fin de siècle imagination and in the everyday reality of Viennese society, politics, and culture. I will examine the history and images of Viennese Jewish women, their activities, affiliations, and writings, in light of the dilemmas and limitations they faced due to gender-based and anti-Semitic stereotypes. Sources such as memoirs, letters, diaries, organizational pamphlets, newspaper articles, and speeches chronicle the lives of Jewish women in fin de siècle Vienna. At the same time, writings by Jewish men in all segments of society about Jewish women document the development of stereotypes which accompanied Jewish women at each stage of their lives and every avenue of their involvement and activity. Jewish women's accomplishments in this period of time will be understood in their integral relationship to the historical and cultural context.

It seems logical to begin with the earliest stages of the lives of Jewish women, by focusing on their girlhood years. Therefore, Chapter 1 explores the feelings of Viennese Jewish girls about their Jewish and gender identity by examining the accounts of childhood in memoirs. The home life and the school environment encountered by Jewish girls are reflected in their recollections and in the writings of leaders in the organized Jewish community about religious lessons and anti-Semitism in schools and the upbringing of Jewish girls in the home.

Continuing the focus on the Jewish community, in Chapter 2 I examine the adult lives of Jewish women in the context of the organized community and the role of prayer and philanthropy. Jewish prayer books for women and the proliferation of Jewish women's charitable organizations are contrasted with the writings of the major rabbinic leaders of Vienna, Adolf Jellinek, Moritz Güdemann, and Joseph Samuel Bloch, as well as other communal leaders on Jewish women. While the former indicate an attachment to Jewish tradition among Jewish women, Viennese rabbis and communal leaders tended to idealize Jewish women of the past, suggesting the need to improve Jewish women of the present. They also demonstrate their conflicting desire to make Judaism relevant in the modern world while retaining Jewish distinctiveness. Their need to clarify the Jewish position on women and the role of women in Judaism resulted from their confrontation with modernity, the women's movement, anti-Semitism, and religious reform.

Their writings demonstrate the centrality of the "woman question" for Viennese Jews, and the ambivalent relationship of the religious Jewish leadership to the cultural context in which it endured.

In Chapter 3, I turn to the lives of Jewish university women and Jewish women in feminist, socialist, and communist politics, as well as in professional careers, looking at the way they used their political involvement to negotiate the tensions of their identity as Jews and women as well as the reactions and negative stereotypes of them that emerged as a result of their activities. The theme of politics continues in the next chapter on Jewish women's involvement in Viennese Zionism in light of the Zionist conception of them. While some Zionist women focused on finding feminine ways to contribute, others incorporated feminist ideas and subtly strove for equality or more political roles, and a third group concentrated on defining the role of women in the *Yishuv* (pre-State Israel). Zionist men stressed women's importance to the future of their people, while criticizing their lack of Jewish feeling, pursuit of assimilation, and love of luxury. They professed that the traditional relationship between the sexes in the East European ghetto would be transformed if the Jews had their own nation. In keeping with the ideas of the German volkish youth movement, they argued that Jewish men would become more manly by working the land, consequently causing Jewish women to become more feminine. Feeling the need to assert themselves as masculine in contrast to the image of the feminized Jewish male, Viennese Zionists in the end relegated Jewish women to a more passive role.

Chapter 5 examines how the climate of rising anti-Semitism, with its heavy sexual emphasis, shaped the way Viennese Jews in the fields of medicine, psychology, and psychoanalysis dealt with the Jewish question and the woman question. In their response to anti-Semitic stereotypes and the myth of the effeminate Jewish male, Jews in these fields challenged negative stereotypes of the Jew, while embracing negative images of women. Jewish women also pursued careers in medicine and psychoanalysis. Stereotypes of women and Jews circumscribed Jewish women's contributions to psychoanalysis and medicine, while their involvement in these fields allowed them an avenue by which to address notions of femininity and feminism persisting in their culture.

Continuing to explore images of Jewish women together with Jewish women's contributions, I turn in the final chapter to Jewish women's creative output and the representations of them in works of art, literature, theater, and journalism. Jewish literary works suggested various solutions to the question of Jewish women's role in the modern world. In ghetto literature, Jewish women often led the way to enlightenment, but sometimes suffered the pain of rejection by the traditional world. Later writers of ghetto stories portrayed Jewish women as the link to tradition. Jewish writers in the *Jung Wien* (Young Vienna literary movement) circle rarely pursued Jewish themes and even less frequently included female Jewish characters. In the instances where they appeared, female Jewish characters conformed to the general stereotypes of women in Viennese culture—as sexual victims, masculine intellectuals, or useless materialists. Jewish women in literature and creative culture faced competing and sometimes conflicting conceptions of womanhood found in the feminist movement and the bourgeois and Jewish notions of femininity. They used their writing and art as a means to negotiate the tensions of life as Jewish women in fin de siècle Vienna.

The purpose of these chapters and this book as a whole is to give a broad picture of the importance of the Jewish woman to the culture of fin de siècle Vienna as both subject and object. These two areas are explored simultaneously in each chapter as much as possible in order to highlight the interaction between image and identity and present a unified view of gender and Jewish culture by focusing on Jewish women's lives and images of Jewish women. Previous works have dealt either with images and stereotypes of Jewish women or "Jewish women's history," addressing the position and status, historical roles, cultural contributions, and/or questions of identity of Jewish women. An underlying conviction—that in order to understand either area, images of Jewish women or "Jewish women's history," they must be examined together—informs my analysis. By examining the specific case of Viennese Jewish women with this dual lens, this book aims to revisit the question of fin de siècle Viennese culture.

1 » Childhood and Youth of Jewish Girls

In her memoirs, the Viennese Jewish socialist, sociologist, and advocate for working women, Käthe Leichter (Marianne Katharina Pick) (1895–1942), recalled that her appearance—lanky, with long blond braids and gray eyes in a rosy-cheeked, boyish face—helped her, but that she did more than necessary in order to fit in. She wore her hair combed back flat, wore socks and a school uniform until the age of fourteen, and sailor blouses and a school bag on her back until the age of sixteen.[1] Minna Schiffmann Lachs (1907–1993) recalled her new teacher hitting her hands for making a cross with her thumbs while reciting the prayer "Shema Israel" during the "religious hour," the time in schools when students were separated according to their religious affiliation for special classes. Her classmates surrounded her at the end of the hour, asking, "Did you really not know that only Christians make a cross?"[2] Filled with memories of incidents such as these, the descriptions of Jewish girlhood in fin de siècle Vienna found in memoirs suggest that feelings of difference and isolation dominated these formative years.

However, memoirs cannot always be considered reliable sources because of the potential for reading the past through the lens of later experiences. For example, many of them were written after the Holocaust and may have a tendency to either exaggerate anti-Semitism in hindsight or to look back to earlier times with nostalgia. These women's later experiences of changing gender roles and opportunities also may influence their memories and depictions of their earlier years. Therefore it is important when using these documents to keep in mind their limitations and to consider sources written during the period as well. Sources and documents from the period, such as newspaper articles, pamphlets, and sermons, also indicate prejudice and isolation in schools and concern over the failure to transmit a clear sense of Jewish identity to girls and youth in school and at home. While Jewish boys often encountered similar difficulties and faced prejudice in schools, the expectations as well as the limitations placed on Jewish girls due to their gender added another dimension to their isolation and had an impact on their experiences and emotional development.

This chapter will examine the identity struggle that plagued Jewish girls growing up in fin de siècle Vienna, a city full of contradictions: promise and pathos; hostility and envy toward Jews, and desire and enmity toward women. In this crucial stage of their lives, Jewish girls struggled to define themselves and understand their place in their families, communities, and the larger society and culture. For Viennese Jewish girls, this struggle took place in the context of the diverse and growing Jewish community of fin de siècle Vienna, and the slowly developing women's movement. The unique characteristics of Vienna and its Jews led Jewish girls growing up there to have distinct experiences and concerns.

Vienna, the capital of the multinational Habsburg monarchy, hosted a diverse and unique Jewish population. As one of several ethnic groups, Viennese Jews tended to assert Jewish particularity more often than their counterparts in more homogeneous nations such as Germany. Viennese Jewry was composed of immigrants and children of immigrants, numbering almost 200,000 by World War I, making it the largest Jewish community of Western or Central Europe. Jews immigrated from the Austrian provinces of Bohemia, Moravia, Galicia and Hungary after 1848, leading to the diverse nature of the Jewish community. The geographic position of Vienna between East and West also influenced the self-conception of Viennese Jewry as mediators between the traditional and progressive movements in Judaism. The Viennese Jewish community did not experience a dramatic split between Reform and traditional movements, and its leaders maintained a spirit of moderation. They also emphasized the importance of making Judaism more modern through reform, or proving that Judaism was already modern. In this atmosphere, Viennese Jewish families focused on providing their children with the education and training necessary for upward mobility and redefining their Jewish identity to meet the times. The education provided for Jewish boys and girls differed due to the divergence in expectations and opportunities for men and women.

Viennese Jews came to occupy important and influential positions in the general society and culture. Due to the influence of the Jewish liberal bourgeoisie and the important role Jews played in the Austrian economy, it seemed that they were becoming less of a distinct ethnic group and more part of the German elite class. In Käthe Leichter's words, "The Austrian culture is significantly influenced and shaped by them [Jews], one cannot imagine the physiognomy of pre-war Austria without this assimilated and cultivated Jewry, disturbed in their position neither by Schönerer's nor by Lueger's anti-Semitic movements."[3]

On the other hand, the overwhelming Catholic nature of the Habsburg State, the politically charged atmosphere due to the rise of the Pan-German Movement of Georg von Schönerer (1842–1921) and the Christian Social Party of Karl Lueger (1844–1910), and most certainly the rise of political and confessional anti-Semitism, also influenced the childhood years of Viennese Jews during this period.[4] Jewish girls faced additional pressures and limitations because of the lack of educational and career opportunities, the attitudes of teachers and parents, and the cultural stereotypes of women. This presents itself clearly in many everyday interactions recorded in Jewish women's memoirs of youth. Both at home and at school, Jewish girls attempted to make sense of the contradictory messages surrounding them. As females they faced social and educational limitations, while as Jews they confronted a world dominated by Catholicism, tainted by anti-Semitism, and plagued by uncertainty about what it meant to be Jewish. In order to understand the lives of Jewish girls in Vienna, I will focus on the following four areas: educational reforms for girls, discrimination in schools, confirmations, and home life. In all of these areas it will be seen that their identities as Jews and women shaped their experiences.

Educational Reforms for Girls

Jewish girls benefited from new possibilities for women's education created in 1868 as a result of the revision of the Austrian constitution. Several new educational institutions for girls emerged in the ensuing years, vastly expanding the opportunities for girls' education as well as their social networks and exposure to new ideas and beliefs. The *Stern'sche Mädchen-Lehr-und Erziehungsanstalt*, founded in 1868, was the first in Vienna to provide some higher education for girls. Later, a new type of secondary school emerged, the *Mädchen-Lyzeum*, or "higher" school for girls, which offered six-year programs for girls from ten to sixteen years old. They included obligatory foreign language study, expanded the age limit to sixteen rather than fourteen, and offered an examination which entitled graduates to attend the University as non-matriculating students. The *Stern'sche* school lost pupils to the *Lyzeum*, but at the same time began to attract more boarding students from Eastern Europe.[5]

In spite of these reforms, the humanistic *Gymnasien* or *Realschulen* still did not admit girls until later. According to the eminent historian of Habsburg education, Gary Cohen, authorities opposed opening secondary educational institutions to girls because women lacked employment opportunities in fields such as law, state service, medicine, and teaching in secondary schools.[6] The curriculum offered in girls' schools therefore consisted of modern languages and electives in sewing, stenography, typing, and, in a few schools, Latin. In her memoirs of life in Vienna, Toni Stopler (1890–1988) explained the separation as a scheme of education which underscored the expectation that women would be in charge of "culture" and men of the professions. "The boys were to become doctors and lawyers and teachers but the girls in their families would take care of *belle lettres*, music and the arts, of 'culture'."[7]

According to many recollections, parents also usually prioritized the education of their sons and did not support their daughters' interest in study. For example, Dora Israel Amann (1894–1992) recalled, "I was fourteen years old and just finished with my schooling. I wanted to go to the *Lycee* and to study, but my parents found that with five sons who should study, the money was not there." Nevertheless her parents promised her she could study at the *Lycee*, and she prepared for the examination. In the end her father's "practicality" won and she was registered in a private trade school.[8] Similarly, Ulrich R. Furst (b. 1913) described his mother's difficulty in procuring an education due to gender limitations.

> Mother would have loved to get an education: she certainly was smart enough to qualify, but did not have the opportunity to study anything. This was partly due to the financial situation, but mainly, because at that time, a girl was not thought of as needing an education: after attending school until the age of fourteen, as required by law, she was supposed to stay home, learn how to run a household, help her mother, and wait until a suitor asked her parents for her hand in marriage.[9]

Nevertheless, she managed to study both French and English over the protest of her family, and obtained teaching certificates in both subjects, "quite a feat for a girl at that time."[10] Fears and superstitions also abounded and shaped parental attitudes toward their daughters' educational aspirations. Esti Freud (1896–1980) attended the Schwarzwald school, which will be described below, and then chose to go to *Gymnasium* in order to prepare for University; however, she recalled that her mother would not permit it, saying she would become blind and hunchbacked. Her parents also did not allow her to go on overnight hikes because it could have endangered her reputation as a sexually inexperienced girl and interfered with her chances of making a good match. "This was an extremely important matter to an upper-middle class family in the Viennese Jewish ghetto."[11]

Lise Meitner (1878–1968), who went on to become a physicist and discover nuclear fission, also commented on the limitations of girls' education in Vienna. She recollected, "Although I had a very marked bent for mathematics and physics from my early years, I did not begin a life of study immediately." "Thinking back to . . . the time of my youth, one realizes with some astonishment how many problems then existed in the lives of ordinary young girls, which now seem almost unimaginable. Among the most difficult of these problems was the possibility of normal intellectual training."[12] Käthe Leichter criticized the education available for girls at that time, describing the *Mädchen-Lyzeum* as a substandard school system which had nothing to do with real life. It did not entitle one to attend university, nor did it provide any practical knowledge. "It was reserved from the start for those circles who could allow themselves to send their daughters away to school for six years, to procure an empty education." The education was nominally concerned with languages, literature, and history, to ensure that the graduates would be able to do well in the circles of the best society.[13]

However, modest improvements in girls' education continued during this period. For example, in 1892, the *Verein für erweiterte Frauenbildung* (Society for Expanding Women's Education) founded the *Gymnasiale Mädchenschule*, which offered a *Gymnasium* curriculum of Latin and Greek, German, history and geography, religion, mathematics, natural history, and philosophy, in a six-year program. A Jewish woman, Ottilie Jeitteles Bondy (1832–1921), one of the moving forces behind the *Verein für erweiterte Frauenbildung*, also co-founded the *Wiener Hausfrauen Verein* (Viennese Housewives Society) in 1875 and advocated for social welfare.[14] The *Gymnasiale Mädchenschule* expanded to seven years in 1901 and eight years in 1910. After 1910, other private women's *Gymnasien* grew from pre-existing *Lyzeen* which added a seventh and eighth year, although without central government funding. By the spring of 1910, Austria had thirteen private women's *Gymnasien* with about 2,600 regular students.[15] In 1907, the physicist Olga

Steindler (1879–1933) together with Olly Frankl Schwarz (1877–1960), wife of Professor Emil Schwarz, also Jewish, established yet another new type of school, the *Handelsakademie für Mädchen* (Business Academy for Girls), to prepare girls for careers in economics and commerce.[16] In 1912, the *Verein für realgymnasialen Mädchenunterricht* (Society for the Instruction of Girls in the *Realgymnasium* system) established a school for girls.

Jewish women played an important, often leading, role in the founding of schools for girls in Vienna. In addition to those mentioned above, the *Schwarzwald Mädchen Lyzeum* and the *Cottage-Lyzeum der Salka Goldmann* were both founded and led by Jewish women.[17] Eugenie Nussbaum Schwarzwald (1873–1940) from Polupanowka, a small Galician village, founded the *Schwarzwald Mädchen Lyzeum* in 1901. One of the first women to obtain a degree at the University of Zurich, a doctorate in German literature, she decided to establish a school for girls to prepare them for University study in response to her own experiences of gender discrimination. She acquired a school on the Franziskanerplatz in which to build her school. She "fought lengthy battles with the authorities for permits, appropriations, and privileges, addressed financial concerns, and obtained support of wealthy parents."[18] Important and prominent figures, such as the painter Oskar Kokoschka, the composer Arnold Schoenberg (1874–1951) and the architect Adolf Loos, taught at her school alongside political leaders, such as Social Democrats Anton Tesarek, Felix Kanitz, and Aline Klatschko Furtmüller (1883–1941), and Communist Otto Eicher.[19] The dancer Grete Wiesenthal (1885–1970) supervised physical training. Hilde Spiel (1911–1990), who later became a prominent writer, attended this school. She described the students, in contrast to other state-educated girls, as a clan, "based not on snobbery but its opposite—a natural, unaffected, eternally curious attitude towards life and people, a determined resistance to every form of fake and fraud."[20]

In her groundbreaking study of Austrian women's movements, Harriet Anderson describes Schwarzwald's educational establishment as including several different types of schools under one roof and administration. A co-educational junior school was added to the existing *Mädchen Lyzeum* in 1903 and a secondary school for girls placing equal weight on natural sciences and languages in 1910–1911. The school grew from 180 students in 1901–1902 to 470 students in 1912–1913, moving locations in 1902 and again in 1912–1913. "In 1915 there was a preschool, a coeducational five-year elementary school, four classes of a

Eugenie Schwarzwald. ÖNB/Wien.

Eugenie Schwarzwald. Caricature.
ÖNB/Wien.

public eight-year high school, a six-year *Lyzeum*, a four-year humanistic
high school for girls, a three-year occupational school for women, and
postgraduate courses for those who had finished the lyceum or high
school." [21] Schwarzwald approached education from a creative and
child-centered perspective. She aimed to provide each child the freedom to develop in her own direction and to find school an enjoyable
experience. She believed that learning should be a joyful experience
for children and aimed to remove fear and coercion. In her emphasis
on non-interventionist education and naturalness, she echoed the approach of Austrian feminists such as Rosa Mayreder and Marie Lang.
Other values she shared with the Austrian women's movement included simplicity in dress, opposition to alcohol consumption, and
continued adherence to accepted notions of femininity.[22] Schwarzwald
also engaged herself in charity work and held a salon in her home in
the eighth district, but her salon was unlike those of her contemporaries. "A kind of 'scurrilous Viennese' atmosphere predominated in
this circle of artists, writers, philosophers, and others, many of whom
were social nonentities and outsiders." [23]

Schwarzwald and her school faced widespread criticism and ridi-
cule from her Viennese cultural milieu. An inspection report from

1908 critically remarked that "Frau Schwarzwald would best like to make a University for girls."[24] Karl Kraus (1874–1936), the relentless critic and editor of the journal *Die Fackel* (The Torch), defamed her as "Hofrätin Schwarz-Gelber" in *Die Letzten Tage der Menschheit* (The Last Days of Mankind). The novelist Robert Musil, who spent much time as a guest in her home, immortalized her as the energetic Salon woman "Diotima" in *Der Mann ohne Eigenschaften* (The Man without Qualities).[25]

At the same time, Salka Goldmann (1870–1942) founded a school outside the city in the suburbs. Toni Stopler described her as "a Jewish type, no one could forget that she was Jewish, but she was a highly trained German historian." Trained at the University of Leipzig by the famous historian Karl Gottfried Lamprecht, she went on to receive a doctorate from the University of Zurich like Schwarzwald and founded the *Cottage-Lyzeum* in 1903. The Goldmann school was more modern than the bourgeois Schwarzwald school, according to Stopler. She did not believe in training girls to become "good well-cultured young animals ready to be married."

> She stressed on us from the beginning that we were persons, and that we would have to stand on our own merit, not to wait for someone to come and marry us—to count as ourselves . . . While the other Frau Doktor Schwarzwald, fitted in perfectly in this joyous 'live and let live' current of Vienna, this more serious and interesting complicated person, very north German, didn't fit into the Vienna picture very well.[26]

Girls' education progressively improved through these institutions, and Austrian feminists, such as Marianne Perger Hainisch (1839–1936) and Irma von Troll-Borostyáni (1847–1912), continued to press for further advances.

Statistically, Jewish girls achieved a higher degree of education than was typical. According to Marsha Rozenblit in her social historical study of Viennese Jewry, Jews comprised the majority (57 percent) of all *Lyzeum* students in 1895/96, and 46 percent in 1910. Some of the *Lyzeen* had higher percentages of Jewish students than others. The Amalia Sobel school and the Olga Ehrenhaft-Steindler school were 88 percent Jewish in 1910/11, while the two Christian *Lyzeen* had no Jewish students at all. The girls who attended the Schwarzwald school (69 percent Jewish in 1910/11) came from the upper classes. "They were the daughters of Vienna's most successful and established Jews, those who had already achieved high social status and now wanted to have their daughters become the proper ornament of their upward mobility." Most of their fathers worked as industrialists, large-scale merchants, and high-status professionals. In 1890, two-thirds and in 1910 three-quarters of the Jewish girls at the Schwarzwald school were native-born Viennese.[27]

Discrimination in Schools

While many did eventually attend *Lyzeen* with high percentages of Jewish girls, this was not always the case. Furthermore, in the *Volks-schulen* (public elementary schools), many educated Viennese women remember having felt alienated from Judaism. In part this alienation seems to have stemmed from their experiences of the "religion lesson" at school during which they received separate instruction in Judaism. While Jewish boys also had the experience of being separated for religious instruction, girls also sometimes felt alienated in a tradition which seemed to hold them in lower esteem. For example, Toni Stopler recalled:

> My experience with Jewishness was negative from the beginning, because the teacher who taught us, from whom I learnt the Hebrew alphabet, was a poor, sickly, badly dressed man, not very well groomed, I thought, and he impressed me as counting for nothing. The second crucial negative feature was: when we were attending a family wedding at a synagogue, what happened? Here were the men in the centre, and the women were by themselves, in a separate part, quite divided off, and that didn't suit me at all . . . this funny division from the men, separated by galleries . . . Thus my personal impression of Jewishness was purely negative.[28]

When the majority had their religion class, the Jewish children went to a neighboring school where they learned basic Hebrew letters, biblical stories, etc. Afterward, Stopler attended a very upper-middle-class *Lyzeum* with very few Jewish girls. "There was no question of religious education any more." Nevertheless, she socialized with Jewish girls and did not develop any close relationships with the non-Jewish girls.[29]

School and especially the religion lesson caused a great deal of distress for Anny Robert (1909–1988). She did not enjoy school and was not a very good student, but "the worst for me was the religion lesson." The seven Jewish girls sat around idly while the Catholic classmates received their religion lesson in the morning between other classes. Instead they had to come twice a week in the afternoon and once during school. "With the greatest difficulty, I learned our Hebrew prayer. But I learned only phonetically, and I rattled it off without having any idea, what I was saying. But we also had to learn Biblical stories in German language, to learn to read and write Hebrew, from right to left. It went in and out of my head." [30] Lillian Bader (1890–1920), who also recalled being separated into groups for religious lessons in the public school she attended, wrote that in spite of this separation, she never experienced discrimination during her four years at this school, from either teachers or pupils. "Never once was any reference made to the difference in our creeds." [31] Recalling her experience in a private elementary school, Elisabeth Freundlich (1906–2001) wrote: "For religious instruction we were led by the lady with the long skirt into other classrooms and divided into three groups. I belonged to the larger group, namely to the Mosaic Confession, which was an expression that I heard then for the first time." [32]

Governesses, luxuries, and a good education did not spare the mother of psychoanalyst Marie Langer (1910–1988) from being stigmatized in school. She was born in 1886 and she attended a private school which corresponded approximately to the *Lyzeum*.

> My mother's family was completely atheistic. While my grandfather was indifferent toward religion, my mother suffered being a Jewess. In those days each child was asked: "What are you?" on the first day of school. When my mother, who understood neither this question nor the rough reaction of the teacher, came running home crying, my grandfather said: "They are asking you, whether you are Jewish or Catholic. You are Jewish!" This fact was long repressed by my mother.[33]

Langer's mother gave her the name Marie in order to spare her a typical Jewish destiny. When her mother returned to Vienna in 1955, the Jewish community wanted a large sum of money from her for taxes that were not paid during her exile. She declined to pay and lost her "right" to be buried in the Jewish cemetery.

At her *Volksschule*, which many Jewish girls attended, Marie Langer recalled looking at the Catholic girls and thinking, "on these brows, the cross has been marked with consecrated waters." She knew about holy water from her Catholic cook, who brought her to evening masses and presented her with small treatises on the life and work of the saints. She was frightened by their pain and suffering, but "I also understood that one must be able to suffer and die for an ideal." "At seventeen I had a religious crisis. First I wanted—in opposition to my parents—to seriously declare my allegiance to the Jewish religion, and then—during a long and sorrowful Good Friday—to become Catholic. Thereupon I finally became an atheist and later a communist."[34] She attended an upperclass, exclusive school where a psalm was recited every morning. From there she moved on to the *Schwarzwaldschule Realgymnasium*, which she described as following a Marxist and feminist line. Once Frau Doktor Schwarzwald called her mother, asking her not to send Marie to school with a chauffeur or allow her to go to school in a fur coat.[35]

Prayers in school and the influence of Catholic classmates combined with the lack of religious observance and education at home made it common for Viennese Jewish girls to grow up with confusion about their religious identity. The Roman Catholic Church dominated the public elementary school, which Toni Stopler attended from the ages of six to ten. "Every morning we had to stand up and recite the Lord's Prayer and the Ave Maria before school lessons began." The Viennese poet and essayist, Mimi Grossberg (1905–1997), described her experience of prayer at school.

> In the school I participated every morning, and in complete innocence, in "The Lord's Prayer," folding my hands and saying the words together with my classmates. I still know them by heart, nobody interfered. But on my first day in the new school, something happened. I rose with my new classmates, as I had always done in the other school, folded my hands and prayed with the others. All of a sudden the new teacher rushed towards me with a dramatic gesture, pulled my hands apart and hollered: "Stop child, you are committing a great sin!"[36]

The teacher explained to her that as a Jew, she was not allowed to fold her hands and cross her thumbs and say "The Lord's Prayer." This incident for the first time impressed upon her that being Jewish made her different. "It saddened me terribly. What child wants to be different? Did I experience at this early age an inkling of what this being 'different' would mean later in life? Was this just the overture to the drama?"

A cultural division between Jewish and non-Jewish girls shaped the experiences of Käthe Leichter and her sister Vally, who entered the distinguished *Beamtentöchter-Lyzeum* (Officials' daughters' school) in 1906. They did not attend the *Gymnasium* because their father opposed private schools. The *Beamtentöchter-Lyzeum*, situated in the Josefstadt, had the reputation as the best and strongest girls' school. Supported by a school association for officials' daughters, it consisted of a boarding school and a regular school in order to guarantee a higher education for the daughters of the Austrian civil service. The school also appealed to the Jewish liberal bourgeoisie. Although the school emphasized Austrian tradition and patriotism in its history lessons and ceremonies, top-ranking professors taught the students. "It was above all the Jewish-liberal bourgeoisie that despite the high tuition for non-officials sent their daughters to the officials' daughters' school. The intellectual standard of the school was only raised through the maturely intelligent Jewish girls; the dominant puritanical strictness benefited much from them." [37]

Leichter recounted in detail the social composition of her school, and its impact on her developing world view. Class rank dominated the hierarchy of the school, with a sharp division between the officials' daughters and the Jewish girls. The students grouped themselves according to the class rank of their fathers during the recess. These groups differed in appearance and personality. The officials' daughters dressed simply with black skirts and sleeves over high-necked dresses, their hair combed back flat and dangling in thick braids. They were conscientious students, and had painfully neat homework assignment notebooks. In contrast, the daughters of the liberal Jewish bourgeoisie—university professors, doctors, lawyers, and industrialists—benefited from a good upbringing and manners and were "more tastefully dressed than the others." The gap between the Jewish and non-Jewish girls increased when they reached the age of thirteen.

The Jewish girls experience puberty and maturity earlier, they are growing up when the others are still children, when the officials' daughters still are playing ball in the park, the others are making their first conquests on the ice or in the park; while the one cries bitterly over each bad mark which must be shown at home, the other is already extremely indifferent to school, and while the one reads out of girls' books at the most *Joern Uhl* of Frenssen or Rudolf

Hans Bartsch, the other is secretly already working at Oskar Wilde, Schnitzler, and Sudermann. When the officials' daughters go to their first club, or are taken by their parents to comradeship evening, they are wild about the professors, in the break they put their heads together and giggle, the others already past that stage, suffer from romantic discontent and quote Nietzsche.[38]

The working class could not afford to send their daughters for six years to a purely educational school with high tuition. Instead they went to four-year public schools, after which they helped in the house, learned to do tailoring, or worked in factories. Occasionally, gifted proletariat boys attended middle school, but never girls. "Their world, which I had come to know a little in the elementary school, was supposed to remain closed to me during all the years of middle school."

Wanting to merge into the world of her school, Leichter avoided belonging to either group. "I stood between the social classes, not entirely in either, thus both soon wooed me; I found much affiliation in both." Her strong feeling for community came to life and she began her political activities with the support of her classmates.

> Here finally were people of my age, not chosen by my parents, here there was a coalition against the strict pressure of the school administration and teachers; tricks that depended on boldness and imagination, group education, friendships and antagonists, secrets,—in short everything which my little heart had longed for in vain until my eleventh year. And because I went along with all this with total devotion and passion, because this daily school life from now on stood so entirely at the center of my life, my social desire to dominate was able to come so fully to life. Also, I soon became a center of this small world.[39]

The families of the nobility must have opposed their daughters' involvement with Leichter. "Of the ambitious mothers, who wanted to give their daughters a good education, so that they could marry profitably, the ringleader of the school conflicts was just not accepted."[40]

The Jewish students associated with one another, visiting each other for afternoon teas. These friends remained with her through school and to some extent through life. With them she remained full of fun and wit, knowing how to ease their blasé attitudes. But the others also attracted her.

Their calm assurance pleased me, their simplicity, their childishness, their high German, which had an easy beat in the courtly Viennese, the officials' milieu, of which they told stories. All this pleased me more than the restlessness of the others and magically pulled me in, until I neatly assimilated externally, which would have occasioned the impartial observer to rank me much more easily with them than with the Jewish bourgeois children.[41]

She attributed her career successes in later life to her assimilation in the environment of the *Beamtentöchter-Lyzeum*. "That I have so strongly acquired this calm simple Aryan character that it not only remained a superficiality but became a matter of course, helped me very essentially later in life, in my career and in the workers' movement in getting along with people . . ."[42]

The intense discipline of her school, her resulting activities to counter it, and her social interactions exposed her to experiences she craved, such as community, solidarity, actions, protests, and social acceptance. It influenced her later life as a socialist and an activist for women's rights, particularly for workers as she encountered the limitations faced by working women and the restricted expectations for women in general. She also noticed some holes in the strong tradition of the *Beamtentöchternschule* in the pre-war years. The religious teachers criticized Austrian tradition. She wrote: "The friendly Evangelical Pastor made a German nationalist, anti-Austrian conviction the center of his religious hour, while his colleague, the Rabbi, made painful attacks against Lueger, Bielohlawek, and the anti-Semitism of the city administration."[43]

Erna Segal, who moved to Vienna from Lemberg when she was six, remembered experiencing discrimination in school from an early age.[44] In Lemberg, she attended a Jewish school, spoke only Yiddish, and learned Hebrew and history. The strict teacher sometimes beat the children. When she first arrived in Vienna, she had no knowledge of other religions, and it shocked her when children at school laughed at her poor speech. She soon learned German and improved her situation, but every time the hour came for religion class and the Jewish girls went to another classroom, one of the other students would make cruel remarks.

Her father an Orthodox cantor and rabbi, Segal grew up in a religious setting. "He was very good and tolerant and taught us to always be helpful and good to our fellow-man." He taught his children that all men, regardless of race, class, and religion, were equal in the eyes of God.[45] From an early age, she was proud that Moses, a Jew, gave the Ten Commandments, the foundation of human civilization, to all mankind. "Whenever I was hurt because of my religion, I would hold this up before my fellow students, which most of the time made them silent." Over the years, she heard about the persecution of Jews in Russia and Romania, and learned in religious class about the Inquisition in Spain and persecutions in France, Germany, Prague, and other countries. This shook her deeply, and she could not believe that such horrors occurred. "I began reading about the history of the Jews and determined that Jesus himself was a Jew—what would he say if he knew that his fellow-believers were being persecuted and cruelly murdered until the present time." Discovering that the Church itself was in large part responsible for the persecution of Jews, she wondered how Christians prayed to one Jew and annihilated others. She spent many sleepless nights thinking about this, and when she did sleep she had nightmares. "I was a young girl but always sad and whenever I had the opportunity, I talked about it with a few reasonable classmates who were horrified when I said, that Jesus must have been a great wonderful person and that he was a Jew—most did not know it or did not want to know it." [46]

Dora Israel Amann (1894–1992) also experienced anti-Semitism in the *Volksschule* she attended, despite the fact that her father had her converted to Protestantism. "I was not happy in my first three school years because my teacher was anti-Semitic, which I did not yet understand, but I felt her unfriendliness to me." After that she changed schools to the Cherninschule in the second district, the Leopoldstadt district, where a large part of the Viennese Jews lived. She had a long way to travel to school but felt contented and at home there.[47]

The existence of anti-Semitism in Austrian public schools is corroborated by other sources as well. For example, the newspaper *Freies Blatt*, the organ of the *Verein zur Abwehr des Antisemitismus*, a society for defense from anti-Semitism founded in Vienna in 1891 by prominent Christians, included an article on anti-Semitism in the schools. Written by a Jewish mother, it recounts a series of conversations with her son about his wish to return to his previous school, the Hernalser Gymnasium, because of anti-Semitism in his new school, consisting primarily of verbal insults. When she offered to speak to the Director of the school, her son discouraged her because he believed that would lead to more trouble. After restraining herself for some time, she eventually went to speak to the Director without her son's knowledge.

The very next day, his teacher delivered a strong warning to the class about insulting Jewish students. And this solved the problem. She concluded that "a protection against anti-Semitic mischief in public school is also possible. The authority of the teacher will be respected everywhere. A truly educated teacher, in his top form, who appreciates his calling as an educator of the people in the best sense, will put a check on anti-Semitic excesses." [48]

Minna Schiffmann Lachs described her experiences in a *Volksschule* in Vienna around the period of the First World War.[49] Born in Trembowla, an east Galician town, she moved with her family to Vienna, where she began school. On her first day, she recalled looking around the room while her father spoke to the teacher and noticing a portrait of the Emperor and over it a crucifix. Her class had only three other Jewish pupils, but they were separated for "mosaic religious instruction" with the many Jewish children from another class. At first they had a nice young religious teacher, who took off his hat when he entered the room and put a "small round cap" on his head. He made a favorable impression on her. He wrote Jewish dates on the blackboard and explained why the Jews had a different calendar than the Christians. He also taught them the names of the Hebrew months and told them about Jewish holidays, relating stories from Jewish history and Bible. "I found this all very interesting and always enjoyed this hour." [50]

Lachs first visited a synagogue with her religious class on the occasion of the Emperor Franz Joseph's death in 1916. The episode made a great impression on her. Until then she had only known of the Jewish prayer houses in the second district, "from their covered windows loud sing-song pushed out into the streets." The synagogue, in contrast, impressed her as very ceremonial. There was a boys' choir and a youth service, in which the class took part. The Rabbi spoke to them about the life of the Emperor, about his long reign and all the good things he had done for his people and also for the Jews. "We have lost a good friend with him." [51]

Lachs's next religious teacher, the strict Fräulein Rosenfeld, mistook her ignorance of Judaism for wickedness. "I knew so little of the Jewish customs and laws, because in our family they were not followed." When this teacher told the story of the Creation, she told about the first humans, Adam and Eve, who lived in Paradise and the brothers Cain and Abel. When Lachs asked out of curiosity whom Cain married if there was still no woman in the world other than his mother, the teacher said, "You are not only dumb, you are also fresh." On another occasion, when the teacher told them about how Jacob received the blessing of Isaac by deceiving him, Lachs cried out indignantly, "He was a swindler! I do not want to be descended from a swindler!" Fräulein Rosenfeld hit her fingers painfully with a ruler.

Her father had given her a Hebrew book in order to learn the Hebrew alphabet. She learned the letters in block print with her father and taught herself the handwritten letters. She practiced reading Hebrew out of a small prayer book in order to pacify her teacher. In the next class, she stepped forward to read. Not knowing that it was forbidden to say the name of God (she was supposed to say "Adonai"), she pronounced the word "Jehauvo." This time the teacher lost her composure and concluded that she was a wicked child. After the class, the other pupils surrounded her and told her that God would punish her for sinning. Frightened and disturbed, she went home and shut herself in a closet and said "Jehauvo" over and over again, and nothing happened. After that she no longer believed anything that was said by her teacher or classmates.

When Lachs's father returned on leave, she told him about what had happened at school. He had a long talk with Fräulein Rosenfeld, and from then on she was less abusive. One day she described to the class the bar mitzvah of her son and that his sister had made him a beautiful velvet bag for his *Tefillin* (phylacteries). The entire class was excited and wanted to know about some detail of the ceremony. But Lachs sat there indifferently, not knowing exactly what they were talking about. Noticing this, the teacher thought perhaps she only knew the German word for *Tefillin*.

The teacher wanted to help me this time. She asked, "What does your father do when he gets dressed before breakfast?"—"He puts on his tie."—"What else?"—"He puts on his moustache band."— "But what is something important that he does every day?"—"He goes to the bathroom." I cannot describe the laughter in the class, in which Fräulein Rosenfeld herself joined. But I hear it still today.

My father never prayed in the morning, and I had never before at any time seen Jews pray with Tefillin. I also did not know what a bar mitzvah was. "A type of confirmation," my mother said to me later.[52]

Jewish families often prioritized education as part of their effort at assimilation and integration. For example, Lise Meitner grew up in the

Leopoldstadt district with a high concentration of Jews. However, her family clearly distanced itself from its Jewish past to such an extent that one of her nephews later had the impression that his mother and all the Meitner children had been baptized and raised as Protestants. In fact they were all registered with the Jewish community at birth. Lise became baptized as a Protestant as an adult in 1908.[53] Her parents embraced German culture, and raised their children in an intellectual atmosphere. Her father, Philipp Meitner, a lawyer, was liberal and sympathetic to Social Democracy. The Meitners' home became a gathering place for intellectuals and other interesting people, and all the Meitner children, including the daughters, pursued an advanced education.[54]

Being a girl limited Lise Meitner's educational opportunities. She attended the *Mädchen-Bürgerschule* at Czerninplatz, completing her studies in 1892. "She had learned bookkeeping arithmetic but not algebra, a smattering of history, geography, and science, the requisite drawing, singing, and 'feminine handwork,' a little French and gymnastics."[55] She then went on to a teacher's training school—since teaching was the only professional career possibility for women—and later in 1899, began preparing for the Matura, which she passed in 1901, allowing her to enter the University of Vienna.

Dissatisfied with the schools, some Jewish families had their daughters privately tutored. In these cases, Judaism may not have been taught at all. For example, Elise Richter (1865–1943), an important scholar of Romance languages, and her sister Helene (1861–1942), both of whom were later killed in Theresienstadt, received a progressive education from a private teacher, who introduced them to art, music, and theater.[56] Their non-confessional religious education lacked any Jewish content. "We were fundamentally educated . . . that all confessions were equal . . . So we visited all types of religious services, except the Jewish, but above all the Protestant." They also learned French and English, and later Italian and Spanish.[57] After their parents' death in 1896, the sisters lived together, studied on their own, and attended lectures at the University. When a new ordinance of the Ministry of Public Worship and Education allowed for women to take the matriculation exam at certain boys' *Gymnasien* in 1896, Elise Richter prepared independently and made an application for the Matura, which she passed in 1897.

Articles from the period argued for the importance of religious lessons in schools, giving quite a different perspective from memoirs regarding the accomplishments of "religion lessons" in instilling a positive Jewish identity in children. For example, an article entitled "Schule und Haus" (School and Home) indicated that much had been written about the problem that students almost never saw what they learned at school put into practice at home.[58] The author asserted that the desires of the parents and governesses to suppress the "Jewishness" of the child always frustrated the sincere efforts of the teachers. He used the observance of holidays such as Passover, Rosh Hashanah, and Yom Kippur as examples of the conflict between teachings in school and practices at home. He also asserted the importance of religious instruction in school in light of the inevitable impact of anti-Semitism. For example, in teaching about the Exodus from Egypt, an exciting story which captivates the attention of students, they learned to sympathize with the Jews and to identify with and feel pride in their ancestry. "The sensitive child will certainly take with him some sympathy for this nation and not see the Jews as their enemies see them, as only a greedy, haggling and despised people." The author lamented that even though the Passover Seder was known as one of the most uplifting Jewish acts, and the Christian sacrament of the last supper can be attributed to the Passover meal, Jewish parents tended to support respect for the Eucharist while disdaining or deriding the holiday of Passover.

All these examples suggest that middle-class Jewish girls routinely received formal education as it became available to them. Clearly the Jews hoped that through the pursuit of education for their daughters, new possibilities would open for them. However, they often failed to provide their daughters with a coherent sense of Jewish history and identity with which they could withstand the pressures of insensitive teachers and fellow pupils. Therefore, Jewish girls' experiences in school ranged from a feeling of not quite fitting in, to incidents of outright anti-Semitism. Unlike Jewish boys, they also struggled against limitations in the possibilities for women's education in their times and faced the negative stereotypes of educated and intellectual women which prevailed in fin de siècle Viennese society.

The Introduction of Girls' Confirmations in Vienna

In response to discrimination in schools, the organized Jewish community of Vienna attempted to provide Jewish girls with a positive Jewish identity through the refinement of religious instruction in school and the institution of confirmations. Because of a Talmudic ruling that prohibited a father from teaching certain texts to his daughter, traditional Jewish practice focused more attention on the formal education of boys. Girls were expected to learn by example in the home. However, as a result of emancipation and modernization, the religious education of girls by their mothers could no longer be relied upon, and concern for the lack of formal Jewish training for girls mounted. Reformers introduced the confirmation for both boys and girls in order to address this problem, by drawing attention to the importance of educating children of both sexes.

The Jewish confirmation ceremony began in Germany. According to the American Reform rabbi Solomon B. Freehof, the confirmation was the first religious ceremony introduced by Reform Judaism. He described it as an improvement over bar mitzvah because it applied equally to boys and girls to mark their religious coming of age. Reform leaders chose the holiday of Shavuot (the Feast of Weeks) as the fixed date for the group confirmation ceremony.[59] W. Gunther Plaut concurs that the reform of the bar mitzvah rite was one of the earliest changes of the progressive movement.[60] According to Michael Meyer, the first institution of the confirmation ceremony took place in a new modern school in Dessau in 1803. Leopold Zunz, one of the founders of the *Wissenschaft des Judentums* (science or scholarly study of Judaism), was confirmed in 1807. The first official mention of confirmation occurred in Westphalia among the duties of the rabbis in 1809. According to Meyer, "Clearly this was an institution adopted from Christianity where it represented the culmination of a course of study intended to prepare the young person for adult status in the church." [61] Benjamin Maria Baader adds that the first full account of a Jewish confirmation ceremony comes from the Cassel school in Westphalia in 1810. The ceremony included a speech by Jeremiah Heinemann, a pledge from the boy being confirmed, and a blessing by the rabbi.[62]

Some rabbis indeed objected to the syncretistic character of the confirmation ceremony. Teachers prepared students for confirmation with the question-and-answer technique of the catechism, focusing on universal principles and obligations rather than on particular Jewish ones. However, the German reform rabbis who advocated the confirmation ceremony denied that it meant the same thing in Judaism and Christianity.[63] Unlike Christianity, which required confirmation for acceptance into the church, the Jewish confirmation ceremony signified a commitment to the principles and duties of Judaism. This contrasted with the traditional bar mitzvah celebrating a boy's coming of age and taking upon himself the religious obligations of an adult male.

Although the introduction of confirmations prompted some disagreement, it prevailed in part because of its relevance to and inclusion of girls. If in theory the confirmation applied equally to girls and boys, in practice the inclusion of girls took longer, with Moses Hirsch Bock conducting the first girls' confirmation only in 1814 at his private school in Berlin.[64] Isaac Asher Francolm, a rabbi in Königsberg, held confirmations for boys and girls until his traditionalist opponents protested to the government. Francolm wrote, "There is no definite age at which girls begin their obligation to obey the laws. Hence, no festivity of this kind [bar mitzvah] is held for them. Once again, the female sex is here treated as less capable, as in Oriental custom." He also wrote that Jewish boys and girls should be confirmed separately, and that neither boy nor girl confirmand should hold an address on this occasion, "so that a solemn observance which is meant to make a deep impression upon the young should not be desecrated through pomp and the satisfaction of idle vanity."[65] The report to the Breslau Conference (1846) suggested that the age of religious maturity for both sexes should be thirteen. Later the age for confirmation was raised to fifteen.[66] Jewish feminists in Imperial Germany who desired equal religious preparation for girls supported the confirmation.[67]

In Vienna, the Jewish leadership perceived the weakening of the Jewish family as a mechanism to transmit Jewish knowledge and practice to future generations. As part of their initiative to strengthen the Jewish family, they sought to improve Jewish education for girls and instituted the confirmation rite. Various rabbis and religious leaders discussed the confirmation's educational and ceremonial significance. They justified it as having symbolic value while remaining skeptical about its educational merit and its derivative nature (from Christian ceremonies). The lay leadership, on the other hand, promoted the confirmation of girls as a means to ensure Judaism's survival in the future.

In the 1820s, Isaac Mannheimer (1793–1865) introduced the custom of confirmations for Jewish girls and boys in Vienna. Mannheimer, who had been an ardent reformer in his previous post in Copenhagen, arrived in Vienna in 1826 to consecrate the newly built Seitenstettengasse synagogue. Recognizing the conservative nature of the Viennese Jewish community, he curbed his zeal and adapted himself to the spirit of moderate reform. The only substantive reforms he introduced were the confirmation, reduction of the number of *piyutim* (liturgical poems), and elimination of the *Kol Nidre* service on Yom Kippur.[68] In Copenhagen, appointed first as a teacher and then in 1816 as a royal catechist, Mannheimer worked as an educator, and it became his special task to prepare students for the required public examination, which soon became known as confirmation.

> The first such ceremony took place on May 19, 1817 in a spacious room that had once served as a concert hall. An organ had been placed on the east wall, a table bearing two candles stood on the west in front of a plaque displaying the Ten Commandments. A large crowd gathered to hear Mannheimer conduct the examination and deliver a Danish sermon on the text from Job: "Wisdom, where shall it be found?" Some psalms were sung in the vernacular to musical accompaniment. The ceremony apparently made such a favorable impression on many Jews, and also on Gentiles present, that it prompted the community leadership to initiate regular devotional exercises in the same hall.[69]

Mannheimer, it seems, lost his enthusiasm for confirmations during his tenure in Vienna, holding only nine confirmations in thirty years. There were 85 boys and 125 girls confirmed during this period.[70]

Mannheimer's successor, Adolf Jellinek (1823–1893), came to Vienna in 1857. He was preacher at the second temple in the Leopoldstadt district (dedicated in 1858) until Mannheimer's death in 1865, when he took up his post at the Seitenstettengasse synagogue. More open to reforms than Mannheimer, he nevertheless tried to maintain a moderate position which would alienate neither the liberal reformers nor the traditionalists. Unlike his predecessor, he held annual confirmation ceremonies.[71] In spite of this practice, he expressed skepticism toward the notion that confirmations for girls improved their Jewish education in a sermon delivered in 1864 for Shavuot on the religious education of Jewish women.[72] He described confirmations as "ceremonies in which many girls marched past us in the synagogue."

While he credited the ceremony as a beautiful, sensible, effective, and moving one which left a deep impression, he complained that the community and parents did not take it seriously enough. He concluded that in order to rejuvenate Judaism and bring women to an understanding of their role, the community must focus on the religious upbringing of young girls, by bringing it back into the privacy of home, rather than relegating it only to the realm of the dazzling Temples.[73] He was opposed to changing the nature of public observance to minimize traditional gender distinctions. The beautification of services and the innovation of confirmations had not succeeded enough in bringing about a deeper sense of religion in women. This sentiment corresponded to Jellinek's general conservatism on the issue of women's role in Judaism.

Meir Friedmann (*Ish Shalom*) (1831–1908), a rabbinic scholar and teacher, also criticized the institution of confirmations. Friedmann, summoned to Vienna in 1858, started out as a private tutor. In 1864, he became a lecturer at the newly instituted Vienna Beth ha Midrash, continuing for 44 years.[74] He discussed the matter of confirmations in a responsum written at the request of Wilhelm Ritter von Gutmann (1825–1895), the president of the Vienna Jewish community, who in 1892 raised the question of the participation of women in Jewish religious services, hoping to interest young women.[75] He acknowledged the custom of confirmations for girls as useful and positive in awakening a religious consciousness and leading to greater family observance. Nevertheless, he found the ceremony to lack uniformity and originality.

Most surprisingly, he suggested, "Wouldn't we do better to call our girls as bar mitzvah [*sic*] to the Torah, just as the boys? The impression and the appeal would be more decisive than with the imitative confirmation."[76] Although this suggestion was radical, he also remained committed to Jewish law. Take for example his case for allowing women to be called to the Torah.

> I, myself, would even be in favor of the idea, that women also should be called to the Torah, because today we would lack the feeling that the dignity of the congregation (*cavod ha tsibor*) is violated if a woman were to be called up. On the contrary, the Jewish domestic and communal life would gain extraordinarily, if the women were deemed worthy of this religious practice. It goes without saying that one must erect a covered staircase from the women's gallery directly to the Ark so that the woman who is called up can ascend and descend unseen.[77]

Friedmann, considered traditional in the Viennese context, suggested quite a novel idea. He favored extending as many religious privileges to women as possible without disregarding Jewish law. He did not consider any biological, social, or cultural rationalization valid for limiting women's role in Judaism, in contrast to many other nineteenth-century rabbis. On the contrary, he asserted that Jewish domestic and communal life would gain by a greater participation in public religious observances. He forcefully opposed changing Judaism in ways which imitated other religions, but he also remained committed to looking for solutions to practical problems according to Jewish tradition.

In contrast to the rabbis, the lay leadership of the Jewish community had high hopes for the practice of confirming girls. The *Israelitische Kultusgemeinde Wien* (IKG), the official Jewish communal organization in Vienna, instituted special confirmation lessons independent of the regular religious lessons during the school day. The members of the IKG wanted the lessons to be serious, regarding them as practical, ethical preparation for the real world. Dominated by wealthy notables, the IKG had a vision for the confirmation ceremony that upheld decorum and impression over content. The confirmation ceremony was intended as a festive conclusion to the lessons at which the confirmed girls took a sacred vow in the sanctuary of the synagogue in front of the assembled community.[78] The curriculum for girls' confirmation lessons consisted of four subjects, some taught in German and others in Hebrew: I. The Ten Commandments of God (German), II. The Thirteen Qualities of God (Hebrew), III. The Thirteen Principles of Maimonides (German), and IV. Leviticus, Chapter 19, Verses 1–4, 9–18, and 30–37 (German).[79] The curriculum prepared them to answer six questions at the ceremony. For example, in 1892 the questions were: (1) What is the main Jewish teaching about God? (2) What is the main Jewish teaching about mankind? (3) What is the main Jewish teaching about the duties of mankind toward God? (4) What is the main Jewish teaching about the duties of mankind toward his neighbors? (5) What is the main Jewish teaching about the duties of mankind toward themselves? (6) What is Israel's hope for the future of mankind? The girls were required to answer these questions in Hebrew and German.

The IKG stated the purpose of the confirmation lesson as follows: "The confirmation lesson has the goal to impress upon female youth the most important precepts and the fundamental ethical principles of the Israelite religion, before they leave school and step out into life, thereby offering the maturing female youth a firm grounding and a secure support in later life in all matters." They intended the lessons to provide a precise summary of the principles of Judaism in a clear, easily understood presentation. They wanted the lessons to have an "apologetic character" and to especially emphasize the principles which distinguished Judaism from other religions.

EINLADUNG

zur

CONFIRMATION DER MÄDCHEN

SONNTAG, DEN 22. MAI D. J.,

10 Uhr Vormittags

im Stadttempel

und

DONNERSTAG, DEN 26. MAI D. J.,

halb 10 Uhr Vormittags

im Leopoldstädter Tempel.

Der Bethausvorstand

der isr. Cultusgemeinde.

Wien, im Mai 1892.

Invitation to Girls' Confirmation (Einladung zur Confirmation der Mädchen) 1892. Courtesy of Central Archives for the History of the Jewish People, Jerusalem. A/W 1638.

The IKG also gave specific instructions as to how to teach the classes in order to effectively make a lasting impression on the girls. They suggested that the lectures be lively and free of superfluous phrases. The teachers were to be enthusiastic, and to stress form as well as content. The teachers should ask students questions at the end of the lectures and periodically quiz them in order to ensure that they had properly understood the material. "If the confirmation lesson is taught in this spirit, it can become an important factor in the life of the female youth. The students will listen to the lectures with desire and love; they will adopt the teachings with enthusiasm and remember them. They will understand the tenets and guard them as a sacred treasure and apply the received principles also in later life." [80]

The students practiced speaking loudly and clearly and pronouncing the Hebrew words properly. The lessons were open to students even if they did not intend to participate in a confirmation ceremony. The notions expressed by the Viennese lay leadership in these documents demonstrate a shift in Jewish practice and identity. They aimed to create a feeling of community in Jewish girls, which would be carried over into their future homes.

An exchange on the subject of girls' confirmations in the Viennese Jewish newspaper, *Die Wahrheit*, in 1913 suggests that the debate continued. An anonymous writer suggested, in an article entitled "Mädchenkonfirmation," that while the institution of girls' confirmations was borrowed from the church, this fact did not weaken its usefulness, because actually Judaism often borrowed ideas from other cultures.[81] He acknowledged that even the well-known historian Heinrich Graetz wrote disapprovingly of the confirmation of girls, claiming it made no sense in Judaism. The author countered: "Nevertheless various reforms, which are suited to rouse religious feeling in the hearts of young children and to keep it lively, should not be so carelessly condemned, even when taken from other forms of worship." He argued that positive things should always be incorporated and gave examples of Judaism borrowing ideas from the outside. He concluded that in pre-modern times, confirmations for girls would not have been necessary because religious traditions were transmitted in the home through the family, but that "in our times" religious life completely disappeared from many Jewish homes and all possible means must be employed in order to provide the youth with strong Jewish beliefs.

Two numbers later, Rabbi Löwy of Hamburg argued an opposing viewpoint.[82] He suggested that Herr Fr. failed to distinguish between religious practices and entirely universal human principles. The examples of Judaism borrowing from other traditions given by Fr. fell into the latter category, according to Rabbi Löwy, and did not in any way prove that non-Jewish traditions should be incorporated into Jewish places of worship. "Pure ecclesiastical customs have no place in Judaism! Looking back from the beginning of the reforms up until today and answering honestly with hand on heart: Has organ music strengthened 'yiddishkeit'? Have the perfectly formed girls' confirmations decreased conversions?" He concluded that the answer to the disappearance of Jewish spirit in home and family life should be found within Jewish tradition rather than outside. "Only an honest, self-conscious Judaism, that disdains everything foreign, can stop the decay."

The reflections of the original author followed Löwy's response. He suggested that confirmation of girls was not a religious law but rather merely a form, and therefore it would be permitted to incorporate it from other religions. He also argued against Rabbi Löwy's assertion that his examples of Judaism borrowing from other traditions pertained not to religious matters but only human ones. Finally, he asserted that because something takes place in a church is no reason to reject it in Judaism.

> By this means, it should also be forbidden for Jewish boys to be confirmed in synagogues and in fact for prayers to be said and sermons to be preached there, because in church they not only confirm but they also pray and preach. The blessed Mannheimer did not introduce the girls' confirmation here in Vienna because it is an ecclesiastical custom, but purely and simply to offer those girls, who do not benefit from strong religious upbringing in the home, the opportunity to become familiar with the fundamental teachings of the Israelite religion and enthusiastic and inspired for the beliefs of the forefathers.

According to the author, Mannheimer successfully curtailed the growing epidemic of conversions through the introduction of confirmations for girls, winning women back to religion. Women, the author argued, are traditionally stronger than men in their belief, and therefore by bringing women closer to their traditions, they will in turn influence men.

The dialogue over the institution of girls' confirmations in Vienna demonstrates, perhaps above all else, a discrepancy between the beliefs and desires of the scholarly rabbinic leadership and the elite lay leadership, over which direction would best be followed for the future of the Jewish community. While the rabbis appeared to embrace the confirmation ceremony as having symbolic value, they often betrayed skepticism toward its true educational merit and viewed its derivative nature as a deficiency. The rabbis consciously desired upholding and maintaining Jewish particularity, whereas the lay leadership not only desired integration but regarded it as necessary to the future of Judaism. They believed that Judaism's survival could be guaranteed by keeping it relevant and modern. They promoted the confirmation of girls as a method of achieving this goal. While in general the Viennese rabbis were willing to go along with this innovation, they expressed their reservations about the overall value of such ceremonies.

As for the impression the confirmation lessons and ceremony made on girls themselves, it remains difficult to say. Although confirmation is not mentioned in memoirs, this could mean either that the women who wrote memoirs did not participate in confirmation, or that the ceremony did not leave a lasting impression. Nevertheless, in their autobiographical writings Jewish women did often indicate the perception that Judaism valued men over women. Most of all, the concern over the religious education of Jewish girls on the part of religious and lay leaders demonstrates their awareness that the combination of influences on young Jewish women in the Viennese fin de siècle threatened to weaken their Jewish self-awareness, thus lending support to the descriptions of their childhood experiences in their reminiscences.

Conflicting Influences at Home: The Kinderfrau and the Jewish Family

Assimilated parents, Catholic domestic servants, and traditional grandparents frequently exerted conflicting influences on Jewish girls at home. In most memoirs, Jewish women describe their parents as secular and, in some cases, rejecting their Jewish identities. For example, Toni Stopler described her father as a "non-believer in Jewish law and customs," who declared himself *konfessionslos* (without religious confession). After her fourteenth birthday, the age at which a child could legally declare him- or herself *konfessionslos*, she went to City Hall, unaccompanied, to do so. Dora Israel Amann wrote: "My parents were not religious and that is how we were also brought up. My father feared that we children would have suffered under anti-Semitism, especially with our name Israel. In the year 1897, when I was three years old, he had all the children converted to Protestantism. That was not simple in Austria."[83] Anny Robert's description of her family similarly suggests the lack of Jewishness in the home.

> In my parents' house, we were engaged in neither religion nor Zionism. We were Jews, but I believe in the first place Austrian. That is to say Austrian Jews, or Jewish Austrians. Indeed my mother said a little prayer with me before bedtime, as one can call a *Kindergebet* . . . In any case I spoke German and not Hebrew. It was a prayer that was both for Jewish and Christian children, and certainly was prayed by many.[84]

She described her family as "really rather assimilated" but not ready to convert. At the age of eighteen she considered becoming *konfessionslos* for a short time, while under the influence of socialism, but ultimately gave up this idea, preferring to remain Jewish. Although her family practiced no religious rites, she did learn some things about biblical history, and remembered inventing a game called Noah's Ark as a young child before her school days. Her family housekeeper, Mizzi, brought her along to church now and then, and her parents had nothing against it.

Dressmaker and designer Gertrude Berliner (b. 1908) grew up in an assimilated family in Vienna. "We celebrated Christmas with a tree and Easter with colored eggs . . . And viewed the Catholic ceremonies at Easter and Christmas with the maids."[85] Nevertheless, she received some Jewish education in school, which provided her with a sense of pride. When she visited the Museum of Art on Heldenplatz at the age of eleven, another child asked her if she recognized a painting of the Virgin Mary and her child Jesus. Knowing a little from her Catholic classmates, she thought, "I bet they do not know about Seder and Moses crossing the Red Sea with the Jews and the *manischtana* (the four questions) . . . and the fasting on Yom Kippur our beloved religious teacher Irma Schrötter had taught us. And all that Hebrew Paul already knew."[86]

The presence of Catholic domestic servants and their influence over Jewish daughters presented dilemmas for some Jewish girls. For example, the Galician-born actress and writer Salka (Salomea) Steuermann Viertel (1889–1978) recalled that her nanny, Niania, taught her the Lord's Prayer, and she said it fervently every night. When a new fanatically Catholic governess, Mlle. Juliette, arrived on the scene, she noticed Salka's piousness and decided to try to convert her.

> Sitting at my bedside she whispered gruesome stories of the martyr-dom of Saint Dennis, walking with his head under his arm, Santa Barbara having her breast pinched with red hot irons, Saint Sebastian pierced by arrows, and others. The Crucifixion, in her fanatic version, was the most terrifying of all. She told it with such passionate hatred for the Jews that I was crushed with guilt.[87]

Sometimes Niania or one of their French governesses took Salka and her siblings to church. The children later reenacted the chanting and genuflections of the service to the great amusement of the servants. When Niania overheard Juliette's whispering and Salka's sobbing one evening she called Salka's mother, who stormed into the room and told Juliette to pack her things and leave. "After Juliette left the room, my mother kissed and comforted me, but I pushed her away. I did not want to belong to those who had killed and tortured Jesus." Later her mother told her a more objective version of the Crucifixion, dividing the blame between the Jews and Romans and "revealing the astonishing fact, which Juliette had suppressed, that Jesus himself was a Jew."

Stella Klein-Löw (1904–1986) recalled the influence of a Catholic *Kinderfrau* on her religious perspective.

> Religious duality impressed me for my entire life: My parents were enlightened Jews—Juschka was a fanatic Catholic (otherwise also an anti-Semite, only we were for her not Jews). Where did I stand? What remained from this for my entire life? As a child I could not understand, that God, to Whom one prayed, in Whom one trusted, was doubled. I went along to processions and loved the stillness of the church. Temple was not visited by us, and also we never prayed. Therefore was our God less important? Or was He so far that He could not hear our prayer? Why were we Jews? It seemed so much nicer to be Christian.[88]

She asked her grandfather once why they were Jews. He answered that his father, grandfather, and great-grandfather were Jews. When she asked why they could not be Catholic, he replied, "Because we do not want to be." She protested that no one asked her what she wanted to be. He said, "The Jews are pursued, hated by many. Stelli, do you believe that one should abandon them and their religion? Wouldn't that be cowardly? . . . Religion is not a shirt which you can change every week or each day." She answered him, "I will not constantly change it, only once and forever." In the end he laughed and said, "Stay as you are. Religion is not as important as a good heart and a clear head." [89]

Esti Freud described going to mass every day at St. Stephan's Cathedral with her nanny. "Nanny wanted us, especially me as the oldest, to convert to Catholicism. One of her arguments was that we would never ascend to heaven unless we did. I remember telling her that if my father didn't go to heaven, I didn't want to." [90] Esti asked her mother if there were two kinds of *lieber Gott*, one for the rich and one for the poor, because the servants went to pray at the Cathedral, whereas her mother went to the Temple on holidays. She also recalled a nightmare about reciting the four questions at her grandparents' house on Seder Evening. "For a six-year-old who knew no Hebrew it was a hard task to memorize those questions. I think I did fairly well however, in reality."

Children in assimilated families sometimes developed a sense of curiosity about the religion that their family had struggled to leave behind. For example, Toni Bondy Cassirer (1883–1961), wife of philosopher Ernst Cassirer, wrote about her family's distance from Judaism and her opposing stance. "We were raised without religion. My father's family had not observed the rituals for three generations, and my father was so far removed from the ghetto type, that he quite seriously believed in assimilation and also wished for it. Of us five children, I was the one, who skeptically opposed this outlook." [91] Shortly before her death, Cassirer expressed regret that she did not know more about Judaism. "It is horrible how little I know of my own religion. You know, my grandfather (or was it an uncle or great-uncle) was already a physician—I have forgotten at which German princely court—and we were too far removed not from the faith, but from knowledge about Judaism." Her son converted to Christianity, and she described a feeling of discomfort when he discussed his beliefs with her. [92]

Salka Steuermann Viertel also expressed interest in religious Jews, describing them as mysterious and exotic. Her father went to services in the synagogue on Yom Kippur and resisted conversion even though it would have helped his career. "Although completely assimilated into Polish-Austrian society, he had refused the directorship of a major bank in Vienna because it would have meant having himself and his family baptized." [93] She described "Old Lamet," an innkeeper who was an Orthodox Jew, as "a strikingly handsome patriarch, very tall, erect, his beautiful, noble face framed by a long snow-white beard." On Friday evenings, she used to sneak to the back window of the inn to see him sitting at a white-covered table surrounded by his family, saying the blessings. "As my parents never cared about any kind of religion and did not practice their own, all this was to me very mysterious and fascinating." "I knew that we were Jewish, but certainly did not belong to those strange people in long black caftans, with beards and side-locks, and we did not understand their harsh idiom. Still we were not Christians either, although we had a Christmas tree and sang Christmas carols. Our parents never went to church—but also they never went to the synagogue."[94] About Yom Kippur, she wrote, "I had always been awed by this day; it made me uncomfortable with all the Jewish men and women fasting and going to the temple, looking reproachfully at us apostates."[95]

The presence of religious grandparents encouraged interest in the Jewish religion for some Jewish girls in assimilated families. Käthe Leichter revealed nostalgia for tradition based on the influence of her religious grandfather.[96] "My grandfather, who outlived my grandmother, spent the summers with us in Baden, and though my father was entirely liberal and secular for himself and our education, the strong religiosity of Grandfather was respected with utmost reverence. Food was ritually cooked for him, my sister and I recited the *Shema Yisrael* daily in the early morning to him."[97] Her parents concealed from her grandfather the fact that they celebrated Christmas. She also remembered participating in the Seder with him. "Its venerable patriarchal character with its lights, prayers, foods, under the leadership of the aged grandfather made a very big impression on me." As the youngest child, she recited the four questions and for it received a gold coin. While her older cousins drew in their *Haggadah*s during the ceremony, regarding it as amusing and outdated, she considered their attitudes improper. Under the influence of her grandfather, and later her religious instructor in school, she was "devoutly religious and also fasted on Yom Kippur, against the will of my enlightened parents, because it seemed to me indispensable as training of my determination."

Her grandfather died on Yom Kippur at the age of eighty-four. He insisted on fasting although the Chief Rabbi of Vienna personally advised him against it. His independence impressed Käthe and her sister, Vally. It astonished the parents, who were determined to rid themselves of the grandparents' "primitive religiosity," that the tradition made a greater impression on their children than their own rational superiority. "When we were fourteen or fifteen we finally gave up the traditional ceremony on Yom Kippur, because our corresponding vow not to quarrel one day a year was to us impossible. With this, my religiosity came to an abrupt end."[98]

In conclusion, Jewish girls in Vienna faced the challenges of life as Jews in an increasingly hostile environment, and the additional burden of gender limitations. Most Viennese Jewish girls who later wrote memoirs recalled growing up in assimilated families. In addition to the lack of a coherent Jewish upbringing in the home, young Viennese Jewish girls, who attended public elementary schools, faced a school environment dominated by Catholicism in which being Jewish meant being different. The problem of anti-Semitism in Viennese schools referred to in memoirs concerned the leaders of the Jewish community and became a topic of discussion in Jewish newspapers. Additionally, many found themselves in church on a regular basis with their Catholic nannies, who in some cases actively tried to indoctrinate the girls. For young Jewish girls with little exposure to Jewish religious practices and beliefs, these incidents led to a great deal of confusion. Moreover, separation for religious classes from the other children, often accompanied by discrimination, and the sense that Judaism did not value women as highly as men, led to alienation from Judaism. For most of these young women their Jewishness meant being different. In some cases, families that were determined to distance themselves from tradition found their daughters attracted to traditional Jews and Jewish grandparents as mysterious others. Curious about these others and sensing that their ancestors once belonged to this group, they developed a complex desire for more knowledge about traditional Judaism. In addition to facing the challenges of life as a Jew in a sometimes hostile environment, Jewish girls had the additional burden imposed by their gender. The common ground in the experiences of Jewish women who wrote memoirs about growing up Jewish and female in Vienna was a lingering confusion about what it meant to be Jewish. Their desire to overcome the obstacles they faced as women and Jews would influence their future choices and paths.

Recent historical works on Jewish women have argued that in Western Europe, women held on to Jewish religious practices in the home long after most Jewish men had abandoned traditional Jewish culture.[1] In Eastern Europe, on the other hand, where assimilation did not threaten Jewish group survival, women remained ethnically Jewish; however, they became increasingly secular and drawn to various political movements.[2] Neither of these patterns adequately describes the Viennese Jewish women who wrote about their lives. Because they were living in the crossroads between east and west, their Jewish ethnic identity endured more than in Western Europe, giving them less need for turning to religious rituals. With little Jewish religious practice in the home and somewhat less social isolation than in Eastern Europe, they retained Jewish distinctiveness primarily in educational, social, and political patterns, and were reminded of their identity by anti-Semitism. However, the female Jewish intelligentsia, the daughters of middle-class, highly assimilated Jewish families, were neither typical nor representative of the experience of Viennese Jewish women on the whole.

This chapter will focus on Jewish women who maintained ties to Jewish religion and community through prayer and philanthropy. The involvement of women in the Jewish community provides a counterexample to the trend of assimilation. They participated in prayer and formed societies which organized activities such as charity, burial, and visitation of the sick. While this phenomenon in part is attributable to the general bourgeois values of their surrounding society, the choice of a Jewish framework for pursuing the appropriate female venues of communal giving demonstrates a certain level of group consciousness and identity. I will also examine the images of Jewish women that emerged in the writings of the Jewish religious and communal lay leadership in Vienna. Together these sources will begin to illuminate the actual and perceived roles of Viennese Jewish women in the Jewish community and the impact that this had on their identities. It will also demonstrate the importance of gender as a factor in Viennese Jewish identity, as it will become evident that leaders in the Jewish community focused their attention on Jewish women in their writings.

Jewish Women and Prayer:
The Domestic Ideology of Beruria

A Jewish prayer book for women, entitled *Beruria* after the learned wife of Rabbi Meir from the Talmud, published in many editions in Vienna around the turn of the century, provided a German abridged version of different prayers, such as weekday prayers, the blessings for after a meal, and for the Sabbath and Jewish holidays. It also supplied explanations of prayers and rituals directed at women in the form of short commentaries on various topics. While these essays predictably provide more information on the male writer's perspective of women than on women themselves, the popularity of this book attests to the fact that Jewish women wanted to pray. It represents a genre of Jewish women's prayer books in the German language, similar to the collections of Yiddish Tehines (women's supplicatory prayers).[3] The rabbi and folklorist Max Grunwald (1871–1953), who edited the book, described aspects of Jewish prayer and ritual in commentaries directed at a female audience. For example, in an essay on the "Shema" (Hear O Israel) prayer, Grunwald made the following appeal stressing the importance of women's domestic role as transmitters of Judaism.

> Our daughters must above all know the phrase, which forms the mainspring of Israel as a religion and as a nationality. This applies to girls above all others, because in most cases the woman is the one, to whom the task falls, to maintain Judaism in the home, in the hearts of the children, and even of the husband, as already Moses thousands of years ago first turned to women with his message, and only then turned to the men.[4]

In another commentary, he described a crisis in Sabbath observance, but indicated that women observed the Sabbath as a day of rest by celebrating it in the home and transmitting the traditions to their children.[5]

In addition to the Sabbath and holiday prayers and treatises on Judaism, Grunwald included many pages of prayers and messages of special relevance to female experiences. For example, in a section entitled "On the Infant" he discussed the importance of the relationship between mother and infant. "Not only, what the child receives from the mother, but also what the mother receives from the child, this also creates and strengthens the moral power of the world. This awareness of the moral importance of the infant was comprehended by no other people of the earth so clearly and effectively as by the Jews."[6] This was followed by a poem called "My Child" and special prayers to be recited on the day of circumcision and on the naming of a daughter. He introduced other special prayers for various occasions, such as the confirmation of one's children, for a child in a foreign country, before and after the birth of a child, and during cemetery visitations.

Only the Shema and the blessings for lighting the candles on the Sabbath and holidays were rendered in Hebrew. The book contained an expanded German version of the *Kaddish*, a prayer traditionally recited by Jewish men in mourning. The fact that he encouraged women to say *Kaddish* at all, and in the vernacular, indicates that this prayer book was far from traditional. He also provided an abridged German form of the blessing over a meal. Romanticized images of the position and importance of women in carrying out the Jewish religion characterized the commentaries. In the appendix, Grunwald compiled excerpts from an eclectic group of philosophers, writers, and other sources, such as Henrik Ibsen, Napoleon I, Friedrich Hebbel, Leo Tolstoy, Friedrich Nietzsche, and Adolf Jellinek—not exactly what one might expect in a Jewish prayer book. This suggests that he directed it to Jewish women who had stronger secular educations.

The emphasis on family in the prayer book reflects the domestic orientation of the Jewish religion and community. Women who chose non-traditional paths, such as university studies, politics, and careers, most likely would not have felt drawn to the domestic ideology of Jewish communal organizations or religious observance. Moreover, they fulfilled their ideological and spiritual needs through their careers and/or politics. Those who followed the example of their mothers and grandmothers, making the family the center of their lives, participated more actively in the Jewish community and religion. Thus, it is not surprising that in most memoirs and biographies, usually written by or about professional, "intellectual," and/or political women, Judaism played at best a peripheral role. Jewish women in the lower classes (because their work did not provide satisfaction) and upper classes (who had more leisure time to fill) probably focused more attention on family, religion, and community. Perhaps both these groups prayed with and read Grunwald's *Beruria*.

The Proliferation of Jewish Women's Charity Organizations

The growing participation of Jewish women in philanthropy also indicates that many Jewish women still had ties with the Jewish community. Prominent wealthy Jewish women as benefactors along with the needy as recipients participated most actively in Jewish charitable and humanitarian work. The involvement of Jewish women in these enterprises has been attributed in part to an idealization of female philanthropy in general society. Marsha Rozenblit states that "the decades before World War I witnessed the growth of women's charitable organizations which provided bourgeois Jewish women with the opportunity to fulfill the nineteenth-century ideal of female philanthropy."[7] On the situation in Germany, Marion Kaplan notes that "Jewish social work developed in a context of Jewish culture and philanthropy, economic depression, the rationalization of state poor relief, and a large variety of centralizing, modernizing Christian and secular societies."[8]

In Vienna, the roots of Jewish women's philanthropy dated back to the early nineteenth century, when Fanny Jeitteles founded a poor house and Theresa Mayer Weikersheim established the *Theresien-Kreutzer-Verein* for the encouragement of synagogue attendance.[9] The *Israelitischer Frauen-Wohltätigkeits-Verein* (Israelite Women's Charity Society) was established in 1815. (Until around 1895, it was known as the *Israelitischer Frauen-Verein*.)[10] After a hiatus of over forty years, the *Israelitische Mädchen-Waisenhaus in Wien* (Israelite Home for Orphaned Girls) (1873) emerged.

Around the turn of the century, new Jewish women's charity organizations proliferated in Vienna. For example, Laura Bloch, wife of Rabbi Josef Samuel Bloch, founded the *Israelitischer Frauen-Wohltätigkeitsverein Floridsdorf* (Israelite Women's Charity Society Floridsdorf) in 1880. Others include *"Frauenhort" Israelitischer Frauen-Wohltätigkeits-Verein im Bezirke Alsergrund* ("Women's Shelter" Israelite Women's Charity Society in the Alsergrund District) founded in 1893, the *Brigittenauer Israelitischer Frauen-Wohltätigkeitsverein* (Brigittenau Israelite Charity Society) founded in 1895, the *Israelitischen Frauen-Wohltätigkeits-Verein des VIII. Bezirkes in Wien* (Israelite Women's Charity Society of the 8th District in Vienna) founded in 1896, the *Jüdischer Frauen-Wohltätigkeits-Verein "Zuflucht"* (Jewish Women's Charity Society "Shelter"), the *Erster Simmerlinger Israelitischer Frauen-Wohltätigkeitsverein für den 11 Bezirk* (First Simmerling Israelite Women's Charity Society for the 11th District) founded in 1900, the *Mädchen- und Frauen-Verein "Bikur-Chaulim"* (Girls' and Women's Society for Visiting the Sick) founded in 1903, and the *Hietzinger Frauenwohltätigkeits-Verein* (HFWV) founded in 1906. According to the statistics of the *Israelitischer Frauen Wohltätigkeits-Verein*, before 1866 only eleven Jewish charity organizations operated in Vienna, three run by women. During the years 1866 to 1870, three more emerged; from 1871 to 1880 another nine, from 1881 to 1890 another nine, from 1891 to 1900 another twenty-seven, from 1901 to 1910 another twenty-three, and from 1911 to 1916 another six. Thus by 1915, a total of eighty-eight Jewish organizations operated in Vienna, of which eighteen were women's organizations.

Philanthropic organizations provided bourgeois Jewish women, whose sphere of activity was otherwise limited to the home, with important opportunities to enter into public life.[11] They also allowed Jewish women to fulfill a religious obligation, *Tzedakah* (charity), and a social obligation at the same time. Precisely during this period, social problems for the Jews, such as anti-Semitism and prostitution, heightened. In response the organizations addressed perceived problems, such as cultural backwardness of the Jews in the eastern part of the Monarchy. Taken in combination, these factors help account for the proliferation of Jewish women's charitable organizations in Vienna during this period.

Eleonore Wertheim and Eleonore Nassau, wife of Isaac Wolf Nassau and mother of Wolf Isaac, Elisabeth Kohn, Franziska Goetzl, Charlotte Biedermann, and Judith Loewinger founded the *Israelitischer Frauen-Wohltätigkeits-Verein* (IFWV), the first and most enduring organization of its kind, in 1815. The organization aimed for "the support of needy Jewish women, especially Jewish women in childbed and widows, and to contribute to the dowry of Jewish brides and the education of Jewish girls." It earned the respect and recognition of general philanthropists.[12] The writer J. Biederman donated a substantial amount and raised funds by producing his Yiddish-German satirical dramas about the tolerated class of Viennese Jews. Joseph Fischhof wrote the music for these short plays, which the men and women of the society presented for the benefit of the organization. Some of the titles performed were *Israel in Floribus, Emancipated Jews*, and *The Kobelsdorfers*.[13]

Adolf Jellinek spoke at the celebration of its fiftieth anniversary in 1866.[14] He stressed that the organization's founders responded to economic crisis with the Jewish idea of charity. Women gave anonymous assistance to the needy without causing them shame or embarrassment. In 1873, a year of economic depression, membership in the organization began to decline and continued to do so until the early 1900s. In 1873 there were 1,283 members, and in 1900 membership reached its lowest point at 723. The annual contributions also declined during this period.[15]

Annual reports during the period of decline tried to present an optimistic outlook. According to the 1891 report, the organization ran smoothly, improved its structure, and provided assistance to many women.[16] In 1892 the death of Bettina von Rothschild brought in a large number of donations in her honor, allowing the society to continue its work.[17] In 1901, things temporarily picked up with about 38 new members, bringing the total membership to 761 and an annual contribution of about 10,000 K., allowing the organization to begin to build a reserve fund.[18]

The IFWV politely asserted that the founding of so many new local women's charity groups actually hindered philanthropic work. In 1912, on the verge of celebrating its one hundredth anniversary, the organization's leaders raised the following concerns in the yearly report.

> Our effectiveness extends over the entire Viennese community. Far removed, from wanting to deny the acknowledgment of the work of our sister organizations, we cannot be completely restrained from speaking openly, that the existence of a large number of organizations with similar tendencies brings about just the opposite, of allowing that pure and simple goal-oriented success to mature: Centralization of relief for the poor.[19]

In 1915, the IFWV celebrated its one hundredth year. The ceremony, held at the *Stadttempel* on Seitenstettengasse, included psalms arranged by the cantor Salamon Sulzer, an official speech by Rabbi Moritz Güdemann, and the national anthem. Güdemann spoke about the patience and perseverance of the "oldest and most noble women's organization of our community."[20] He compared the women of the organization to women of Jewish history and classical antiquity and praised their wartime efforts to combat hunger, misery, sickness, and death. The *Jahresbericht* (annual report) also included a text on the history of the IFWV, which described how it developed from its modest beginnings in the early nineteenth century, into a crucial factor in the poor-relief work of the community.

In 1867, the *Mädchen-Unterstützungs-Verein* (Society for the Support of Girls) (MUV) was founded with the goal of supporting schools which prepared poor girls for various types of employment.[21] Like the *Frauen-Erwerb-Verein* (Women's Employment Society), this society strived for the earning capacity of female youth and their economic independence. Thousands of poor young girls attended their schools over the years and successfully pursued careers as office workers, merchants, teachers, and seamstresses. Every year the schools of the MUV were full to capacity. At the general assembly in 1889, the president, Paula Frankl, gave a speech describing the development of the MUV, in which she asserted that the organization had blazed a path toward the awareness of women's ability to work. "The revolution, which has taken place in recent years, is essentially attributable to the changing relationships in Vienna and in the Monarchy, but the fact that families have come to the insight that women's work eases pressure just as men's work, also plays a part."[22]

The *Israelitische Mädchen-Waisenhaus*, founded in 1874, provided for young Jewish orphaned girls, giving them a "family life," an education, and the means to live independently.[23] Charlotte von Königswarter served as the president of the women's committee (*Schutzdamen Comite*) in charge of the school. Marie Kompert and Ida Gutmann served as vice presidents, and Charlotte Berhrend, Ottilie Bondy, Emilie von Ephrussi, Anna Friedländer-Delia, Mina Gomperz, Sophie Gutmann, Emilie von Pfeiffer, and Henriette von Wertheimer comprised the board. The members of the women's committee visited and inspected the home on a regular basis. They recorded 196 inspection visits during the first two years. The yearly report described the origins of the home on July 1, 1874, when seventeen orphaned girls were taken into the home by the Gutmann brothers. The women's committee undertook the mission "to educate them, who were for the most part physically and spiritually badly neglected creatures, into self-reliant and fully employable persons in a few years."[24]

They declared as their leading principles religious education, schooling, training for female work, and experience in domestic work. They taught the girls religion, practical arithmetic, preparation for female work, and health and diet. The women's committee of the Home assembled every month. "The spirit of filial obedience and sisterly unity ruled in the Home." They attributed their success to the dedication of the House Mother, Flora Bruck. Also the preachers Adolf Jellinek and Moritz Güdemann, the renowned and talented cantor

Salomon Sulzer (1804–1890), and the professors Dr. Jonathan Wolf and Dr. Längfeller presented the students with speeches and song.

Gottlieb Bettelheim, the president of the Temple society of the ninth district, founded *"Frauenhort" Israelitischer Frauen-Wohltätigkeits-Verein im Bezirk Alsergrund in Wien* in 1893. Rosa Zifferer served as president and led the organization until her death in 1911. Clothilde Benedikt, the secretary of *Frauenhort* and daughter of the neurologist Moritz Benedikt, wrote the following description of Zifferer after her death.

> . . . how can the magic of your essence be grasped by words, that you have the spirit and refinement of a French Salon woman, the pride and control of the Northern Germans, the heart of the Jewish people, the ripe intellect of a man, the mild worldly wisdom of a woman who has been placated by her destiny in life, the purity of heart and receptiveness for all good and beauty, which is otherwise only possessed by the youth, united in you in a rare mixture.[25]

This gives an interesting perspective on the qualities expected from the ideal Jewish woman in fin de siècle Vienna.

Frauenhort's main purpose was to assist poor families. For example, they distributed money, provided matzah and wine for Passover, gave support for emigrating families, provided clothing, shoes, and school supplies for children, and provided fuel for many families.[26] They eventually built a convalescent home for female workers, in order to "take care of twice the number of female workers with the same means and through suitable supervision improve the physical and moral health of these step-children of destiny."[27] This home gave working women a place to stay, and provided for their physical well-being during illness and recovery, so that they would not return to work prematurely out of financial desperation. In 1904 they had the land for the building, but did not yet have the means to build. Benedikt described how the idea for the Home eventually became a reality.

> When Frau Rosa Feigenbaum, the valued contributor to this newspaper and my most worthy predecessor in "Frauenhort," conceived of the bold idea, to erect a working women's home in Austria, Rosa Zifferer, with indefatigable persistence and strong sense of reality slowly brought the beneficial idea of her colleague to maturity and so

the magnificent *Kaiser Franz Josephs-Arbeiterinnen-Erholungsheim in Seebenstein*, the "Frauenhort" creation of the Kaiser's anniversary year, is finally drawing attention to the self-sacrificing spirit of Viennese womankind at the beginning of our century.[28]

Frauenhort also cooperated with other Viennese charity organizations. For example, they worked together with the Jewish women's organizations in the Leopoldstadt and Brigittenau districts, and in the eighth district.

The Brigittenau, a very poor section of the Leopoldstadt, or second district, became a separate district (XX) in 1900, and was 14 percent Jewish in 1910; many of the Jews there depended on charity. The *Brigittenauer Israelitischer Frauen-Wohltätigkeitsverein* (BIFWV) was founded in 1895 with the goal of "supporting poor orphans, widows, and maternity cases in our district," with Emilie Weiss as president and Marie Kohn as vice-president. In 1910, they distributed a total of 13492 K., which seemed "small and unimportant . . . with regard to the bitter state of distress of our district," but was actually 60 percent more than other charity organizations when compared in proportion to the number of members.[29]

One of the joint enterprises of the different organizations was the *Verbande zur Unterstützung armer israelitischer Wöchnerinnen* (Union for the Support of Poor Jewish Maternity Cases), which originated in 1900.[30] The BIFWV took a leading role in creating and supporting the *Verband*, and a high percentage of the cases came from their district. In the year 1909, the *Verband* supported 547 maternity cases, of which 229, about 42 percent, were from the Brigittenau district.

> From this summary it follows, how right we were to greet the foundation of this *Verband* with great pleasure, and how right we are, that in spite of great quantities of troublesome inquiries and paperwork, we rank among the most enthusiastic colleagues of the *Verband*. Much more than a third of the total supported maternity cases and more than a third of the total expenditures fall to the Brigittenau.[31]

In addition to their support and work for the *Verband*, the BIFWV also contributed to relief work for poor children, by belonging to the Leopoldstadt Council for Orphans, contributing to the Jewish kindergarten in the Brigittenau, and providing clothing and shoes for school children.

In contrast to the Brigittenau, Josefstadt (VIII.), a middle-class district, attracted very few Jews. In 1890, it was 4.2 percent Jewish, in 1900 5.8 percent, and in 1910 8.8 percent.[32] A similar organization (the *Israelitischer Frauen-Wohltätigkeits-Verein des VIII. Bezirkes in Wien*) emerged in the Josefstadt district in 1891, with Amalie Beck as president and Wilhelmine Steiner as vice-president. The organization contributed to the *Verband*, to supporting widows, orphans, and sick people, poor children, etc. The charitable contributions of this organization totaled 5675 K. in 1904.

The Simmering (XI.), another minimally Jewish district, also maintained a Jewish women's charity society. The Simmering was an outlying neighborhood of Vienna which was less than 2 percent Jewish. Netti and Karoline Vogel founded the *Erster Simmerlinger Frauen-Wohltätigkeitsverein für den XI. Bezirk* in 1900. They aimed to support poor Jewish widows and orphans, and arranged cultural evenings in order to raise money for poor Jews of the Simmering district.[33]

Zuflucht was founded in Vienna, with the goal of offering "adequate assistance to the worthy, deserving poor either through securing their unsteady existence or through the establishment of new helpful earnings."[34] *Zuflucht* took great care in determining who was worthy and deserving of support, emphasizing the need to assist those deemed worthy in establishing their own earnings and becoming self-sufficient, and the need to eliminate "professional beggary." Their written statutes included provisions stating that committee members would decide whom to support.[35] Funding came from the membership contributions and fund-raising events. Each year in January, the opera singer Selma Kurz performed at an "Akademie," along with other men and women, in order to raise additional funds.

The third yearly report opened by describing the event which motivated the founding of *Zuflucht*.

At the beginning of the harsh season of 1900, one of the seven children of a poor woman came home joyfully having been given a gift of new clothing from a charitable neighbor. The widow, however, who had once seen better days, having lost not only her entire wealth, but also her husband, confessed to a nearby woman that the joy of this child gave her no joy, but instead gave her pain at the bottom of her heart. She would much prefer to buy all her children old and less beautiful clothing, if some means were at her disposal, in order to obtain with her own energy a livelihood for herself and her children.[36]

This story well illustrated the ideology behind *Zuflucht*: that in order to truly help the poor, one needed to stand them on their own feet. Most important, one must help them establish livelihoods before they had the misfortune of becoming professional beggars, to maintain their moral sensibility and sense of honor. According to the report in 1904, one man who had earlier been supported by *Zuflucht* since became a contributing member.[37] This trend increased in subsequent years, with more formerly supported families paying back their debts and becoming contributors. By 1907, there had been twelve such cases. "This illustrates most plainly the systematic and modern poor-relief of the organization '*Zuflucht*'."[38] In order to fulfill their goals, they delivered cash, provided machines, purchased materials, wrote recommendations for jobs, defrayed the costs for studying a trade, and sometimes paid for housing. In 1908, *Zuflucht* took over control of the *Verband zur Unterstützung armer Wöchnerinnen* in the second district under the leadership of their treasurer, Ida Figdor.[39]

In 1907, Eugenie Hoffmann created a women's charity organization in the Hietzing district (XIII.), an outlying "villa district" in the southwest with only a small percentage of the most wealthy Jews. After her resignation, Laura Krenberger was elected to replace her and served as president for the next several years.[40] The original purpose of the *Hietzinger Frauenwohltätigkeitsverein* (HFWV) was to decorate the Hietzinger Temple, but its activities soon expanded to supporting poor Jewish families in the outskirts of their district.[41] It worked to raise and distribute funds to the poor, organized Hanukkah celebrations for poor children and monthly lectures by prominent individuals such as the children's writer Helene Scheu-Riesz (1880–1970) and writers Siegfried Fleischer and Max Kaiser to encourage sociability and attract new members, and organized an annual "Akademie" with dance and an annual general meeting.

Beginning in 1909, the organization changed its orientation, focusing on providing for the physical and spiritual well-being of poor children. The women of the organization aspired to establish a parental bond with the children, particularly in order to strengthen their spiritual lives.[42] They established relationships between poor orphaned children and patron women. In order to accommodate their new focus, they revised the statutes so that a greater number of women could serve on the board of directors. The assistance of abandoned and orphaned children occupied them more fully in the following years, and the society renamed itself the *Hietzinger Frauenverein zum Schutze Armer,*

Verlassener Kinder (Hietzinger Women's Society for the Protection of Poor Abandoned Children) in 1915.[43]

In 1910, twenty patron women or *Schutzdamen* sponsored eighty-five abandoned children. Rudolf Kraus, the leader of the IKG charity office, helped organize the children's protection. The women visited each child at least once every three weeks, checked the condition of their clothing, and reported on their health and their progress in school. They attended to the spiritual needs of the children in an effort to provide them with a Jewish upbringing. For example, when a boy reached bar mitzvah age, delegates from the board attended the ceremony and gave gifts of special clothing and a silver watch.[44] They arranged apprenticeships for orphans above the age of fourteen and excursions for the smaller children. For example, in July 1909 they took 27 children from various districts on an outing to Gatterhoelzel bei Schoenbrunn. "With lively thanks and loud cheers, the children parted from us that evening. It was also a beautiful day for the participating *Schutzdamen*."[45] The activity evidently fulfilled a need on the part of the women volunteers to feel they provided for needy children, while it also gave the children some protection and caring.

Lack of coordination among these various groups emerged as a result of the proliferation of charity organizations. At the general assembly in 1909, Kraus delivered a lecture entitled "Centralization of Poor-Relief," in which he described the importance of the *Zentrallstelle für das Jüdische Armenwesen* (Coordinating Office for the Jewish Poor-law Administration) of the IKG. He asserted that the large number of charitable organizations, some overlapping each other, not to mention private philanthropists, necessitated coordinating welfare work in a central office. He proposed that all charity organizations be required to join the Coordinating Office, which would ensure cooperation and improve the overall structure of Viennese Jewish poor-relief.[46]

Jewish women also formed organizations to engage in the Jewish religious obligation of visiting the sick. The *Mädchen- und Frauen-Verein "Bikur-Chaulim"* (Girls' and Women's Society for Visiting the Sick), founded in 1903, focused on visiting Jewish patients in Viennese hospitals and providing them with free refreshments.[47] They visited and comforted poor Jews who had no family, helped them get admitted to hospitals when necessary, and provided them with transportation, clothing, and other items. The president, Gisela Kohn, and vice-president, Rosa Stransky, led the organization, not only assisting those who requested aide, but seeking out the poorest and most abandoned.[48] Members attended to the Jewish needs of the sick, recognizing that most hospitals ignored them.

> Our Jewish brothers and sisters, interned in unfamiliar, often unfriendly surroundings, very frequently suffer moral and spiritual agonies alongside their physical pains, which disappear through our visit and sympathetic conversation and the promise to come again, and give way to a more optimistic, more cheerful mood. The two hour visiting time in the hospitals should connect the patients with the outside world; but how wretched those feel to whom nobody comes, whose bed everybody apathetically ignores. How afraid the strangers, the forsaken become there.[49]

In addition to this description of the impact of their visits to patients, they made an appeal for more women to participate in visitations. They asserted that *"Bikur-Chaulim"* needed female qualities, such as a "noble strong female heart" and the exercise of philanthropy in "sisterly ways."

Charity work rewarded not only the recipients of care, but also female Jewish philanthropists. The leaders of *"Bikur-Chaulim"* recognized feeling a sense of accomplishment by fulfilling a religious commandment and helping mankind at the same time. "'Bikur Chaulim' is a pious action according to our holy scripture, which finds rewards with God in this life and the life to come! But the awareness, to have exercised noble human responsibility, raises our chest and fills us with self-worth and satisfaction, when we complete such hospital visits."[50]

Philanthropy provided an important outlet for the religious sensibility of Viennese Jewish women. The number of Viennese Jewish women involved in charity work in some measure was in the thousands. The IFWV, one of eighteen Jewish women's charity societies, alone had around 1,000 members. Philanthropy became recognized as the official avenue by which Jewish women served the community. Viennese Chief Rabbi and preacher Adolf Jellinek wrote that "the Vienna Jewish Community (IKG) can point with pride to its women, who are active in holy service to humanity, descend from their palaces and sympathetically care for the needy lower classes." He reported that on Hanukkah, they provided one thousand needy children with warm winter clothing. "And who collected the means to give pleasure to these one thousand children and protect them before the coldness of winter! Women, only women of the Viennese Jewish Community."[51] Nevertheless, he con-

Naemah Beer-Hofmann with pogrom orphans at the Anitta Müller Heim; Vienna, 1921. Courtesy of the Leo Baeck Institute, New York.

cluded that "charity alone is not able to preserve religion, and that Judaism demands more from its women than a pleading and helping hand. Religious loyalty is the most beautiful ornament of the Jewish woman."

During and after the First World War, the need for orphanages for refugee Jewish children increased and Viennese Jewish women answered the call. Anitta Müller-Cohen (1890–1962) founded the *Soziale Hilfsgemeinschaft Anitta Müller* (Social Relief-Organization Anitta Müller) at the outbreak of the war, which helped a large number of Jewish refugees and became one of the largest private Jewish relief organizations in Vienna.[52]

The plethora of Jewish women's charitable organizations is a reminder that female memoir writers do not represent Viennese Jewish women as a whole. Although the female Jewish intelligentsia devoted themselves to study, politics, and careers, and did not fit into the family-oriented institutions of the Viennese Jewish community, significant numbers of Jewish women participated in the Jewish community through their involvement in Jewish philanthropy. Poor and newly immigrated Jewish women in Vienna led more traditional lifestyles. That charity organizations provided religious articles and foods for Jewish holidays suggests that the Jewish calendar still guided the lives of a significant segment of the Jewish population of Vienna. In contrast to the women raised with Christmas trees and Easter eggs, the women involved in Jewish charity incorporated Jewish values such as *Tzedakah* and *Bikur Cholim*, providing for the spiritual needs of orphaned Jewish children, and providing items necessary for ritual purposes to the poor. Even with this in mind, most of the goals and activities of the Jewish women's charity groups lacked religious content. Their statements of purpose rarely gave an indication of anything particularly Jewish about Jewish philanthropy. The IFWV, founded in 1815, came close to having a Jewish content in its statement of purpose, including in its provisions the contribution to the dowry of Jewish brides and the education of Jewish girls. The *Israelitische Mädchen-Waisenhaus* actually listed education in the sense of true religiosity as its first goal. The girls were taught religion, and religious leaders such as rabbis Jellinek and Güdemann visited them. Other charity organizations aimed to educate Jewish girls for employment purposes or to provide for Jewish orphans without mentioning religion.

The Jewish women's prayer book, *Beruria*, also combined Jewish and modern European bourgeois values in a uniquely Viennese manner. Emphasizing the role of the Jewish woman as the upholder of Judaism in the home, and putting family and children at the center of the lives of Jewish women, the prayer book reinforced Viennese bourgeois values by presenting them as Jewish. The prayer book mixed traditional Jewish elements, such as the *Kaddish* prayer and the blessings for lighting candles and for after a meal, with new religious innovations, such as a prayer to be recited at the confirmation of one's child, and excerpts from non-Jewish sources about women. In attempting to reach out to Jewish women who may have had stronger secular than religious backgrounds, Grunwald created a Jewish prayer book that fundamentally incorporated bourgeois gender stereotypes of domesticity, defining them as Jewish.

Images of Jewish Women in the Organized Jewish Community

Jewish women in Vienna participated in Jewish religion and community through their prayers and philanthropy. How did this affect the way they were viewed by prominent rabbis and communal leaders who frequently addressed the topic of women in pamphlets, articles, lectures, sermons, and books? Despite Jewish women's contributions in the community, the writings of Viennese Jewish leaders tended to idealize Jewish women of the past at the expense of Jewish women of the present. Although the depiction of Jewish women and the underlying messages of their work varied greatly, this common thread runs through the literature.

The writings of the most prominent rabbis of Vienna, Adolf Jellinek (1823–1893), Moritz Güdemann (1835–1918), and Joseph Samuel Bloch (1850–1923), demonstrate their conflicting desires to make Judaism relevant in the modern world while retaining Jewish distinctiveness. Their need to clarify the Jewish position on women and the role of women in Judaism resulted at least in part from their confrontation with modern ideas such as the women's movement, modern anti-Semitism, and religious reform. Their writings demonstrate the centrality of "the woman question" for the Jewish community and the ambivalent relationship of the religious Jewish leadership to the cultural context in which it operated.

Each one of the three rabbis had different intellectual interests and therefore considered different aspects of Jewish women. While Jellinek wrote and spoke about women in the context of his interests in philosophy, in his sermons, in his ethnographic studies, and in his articles, Güdemann studied and wrote about the history of Jewish women. Bloch's concern for Jewish women grew out of his political activities and his involvement with the question of white slavery (prostitution) in Eastern Europe, as well as his general efforts to refute the anti-Semitic assertions regarding the status of women in Jewish texts. While they each used Jewish women of the past as role models, their work also developed in the context of modernization and the rise of bourgeois values. The influence of this context can be detected to greater or lesser extents in the works of Viennese rabbis. In meeting the challenges of their time, the stereotypes of Jews, and the need to make Judaism relevant for modern Jews, they created images of Jewish women.

The preoccupation with the Jewish woman extended beyond the works of these three rabbis. Organizations such as the *Österreichisch-Israelitische Union* (OIU), a political organization founded by Rabbi Bloch in 1886 in response to the challenges of anti-Semitism and assimilation, and the *Jüdische Toynbee-Halle*, established and staffed by Viennese Zionist leaders in 1900, held numerous lectures about Jewish women. Furthermore, articles, feuilletons, *Familienblatter*, and notes pertaining to the question of Jewish women frequently appeared in the Viennese Jewish press. The three leading non-Zionist papers—*Die Neuzeit* (1861–1904), edited by Simon Szanto (1819–1882) and Leopold Kompert (1822–1886) and later by Adolf Jellinek; *Öster-reichische Wochenschrift* (1884–1921), edited by Josef Samuel Bloch; and the emphatically assimilationist and anti-Zionist weekly *Die Wahrheit* (1899–1938), founded by the senior cantor Jacob Bauer—all gave substantial coverage to the theme of Jewish women.[53]

Images of Jewish women and women in Judaism came to occupy a central place in the Jewish response to the tensions and crises of identity resulting from the emancipation of Viennese Jewry. Communal leaders and rabbis had the onerous task of keeping the spiritual side of Judaism alive and relevant in the lives of Jews who were occupied with the challenges of achieving social integration, occupational success, and defining their place in Viennese society and culture. With the incorporation of bourgeois definitions of womanhood on the one hand, alongside an unyielding insistence on Jewish particularity and superiority, these figures fixed on the topic of Jewish women as a way of demonstrating both the relevance and uniqueness of Judaism. The desire to demonstrate that Judaism's view of women kept up with the general society and modern culture conflicted with the impulse to retain a sense of Jewish distinctiveness.

While the discourse on women's position in Judaism among German Jewish leaders reflected a climate dominated by the tension and competition between Reform and Orthodoxy and took the form of a heated debate, the situation in Vienna was very different. The Viennese Jewish community always maintained formal unity and avoided an open split in the community. According to Michael Meyer, the Viennese Jewish community placed "communal unity above ideology, to avoid labeling its official practice as anything other than the 'Vienna rite.'"[54] Furthermore, due to Vienna's location between east and west, the Jewish community came to serve as a bridge between the Jewries of eastern and western Europe. As Robert Wistrich has demonstrated, Vienna's most important role in Jewish scholarship was as a bridge between east and west.[55]

The importance of unity and mediation also influenced discussions of Jewish women in Vienna. Rather than trying to show that Judaism treated women according to western values, the rabbis in Vienna maintained that Judaism held a unique position between east and west. There was a lesser tendency to idealize the western tradition, and more incentive to coddle the east. This tendency to assert proudly a Jewish particularity will be found in varying degrees in the works of Vienna's rabbis.

Adolf Jellinek

Of all the Viennese Jewish leaders, Adolf Jellinek wrote the most on the subject of women. Born in Moravia, he arrived in Vienna in 1857 and succeeded Isaac Mannheimer in 1865 as Vienna's foremost preacher.[56] Jellinek, the preacher at the second temple in the Leopoldstadt district (dedicated in 1858) until Mannheimer's death in 1865, when he took over for him at the Seitenstettengasse synagogue, instituted many reforms and was apparently lax in matters of personal observance.[57] He placed his faith in German culture, liberalism, and the emancipation of the Jews in the new dual monarchy in 1867. He gave a liberal humanist and universalist account of Judaism's mission. He sought nevertheless to blend this universalism with a commitment to particularistic aspects of Judaism. He favored a moderate reform that would not alienate the reformers or the Orthodox, a characteristic of Viennese Jewish leaders in general that had been formulated by Mannheimer. His sermons, which had such rhetorical power and artistry that they revolutionized the traditional homily, neatly combined Jewish and general sources.[58]

Jellinek believed that the Jews naturally mediated between east and west. In *Die Neuzeit*, the organ for liberal Viennese Jewry founded in 1861 that became his mouthpiece, he praised a speech given by Minister of Finance Kallay in Budapest in which he had stressed the importance of a nationality which united all residents in spite of differences in religion or race.[59] He concluded that Hungary, which stood on the border between Orient and Occident, ought to play a mediating role. Jellinek pointed out that the Jews of Hungary were especially equipped to build a bridge between the Orient and the Occident. Throughout history this had been the role of the Jews, and he regarded it as the Jews' mission to bring the two worlds and cultures closer together.

In a lecture held in Vienna in 1872, Jellinek discussed the position of women on the basis of a philosophical analysis.[60] While he did not address the issues of Judaism or Jewish women, a metaphor loomed with the Jews. He focused on the speculations about the position of women by philosophical and historical writers such as Auguste Comte, the founder of the positivist school in France. Comte argued that the renewal of society depended on three factors working together: thought, i.e., speculation of philosophers; deed, i.e., energy of the masses; and love, i.e., the hearts of women. Women upheld universal love as the highest principle because of their dominance, selfless giving to others, and outspoken inclination to be connected to society. "The main feature of the female psyche in contrast to the male is a prevailing receptivity, or psychic composition, which lets itself be influenced by the events of the outside world, to feel alive to overriding impressions, to treat them quickly, to penetrate her personality and to assimilate them into her deepest sense." [61] Jellinek's view of women was not all positive. He held not only that the female psyche differed from and complemented the male psyche, but that the woman lacked originality and creativity. Drawing on contemporary notions, he noted that the French resembled women in this and other respects.

In addition to her receptivity and passiveness, the woman was ruled by compassion, sympathy, and emotions, which could lead to either positive or negative consequences. This explained the woman's devotion to family and her concern for people in need, as well as her lack of objectivity and her distorted sense of justice. Drawing on the contemporary Viennese social milieu, he believed women could be general practitioners or compassionate nurses because of their ability to quickly assimilate information and reach a diagnosis, and their ability to make the patient the center of attention and care. Also, women had good memories because of their receptive psyche. They learned things and repeated them well, but had trouble figuring out complicated matters. They had a talent for deductive or hypothetical method, but not for induction.[62]

Jellinek's ideas about the psyche of women reflected the attitudes of his society and his contemporaries with their emphasis on mediation, and lack of creativity and originality. He sympathized with the idea of emancipation and equal rights for women, but his discussion of the female psyche suggested that the natural distinction between the sexes should not be blurred. What drew Jellinek to be interested in the female psyche in the first place? The answer lies in his linking of Jewish and female characteristics, leading him to the conclusion that an examination of the female psyche would shed important light on the nature of the Jews. "Whoever wants to understand the Jews, to value them according to justice and merit, to judge them without bias and without preference, and to solve some contradictions in their nature, must study the female psyche." [63] As a newly emancipated Jew, he identified with the cause of women, who were not yet emancipated.

Jellinek often drew parallels between women and Jews and asserted that the Jews had feminine traits. For example, in *Der jüdische Stamm* (1869) he discussed women's preference for deductive rather than inductive reasoning, and made a three-way connection between women,

Jews, and the French.[64] Also, in a chapter entitled "The Femininity of the Jewish Race," he stated the following. "In the examination of the various races it is clear that some are more masculine, others more feminine. Among the latter the Jews belong, as one of those tribes that are both more feminine and have come to represent [repraesentieren] the feminine among other peoples."[65] In a note he went so far as to remark that among Jews, bass voices are found much more seldom than are baritones.

Jellinek described three main areas in which the similarities between Jews and women manifested: the centrality of the heart, the quickness of the mind, and the creativity of the imagination. Both had a tendency toward luxury; they liked to display pomp and magnificence. Women enjoyed pleasing men, and Jews enjoyed receiving the praise of non-Jews. This imagination along with the powerful heart and quick mind of Jews and women also influenced their artistic creations. In poetry they distinguished themselves more in the lyrical rather than the epic or dramatic fields. In addition to the three areas of heart, mind, and imagination, women and Jews shared some other characteristics, according to Jellinek. Both distinguished themselves less as individuals than did men, or non-Jews; they had stronger kinship ties; and, in spite of their subordinate position and narrow sphere of rights, they were able to exert influence and domination. He concluded with the practical advice that women must not be forgotten in the transformation of society. Women would have a great deal to offer society if freed from oppression, just as did the newly emancipated Jews.[66]

Jellinek again made his case for the femininity of the Jews in the *Neuzeit*. "The reader of the *Neuzeit* already knows my outspoken thesis which has been repeated many times in this paper, that the Jews represent the female element in the family of nations, that their tribal nature is more female and that they have merits and faults in common with women."[67] He noted a deep similarity between anti-Semites and the enemies of women who made sexual difference the point of departure for an irreconcilable polemic against women. The aversion against Jews and women was united in the pessimistic philosophy of Schopenhauer, who criticized both groups for possessing an innate optimism.

Jellinek's preoccupation with the linking of Jews and women seems peculiar in hindsight. This is an argument one would expect to find only among anti-Semites, self-hating Jews, and perhaps Zionists who believed the Jews' femininity resulted from the restrictions of life in the ghetto and Diaspora. His emphasis on the "femininity" of the Jews shows he did not try to prove that the Jews were modern and western.[68] The importance of maintaining a clear line between male and female was an ideal of nineteenth-century European culture.[69] Rather, Jellinek linked Jews and women with images of mediation, mildness, receptivity, and other qualities which reinforced the idea of Viennese Jews as the mediator between two worlds.

In addition to Jellinek's writings on women and their similarity with Jews, he also wrote and sermonized on Jewish women and their position in Judaism. In this area, which he addressed primarily in speeches and sermons, he followed a much more apologetic line of argumentation, idealizing Jewish women of the past and the status of women according to Jewish tradition. At the same time, he criticized the state of Jewish women in his own community, and argued that greater participation of Jewish women through education would strengthen Judaism. He found the solution to the contemporary problems of Jewish women by looking back to the past and Jewish tradition.

The previous chapter discussed Jellinek's sermon on the religious education of Jewish women in the context of his views on girls' confirmations.[70] He also concentrated on the role women should play in Judaism, how it differed from that of men, and how to educate Jewish women so that they could best serve and strengthen Judaism. He emphasized the female nature and its affinity for matters relating to the heart and emotions, such as compassion and beauty, as opposed to intellectual matters, discussions of legality, and technical matters.

He asserted that Judaism always acknowledged the importance of women for the development of national freedom and for the upholding of religious belief. This contrasted with the medieval tradition of worshipping women, as well as with the modern belief in equality and the erasing of all differences between the sexes. Judaism accorded the woman a high position because her heart was more receptive to belief than that of man. "The love of God as the father of all people, God's love for his creations as his children, the regulations regarding sympathy and benevolence, goodness and compassion, all the beautiful, I would like to say, female sides of Judaism grasp the female heart as a friend and relation."[71] Women helped to balance Judaism away from the tendency toward legality and conformity. They made the Sabbath a special day for the family. "Female charity is more than a cold fulfillment of a duty to give her surplus to the needy, but a deed of the heart which is often accompanied with a tear in the eye, a friendly laugh, or some sympathetic words."[72]

For all these reasons, Jellinek concluded that the education of Jewish women would ensure the strengthening of Judaism. It would not be enough to present them with abstract, superficial notions of truth, beauty, and morality, to clothe Judaism in beautiful and shiny colors. In order to make women into true believers and guardians of the Jewish people, the truth had to be substantial, the beauty deep and organized, and the moral idea, tangible and pronounced. He reinterpreted the well-known Talmudic saying that "he who teaches his daughter Torah, teaches her lechery" (Mishnah Sota 3:4) to mean that teaching one's daughter through theories, without instruction in belief, was like giving her food without spices, leaving no aftertaste, or offering her veneer or paint, which touched the surface but disappeared in the course of time.[73]

In his 1866 speech at the celebration of the fiftieth anniversary of the establishment of the *Israelitischen Frauen-Vereins* he praised the organization as living up to the example of the Jewish women of the past, strong and loyal in their belief, and more persistent and steadfast than their husbands. He cited biblical examples to make his point. For example, when men demanded an idol from Aaron, women struggled against it (Tanhuma Parshat Ki Tezeh). When men received a report on the strength of the inhabitants of Canaan, they wanted to return to slavery in Egypt because they feared war, but the "weak" women remained firm and steadfast in their belief in God's promises. In that generation, said the sages, loyal women shamed skeptical men, the women were braver in spite of their physical weakness than the men (Tanhuma Parshat Pinhas).[74] He mentioned that the prophetess Hulda helped to ban paganism from Jerusalem (Chronicles 2) and that although women had a low status in general society in antiquity, the Torah commanded that once every seven years on Sukkot they would be allowed to take part in the public ceremonial reading of God's law (Deuteronomy 31:10–12).

Jellinek used the occasion to praise the positive characteristics of Jewish women, such as their inclination for charity work for the community, as well as to define the proper areas of activity for women. He clearly saw communal social work as an appropriate activity for Jewish women. Along with mothering, women could not only successfully participate in this area, but had a special affinity for it. Because of the importance of the feminine side of Judaism, he concluded that Jewish women's activities deserved high praise and recognition.

In his book *Der jüdische Stamm*, Jellinek commended the sense of family as a unique and noble quality of the Jewish tribe.[75] Family stories were the crux of every page of Israel's history, distinguishing the Jews from other peoples who immortalized the war heroes and the cities of the past. The names of the Jewish people, such as House of Jacob, House of Israel, House of Judah, children of Israel, children of Judah, were those of the ancestors, while other peoples named themselves after the land in which they lived. Furthermore, the Jews found their festive enjoyment in their homes, being together as a family, rather than in competitions and fighting.[76]

Jellinek also upheld the Jewish conception of women's work as laudable.[77] He asserted that Jewish women were "neither shut out from active participation in the matters of their people in the oriental manner, nor did they 'wear men's clothing,' and a 'female speaker' such as Miss Anna Dikinson [sic] in New York would have excited less sensation among the old Hebrews than among the practical Americans."[78] He stressed that Jewish tradition carefully maintained a distinction between the male and female. Fundamental differences between the sexes explained their different treatment.

Jellinek referred to a faction that wanted to deny the differences between the sexes and to oversee a religious emancipation of women in Judaism. "The theory sounds good, but does it hold in practice?" he asked.

> Are man and woman actually like one another in the observation of religious ceremonies? Is it an accident that women of every confession cling with loving piety to certain religious customs, which are neglected by men, while on the other hand certain practices are treated as unimportant by the former? The woman has by nature in all respects, more sense and receptivity for the form, more inclination and propensity for the precise forms and in the religious domain, should this psychic difference not acquire expression?[79]

He argued that, overall, Judaism's treatment of women occupied a middle ground. It did not deny differences in the female and male psyches, as was clear in the area of religious observances, but it did advocate equality in the areas of belief and work.

Elsewhere, Jellinek criticized assimilated Jewish women, specifically when he took up the themes of fashion and jewelry. He discussed the critical Hungarian expression, "On the Jewish woman something always hangs," which reproached Jewish women for being partial to jewelry and ornaments, claiming that some shiny object of gold or gems always hung on them.[80] Rather than seeing this as a stereotypical presentation of the Jewish woman as ostentatious and of the wealth and conspicuousness of the Jew in general, he saw this expression as having a valid message for the Jews. He wrote that Jewish sources commonly addressed the theme "Hebräerin am Putztische" (Hebrew woman at the jewelry table).[81]

Jellinek suggested that if young Jewish women had known all the opportunities Jewish law and custom offered for the purchase of new clothes, they would surely have all become pious daughters of Zion. One such young, pretty, and pious Jewish woman could have held the following pious and solemn speech in front of her husband.

> Dear husband! Something must happen with which our young women will not be entirely estranged from Judaism, and with which a religious mood will again be promoted. Cooking no longer suffices because they have given up the purchase and preparation of meals to cooks, who cannot always read and write, but are very good at calculating their profits. We women do not understand the Hebrew prayers and we can scarcely read them. This is entirely excusable. We must study French, Italian and English, in order to make a long honeymoon to Italy, France and England after a short wedding ceremony. There is only one sure way to lead us women again to Judaism, this is the Talmudic specification, to celebrate and distinguish the Sabbath and holidays with beautiful clothes. Oh, my dear husband! I have a new Shulhan Arukh ready for us, pious dressing! There is a Sabbath, on which one reads of a half silver shekel from the Torah. For this Sabbath it would be proper to wear a dress woven with silver. Before Purim, there is a Sabbath on which the bloodthirsty Amalek is remembered. For this next fine Sabbath I would choose a dress of bright red silk with lace. Before Passover one becomes reminded through the lessons of the Torah of the cleansing ash and the new moon; for that Sabbath, I would suggest a dull ash colored and for the other a dull yellow dress . . . That, my dear husband, is my Shulhan Arukh; through its colorful paragraphs the leaders and keepers of Judaism will succeed in again inspiring us young women for the beliefs of our fathers wrapping them in silk and furnishing them with a shiny trimming. If you agree with my views, let us make our influence count with the young rabbis, with which they will call together a Synod and sanction the new female Shulhan Arukh.[82]

This section of Jellinek's work was on the whole extremely patronizing toward women. On the one hand, he may have been serious when he suggested that women might have become interested in Judaism again if they learned about Jewish laws and customs which related to fashion. On the other hand, he clearly mocked the Jewish woman, who felt her honeymoon more important than her wedding ceremony, that learning French, Italian, and English was more important than Hebrew, and who decided her favorite holiday on the basis of which clothing flattered her most. The "woman's speech" made Jewish women appear extremely superficial and self-centered, in stark contrast to the idealized representation of Jewish women of the past.

In response to the anti-Semitism of the early 1880s, Jellinek remained committed to liberalism. He believed in the Jews' responsibility to show non-Jews what Judaism had to offer, to demonstrate the unique and important messages of the Talmud and Jewish teachings for Jews and non-Jews alike. Regarding women's participation in anti-Semitism, he singled out women who resisted anti-Semitism as exemplifying the true nature of women, while those who succumbed to it were seen as even more despicable than male anti-Semites because they denied their female nature.[83]

In the context of late-nineteenth-century Vienna, Jellinek's ambivalent attitude toward women was typical. He identified to a certain extent with women, because they shared with the Jews an outsider status in Viennese society. This also colored his attitude toward Jewish women when trying to appeal to them in some of his speeches and sermons. On the other hand, Jellinek comes across at times as patronizing, and even demeaning toward women. He did not, in general, have a real vision of their role other than to be supportive of men.

Moritz Güdemann

The newly elected Orthodox President of the Kultusgemeinde, Jonas Freiherr von Königswarter (1807–1871), brought Moritz Güdemann (1835–1918) to Vienna as a response to increasing Orthodox pressure to balance Jellinek's liberal influence.[84] Güdemann, who followed Jewish law more strictly, rejected the proposed introduction of the organ into the synagogue and the suggestion to cut out passages in the prayer book referring to the return to Zion and the reestablishment of Temple sacrifices. On the other hand, Güdemann was liberal in his approach to scholarly research. He studied at the Breslau Jewish Theological

Seminary under Zacharias Frankel, the founder of the Positive Historical School of Judaism, the historian Heinrich Graetz, and the scholar Jacob Bernays. There he developed an interest in historical scholarship. His interest in the question of women fits into his larger scholarly interests in social and cultural history.

Güdemann's work represented an important turning point in that he went beyond reliance on biographical and literary sources and approached Jewish history from below by examining customs, manners, superstitions, morals, language, and literature. While biographical and literary sources generally shed light on the upper strata of society and gave little insight into the lives of the ordinary people, and women in particular, his inclusive approach shed some light on the role of women in Jewish history. Partially motivated by an apologetic interest in demonstrating the interaction between Jews and non-Jews in history, he used non-Jewish sources and a comparative method.

In contrast to Jellinek, whose attitudes toward women were dispersed among a number of different types of works, Güdemann wrote about women always in the context of his academic interest in Jewish history. In the first of these works, written shortly after he completed his dissertation (and before his arrival in Vienna), he focused on women in the Mishnaic-Talmudic epoch.[85] He did not defend the position of women in Jewish law, but argued that a large gap between their status in theory and in practice persisted. In practice, Jewish treatment of women was guided by morality. The theory, an abstract discussion of the law, had little bearing on actual practice. He tried to demonstrate, through various examples that the Jewish people responded to moral developments, creating "the very peculiar relationship between the theoretical normative and practical position of the female sex in Judaism."[86] He believed that in order to get to the true picture about the status of women in Judaism, one had to look beyond the legal position and turn to social and cultural sources—i.e., history from below. By looking at the lives of women and what they achieved in this period of history one could provide a more accurate and (incidentally) a more positive portrayal of the place of women in Judaism.

Güdemann began with the childhood and education of girls. Despite rulings against the education of girls, most notably that of R. Eliezer b. Hyrcanus, who declared that one should not waste education on one's daughter (Sota 20a), in practice many women in Jewish history became learned. Beruria, for example, the daughter of R. Chanina b. Teradion and wife of R. Meir, demonstrated a deep knowledge of the law as well as a sharp wit, and at the same time did not lack a genuine feminine nature (Avoda Zara 18b, Rashi; Erubin 58b; Yalkut Mishle, end). Also, Ima Shalom, sister of R. Gamaliel and wife of R. Eliezer ben Hyrcanus, was a knowledgeable, witty, and yet gentle-minded woman (Sabb. 116b; Bab. mez. 59b). The daughter of R. Chisda, who served as a judge in the case of her husband, Raba, decided to defer the oath on the halachic (Jewish legal) grounds that someone was suspected of perjury (Ketub. 85a; Shevuot 44b). This story demonstrated that a woman practiced law. Yalta, the wife of Rabbi Nachman, demonstrated the level of knowledge of her sex and a quick wit when she said that for everything which Scripture forbids we are compensated with an allowance in a corresponding theme (Chullin 109b). From these examples, he concluded that women in Mishnaic and Talmudic times often enjoyed a deeper education and familiarity with the law than is suggested by legal sources alone.

Güdemann gave numerous examples of Talmudic sayings which emphasized the importance of marriage and children. The early age of marriage ensured a high morality. It protected girls from excesses and errors (Pesachim 113a). "The entire literature of that time is full of expressions, which glorify love and the creation of marital happiness." [87] He claimed that these marriage ceremonies followed the morality of modern times. He described the ways in which young people met each other and became engaged. Women looked for educated men, while men looked for daughters of educated men (Pesachim 49b).[88] Marrying for money was discouraged by the saying that one who married for money would have ugly children.

Güdemann viewed the issue of the marital relationship in terms of the morality of Judaism's treatment of women.

It is the best sign of the morality of a nation, when awareness of the wife appears as the cause of good fortune rather than misfortune. For this view includes the appreciation of the house as the proper arena for the manifestation of good fortune. With the Jews, we find this view impressed in its most complete purity, and the Talmud is full of maxims, which reflect it once more in the brightest light. Fortunately we are given opportunities to look into the homes of the time, to which our sketch is dedicated, and our eyes rest with true joy on the inner, gentle relationship of the spouses to one another.[89]

He presented the social position of women in Mishnaic and Talmudic times as evidence of the overall morality of the Jews' treatment of women.

Women enjoyed high esteem, according to Güdemann, as evident in the influence which they exerted on men, although men eagerly tried to deny it in theory. The sages of the Talmud expected an unquestioning obedience from wives to husbands. In one example of subservience, a woman spat into the face of the famous scholar Rabbi Meir at a public gathering at the command of her husband (Lev. rab. 9.—Bamidb. rab. 9.—Jer. Sota cap. 1). But Güdemann found counterexamples in the sources proving that "subservience was in no way a general character trait of women in those days, that they much more often exerted a decisive power over their husbands."[90] He concluded with the expression, "The wife can lead a bad man to good and a good man to bad,—so everything happens through the influence of women" (Wer. Rab. Sect. 17, ed. Frankf. p. 14b, col. 2.).

Güdemann's interest in the topic of Jewish women did not end with this early work. In his most significant historical contribution, the history of the educational affairs and the culture of western Jews, he also included women. Ismar Schorsch, in his article on Güdemann, dismissed his attempt to confront the issue of women as a misuse of the comparative method in order to prove the moral superiority of the Jews, stating that "similar efforts to compare the morality of Jewish and Christian women and clergy ignored the fundamentally different circumstances."[91] He thus glosses over Güdemann's pioneering work in including women in Jewish history and fails to account for some of his assertions—for example, that the education of Jewish women was far inferior to that of Christian women.[92]

In the first volume of his history of education and culture, which covered France and Germany from the tenth to the thirteenth centuries, Güdemann used both Jewish and non-Jewish sources in order to discover as much as possible about women in this period. He concluded that Jewish women did not become educated. While in the Christian world, women often became scholars or poets, in Judaism the education of women was made impossible by traditional religious fears and prejudices. They believed that one should educate girls exclusively for their future wifely and motherly duties, such as the care of domestic chores. They often married at such a young age that little time or opportunity remained for education.[93]

For these reasons the education of women was limited to practical matters helpful to successfully running a household. Women did not learn Hebrew and prayed in the vernacular. There was an exception of a pious man who taught his daughters to write, so that they would be able to help their husbands in business. This demonstrated that in unusual cases daughters were educated and that women could be involved in their husbands' business. Women helped their husbands to have time to pursue an education by managing the business during their absences, "and this service formed a highlight in the otherwise very simple and modest life and work of the Jewish women of the Middle Ages."[94]

Güdemann claimed that Jews of all social classes upheld the strongest morality in the home. Boys and girls did not play together, in order to encourage the idea of modesty and women's honor. He asserted the superiority of Jewish marital relationships, attributing it at least in part to the decree formed by Rabbenu Tam and his brothers, according to which an abused woman should be withdrawn from her husband's domain and granted means for subsistence. Rabbi Meir of Rothenburg said that wife beating was rare among Jews compared to other peoples.[95] In contrast, Rabbi Elasar of Worms said that a man should endure insults and maltreatment from his wife with pleasure because his suffering spares him punishment in the world to come (Agudda 85b).

Like Jellinek, Güdemann had something to say about the jewelry of Jewish women, asserting that gifts of jewelry and ornaments proved the high position of women in the Jewish household.[96] He commented on the jewelry of Jewish women in the twelfth and thirteenth centuries, asserting that it not only demonstrated the high position of Jewish women, but also that Jews borrowed from their surroundings in spite of barriers and persecution. He observed that such borrowings contradicted the Talmudic saying that in times of religious persecution, one had to be very particular about one's individuality "up to the shoelaces." He recognized that in practice it was difficult to carry out individuality. Though he did not state it explicitly, this observation must have had a great deal of relevance for his own dilemmas in an increasingly anti-Semitic Vienna.

The second volume of the *Geschichte des Erziehungswesen*, covering the Jews of Italy in the Middle Ages, also included a discussion of women.[97] Again, his comparison of Jewish and Christian women was more complex than just an assertion of Jewish moral superiority, and he considered a wide range of sources. He wrote that in Italy, the female sex enjoyed greater freedom than in other places and took part in educational efforts and the pleasures of the world of men. One exceptionally scholarly woman, Paula, who descended from R. Nathan ben Jeniel of Rome, was a skillful writer.[98]

Accompanying the greater intellectual freedoms, moral standards fell and intimate relationships between men and women developed. Jews tried to uphold morality by regulating the length of trains on dresses, the types of jewels and ornaments, and the number of rings women were allowed to wear. Christian preachers threatened women with the wrath of God or appealed to their practical side by pointing out the need for larger and larger dowries. One Jewish moralist of the thirteenth century said that "it is unbecoming for Israelites, to wear luxurious gowns, such as red-colored, brown-colored and multi-colored dresses, they should be much more simple and modest, shrouded in the gown of humility." Only on the Sabbath were better dresses allowed, but they were still required to be modest.[99] This moralist went so far as to embrace monastic attire, and to call it Jewish. He recommended wearing a rough gown made of sackcloth, and wearing linen only on the Sabbath and holidays.

According to Güdemann, however, it would be reasonable to conclude that most Jewish women in that period were modest and virtuous because even one of the strictest moralists of the period had no major complaint against them. He concluded that even in medieval Italy, which was characterized by extravagance, luxury, and immodesty, Jewish women remained on the whole morally pure.

Güdemann demonstrated that throughout ancient and medieval history, Jewish women fared well in practice. While Jewish society and culture was always influenced by its surroundings, for the most part this influence was regulated and had an overall positive effect.[100] Like Jellinek he emphasized the complementary relationship of women and men in Judaism, seeing women's role mainly as being supportive to their husbands. Both believed that Jewish women were prone to become ostentatious and were critical of this tendency. While their goals and styles may have differed, the overall images which emerged have much in common.

Joseph Samuel Bloch

The third of the trio of important fin de siècle Viennese rabbis, Joseph Samuel Bloch (1850–1923), was born in Dukla (East Galicia), and educated in traditional Jewish sources, as well as European culture and the German language. Soon after he completed his education he was appointed rabbi in Floridsdorf (the twenty-first district), a proletarian suburb of Vienna with a small (2 percent) Jewish population. He also served as a teacher at the *Beth Hamidrash* in Vienna.[101] He slowly but steadily became influential in Viennese Jewish affairs, eventually emerging as the most outspoken opponent of Austrian anti-Semitism, the founder of an Austrian Jewish weekly, a member of the Austrian parliament, and a founder of the *Österreichisch-Israelitische Union* (Austrian-Israelite Union). His writings on women fall predominantly into the context of his fight against anti-Semitism.

Adolf Fischof (1816–1893), a Jewish politician who believed in the importance of resolving ethnic tensions in Austria through a federation of nationalities, influenced Bloch, who applied Fischof's ideas to the Jewish situation in Austria. He considered national harmony to be vital to Jewish interests. He saw this as compatible with the traditional role of Jews as mediators between the nations.[102]

In his apologetic work, *Israel and the Nations*, Bloch showed that people blamed Jews for any political or social unrest, and said Jews had no morality.[103] Jews were accused of ruining the Germans' health and dominating "the fashions as they do everything, and *as they are (by the way) very sensual* they compel the poor Germans to wear close fitting and deeply cut garments whereby they squeeze their lungs and expose their throats" (my emphasis). Jewish women had been accused of spreading disease. "The cookery books, mostly compiled by Jewesses such as Henriette Davidis, etc. systematically ruin the stomachs and health of the Germans." Bloch pointed out that the paper that printed this accusation later had to retract its allegation and to state that Henriette Davidis actually came from an old family of Lutheran pastors.[104] He concluded that anti-Semitism was a mental disease, a political insanity, and a mental derangement.

In response to August Rohling's book, *Der Talmudjude* (1871), an anti-Semitic pamphlet which went through seventeen editions, Bloch became very vocal and prominent. Rohling attacked the Talmud and the Shulchan Aruch (a Jewish law code) using quotations which made it look as if he were an expert, while he actually relied on *Entdecktes Judentum* (1701) by Johann Andreas Eisenmenger (1654–1704). He argued that the Talmud degraded and insulted non-Jews, particularly Christians.[105] By attacking the Talmud, he sought to justify his anti-Semitism. His seemingly "scientific approach" gave the book an air of legitimacy.

Like many anti-Semites, Rohling attacked the Jews for their supposed exploitation of non-Jewish women. He began with the biblical quotations "You should not covet your neighbor's wife" (Exodus 20:14) and "He who commits adultery with his neighbor's wife, is deserving of death" (Leviticus 20:10). Then he looked at Tractate Sanhedrin (52b), which interpreted "his neighbor's wife" to mean only Jewish women, making an exception of non-Jewish women. He added that the Tosafot and Rashi, two important scholarly sources, both interpreted this to mean that non-Jews had no marriage. He concluded that these axioms denied the non-Jew any human dignity; marriage, however, was a moral institution which belonged to humans and distinguished them from animals. He argued that Jewish men lacked respect for non-Jewish women, and that Jewish law permitted adultery with them. He claimed that according to several rabbis no adultery is committed in the case of a Jewish man and a Christian woman. One rabbi allegedly remarked: "It is allowed to take advantage of a non-believing woman."

Rohling also argued that the Jews lacked morality in their laws regarding women. He claimed that according to the Talmud, *Berachot* 57a, if one shamed his mother in a dream it meant that he hoped for wisdom, for thorough knowledge of the law, for a fiancée, for eternal life. The Talmud (*Niddah* 47b), he claimed, also permitted a man agonizing from temptation to follow his desire as long as he did so secretly and did not blemish the holy name of Israel. He wrote that in Tractate *Yoma* 18b, the Rabbis Rav and Nachman were said to have claimed that a man coming to a foreign city could take a wife without her consent. He claimed that the sages taught that a man was allowed to do whatever he wanted to do with his wife, as with a piece of meat that comes from a butcher; that a man could eat fried, cooked, stewed, or even with a fish from the fish seller. In another example, a woman complained to the rabbi that her husband was a sodomizer. The rabbi answered that he could not help her, the law had given her a price. He (the rabbi) also commented that the woman in Judaism was nothing because public prayer in the synagogue required the presence of ten men, while one million women did not make a full standing assembly.

In every new edition of his book, Rohling declared that "he was ready to pay the round sum of 1000 Talers if Judah managed to get a verdict from the German Association of Orientalists that his quotations were fictitious and untrue."[106] He wrote this knowing that the German Association of Orientalists was composed mainly of scholars of other Eastern and Near Eastern languages and only to a very small extent of scholars who specialized in Talmud.

"It was then that I made up my mind to grapple with the author of these incendiary writings," wrote Bloch.[107] He wrote a long article which rapidly sold over 100,000 copies and was reprinted again and again and translated into Hungarian, Polish, Czech, and Italian. He received hundreds of telegrams and letters, from Jews and Christians, professors and noblemen. But Rohling continued his calumnies and testified in the courts against Jews as a witness that they were allowed to commit any crime against Christians. On the occasion of the Tisza-Eszlar ritual murder trial (1882) in Hungary, he offered to take an oath "that it was an extremely sacred ceremony with the Jews to shed the blood of a non-Jewish virgin, that this blood was very acceptable to Heaven and procured to the Jews the mercy of God."[108] This repeated the theme of the supposed Jewish victimization of non-Jewish women and also demonstrated the sexualization of the traditional ritual murder accusation. This prompted Bloch to take further action against Rohling. In a series of articles in the *Wiener Morgenpost*, he made charges against Rohling, including the accusation of taking false oaths and committing perjury, compelling Rohling to bring an action for libel against Bloch in the Vienna law court. Bloch went ahead and had the court name two experts authorized to translate from the Talmud and rabbinical literature. He put together a collection of texts from Talmudic-rabbinical literature, including all the quotations used by Rohling and many others, with his own commentary attached. The material was transmitted to Rohling by the court with permission to add as many supplementary questions as he wished, which he declined to do. The papers were then sent to the experts, Theodor Noeldecke and August Wuensche. The translations of the experts exposed all of Rohling's falsehoods, and the trial was set to begin on November 18, 1885. Immediately before the trial, Rohling withdrew his charge, thereby admitting that he had sworn false oaths before the law courts. He could no longer remain lecturer in the University of Prague, and he was sentenced by the Court to pay all the costs.[109]

In *Israel and the Nations*, Bloch countered Rohling's anti-Semitic arguments, demonstrating that Jews did not discriminate against Christian marriages. He also devoted an entire chapter to Rohling's charge of Jewish sexual immorality and his claim that the Talmud justified adultery with Christian women. Bloch endeavored to prove that

Jewish tradition actually taught the exact opposite of what Rohling claimed, arguing that according to the Bible, the Jew caught in an adulterous act with a non-Jewish woman could have been killed immediately. While Rohling asserted that, according to the Talmud, a Jew was permitted to commit adultery with a non-Jewish woman with impunity, Bloch demonstrated that the Talmud was actually very strict on this subject and forbade the Jewish man to be alone with a woman other than his mother or sister, whether she was Jewish or non-Jewish (*Kiddushin* 80b, *Avoda Zara* 36b).[110]

Bloch pointed out that the Talmud required a man to treat his wife kindly, since the house was blessed only on her account (*Baba Metsia* 59a). God had given her to him so that she would enjoy life with him and not so he would be allowed to cause her distress by bad treatment (*Ketovot* 61a). In *Sanhedrin* 76b it was written that he should love his wife as himself, and honor her more than himself. According to *Sota* 17a, the husband was supposed to strive to advance the well-being of his wife, and to live in peace with her. Bloch countered Rohling by demonstrating that the Talmud actually demanded that the husband honor his wife. He responded to Rohling's assertion that women held a low position in Judaism, pointing out that in the Middle Ages women took an active part in economic life. He cited R. Eliezer b. Nathan of Mainz (Responsa Nr. 40) that women in his time were guardians and shopkeepers, did business, borrowed and lent, paid and accepted payment, took and gave in deposit.

Bloch also addressed the question of the third benediction recited in the Jews' daily prayers, "Blessed art thou, O Lord, our God, who hast not made me a woman." This benediction was considered a scandalous disparagement of the female sex. The Vienna Supreme Court of Justice of June 11, 1908, ruled, "The daily thanksgiving, 'Blessed art thou, O Lord, our God who hast not made me a woman,' may voice the conviction of orthodox Jews of the total inferiority of woman, a conviction rooted in the ordinances, habits, and customs of the Oriental peoples, but it does not hold before the penal code."[111] Instead of simply arguing that Judaism was not oriental, Bloch, himself of East European origin, argued that the benediction originated in non-Jewish western culture. According to Lactantius, Plato was said to have thanked nature for having been a man and not a woman, and this prayer was also attributed to Socrates by Diogenes Laertius and to the Parsees by James Darmsteter. The first to mention these benedictions in Judaism was Rabbi Meir (Menahoth 43b), the disciple of Elisha ben Abuya (Acher), an enthusiastic admirer of the Greeks. Hence the thanksgiving was absorbed into Judaism, from the Greeks to Acher to Rabbi Meir.[112] Bloch did not apologize for the benediction, but searched for its true origin. Because he did not fall prey to that tendency to judge all that is western as positive, there was no need to try to identify Jewish values with Greek or western values. Instead he demonstrated that the benediction which, according to the Vienna Supreme Court, attested to "the total inferiority of women" actually came from their own cultural heritage.

Bloch asserted that the position of women in ancient Judaism compared favorably to both the civilizations of the east and the west, and specifically refuted many of Rohling's claims. Overall, his defense of the Talmud regarding the status of women and the sexual morality of the Jews aimed to contradict the negative image of the Talmud and of traditional Judaism which was put forward by Viennese anti-Semites. In contrast to the attitude that the Jews should not draw too much notice to themselves by fighting anti-Semites, his strategy was to draw as much attention as possible. He did not fear bringing attention to the Jewish community, but rather the consequences of not fighting back— namely that people who did not know better would assume that the anti-Semitic accusations were justified. In his defense of the Talmud, Bloch set out to demonstrate that the Jewish treatment of women was moral. He exposed the errors of anti-Semites who claimed to be Talmudic experts and demonstrated Judaism's attitude toward women as far superior to both the "oriental" and the western attitudes.

Anti-Semites also attacked the Jews' sexual morality by blaming them for the white slave trade, i.e., prostitution. Austrian anti-Semites accused Jewish traffickers of kidnapping and abusing Christian girls, distorting reality by failing to mention that many of the victims were Jews, in order to promote fear of the corrupt Jewish trafficker who stole Christian girls and turned them into prostitutes. As Edward Bristow noted, the white slavery charge represented a sexualization of the ritual murder charge.[113] The non-Jewish woman was made into the victim. The hostility was directed at Jewish men's alleged abuse of Christian girls, and not at Jewish prostitutes.

Viennese anti-Semites exaggerated the problem of the Jews' involvement in white slavery much beyond its true proportions.[114] As Vienna began to grow, it attracted immigrants, most of whom abided by the law; however, "some Jews were involved in commercial vice and that was particularly unfortunate in Vienna, one of the breeding grounds for racial anti-Semitism."[115] White slavery resulted from the difficulties of immigrant life in the Leopoldstadt and other immigrant districts of Vienna. A handful of traffickers took advantage of penniless women, most of whom were Jewish. Vienna's anti-Semites exploited this and associated Jews with prostitution. Following the Lemberg trial of 1892, the biggest, longest, and most publicized white slavery trial, in which twenty-two traffickers were convicted for procuring girls, the issue of white slavery became important in Austrian anti-Semitism.[116]

On November 11, 1892, an anti-Semitic deputy in Parliament, Joseph Schlesinger, introduced a parliamentary question signed by fourteen of his colleagues, including Karl Lueger and Franz Schneider, which read: "What precautions does his Excellency the Minister President think of taking in order to build an effective claim against the shameful outrages of the Jewish people in Austria?" In an attempt to gain as much as possible from the post-trial climate, he prefaced the question with the statement "that he wondered what some minister would feel if his daughter fell into the hands of the mentioned trafficker, and that even liberal deputies would not want their daughters exposed to the filth of such people."[117] Schlesinger was disciplined by the president of the Austrian *Reichsrat*, Franz Smolka, for violating public decency and insulting the ministers, but not for the offensive question about the Jews. According to Bloch, Smolka said that Schlesinger's question "contains so many offenses against decency and morals that I cannot find words to express my indignation at it." On November 24, Schlesinger and Schneider made venomous speeches on the white slave traffic.

On November 25, 1892, Bloch stood up to defend the Jews before the Parliament, asking the following question. "Does he not know that there are in Upper Austria, Lower Austria, Silesia, Styria, Bohemia, Moravia, one or several b . . . s [brothels] [*sic*] (loud laughter) in every large town? And do you know that the owners of these shameful houses are, every one of them, thoroughbred Aryans of the same race and the same faith as the interpellant? (Laughter)."[118] He pointed out that many "Aryans" worked in prostitution in Vienna. He asked sarcastically if this was an exclusively "Aryan" trade "because you are so indignant that a Jew has encroached upon it, because a few Jews have tried to compete with you?"

He remarked that the anti-Semitic German-National leader in Austria, Georg Ritter von Schönerer, had transformed the house he had inherited in Vienna into a brothel in order to force his mother and his sister to clear out.

I once asked a German nationalist student, one of Herr Schönerer's worshippers, how it happened that Schönerer had made his house in the Krugerstrasse a b . . .? [brothel] And he said: "That is an ancient German institution." Well, a few Jews have Germanized themselves, that's all. (Noise on the left side of the House.) I beg your pardon, I wish the Jews would not have had to suffer offence; but if one shoots at them it must be permitted to return the compliment.[119]

In spite of Bloch's efforts the connection between the Jews and prostitution remained notorious in Vienna on every level of society. When it came to public attention in 1906 that Regina Riehl, a non-Jew who ran a tolerated house, locked up and exploited prostitutes, the role of Antonie Pollack, Riehl's sixty-eight-year-old servant and procuress who happened to be Jewish, was prominently broadcast.[120] However, Bloch served a vital and much appreciated role in Vienna as a defender of the Jews against anti-Semitism. Because anti-Semites often focused their attacks on the Jews' treatment of women, Bloch's defense of the Jews also dealt extensively with these issues, developing a detailed explanation of the position of women in Judaism. Bloch's interest in Jewish women can therefore be seen as a direct result of the centrality of gender and sexuality in Viennese anti-Semitism.

Other Works

Many other articles, books, and lectures in Vienna addressed the topic of Jewish women, demonstrating a high level of interest and concern with these issues. Much more could be written on these works; however, for the purposes of this study, it will be sufficient to look at a few examples, dealing with Jewish women during different periods of Jewish history: Adolf Schwarz's lecture series on Jewish women in the Bible, Leopold Goldhammer's and Moritz Friedlaender's articles about Jewish women in antiquity, Stephan Darnau's lecture on the appearance and wardrobe of the Jewish woman of Palestine, Naum Klugmann's book defending the position of the Jewish woman in the Talmud, and Max Grunwald's speech on the Jewish woman in modern times.

Adolf Schwarz (1846–1931) was born in Hungary and studied at the Jewish Theological Seminary in Breslau. From 1875 to 1893, he was a rabbi at Karlsruhe. In 1893, he became the first rector of the *Israelitisch-theologischen Lehranstalt* in Vienna. He was one of the most important personalities of the Viennese Jewish community. His arrival in Vienna in the same year that Jellinek died and Güdemann became the sole chief rabbi of Vienna signified a strengthening of Orthodoxy.[121] In 1903, he presented a lecture series on the women of the Bible at the *Jüdische Toynbee-Halle* in Vienna, a settlement house established by Viennese Zionists in 1900.[122]

Schwarz's central point was that one could learn lessons from looking at biblical women. These women demonstrated the important contribution women could make to the future of a people, because, as mothers, they raised children, and as wives, they created their husbands' destinies, for better or worse. Furthermore, some biblical women contributed on their own without any connection to men. These women, according to Schwarz, demonstrated an important point for women involved in the women's movement, namely that women could become emancipated through their femininity rather than in spite of it. The lectures asserted the importance of women, and also reflected a certain tension between universalism and particularity which plagued the Viennese Jewish community at a time of heightened anti-Semitism, the rise of Jewish nationalism and the women's movement, and the growing trend toward intermarriage and assimilation.

Dr. Leopold Goldhammer, a colleague of Heinrich L. Reich in the publication of the short-lived weekly *Der Reichsbote*, compared Jewish and non-Jewish women of biblical and rabbinic times. Goldhammer asserted that in all stages of development, the Israelite people guarded the spiritual equality of women and men. This was evident even in the naming of woman, *isha*, which has the same root as the word for man, *ish*. This showed an awareness that men and women were related in essence, in contrast to the Greek naming of woman, which regarded her exclusively as an instrument for producing children. He praised the family life of the Jews, which he claimed was "ideal in all times and also is so today." He argued that Jewish marriages were morally superior to those of other nations. While polygamy was tolerated in spirit (Deuteronomy), the Jewish religion only intended for monogamous marriages. Isaac had only one wife, Abraham only took Hagar as a concubine according to Sarah's wishes, and Jacob had two wives only because of Laban's trick. He blamed Judaism's tolerance for polygamy on the influence of surrounding "oriental heathenism." Even so, polygamous marriages were very rare, and in the tenth century, polygamy was forbidden by law according to the ordinance of Rabbenu Gershom (Gershom ben Juda, light of the Diaspora).

The social position of Israelite women was much higher than that of all the other peoples of antiquity, they did not live shut out in women's chambers, but were allowed to move around freely outside the home as well. As a consequence of the free position of women, a few prominent women influenced the destiny of their people. The Israelites remember the Matriarchs as the paragons, who were independent and shared equality with their husbands and were treated by them with special attention. The law made men and women entirely equal and warned the children to honor the mother as much as the father.[123]

He mentioned that although women were not permitted to bring a sacrifice in person, i.e., to lay their hands on the sacrifice, exception was made for Nazarite women (women who took a vow to be especially strict) and women accused of adultery. He concluded that Judaism venerated family and marriage and respected women in all times including the present.

Moritz Friedländer (1844–1919), a communal worker and educator who established schools in Galicia, also compared Jewish women to Roman women in order to show that Jewish women were more civilized due to their privileged position in Jewish law.[124] He described the Jewish woman as virtuous and devoted to her husband. Jewish law rewarded her by considering her an individual with spiritual power and a warm heart. Therefore Judaism spared the Jewish woman from the unbecoming and aggressive fight for freedom. Roman women wanted to be emancipated, and they became licentious through their granted freedom. Jewish women, on the other hand, never demanded freedom because they were to a certain extent free from the beginning.

Friedländer claimed that the Romans' worship of money motivated marriage, leading to disharmony, carelessness, and divorce. Jews did not take marriage so lightly. "An entire lifetime depends on it [the marriage], and Rabbi Yossi lets the Roman woman feel the full reproach of her frivolous proceedings in these laconic words, which he called out to her twice; 'For you it may be looked upon as easy, to enter in a marriage, not so for us!' "[125] He attributed traditional negative stereotypes about Jewish marriages to the Romans. He concluded that the woman was held in higher esteem by the Jews than by any other people of antiquity.[126]

In 1909, Stephan Darnau, member of the *Wiener Bürgertheater*, delivered a lecture at the *Österreichisch-Israelitische Union* highlighting different aspects of the appearance and wardrobe of the Jewish woman of Palestine. He stressed the exotic and unusual, all the while making sure to emphasize that the Jewish woman was the ideal housewife. He compared and contrasted the Jewish woman to the so-called "oriental" woman. His goal, he claimed, was not to be a moralist or reformer, but only to describe the lives of these women. Nonetheless, the lecture contained many judgments and stereotyped images of women. He described their lives and surroundings with a discourse of otherness. They were confined to women's rooms, usually the most interior rooms of the Palestinian houses, and were shut out from the world, devoted to their immediate surroundings. His description of their rooms emphasized the exotic and mysterious.

> Doubtless, the chambers were furnished with the highest refinement of the times. The most precious rugs covered the floors and walls and pleased the eyes and mind through colors and lines; doubtless, the house was immersed in the most desirable perfumes of the Orient, but the bird lacked freedom. Through the windows, actually openings in the walls with net-formed curtains, or Venetian blinds made from red-colored cedar wooden rods, which could be pushed up or to the side, one certainly had a view, but only of the large courtyard of the house, where oftentimes blooming trees and graceful fountains were to be seen, however nothing of the world.[127]

According to Darnau's analysis, the Palestinian woman focused her attention on her home, her family, and herself because she lacked outside diversions. "And thus she began to decorate herself." "She spent hours and hours in the bath, anointed herself, massaged herself with scented oils, covered herself in incense, draped herself with gold and rare gems, dressed herself in delicate and colorful material, and if she had the opportunity to show herself before others . . ."

He described her awaking in the morning, taking her morning bath, and slipping into her several undergarments, which he described in great detail.[128] The hair of the Hebrew woman was abundant and was decorated with ornaments. He asserted that for Jewish women, only black hair was considered beautiful. He described the hand-held mirrors used by the Jewish woman, and hair coverings, such as gauze veils and caps, which he claimed were removed whenever possible in order to show the hair. About their hair he concluded, "I believe that in these respects, the Palestinian woman had nothing to fear from the comparison with our own days." She beautified herself with make-up, perfume, and jewelry. Particular attention was paid to the eyes, the nails, and especially to jewelry. "It seems deeply grounded in the psychology of the woman's soul that she in all times so gladly wore expensive and genuine jewelry." He described the earrings, nose rings, and necklaces, strings of pearls, chains, belt ornaments, bracelets, and rings worn by the Palestinian woman.[129]

He concluded that the Palestinian woman's attention to her physical appearance and love of ornaments stemmed from her female nature, the climate of Palestine, the influences of the Orient, and her isolation from the outside world, which left her free to devote all of her time to her household and herself.

Naum Klugmann, writing about women in the Talmud, claimed that "the Talmud was frequently reproached for being, *according to the oriental outlook*, against the education of women"[130] (my emphasis). He defended the Talmud by pointing out that this reproach was based on isolated sayings of the Talmudist R. Eliezer. He pointed out that there were special circumstances of R. Eliezer with his wife Ima Shalom, namely that she accused him of being responsible for the death of her brother, R. Gamliel. For the most part, however, the Talmud was in favor of the education of women. The only difference—that Torah study was a duty for men and not for women—could be explained by the physical weakness of women.[131] Elsewhere in the Talmud, Ben Azzai (who was especially impartial because he never married) asserted that "everyone is obliged to teach his daughter."

Klugmann asserted that money did not motivate Jewish marriages and that Jews had a choice of marriage partners, in order to counter two popular stereotypes about Jewish marriage. Just as Goldhammer and Friedländer had done for an earlier period, Klugmann argued that the oriental attitude toward women was barbaric, the European attitude was only slightly more humane, and the Jewish attitude toward women was by far superior. Other works on the Talmud and women used similar arguments.[132]

Max Grunwald, editor of the prayer book *Beruria* examined earlier, spoke about the modern women's movement and Judaism at the *Österreichisch-Israelitische Union* in 1903. He discussed what he saw to be the questions facing the modern women's movement: the problem of finding occupations for women without bringing about competition with and hostility from men, and the problem of making women, who had become passive, seek an active life.

Grunwald asserted that Judaism provided answers to the questions raised by the modern women's movement. In the Bible, Talmud, and throughout Jewish history, tradition was seen as a paradigm by which the burning questions of the day should be gauged. But he also implied that the modern Jewish woman needed to be recharged. "Formerly, firm loyalty to the people and sincere love of Judaism were numbered among the highest properties of the Jewish woman."[133]

He concluded:

> Ladies and Gentlemen! If an era appears decayed and insignificant, so must its women be decayed; on the high-mindedness of its mothers lies the durability and the future of a people. If we succeed to fill our women and daughters with pride and love for our magnificent past again, they will not regard it as their main task, to bless the outside world through the magic of their physical appearance, but as in former times instead see it as their task to train their soul to be beautiful and noble; then our daughters will not be satisfied with only the art and literature of the nations, but moreover will also be at home and place her pride in the rich literature and wonderful history of her own people, to be the nurse of Jewish conviction at home and an apostle of Jewish thought in society, then the future will bring us a new blossom.[134]

Thus Grunwald's speech was a thinly veiled criticism of the Jewish woman's extent of assimilation. If they want to be emancipated, they need only look back to their own roots. In their tradition they would find the resources and tools necessary to transform society.

Conclusion

The organized Jewish community in Vienna professed that modern Jewish women needed improvement and strengthening in addressing what they regarded as the challenges of modernity, such as the threat of assimilation and the fight for women's emancipation. By looking to their distant past for role models and deepening their identity as Jews, Jewish women would become more capable of standing up to these challenges.

The works on biblical women and Jewish women of antiquity tended to present idealized images of women and Judaism's treatment of them compared to other ancient peoples. On the other hand, the works on women in the Talmud focused on defending the position of women in the Talmud from anti-Semitic attacks. The works on modern Jewish women were more directly prescriptive and critical, blaming the state of Viennese Jewry on the lack of Jewish feeling among women.

These writings demonstrate several points. First, leaders of the Jewish community in Vienna occupied themselves with the topic of Jewish women. This can be understood as resulting from their own need to define or explain women's role in Judaism in the face of the new challenges posed by modern ideas, bourgeois culture, anti-Semitism, and social integration, as well as a heightened interest in this topic on the part of their audience. In addition to sheer volume, certain tendencies in the way the woman question was handled by the organized community leadership are distinctively Viennese. First of all, Jewish particularity and superiority emerge as common themes. Likewise, the Jews were often presented as mediators between east and west, rather than as modern and western, or exotic and oriental. And finally, the proposed solutions to the woman question had a reactionary ring to them, for the most part. If the position accorded to Jewish women in Jewish tradition was ideal, and the Jewish woman of the past was to be a role model, it follows that turning back to the past was the key to solving the problems of Viennese Jewish women and Viennese Jews in general.

Modern Viennese and bourgeois views of womanhood were also consciously, or subconsciously, incorporated into the conception of Jewish women found in the works of the organized Jewish community. Viennese bourgeois values favoring domesticity for women reinforced values attributed to Judaism found in these works, such as an inherent difference between the sexes, modesty, womanly virtue, and the woman as the priestess of the home. Nevertheless the influence of modernity is not as direct as in other communities. Rather than simply asserting that the Jews were modern, Viennese Jewish leaders argued that the Jews solved modern problems long ago in their own simple and unique way. In the description of the "Jewish" solutions, it is possible to find the impact of modern ideas.

In this way the leadership of the organized Jewish community addressed their specific problems of identity in the face of modernity and also attempted to address the conflicts afflicting Viennese Jews in general. They hoped to point their constituency toward Jewish tradition in order to address the problem of maintaining a Jewish identity in the modern world, and in the face of growing anti-Semitism. It was this agenda which shaped much of the material on the Jewish woman produced by the Viennese Jewish leadership. In addition to directing Jews to the past and to Jewish tradition, some of the spiritual leaders also blamed Jewish women for the state of affairs of Viennese Jewry and incorporated negative stereotypes of women from the Viennese cultural milieu, such as materialism (specifically love of fashion and jewelry). In this way they addressed their own problems of identity, in particular being cast as the "other" by Viennese society and culture, by displacing many of the qualities attributed to the "Jew" onto the woman.

Modernization caused a crisis of Jewish identity for Viennese Jewish men and women. It led to the creation of a class of female Jewish intelligentsia distant from Judaism, and to self-definitions and activities on the part of Jewish women which incorporated so much from the external culture that there was little left that was identifiably Jewish. In this chapter, it has been shown that some Jewish women remained identified with Judaism and the Jewish community by taking part in prayer and philanthropy that combined Jewish and modern European values. Concurrent with the participation of Jewish women in the community an unprecedented level of interest in the topic of Jewish women developed. Their need to clarify the Jewish position on women, and the role of women in Judaism, resulted at least in part from their confrontation with modern ideas.

3 ﹥﹥ *University and Political Involvement*

Viennese Jewish women who entered the University as well as those who entered politics differed from those who looked to the community and spirituality as the means to negotiate their way into modernity. However, both groups clearly shared a tendency to combine modern and traditional values and to attract attention and sometimes criticism. This chapter will focus on those women who pursued a higher education, those who dedicated their lives to careers in areas such as academia and science, and those who turned to politics, such as socialism, communism, and feminism. In most instances these categories overlap, with university women continuing on to careers and politics, but not in every case. One question that arises is what motivated Jewish women to dedicate themselves to study, careers, and politics in a climate that was still generally unfavorable to women's self-assertion. To what extent can these choices and affiliations be seen as a way that Viennese Jewish women negotiated the tensions of their identity in the context of increasing secularization, assimilation, anti-Semitism, and the persistence of limitations and negative images of women, particularly those seen as too assertive and "masculine"?

Life in the University of Vienna

Marion Kaplan demonstrates that German-Jewish women disproportionately entered the universities when they opened their doors to women, attributing the phenomenon to aspects of modernization, such as economic prosperity, urbanization, desire for social status, and later marriage, as well as the traditional Jewish veneration of learning.[1] Moreover, she reveals the existence and impact of discrimination against women and anti-Semitism that confronted them. In Vienna, Jewish women comprised an even higher percentage of the total number of women in universities than in Germany and faced similar obstacles to their pursuit of a higher education.

The University of Vienna was ironically both "an avenue of social mobility" for the Jews and "a veritable hotbed of nationalist and anti-Semitic hostility" during this period.[2] Between 1800 and 1890 Jews made up one-third of all students there. In 1885, the Jews constituted 41.4 percent of the medical students in the University. The figures dropped by 1900 to 24 percent of the student body and 25 percent of those studying medicine, probably due to the impact of anti-Semitism. While the percentage of Jewish students declined overall, a disproportionately large number of Jewish women entered the University of Vienna.[3]

Jewish women played an important role in the beginning years of female university study in Vienna. According to one study of Jewish women at the University of Vienna, they were the "daring pioneers of female university study."[4] They were among the first and most eager to take advantage of the new opportunities opening up in higher education for women. The faculty of philosophy opened to women in 1897; the medical and pharmaceutical faculties followed in 1900. The law faculty did not admit women until 1919, the evangelical theology faculty until 1923, and the Catholic theology faculty until 1946. In 1897, the first year of women's study at the university, women constituted only .4 percent of students. By 1913/1914, the percentage had climbed to 7.7 percent. In 1897/98, eight Jewish women studied in the philosophy faculty, comprising 25 percent of the total number of women. The percentage of Jewish women climbed to 31.2 percent in 1902/03, 37.5 percent in 1907/08, and 37.7 percent in 1913/14.[5] In the medical school, Jewish women comprised an overall higher percentage of female students. The percentage fluctuated during the fourteen-year period from 1900 to 1914. In the first year that women studied in the medical faculty, 63.6 percent were Jewish (7 out of 11). The percentage ranged from 51.2 percent in 1906/07 to 68.3 percent in 1908/09. At all times during this period, Jewish women comprised the majority of female students in the medical faculty at the University of Vienna.[6]

Female Jewish medical students at the university came from all parts of the Monarchy. Over the years, though, more and more started to come from Galicia. In 1913/14, 44.5 percent of all female Jewish medical students came from Galicia, while 21.8 percent came from Vienna, 13.6 percent from Bukovina, 4.5 percent from Bohemia, and 2.7 percent from Lower Austria. Clearly a large number of Galician Jewish women entered study at the medical faculty of the University of Vienna. The students coming from eastern parts of the Monarchy had an ambivalent relationship to the native Viennese. The women born in Galicia felt bound to Polish or Jewish nationalism, while those born in Vienna rejected Zionism and remained distant from traditional Judaism.[7]

What motivated so many Jewish women to attend the University? Perhaps they saw education as a means for bourgeois emancipation and social climbing, as Heindl and Wytek suggest.[8] Similarly, Edith Prost writes: "For the enlightened Jewish bourgeoisie it was self-evident to also confer upon the daughters a serious education. *Bildung* was a possibility for emancipation—emancipation as a Jew and as a woman."[9] However, recollections of university women imply that they actually decided for themselves, often without their parents' approval, to pursue university studies. In spite of many obstacles, such as the lack of the required *Gymnasium* education, Jewish women worked extremely hard in order to prepare for the Matura and gain entrance to the University. Young Jewish women made significant sacrifices in order to enter the University. The opening of the University to women gave Jewish women opportunities to embark on careers which provided meaning in their lives. University attendance, and the careers and politics that often accompanied it, gave Jewish women a means of asserting themselves as both women and Jews.

The first three female students matriculated in the philosophical faculty of the University of Vienna in the winter semester 1897/98. Among them was linguist Elise Richter, who studied with the classical philologists Theodor Gomperz and Friedrich Marx, the Indo-Germanists Rudolf Meringer and Paul Kretschmer, the Germanist Richard Heinzel, and above all the Romanists Adolf Mussafia and Wilhelm Meyer-Lübke. She received her doctorate in French in 1901. Even slower in coming than the admission of women to study at the University was the appointment of a woman as *Privatdozentin* at the University. In 1907, following a long battle, Elise Richter became the first female university lecturer in Austria and Germany, and the only woman to do so before the First World War.[10] Nevertheless, she dissociated herself and her career from the women's movement. "I entered the university not as a feminist. Still less did I think of this career as a livelihood . . . I avoided the women's movement . . . as a feminist I could not have made my way in the university. I had to direct my entire strength not only toward my work, but also to avoiding the appearance of feminism."[11] Elise Richter's motivation to study in the University of Vienna, a single-minded devotion to scholarship, typified Viennese Jewish university women.

Often, their interests in certain fields originated in their childhood. For example, Lise Meitner had an early interest in mathematics and physics. She developed this interest as a student from reading

Elise Richter. ÖNB/Wien.　　　　　*Lise Meitner. ÖNB/Wien.*

newspaper accounts of the discovery of radium by Pierre and Marie Curie. From 1901 to 1905 she studied mathematics, physics, and philosophy at the University of Vienna. The lectures of her physics professor, Ludwig Boltzmann, inspired her. She was the second woman in Vienna to obtain a doctorate in physics.[12] While a student, she benefited from Boltzmann's acceptance of women, and she was welcomed into his community of students. After attaining her doctorate, she faced discrimination and severe limitations in her career. With no career prospects in Vienna, she went to Berlin in 1907. There she spent the first years working in a small room originally planned as a carpenter's workshop because the director of the Chemical Institute, Emil Fischer, did not allow women to work in his laboratory.[13]

Hilda Geiringer-Mises (1893–1973) similarly devoted herself to the academic study of mathematics. She graduated from the University of Vienna in 1917, with a dissertation which is still valuable today.[14]

In many cases, Jewish women discovered that additional study was necessary to become accepted at the University of Vienna. Toni Stopler, for example, realized when she graduated from the "Cottage" *Lyzeum*, that she was not qualified for entry to the University as a full student. *Lyzeum* graduates could attend courses and lectures, but were excluded from examinations. For a couple of years she took law courses at the University and decided to study law. She was allowed to go to all lectures and to take the "colloquium," a course exam at the end of each term, to get examined on the term curriculum. The Austrian system considered law as formal preparation for government service, and the exams, which the government sponsored, were not permitted for women. Stopler also took art history with Professor Max Devorak. She realized that this informal study did not satisfy her and asked her father to finance private education in order to catch up to the *Gymnasium* level. She began private study with two students as her teachers. Her cousin Robert taught her Latin and Greek, and Frieda Meitner, sister of Lise Meitner, taught her mathematics and science. This private education lasted for two years (1909–1911). At the age of seventeen she was ready for the Matura, and in 1911 she became a full student at the university.[15]

Stopler took law courses at the university and became a young member of the student world. She described the beginnings of women's attendance at the university in her memoirs.

> Women were already plentiful at the university when I started in—less so when my sister Julchen started in. While Anna and I went to Lyceum, Julchen went to the newly founded Girls' Gymnasium. It was the very beginning of serious studies for women. There she took the entire curriculum of gymnasium studies.[16]

One year behind Lise Meitner, Julchen began to study the natural sciences of botany and biology, but then turned toward pure philosophy, and received a doctorate in philosophy with a thesis about Kant's notion of teleology. "So when I got to the University there were already plenty of girls around, partly gymnasium graduates (a minority) but mostly Lyceum graduates taking art history, history, etc."

Stopler described a room at the University assigned to female students, "a kind of club where they could congregate and rest and talk." During her time in the University, she joined a club of socialist students, not because she considered herself a socialist, but because she felt they alone took the nationality problems of Austria-Hungary seriously.

However, Stopler recalls feeling isolated as a woman in her law courses. In the introductory lecture on Roman law, given by Professor Wlassak, she was the only woman among the hundreds of students. She took the foundation of law studies, Roman Law, Germanic Law, History of Austrian Law, and British Common Law, in three terms.

She also took a lecture on penal law by a "brilliant professor," and was again the only female student.

> And one day I received an open postcard from my professor which said: "Liebes Fräulein Kassowitz, in the next lecture I will treat so and so. I suppose you will prefer not to attend." It happened to be the paragraph about rape and all these sexual crimes, and he was kind enough to warn me because I might be embarrassed and he told me not to come. So that was still the stage of things. I didn't go. I could read all about it, I didn't need to be there.[17]

She pursued law studies because she thought women would soon be admitted to exams and maybe she could still get into regular studies and graduate. In fact, women were not admitted to regular study in the faculty of law until after the war in 1919, and therefore she eventually switched to humanistic studies.

In the case of Lillian Bader, the decision about her future was made when she was eleven years old and entering secondary school. Her teachers urged her mother that she should be prepared to attend the University.

> At that time it was no easy decision to launch a girl on such a career. At the time that this future was being considered for me, only a very limited number of women registered yearly at the University of Vienna. Not all studies were yet available to women. They could become doctors of medicine, could study sciences or languages, but not yet, for some strange reason, become lawyers. The "girl student" was a type offering great possibilities to the cartoonists of the time, who depicted them smoking cigarettes in mantailored [sic] suits and in high collared shirt waists. They were thought to be "emancipated," which set them apart from the average and which gave them a definite handicap as far as getting married was concerned.[18]

Despite the indecision of her mother and illnesses which set her back, Bader did eventually succeed in passing the Matura in 1913 and attended University. Judaism did not play a significant role in the lives of most of these women. University study seemed to be incompatible with Jewish practice or affiliation for Jewish women at the University of Vienna. According to Harriet Pass Freidenreich's study of the Jewish identity of German and Austrian university women, many lacked

Portrait of Toni Stopler, 1924. Photograph by A. M. Schein.
Courtesy of the Leo Baeck Institute, New York.

a strong, positive Jewish identity.[19] Most of them came from upper-middle-class families and received excellent secular education, but little formal Jewish training other than the required religious classes at school. Their families aspired to assimilation and observed few Jewish practices in the home. Instead of following the expected path of Jewish wife and mother, they chose professional careers and often along with this, political involvement. Many of them never married, and of those who did, many did not have children. Some officially left the Jewish community, either becoming Christian or *konfessionslos*. Most of them never formally left the Jewish community. They "accepted their Jewishness as a fact of life, even though this aspect of their personal identity did not always play an important role in their lives before the advent of Nazism." [20] They rarely attended synagogue and, in contrast to men in similar positions, played virtually no role in Jewish communal governance. Neither did they become actively involved in Jewish women's organizations. Jewish female students seldom established their own societies, but joined mixed-sex socialist or Zionist student societies more often than women's organizations. A minority of Jewish university women actively affirmed their Jewish identity, either through Jewish observances in their homes, involvement in Jewish organizations, acknowledging a Jewish nationality, or seeking to acquire more knowledge about Judaism. [21] They suffered more from discrimination and obstacles due to their gender than their religion at this time, although that would change later on.

Through university study, Viennese Jewish women found a way to assert themselves. Although they rarely became engaged in feminist politics, the mere act of matriculating, and attaining a degree, despite the persistence of obstacles and opposition, represents an action defying cultural norms and expectations. The opening of higher education to women in Austria in certain respects took place at a faster pace and earlier than in other German-speaking countries. For example, the examinations leading to the Matura had been available to women since 1872, although women did not earn the right to matriculate at the University until much later. In other ways, Austria lagged behind in terms of women's education, such as the male-dominated teaching staff at the *Lyzeen*, in contrast to the situation in Germany. Although in both Germany and Austria, Jewish women were over-represented in the University, the discrepancy in Austria was much greater. [22] These distinctions in the German and Austrian case suggest that in Austria, progressive forces and perseverance on the part of women, particularly Jewish women, competed with extremely conservative forces and institutions, such as the dominance of the Catholic Church. This created a situation ridden with contradictions in the development of female education in Austria.

Gender and Politics in Vienna

Jewish women entered into political life in Vienna as a result of changing ideologies of gender and public roles. As Jewish women entered the world of politics, Jewish men formulated their opinion of Jewish women's political roles. Jewish women's political activity was influenced by three developments: the emergence of women's organizations, Jewish women's involvement in general women's movements, and Jewish women's entry into non-feminist politics.

Outside of Austria, Jewish women joined public life under the rubric of Jewish women's organizations. Occasionally these organizations evolved into what have been labeled "Jewish-feminist movements" which offered Jewish women the opportunity to become involved in politics without risking their affiliation and identity as Jewish women. The most famous example of this type of organization was the *Jüdische Frauenbund*, or League of Jewish Women, founded in 1904 by Bertha Pappenheim in Frankfurt/Main.[23] However, this did not seem to be the case in Vienna, it is interesting to note, despite the fact that Pappenheim herself was born in Vienna. Many Jewish women's organizations came to fruition in Vienna, as seen in the previous chapter, but they focused primarily on social work and steered clear of politics.

Some Viennese Jewish women did participate in the general women's movement in its various branches, socialist and bourgeois. The acceptance of Jewish women by the non-Jewish leadership of these circles varied over time and circumstance. Nevertheless Jewish women joined in the struggle for women's rights in all its incarnations. They confronted social problems such as prostitution, women's work, and education, while also striving to increase the political rights of women, and to gain rights for women in the religious community. They employed a variety of tactics which ranged from debating issues through texts to social work and political activism.

The central figures of Viennese feminism were not Jewish. While the reasons for this are complex, the unusual nature of the Austrian feminist movement, its small size, representing a narrow segment of society, and its slow development compared to the situation in England and Germany, led to its homogeneous composition.[24] The Jewish women who joined politics tended to align with the Social Democratic party, the Zionist movement, and later communism. While they were often sympathetic to the women's movement, Jewishness determined their choice when it came to affiliation. Their gravitation to Zionist and socialist politics mirrored that of their male coreligionists.

The Austrian women's movement consisted of four distinct groups: the radical bourgeois feminists, the moderates, the socialists, and the Christian Social women. The radicals included the members of the *Allgemeiner Österreichischer Frauenverein*, the free-thinking, bourgeois union founded by Rosa Mayreder (1858–1938). Together with Auguste Fickert (1855–1910) and Marie Lang (1858–1934), Mayreder established a feminist journal in 1899, the *Dokumente der Frauen*. The moderate group, led by Marianne Hainisch (1839–1936), worked toward achieving concrete goals, aiming for social reforms without risking feminine identity, in contrast to the radicals who sought more fundamental changes.

Adelheid Popp (1869–1939) led the socialist women's movement. Officially under the auspices of the Social Democratic party, the socialist women's movement focused concern on the plight of women workers. Popp's book, *Die Lebensgeschichte einer Arbeiterin* (The Autobiography of a Working Woman) (1909), described her life as one of fifteen children in a provincial weaver's family. After three years of school, she worked in a factory. The hard physical labor of the factory led to her physical deterioration to the point of a breakdown. In 1885, she joined the Social Democratic party and became an agitator and writer for the *Arbeiterinnen-Zeitung.* She fought for women's rights at work, in the family, and in public life and for a better understanding between women's rights activists and workers.[25]

In her history of the women's movement in Austria, Marianne Hainisch described herself as engaged in the same struggle as both the socialist women and the radicals. They all belonged to a small and distinguished group of women's rights activists. They shared the goals of equal rights to education and employment, equal morality for men and women, reform of personal rights in marriage legislation, equal rights of assembly for both sexes, and the passive right to vote for all representative bodies. On the other hand, she drew a sharp line between these groups' shared purpose and the Christian Social Women's organization, which agitated on the behalf of men in their party rather than for women's rights. Their organ, *Die Österreichische Frauenzeitung*, the leitmotifs of which were compulsory education and Jew-baiting, kept a great distance from the question of women's suffrage.[26]

The nineteenth century witnessed the beginning of a transformation in women's status in Austria, particularly in the areas of education and employment.[27] The rise of collective consciousness of women evidenced by the women's movement followed in the wake of the improved situation in these areas, coupled with restrictive legislative decisions such as the Association Law of 1867. Nevertheless, women did not attain civil equality in Austria until much later. For example, women's suffrage was introduced only in 1918, following the Monarchy's dissolution and the establishment of the Austrian Republic.[28] Women's representation in the Austrian Parliament remained under 6 percent until 1975.[29] Resistance to changing the status of women persisted also in the cultural realm, with the Vienna Philharmonic voting to open its ranks to women only in 1997 in response to internal and external pressure.[30]

Even in the limited cases where Jewish women supported the women's movement they subordinated it to their class or ethnic political loyalties. For example, Therese Schlesinger-Eckstein (1863–1940) and her younger sister Emma Eckstein (1865–1924) both joined the *Allgemeiner Österreichischer Frauenverein* in the 1890s. They came from a liberal bourgeois Jewish family in which there were ten children. Therese referred to her mother, Amalie Wehle, born in Prague and well-educated for a woman of her day, as a masculine type and always healthier and stronger than other women.[31] The lack of girls' educational opportunities in her day limited their training.

Therese supplemented her schooling with private lessons in history, primarily on the Enlightenment and the French Revolution. She read a great deal and loved the German classics, especially Schiller. She married Viktor Schlesinger in 1888, and they had a daughter. He was fifteen years older than she was and died of tuberculosis in 1891. After his death she returned to her parents' home, where she lived with her mother, her sister Emma, and her daughter.[32] She also had many physical problems following the birth of her daughter.

During the 1890s, Therese worked in the legal protection position, writing the announcements which appeared in the *Volksstimme*, and spoke at gatherings. She stressed two issues, the importance of education and the rejection of women's traditional humility.

> The girl must be educated, to seek happiness and love in marriage and not only subsistence, to strive for the highest development of her humanity, she must be educated to feel herself equal to man, if necessary to fight for her dignity, instead of selling out for some timid harmony: . . . She must learn that there is nothing more hostile to

culture than the humility of women and that the final dawning self-reliance of the woman signifies a new era of cultural development.[33]

She first came into personal contact with Social Democratic delegates such as Viktor Adler (1852–1918) and Adelheid Popp in 1896 at an *Enquête* on the position of Viennese female workers. The conditions of the female proletariat directly confronted her for the first time. Her socialist sympathies soon placed her somewhat at odds with the *Frauenverein*. In 1897, she announced to Fickert her decision to put her "weak energy" in the service of the Social Democratic cause.[34] After that point she became increasingly involved in Social Democracy.

During the years of the beginning of the Viennese workers' movement, she lived in isolation caring for her sick daughter. A wish for liberation combined with her romantic attitude toward revolution motivated her sympathy with the movement, rather than a political awareness.

Political engagement was for her psychic salvation, amid all of her difficulties.

> But how much less such grief means opposite the infinite enrichment, which my spiritual and emotional life has experienced through my membership in Social Democracy! It has made it possible for me to raise myself above the wretchedness of a merely personal sphere of interests, to strengthen my weak powers thereby, that I might use them in the service of a freely chosen cause, to ripen spiritually, to gather experiences, to sharpen my view for the world and humanity and to remain true to the ideals of my youth.[35]

While shifting her main allegiance from feminism to socialism, she continued to support women's rights. In reconciling the two competing ideologies she presented women's rights as a tool with which to achieve socialist goals. Thus she wrote in 1910, "Equal suffrage for all men and women is certainly not our highest and ultimate goal, but it is one of the most important and indispensable means to get nearer to our goals. It shall help us to bring the exploitation of the working class and the special oppression of the working class woman to an end."[36] Like other Social Democratic women, Schlesinger-Eckstein believed in the primacy of class over gender. In fact, one criticism of the socialist branch of the women's movement in Austria was its failure to fight for women's suffrage, deferring to the leaders of the party who made

Therese Eckstein. ÖNB/Wien.

the decision to demand only unrestricted male suffrage for the time being. After being attacked at the 1907 International Socialist Congress
for this decision, Austrian socialist women reconsidered and decided
that women's suffrage was an inalienable right.[37] Nevertheless, her involvement with the party was not without tensions. Her background
in radical feminist politics along with her bourgeois origins and continued support for women's rights led to the distrust and animosity of

many Social Democrats.[38] Schlesinger-Eckstein was the first Jewish woman to become active in Social Democracy. This may have been an additional factor in her lack of acceptance. However, many Jewish men joined the party and attained leadership roles in it.

As for Emma, her work for the women's movement was hindered by the mental illness which she called her "evil nervousness." Around 1895 she became one of Freud's first patients. Although she did continue her work for the women's movement, she remained a marginal figure.[39] Ida Baumann (1845–1913), the companion of Auguste Fickert, was from a poor Jewish family and faced many hardships due to her Jewishness. Despite her affiliation with the bourgeois women's movement she resented the political and public activities of Fickert, which led to difficulties in their relationship. She ultimately committed suicide following Fickert's death.[40]

Despite the modest level of Jewish women's participation in the women's movement in Austria, anti-Semites blamed Jewish women for feminism in Austria as they did in Germany. Georg von Schönerer, the leader of the anti-Semitic Pan-German Movement, asserted that only women who have failed in their calling as women or who have no wish to answer it and Jewesses devote themselves to the idiocy of female suffrage.[41]

In the fight against prostitution, non-Jewish Austrian feminists, such as Rosa Mayreder and Irma Troll-Borostyáni (1847–1912), limited their response to discourse and text.[42] Rabbi Joseph Samuel Bloch, an ardent opponent of anti-Semitism, defended the Jews in Parliament against the accusation that prostitution was a Jewish vice. However, in spite of the attention given to Jewish white slavery by Viennese anti-Semites, Jewish women's involvement in the fight against white slavery lagged in comparison to other countries.[43] The writer Grete Meisel-Hess (1879–1922), born in Prague and living in Vienna from 1893 until 1908, grappled with the problems of Viennese anti-Semitism and anti-feminism. She put forward the idea that Jewish emancipation and women's emancipation would help bring about the evolutionary progress of humanity, seeing anti-Semitism and anti-feminism as signs of illness and degeneration.[44] She addressed the problem of prostitution in her literature, as did Else Kotányi Jerusalem (1877–1942?), particularly in her best-selling novel, *Der heilige Skarabäus* (1909). However, more Jewish women became involved either in leftist political movements such as Social Democracy and communism or in Zionism (to be explored in the next chapter). In some instances these women formally left the Jewish community.[45]

Later, more Jewish women joined the ranks of the Viennese Social Democrats. Aline Klatschko Furtmüller (1883–1941) studied French and matriculated at the University in 1908. Since 1900 she had a close alliance with the *Sozialwissenschaftlichen Bildungsverein* (Sociological Educational Society) and belonged to the Social Democratic Party. She taught French and German at the Schwarzwald school.[46] Marie Langer described the impact she made on the students there in her memoirs.

> She was a Social Democrat and very progressive. I can still today remember a poem, which she often recited to us: A girl—around the turn of the century—explains to her parents, that she wants to marry the man she loves. The father has already decided upon another bridegroom for her: "I do not want him, I do not love and esteem him" says the daughter. Indignant, the father turns to his wife: "Do you know, what is the news?—Did we esteem one another? Did we love one another?"[47]

The psychoanalyst Helene Rosenbach Deutsch (1884–1982), born in Przemysl, Galicia, had early contacts with socialism. Her romance with the Polish Jewish socialist Hermann Lieberman first exposed her to socialism and continued her involvement while studying in Zurich. In medical school in Vienna, she remembered no special difficulties as a woman. Some individual professors discriminated against her, but on the whole she had no complaints. In 1910, she broke off her relationship with Lieberman and later married the native Viennese internist, Felix Deutsch.[48]

Marianne Springer Pollak (1891–1963), who grew up in a bourgeois Jewish home, studied French and English and was an avid reader. She became a language teacher, a Social Democrat, and a feminist. Oskar Pollak introduced her to socialist politics. Together they read socialist literature, and he brought her to political gatherings where she met many personalities with whom she would later work. Otto Bauer made a strong impression on her.[49]

Käthe Leichter, who also became a prominent Social Democrat, recalled having an early sensitivity to social injustice. For example, the status of the servants in her own home disturbed her at a young age.

> But first the world of social opposition opened itself up to me in my own home, with the domestic servants . . . The world of the employers are the large well lit rooms, which lead to the square—the world

of the domestic servants are the kitchen and the servants' chambers, a bare room without a carpet, without curtains, in the winter without heat, both of which lead to the yard.[50]

As she became aware of class conflicts, demonstrations, and strikes, her sympathy with the working class grew. At the age of eleven, she recalled feeling guilty that she lived in security while others lived in misery and poverty. She later studied sociology and engaged in socialist and feminist politics. She married the socialist Otto Leichter in 1921 and had two children. Although Leichter wrote in her memoirs that she "until the year 1938, knew no anti-Semitism," discrimination affected her career. In 1924, when she received an assignment to establish a women's lecture in the workers' cabinet, colleagues influenced the shorthand typists not to work for this *Jüdin*. She learned nothing of this, and these people were friendly to her face-to-face.[51]

The *Sozialistische Arbeiterjugend* (SAJ) attracted young Jewish women with an intellectual and ideological orientation. Born in Przemysl, Galicia, in 1904, Stella Klein-Löw joined the SAJ as a young student. She became a member of the Social Democratic Party in 1922. At the University of Vienna, she studied classical and modern philology and psychology with the professors Karl and Charlotte Bühler and Wilhelm Reich. Later, she taught at a Jewish private *Gymnasium*. "As a Jew and a Socialist she had no chances for another position."[52] In the party, she worked in the Workers' Library in the ninth district (Alsergrund). Many of her patrons were poor Jews, and among them were some religious Jews who did not come to the library on Saturday.[53]

Still other Jewish women became active in the Austrian Communist Party (KPDÖ). Elfriede Eisler-Friedländer (later Ruth Fischer) (1895–1961) was one of the founders of the KPDÖ.[54] In the case of Marie Langer, she described her attraction to communism as having a connection to her identity as a Jewish woman. "In spite of my wealth, I was always aware of my disadvantages: being a Jew and a woman. And to these disadvantages another was later added: being divorced. It was logical that I wanted to join the Left; because I was certain, these injustices would be lifted in Communism."[55] Genia Quittner (1906–1989), also from a Jewish background, joined the KPDÖ as well. From a poor Jewish petty bourgeois family, she was forced to work in order to support her family when her father died, but still managed to complete her university studies. Due to discrimination, she could not find adequate

work and took a position for which she was overqualified.[56] She joined the SAJ during her school days, the Communist Youth in 1925, and the Executive Committee of the International Communist Youth in 1928. Her husband, Franz Quittner, an assistant at the Physical Institute at the University of Vienna, lost his position due to his membership in the Communist Party. For political reasons, he and his wife emigrated to the Soviet Union in 1929.[57]

Jewish reactions to the women's movement and Jewish women's involvement in politics and pursuit of higher education ranged from support of the cause to extreme opposition, negative stereotyping, and satire. Three themes commonly appeared in the writings of Jewish men about the women's movement: the assertion that in Judaism women already had a high status and therefore did not need modern feminism, the fear that Jewish women's involvement in the women's movement would lead to assimilation by weakening their Jewish identity, and the notion that the women's movement was dangerous because it blurred the natural boundary between masculine and feminine. Hence, Adolf Jellinek, Vienna's most prominent rabbi and preacher, as was seen in the previous chapter, proclaimed that Jews knew intuitively what modern society arrived at much later with complicated theories, and that Judaism, unlike feminism, understood that men and women naturally differ in the observance of religious ceremonies.[58] Adolf Schwarz concluded his second lecture on women of the Bible by saying that the biblical women he described were in the best and most beautiful sense of the words *Dokumente der Frauen*—a reference to the Viennese feminist journal founded by Mayreder, Fickert, and Lang in 1899—because they documented the towering heights to which women could rise. He continued: "They rise up, and call to the women and young women of the present to fight for your women's rights, but do not forget your women's dignity, emancipate yourselves from all that oppresses and restricts you, only guard one thing in order to emancipate yourselves and remain emancipated, your femininity."[59] Rabbi and folklorist Max Grunwald also argued that Jewish tradition provided answers to the questions raised by the modern women's movement.[60]

Discomfort with the women's movement extended to Jewish writers and journalists as well. For example, Karl Kraus, the satirist and editor of *Die Fackel* (The Torch), initially sympathized with the women's movement; however, in his later writings he rejected the concept of women's emancipation on the grounds that women who seek to assume masculine roles deny their femininity. He targeted Alice Therese Schalek (1874–1956), the first female journalist in Austria and feuilleton editor for the *Neue Freie Presse*, as a symbol of the destruction of the barrier between feminine and masculine. Her activities as the only female reporter during the First World War as well as her Jewishness became the subject of Kraus's satire.[61] Similarly, Arthur Schnitzler portrayed the socialist agitator Therese Golowski in *Der Weg ins Frei* as having become masculine and unattractive because of her political engagement.[62]

Meanwhile, psychoanalysts in Vienna linked the women's movement to female hysteria. The psychoanalyst Franz Wittels (1880–1950) wrote in an article that hysteria was the basis for women's desire to study medicine and struggle for equal rights. The prevailing perception that feminism and Judaism were at odds with one another hindered Austrian Jewish women's participation in explicitly feminist politics. All segments of the Viennese Jewish community argued that Judaism highly regarded the Jewish woman, and had answered the questions of the modern women's movement long ago. They also warned that involvement in the women's movement could lead to assimilation, and a blurring of the differences in the sexes.

On the other hand, some Jewish men became supporters of women's rights movements, in the context of their struggle for universal rights, most notably Julius Ofner (1845–1924) in Vienna. The Bohemian-born lawyer was a founder of the Viennese Fabian Society, which developed into the Sozialpolitiker, a non-Marxist radical association which demanded universal suffrage and prioritized the social question. He supported women's rights and removing marriage and divorce laws from the jurisdiction of the Catholic Church.

The centrality of gender to the definition of Jewish identity forms the backdrop to Jewish responses to the women's movement. The prevailing association of Jewish men with femininity led to a concerted Jewish effort to maintain their sense of masculine men and feminine women. Furthermore, anti-Semites and anti-feminists blamed the Jews for feminism, asserting that Jewish women disproportionately joined European women's movements. The reactions of male-dominated Jewish communities to women's movements derived partially as a response to the anti-Semitic assertion that Jews were like women and responsible for feminism, the attempt of women to be like men. The Jewish ambivalence toward the women's movement and women's political activism may correspond to the desire to affirm Jewish manliness.

Other Jewish women dedicated themselves to their careers and/or families and remained uninvolved in politics. Viennese Jewish women pursued just about every career imaginable. Some of the common careers for Jewish women were in medicine, education, and nursing. A number of Jewish women, such as Helene Deutsch, Else Pappenheim, Marie Langer, and Margaret Mahler, aspired to careers in medicine and psychoanalysis, as will be seen in Chapter 5. Many others, such as Eugenie Schwarzwald, Aline Furtmüller, Salka Goldmann, and Ottilie Bondy, devoted themselves to education, either running schools of their own or teaching in them. Many Jewish women became writers, such as the journalist Alice Schalek, the literary essayist Marie Herzfeld, writers Lilly Körber, Gina Kaus, Franzi Ascher, Elisabeth Freundlich, Veza Canetti, Mimi Grossberg, Else Jerusalem, Grete Meisel-Hess, Ida Barber, and Fredrike Zweig. Some Jewish women, such as the actress and founder of the "Theater of Courage," Stella Kadmon, pursued careers in theater, as will be seen in Chapter 6. These women faced obstacles in their careers due to their Jewishness and gender. Some writers wrote under male pseudonyms. The art historian Hilde Zaloscer (1903–1999) tried to establish her career in Vienna three times without success. Although she finally succeeded in 1975, she is still more widely recognized as an art historian abroad than in Austria.[63]

The vast majority of Viennese Jewish women did not attend the University. Many went to other institutions of higher learning and also pursued careers. In some instances anti-Semitism created career opportunities for Jewish women. For example, an article on Jewish nurses suggested establishing Jewish nursing schools in response to incitement against the Jews.[64] As a result, Jewish nurses pursued careers without competition, benefiting the sick because nurses of their own confession better understood their needs. Non-Jewish women also promoted career opportunities for women. Emilie Winiwarter Exner (Pseudonym, Felice Ewart) (1850–1909) was highly educated and put her literary and practical talents in service of her times, dedicating herself to women and education. From 1901 to 1906 she served as president of the *Wiener Frauen-Erwerb-Verein* (Viennese Association of Working Women), and in this capacity she gave a lecture on pharmacology, which required two years of university study, as a career for women.[65]

Modernization presented Jewish women with an array of choices in terms of politics, careers, and education. Furthermore, Jewish women led in the entry of women into these domains that had been thought of as exclusively male. Through these activities they confronted gender stereotypes and re-negotiated their identities in light of modern ideologies. The ubiquity of gender discrimination in Vienna at the turn of the century infiltrated the Jewish community and culture as well. The Viennese preoccupation with sexuality combined with the discourse about Jewish sexuality compelled many Viennese Jewish men and women to confront the question of Jewish women's otherness. As a result, Jewish men displaced anxieties of their own sexual difference onto women. Jewish women's scope of involvement in society, culture, and politics remained circumscribed by these myths, but their activities allowed them an avenue by which to negotiate their way through the conflicting ideologies of their environment. The experiences of Viennese Jewish women in the University and politics represent an early attempt to forge a positive Jewish female identity amid a male-dominated non-Jewish host culture.

4 ›› *Women and the Zionist Movement*

In an address before the Women's Zionist Association in Vienna in 1901 (*Wiener Zionistische Frauenverein*) Theodor Herzl (1860–1904), the founder of political Zionism, declared that women had not contributed significantly to the Zionist cause.[1] He began the speech (which he described in his diary as "a rather absent-minded lecture")[2] by suggesting that while women had contributed practically nothing to Zionism, they could potentially, through the use of successful propaganda, become everything. Poor women, he asserted, would make good Zionists, except that they lacked the means and free time to devote to the cause. Traditional observant women, while praiseworthy for their devotion to home and family, lived sheltered from the realities of Jewish misery and suffering. "That is the type of woman for whom I have the greatest respect, because in her all the fine qualities, all the great and eternal things that were particularly precious in dark days have been preserved in their purest and most beautiful form." He referred to a third group as a "new breed of Jewish woman." Unlike traditional Jewish women, they did not observe the Sabbath or devote themselves to family, but still, they had no contact with the real world. Herzl proposed using poetry and art in order to attract women to Zionism. Once attracted to Zionism, women would spread the Zionist idea in their social circles. He also claimed that Zionism would make women into better mothers. As they became more educated, he explained, they would understand the importance of Zionism for children, the citizens of the future.

Herzl's assessment and typology of Jewish women reflected fin de siècle middle-class values and understanding of the proper feminine sphere. This notion of "femininity" equated the essence of woman with maternal feelings. Therefore women could be expected to focus on caring for the home, children, and family. "Feminine" careers such as teaching, nursing, and child-care were tolerated.[3] Jewish communal leaders adopted this view as their own and accepted it as the Jewish view of femininity, as did Viennese Zionists for the most part.

This notion of "femininity" also infiltrated the consciousness of fin de siècle Viennese Jewish women. To a certain extent, however, the emergence of feminism—that is, the political movement for women's rights in the nineteenth century—challenged the self-definition of Jewish women. Feminism and femininity stood in a complex relationship to one another, different but not entirely antithetical. Jewish women attempted to incorporate these two ideologies in their negotiations of modern female identities. In this chapter, I will address these issues by examining Jewish women's participation in the Zionist movement as a way to negotiate their identities, and images of Jewish women in Viennese Zionist works.

The search for Jewish identity in a climate of intensifying anti-Semitism further complicated things for Viennese Jewish women. I will argue that the quest for a national or ethnic identity in the face of assimilation and growing anti-Jewish sentiment, alongside the need to reconcile femininity and feminism, led some Jewish women to Zionism. The Zionist movement afforded Jewish women the opportunity for solidarity with fellow Jews. It provided a framework for negotiating female identity and Jewish identity, and for confronting gender stereotypes.

Viennese Jewish women dealt with the conflicting values and attitudes of their world. While some Jewish women turned to study, politics, professions, or philanthropy in their efforts to confront gender stereotypes, the women discussed in this chapter used Zionism as a framework for the negotiation of those tensions. Jews became Zionists for a variety of reasons, including the desire for a Jewish national identity in the Diaspora.[4] Likewise, Zionism offered Jewish women ways to negotiate their identities as women. Some found feminine ways to be Zionist, while others sought political roles or believed that gender troubles could be rectified through the settlement of Palestine.

Zionist Women and Girls

Over a dozen Zionist organizations of girls and women operated in fin de siècle Vienna, attesting to the active role of women in Viennese Zionism.[5] Simply by becoming Zionists, Jewish women consciously identified as Jews. They stressed the importance of a national identity regardless of different approaches, concentrating their efforts on getting more women involved. They spoke harsh words about Jewish women who did not participate in the Zionist movement. In their position toward the question of feminism and femininity, three approaches can be identified: (1) the desire to find feminine ways to be Zionist, (2) the struggle for political roles, and (3) the conviction that gender roles could only be properly reconstructed in the homeland.

According to the first approach, Zionism provided Jewish women with the means to work for Judaism in feminine ways. Women understood their contributions to the movement as complementing the activities of Zionist men rather than competing with them. For example, in a statement published in 1907, the organization *Verein jüdischer Mädchen "Miriam"* (Society of Jewish Girls: Miriam) excluded women from political roles. Submitted by Sophie Thau, the president, and Gisela Kohn, the secretary, the appeal read as follows:

> We want to foster Jewish knowledge and sensitivity. We encourage Jewish sociability as well as motivate members to pursue private study and spiritual work through literary speeches and popular science courses. We are considering the foundation of a reading room and a Jewish library. We direct our call without prejudice to national-minded girls and to our opponents: Join our organization "Miriam." We want to strive for our goal through silent serious work of high perspective—not through dabbling in politics and empty debates: to be equivalent to men, in true work for people and home![6]

The words "spiritual work," "serious," and "silent" counteracted the image of the frivolous, loud, idle, bourgeois woman. Women and girls needed not become political and de-feminized in order to be Zionists. They could work for Zionism in respectable feminine ways, without competing with men.

Lectures by Zionist women often focused on finding feminine ways to become active in Zionism. For example, Olga Kadisch spoke on the duties of the modern Jewish woman on April 6, 1901, at the *Allgemeinen jüdischen Arbeitsverein* and on May 11, 1901, at the *Verein jüdischer Mädchen*, Hadassah, an organization which sponsored lectures and study sessions. She stressed the need for Jewish women to raise their self-confidence, to feel proud to be Jewish, and to educate their children on the importance of Zionism. She said that there was a rich field of activity offered here in which women could utilize their special qualities as wife and mother to obtain success.[7] Similarly, the women of the *Jüdischer Frauenbund für Kulturarbeit in Palästina*, founded in 1907, saw their natural role in setting up cultural institutions and working in accepted feminine vocations. They stated in their program that Jewish women of the entire world should gather together to participate in the cultural work of the Zionist movement in Palestine. "The organization should recruit members for this proposal, and aim at founding first of all a Jewish school of domestic science, connected with a boarding school for Jewish teachers and nurses in Palestine."[8]

This approach firmly opposed Jewish women's involvement in the general women's movement, seeing it as a violation of femininity and a vehicle of assimilation. Marta Baer-Issachar (also known as Martha Baer) took up this theme in an article directed "to our women."[9] Baer, who trained as a social worker in Hamburg and set up classes in reading and sewing for girls, was active in the fight against white slavery (prostitution) and lectured on this and other subjects.[10] More sympathetic to East European Jewish women, she had direct experience with both Western and Eastern European Jewish women, and her ideology reflected this background.

Baer asserted that the women's rights movement naturally attracted Jewish women, because they eagerly embraced ideas of rights and freedom. But when they aligned themselves with women of different nationalities, they lost touch with their own people. "In the eagerness, with which Jewish women championed the women's cause, they divided themselves more and more from their people." She claimed that never in the history of nations were women so alienated from their race (*Stamm*). Jewish women's desertion and lack of interest in their race (*Stamm*) resulted from their loss of all sense of belonging. "What was it to them to belong to a people about whom they know nothing, a religious community that had no religion, and a nation that they believed to be dead?"

To those who still dedicated their energies and placed their hopes for the future in the women's movement, Baer-Issachar wrote:

We call on her for cooperation. We want to recruit her for ourselves, to inspire her for our effort. We want to show her a task that is worthy of her: to bring hope and redemption to her deeply afflicted people. We want to educate her with a noble national feeling, stressing its strong and proud individuality, however, free from vain arrogance, which destroys all healthy self-consciousness. She should feel herself as a lively, strong member of a chain, which connects us to our ancestors.[11]

She asserted that women's contribution to Zionism should not contradict their female nature; she envisioned a "New Woman":

The new woman! A strong woman who does not see her future in denying the feminine and does not believe she will only be happy in men's work. But the other type who will heal our nation: instead of precious stones, she adorns herself with accomplishments, and work for her people is her favorite recreation. She does not fight for women's rights, but strives for women's duties with moral seriousness.[12]

In every nation women had "special duties" which were "specifically female." "These special duties are dictated by nature and thus it is self-evident that woman's way of life is so infinitely different from that of man."

The natural areas of the Jewish woman were home and family, and by extension, the family-community—in other words, the nation. Therefore, she prioritized education of Jewish women and children about the poor and needy Jews of the East, their animated life of the spirit oppressed by the narrow ghetto boundaries and the stale ghetto air. This spiritual life needed the fresh breeze of a homeland. Unlike the Jews of the West, who felt a rift in their souls between the Jewish nation and western culture, the eastern Jews were completely prepared for Zion. The new Jewish woman would teach her children Hebrew and Judaism, celebrate the Jewish holidays, and tell them about the deeds of the ancestors and the meaning of the festivals. The Jews of her day needed a reminder and a warning. "Instead of the Christmas tree, the Menorah lights will shine. Certainly, they will not flicker as cheerfully as the Christmas candles—they radiate quietly, but for that reason they make the heart and soul free and wide and support the seekers. And one will sing no hymn other than our victory song."

She assigned two additional tasks to Jewish women, which fell outside the bounds of traditionally feminine duties. First, incorporating Nordau's concept of degeneration, she argued that Jewish mothers should cultivate their own bodies, through sport and physical training, and urge their children to maintain a reasonable level of physical fitness. A final task of the Jewish woman was fund-raising. A great deal of money was required for the acquisition of land in Palestine. Full of passion for Zionism and inspired by her awe for the spirit of eastern Jewry and her concern for their future, she drew her motivation from the inherent problems she saw in western Jewry, particularly their ignorance of their heritage and religion. Zionism provided a solution for the Jews of both the East and the West. Like many other Zionist women, she called upon women to work for Zionism in a feminine role. She saw the involvement of Jewish women in the general women's movement and the fight for equal rights as distasteful examples of assimilation.[13]

Rosa Pomeranz (1880–1934) also opposed assimilation and gave historically based explanations of the importance of women in Zionism. Born in Tarnopol, Galicia, Pomeranz (also known as Roza Melzerowa) studied in Vienna, Leipzig, and Paris, later returning to Tarnopol. In addition to her Zionist writings, she also authored novels, including *Im Land der Not*, about Galician Jews.[14] In her Zionist writings, she aimed at attracting women to Zionism, and demonstrating the failure of assimilation. She also addressed the religious opponents of Zionism who believed the Jews must wait for Messiah before returning to Palestine.

Using examples from history, such as women's giving their ornaments for the decoration of the Ark of the Covenant when the Temple was built, their role in the liberation from Egypt, and the importance of Eastern European Jewish women who remained true to their God and nation in exile, Pomeranz argued that women must become active in Zionism. "Our nation had to thank the moral purity and national trust of the woman for its first liberation and will also have to thank them for its last liberation."[15] She lamented that devout and pious Jewish women believed that liberation from exile would only come with the Messiah, while educated Jewish women had no interest in Judaism. To assimilated women she wrote, "only complete ignorance of your own unrivaled spiritual treasure, your entire historical and cultural past, could mislead you to them."[16]

Most tragic, according to Pomeranz, the Jewish youth suffered from a lack of self-respect and pride in knowing they represented the oldest living nation, due to the absence of Jewish education. Due to the persecution and humiliation they endured as Jews without the compensation of understanding the positive value of their heritage, they came to despise and hate their nation and themselves. She held Jewish mothers accountable for the misfortune of a falsely educated youth. "The Jewish mother, this embodiment of the most limitless and selfless, all-powerful love, prepares her children, in inconceivable, foolish blindness for an existence full of inner confusion and moral miseries, that accompanies them until their last breath of life."[17] She warned Jewish women that they must pull themselves together and carry out their duty. "Learn the language, literature and history of your nation . . . And out of these feelings, the love for the nation and fatherland must emerge in your female hearts, actually re-emerge, because it never vanishes from the soul of a Daughter of Judah."[18]

Pomeranz also noted that Jewish women had become involved in various movements such as liberalism, socialism, and the women's movement. In working for these causes, they forgot about their own needs. The rise of anti-Semitism took these women by surprise. They learned that in spite of all efforts to the contrary, the Jewish woman remained Jewish in the eyes of others. Pomeranz asserted that the Jewish mother must lead her children to Zionism, instead of hiding their Jewishness from them in an attempt to protect them.[19] In the end her vision of the role of Jewish women, shaped by the notion of femininity, drew on using their innate religious belief in the biblical prediction that the Jews would return to Palestine in order to educate their children with positive Jewish identities. But her call for women's active involvement in Zionism and the need to become educated in Jewish subjects demonstrated a desire to make women aware of their national identity.

The *Literischer Geselligkeitsverein jüdischer Mädchen: Moria* (Literary-Social Society for Young Jewish Girls: Moria), founded in 1892, officially promoted the study of Jewish history, literature, and the role of Jewish women in history while also working to revive Jewish nationalism. Rosa Kollman, the vice president, whose premature death from heart failure in 1901 shocked the Zionist community, viewed the goals of her organization as much more political. Shortly before her death, she delivered a speech on "Agitation" in which she asserted that "Moria" had "importance for agitation." "We are not always allowed to freely say that we are a Zionist girls' organization, so when asked about the tendency of our organization, we declare ourselves as a 'literary society for Jewish girls.'"[20] She clearly understood the organization as having political repercussions. The task of "Moria" was to bring non-Zionists and anti-Zionists back to Zionism. Completely de-Judaized girls came into the society and returned to Judaism and Zionism as a result of the lectures.

Rosa Feigenbaum (1853–1912), a Viennese Zionist, a delegate at the sixth Zionist Congress, a leader in Jewish charity work, and a regular contributor to the *Österreichische Wochenschrift* and the *Neuzeit*, two prominent liberal Jewish newspapers, as well as the feminist newspaper *Neues Frauenleben*, addressed a gathering of Viennese Zionist women and girls in 1901. One of the few women who crossed over into both the Jewish and the feminist worlds, she argued in her speech that Jewish women could be immensely important to Zionism. Just as women assisted anti-Semitic leaders such as Fürst Lichtenstein and Karl Lueger, so Jewish women could prove valuable if they put themselves into service of the movement.

She asserted that the rise in anti-Semitism necessitated a more politically assertive role for women. For example, when a decree introduced the division of children in the schools according to confession in 1888, she had suggested to a well-known, respected Jewish woman that a meeting should be called to protest against the "*Judenclassen.*" The woman answered, "What are you thinking of, what is that to us women, not even reasonable men are concerned with such a thing!"

> And still, many other women with whom I have fostered discussions about this concern [division of children in schools according to confession], answered in the same way. "What is it to us?" With this they dismissed it. The Jewish woman today does not feel the pulse of public life, she does not see that we live in a time where the woman must also take a stand, and know the relevant questions that are the mainspring of Judaism. This woman is not worthy of the name "Jewess." [21]

She criticized Jewish women for not understanding that extreme times demanded them to become politically engaged. She admonished women who did not react when a school association announced a condition for filling the position of a teacher as "Christian confession" and for working with the wife of a known anti-Semite in organizing a ball. She continued her speech as follows.

> And these women are not red with shame! Our modern Jewish woman apparently does not understand, in which agitated time she lives, as right and justice of the Jews is stepped on, she does not hear the "Hepp, Hepp" call and does not see the "yellow patch" that one wants to pin on her again; and she has lived with Tisza-Eszlar and Xanten, Konitz and Polna. But the better her social position, the less she feels herself a Jewish woman. She has an ostrich-like attitude and is of the opinion that it is not her business, if one tied up the life thread of our poor peddlers, if in parliamentarian bodies inflammatory addresses are held un-censured against the Jews. She turns the other way with so many Christians, who so often assure her: "Yes, if all the Jews were like you!" and she is delighted, when they lower themselves to take their place at her richly set table.

Feigenbaum's assertive Jewish identity coupled with her feminist inclinations led her to argue for women's need to become political. She appealed to women to work for Zionism in order to create a home for hundreds of thousands of poor Russian, Polish, and Romanian Jews. Her Zionism did not reject the Diaspora, but asserted that Jewish women should be proud of their heritage and come to the assistance of less fortunate Jews. "The Jewish woman should and must learn above all, to feel herself as a Jewish woman and to hold Judaism high. Then national thinking will also take root deep in the Jewish people because it is only the woman who educates the people." The incorporation of the notion of women's special role as educator demonstrates the influence of the notion of femininity on her outlook.

Similarly, Hermine Schildberger challenged the position of Jewish women in Zionism and demanded a more active, political role.[22] She recalled a time when she did not identify with the suffering of the Jews in Russia. In retrospect, she did not understand how she could have held such an attitude. She felt she had been like a sleepwalker, blinded to the suffering of her coreligionists and not understanding that the injuries they suffered were an affliction for all Jews.

> I want to call back these lost years, so that I would be able to use them for the advantage of my people. For the advantage of my people! Once again I ask myself fearfully, will we women really be capable someday of working in public life somewhere or other for the well-being of our sisters and brothers? Can the ardent desire, the burning wish to help, replace the lacking strength? But then what strength, what might lies in the hands of a woman in a land that forbids her, at least for the time being, every participation in political life?[23]

While the Jewish woman naturally worked for Zionism in her capacity as mother and wife in the home, Schildberger asserted she should also feel free to engage in public life, if she wished to do so. For a long time the woman functioned as more than merely a housewife, out of necessity. Helping her husband in the struggle to earn a livelihood, the woman did not hesitate to enter into the struggle for survival of her family. She asked, "Why shouldn't she also have the right like a man to make her views known and to spread them through spoken words and writings?" While she typically received the reply that women counted as delegates at Basel at the Zionist Congress and thus were equally regarded, she found this to be setting aside the real issue with an empty slogan. Perhaps women could speak in Basel, but they were expected to keep quiet the rest of the year! She proposed that Zionist leaders needed to remedy this situation by holding lectures and discussions in which women participated.

Schildberger gave examples of women, Frau Prof. Emma Gottheil in America and Frau Dr. (Sidonie) Kahn in Vienna, who proved that women could work successfully in public life. She avoided criticizing Zionist women's organizations and discussing women's rights; however, she clearly favored a more public role for Zionist women. Jewish women's struggle for equal rights, i.e., feminism, and the struggle to help the Jewish people through Zionism went hand in hand, in her view.

In addition to forming organizations, holding lectures, and writing articles aimed at attracting women to Zionism, women occasionally spoke at the Zionist Congresses, which in itself indicates their willingness and desire for public roles. Rozia Ellman spoke at the second Congress in Basel in 1898, and Emma Gottheil spoke at the fourth Congress in 1900 in London.[24] Miriam Schach, an active Zionist in Paris, addressed the tenth Zionist Congress in 1911. She analyzed Zionist images of women, noting that in early Zionism women had merely a symbolic role as the "personification of Zionism," and later they were seen primarily in supportive roles. She presented the Matriarchs as Zionist heroines and models for the new Zionist woman and called for a more active role for women in Zionism.[25]

At the eleventh Congress in Vienna, Johanna Simon-Friedberg of Heidelberg also argued that women needed to become more active in Zionism. Like Schach, she referred to Herzl's speech on women and Zionism, disagreeing with his assumption that women needed special incentives to be attracted to Zionism, and that women had special duties in the movement. In response to Herzl's assertion that poetry would attract women to Zionism, Simon-Friedberg said, "In general, with or without poetry women have no great ability to be interested in politics, but in times of need of a people women always become heroes like men."[26] While Schach blamed the Zionist movement for limiting women's role, Simon-Friedberg asserted that Zionism gave equal rights to women and therefore demanded that they use their rights to fight alongside men. She lamented that women had not created any Zionist women's journals and had not become leaders in Zionist corporations. Zionist women could be proud when their rights existed not only on paper but also were exercised, not only symbolically, but in real ways. Zionist women had two tasks, according to Simon-Friedberg—inner tasks and outer tasks. The inner tasks related to the home and family, the feminine realm, while the outer tasks involved becoming active and knowledgeable in social work. By learning general social work skills, Jewish women would gain the experience necessary to prepare them for their specific Jewish task.[27] They would be able to address Jewish issues such as vocational guidance for girls, the fight against white slavery, and the organization of evening clubs for working girls.

Simon-Friedberg attributed the lack of involvement of women in Zionism to their distance from Judaism and their desire to assimilate, and in her solution she adopted the third approach to the question of femininity and feminism, the belief that the problem of gender roles could only be sorted out in a Jewish homeland. This followed the logic of male Zionist leaders Max Nordau and Herzl, who blamed the feminization of the male Jew on life in the Diaspora and believed that in the Jewish state, Jewish men would become more masculine by working the land. As a spokeswoman for the *Verband jüdischer Frauen für Kulturarbeit in Palästina* (Association of Jewish Women for Cultural Work in Palestine), she believed that Jewish women would only reach their potential in the natural environment of Palestine. With an interesting blend of Zionist and European notions of health, she explained that the schools taught "European hygiene," especially important in Palestine as a protection against Egyptian eye diseases, and attended to the girls' physical and intellectual development, introducing gymnastics and Hebrew lessons. She wrote about the girls' farm maintained by the *Verband*, especially interesting in light of the entire world's desire for more healthful and natural work on the land. She argued for the central importance of involving women in agriculture, asserting that agricultural work would be unthinkable without the participation of women.

> We want to educate our girls to be good, scholarly and full of interests; one who works most of the day quietly in the fresh air, is able to enjoy a book, a song, or a game in her spare time very differently and more deeply than one who spends her entire day with books. One must realize and understand—and this is not only true for Palestine—that feeding chickens, planting tomatoes, watering trees is a thousand times more beautiful than sitting at a typewriter from 8–12 and 2–6 or doing service in the railway ticket booth or the telephone table.[28]

Her idea of agricultural life was thoroughly romanticized, influenced directly or indirectly by the German youth movement's idealization of nature and the outdoors. On the other hand her preference for action and practical work over emotions demonstrates her desire for a meaningful way to participate as a woman in the Zionist movement.

Rahel Strauss (1880–1963), the German Jewish physician, wrote a "feuilleton" on women's work in Palestine, which appeared in the Viennese Zionist paper, *Jüdische Zeitung*, in 1908. She also stressed the importance of women's participation in the settlement of Palestine. However, she also cautioned women that because of their conservative nature and attachment to their homes, adjustment to the new surroundings, the unfamiliar climate and the sicknesses associated with it, the different food and the shortage of water, and the new types of work would prove difficult. She wrote: "A Jewish woman who goes into the stall, and milks the cows, takes care of the chicken yard, plants the garden! These were in her conception unusual things. And suddenly, these things were being demanded from her!"[29] Nevertheless she expressed optimism that women could make the transition.

City life in Palestine did not entail such drastic changes. However, Jewish women in the city did contend with the inferior status of women. "Whether our religion carries the blame—it preferred the man throughout—or the influence of the oriental surroundings had an effect, I cannot determine; it is certain, that the position of the woman is considerably inferior. The woman is not the man's associate, not the mistress of the house." The woman question in Palestine, she concluded, differed from that in Europe. Jewish women must work for its solution by founding schools and providing teachers who could serve as role models. Her concerns for health and fitness mirrored those of male Zionists. As a physician, she worried about young women giving birth under primitive conditions and discussed the need for midwives and nurses.

Femininity, feminism, and Jewish identity shaped the contributions of Viennese Zionist women at the fin de siècle. They negotiated the tensions among these ideologies, which complicated their identification as Jews and as women. As women, they faced an audience eager to condemn them for crossing gender boundaries. The effort to gain acceptance and legitimacy demanded a certain amount of submission to prevailing ideas. It proved difficult for these women, firmly entrenched in their culture, to transcend that culture's notions of femininity and masculinity. On the other hand, in that they strongly desired an active role in Zionism, women's rights and feminist ideology attracted them. While some Zionist women equated Jewish participation in the women's movement with assimilation, others implied that only feminist notions of women's participation in politics and the public realm could make possible true work for the Zionist cause.

Women in Zionist Ideology

Research has begun to focus upon the discourse of gender in the Zionist movement.[30] David Biale writes, "Zionism promised an erotic revolution for the Jews: the creation of a virile New Hebrew Man as well as rejection of the inequality of women in traditional Judaism in favor of full equality between the sexes in all spheres of life."[31] In practice, however, the notion of a virile New Hebrew Man inhibited the realization of an egalitarian society. According to Michael Berkowitz, Zionism was "a predominantly and self-consciously male affair."[32] Despite Zionism's proclaimed openness toward women, they remained marginal in the movement. "In part the luster of Zionism derived from its claim to have created an equitable order between Jewish men and women. It is no surprise that this myth does not hold up to scrutiny, regarding the movement in Europe or the yishuv."[33] The Zionist movement concentrated on distancing itself from perceived traditional gender relationships of the East European shtetl, in which the physically weak (yet at the same time privileged, due to his access to Jewish learning) Jewish man was dominated by his strong-willed and worldly wife. In contrast, Zionism criticized the bourgeois Jewish woman for not working for the Zionist movement, as well as for failing to attend to the Jewish religious and cultural needs of the family. In this sense, Zionists idealized the domestic attributes of the traditional Jewish woman.

In responding to a long-standing stereotype of the femininity of the Diaspora Jewish male, which had so deeply entered into Jewish self-consciousness of the period (evidenced in the writings of Otto Weininger in particular, as well as many others), Herzl and his contemporaries saw in Jewish nationalism a redemption of sorts.[34] In achieving nationhood through the political establishment of a Jewish state, the Jews would also transform their nature and refine their masculinity through engagement in the productive physical work of nation building. Klaus Hödl argues that in attempting to modernize the traditional relationship between the sexes in Judaism, Viennese Zionists defined the role of the woman primarily as educator of the family. "The 'Eshet

Hayil' of the Shtetl world, namely the hard-working, dynamic woman of traditional Jewish society, became the housewife, who was entirely dependent on her husband. The earlier 'masculine' type of East European Jewish woman was detached from the ideal of the 'lady,' that is, she was 'feminized' through the attribution of new qualities."[35] In fact, the Zionist image of women differed significantly neither from its counterpart in the mainstream Viennese Jewish community nor for that matter from that of the Viennese bourgeoisie in general.

The "gendered politics" of European and, more precisely, German nationalism also influenced the way Jewish nationalism incorporated gender. In his pioneering study on the relationship between nationalism and respectability, or the need to control sexuality, George Mosse pointed out that modern nationalism and respectability emerged at roughly the same time, and formed a mutually beneficial alliance.[36] This alliance served to strengthen the distinction between the sexes by asserting it as a bourgeois ideal. "Woman was the embodiment of respectability; even as defender and protector of her people she was assimilated to her traditional role as woman and mother, the custodian of tradition, who kept nostalgia alive in the active world of men."[37] More recently, describing the emergence and interaction of ideologies of national identity and gender identity among middle-class German-speaking Austrians during the 1880s, Pieter Judson demonstrates that assigning sex identity to national categories like patriotism co-opted the support of women. At the same time, nationalism aimed to unite divergent groups that otherwise may have erupted into conflict, such as social classes and sexes. For these reasons, ideologies about gender emerged alongside ideologies of nationalism.[38] Zionism, like other nationalist ideologies, drew upon a discourse combining the language of nation and gender. It has been suggested that this language was spoken as a matter of course from a masculine voice. As Margalit Shilo remarks, "the Zionist revolution, like other national movements, centered on masculinity. . . . The Zionist movement encouraged male solidarity as a central constituent in the building of the nation. Zionism and masculinity were practically synonymous."[39]

Political Zionism

Zionist ideology espoused the idea that the Jews of the Diaspora were physically and sexually degenerate and "feminized" and needed to become masculine. In light of the companion image of the Diaspora Jewish woman, or more specifically the shtetl woman, that she was domineering, assertive, and "masculine," what sort of transformation was required for women to become Zionists? Was it possible for Jewish men to become "muscle Jews" without Jewish women receding into a passive role? How did Zionists address Jewish women in order to attract them to the Zionist movement? How did Zionism view women's liberation in theory and in practice?

Zionist leaders were critical of Diaspora Jewish culture, and had a precise idea of what was needed to create the "New Jew." For example, Max Nordau (1849–1923) popularized the notion of "Judaism with muscles," suggesting that the Jews needed to become physically and sexually healthy by returning to nature, sports, and physical work.[40] However, his image of the new Jewish woman remained ambiguous. At first he opposed the movement for women's emancipation; later, he felt that emancipation would make little difference because women would not be able to overcome their family-centered nature. According to Nordau, women were needed to temper the harshness of life by serving as mothers and homemakers.[41]

In *Die Conventionellen Lügen der Kulturmenschheit (The Conventional Lies of Our Civilization)* (1883), Nordau mounted a critique of the bourgeois conceptions of marriage and sexuality.

Marriage is the only kind of union between man and woman countenanced by our society. But what have the lies of our corrupt civilization done to marriage? It has been diminished to a business agreement that gives as much place to love as the contract between two capitalists who form a commercial partnership. The pretext of marriage is still, as ever, the preservation of the species, but this is a pathetic lie, for the contemporary marriage has nothing to do with the mutual biological attraction of two sexual beings but with common material interests . . . When a wedding is planned, everything is considered—the living room and the kitchen, the caterers and the honeymoon; only one thing is forgotten—the bedroom, in which the future of the family, the nation, the human race is created. Must not decay and ruin become the fate of nations, in which the egoism of the couple triumphs in the marriage, while the child in the same is an undesirable, at best, an indifferent accident, a not easily avoidable, but thoroughly unimportant consequence?[42]

If the bourgeois notion of marriage, which centered on meeting the material needs of the two parties rather than their sexual needs, would lead to the doom of the nation, it follows that the reorganization of marriage and family would be essential in securing the survival of a new nation. The solution could not be to dissolve the institution of marriage, because that would leave women at a disadvantage. Rather, Nordau's solution lay in requiring that any civilized society provide for the material needs of its women to alleviate the need for them to sell themselves through marriage or prostitution.[43]

Nordau repeated this message in his plays, *The Right to Love* (1893) and *Doktor Kohn* (1902).[44] Both told stories of tragic love affairs, which resulted from the limitations of society's conventions in love and marriage. In *The Right to Love*, the wife decided to leave her husband for her seducer, only to discover that the seducer had no interest in marrying her or in raising her children. She returned to her husband to live a loveless bourgeois marriage of convenience rather than a marriage based on physical attraction. In *Doktor Kohn*, written after Nordau became a Zionist, a Jewish university lecturer in mathematics refused to convert to Christianity in order to attain a professorship. A proud Zionist, he also loved and planned to marry a Christian woman. It so happened that her father was a baptized Jew who would allow Kohn to marry his daughter only if he converts. This brought about a complex set of circumstances leading her brother to insult him, exclaiming, "A man of honor would not bring discord into a united family." Because Dr. Kohn felt that he had not only to defend his own honor but also that of the Jewish people, he was forced to fight a duel in which he was shot and killed. Thus, due to the social conventions of the times, which determined the suitability of matches—in this case anti-Semitism—the fate of this couple was tragic. These plays and the ideas put forward by Nordau in *Conventional Lies* demonstrate his belief in the importance of family serving and strengthening the nation. However, when Nordau spoke of the Zionist solution in his well-known address to a Zionist gymnastic club in 1903, calling for the creation of a *muskeljudentum* (Jewry of muscles), he focused exclusively on the transformation of male Jews from the persecuted and weak ghetto Jews to "deep-chested, tightly muscled, courageous men."[45]

Herzl also lacked a clear, consistent notion of the role of women in the Jewish state. Like other Zionists, when it came to women and Zionism, he stressed their passivity. His views have been attributed to everything imaginable, including the influence of his cultural milieu and his personal relationships with women.[46] In much of his work, he suggested that women's dedication to building Jewish families would attract them to Zionism. He aimed to redirect the virtues of Jewish women for the Zionist cause and at the same time to rehabilitate their negative traits (just as with Jewish men) through their work on behalf of the Jewish state. In all his writings, he regarded the upper-class Jewish women, and with them the typical bourgeois families of Western and Central Europe, with great disdain. Yet he idealized the self-sacrificing, hard-working woman who devoted herself to the Zionist cause, and praised the Jewish woman who left politics to men and devoted herself to family.

In 1894, shortly before coming to the Zionist solution, Herzl wrote the play *Das Neue Ghetto*. He concerned himself with the "Jewish question," negatively portraying the assimilated Jewish middle class as materialistic and superficial. The female characters, Hermine Hellmann, who married the idealistic Jewish lawyer Dr. Jacob Samuel at the beginning of the play, and even more so her sister Charlotte Rheinberg, were particularly shallow. In the words of the stockbroker Wasserstein, "Remember, Miss Hermine will want to live in the same style as her sister, Frau Rheinberg. Fine clothes, jewelry, the theater, concerts. That means a lot of money."[47] In contrast to these pseudo high-society Jewish women, Herzl depicted the traditional Jewish family life of the ghetto (meaning Eastern Europe) sympathetically. Rabbi Friedheimer spoke defensively of the ghetto. "True, the ghetto was crowded and dirty, but the virtues of family life flourished there. The father was a patriarch. The mother . . . (lays his hand lightly on that of Frau Samuel) lived only for her children, and they honored their parents."[48] The image of Jewish women in this play, Herzl's favorite, should not be taken out of context. He also portrayed the male Jewish characters, with the exception of Samuel, as stereotyped caricatures of the materialistic and morally bankrupt Jew. He aimed not for a sympathetic positive portrayal of the Jews but, on the contrary, for a "self-emancipation from negative Jewish qualities."[49]

Herzl further developed his vision of the ideal Jewish future in his utopian novel *Altneuland* (1902). The novel tells the story of a heartbroken Jewish lawyer, Friedrich Loewenberg, who left Vienna with a non-Jewish misanthropic officer, Mr. Kingscourt. Together they set sail for a remote island, visiting a primitive Palestine on their way. After twenty years in isolation, they returned to find that a "new society" had emerged. Herzl painted the New Society as an ideal world without any conflicts, religious antagonism, economic troubles, or social problems. Technology also played a central role in his vision of the future state, both in *Der Judenstaat* and in *Altneuland*. Herzl envisioned a land of peace, prosperity, and progress, where Jews, Arabs, and Christians lived beside one another in complete harmony. The cultural life in *Altneuland* bore a very strong resemblance to European culture, with the characters speaking German or their native languages rather than Hebrew. Although Herzl rejected the idea of Jewish assimilation into European society, he seemed content with the Jews taking the positive and progressive elements of Europe with them to the new state. "With pride, Herzl speaks of transferring into the renascent state the most advanced values that the Jew can bring with him from his former homes." [50]

On their return to Palestine, Loewenberg and Kingscourt found the Litwak family, whom Loewenberg had saved from starvation before he left Vienna, and their antithesis, bourgeois families such as the Loefflers. While the impoverished Litwak family underwent a complete transformation in their new habitat, living a comfortable and contented life as full participants in the New Society, the bourgeois families remained essentially unchanged. The Litwak family had immigrated to Vienna, where they lived in dire poverty in a one-room apartment. When Loewenberg came across them twenty years later in Palestine, he found that David, once a little beggar Jewish boy, had become "grave and free, healthy and cultured, a man who could stand up for himself." [51] The baby had grown into a woman, Miriam Litwak (modeled on Herzl's sister Pauline, who died at the age of nineteen), who completely devoted herself to the New Society. David described her work as a teacher. "She isn't doing it for the salary. I should be well able to keep my sister. But she is performing the obligations, which she has because it also gives her rights. In our new society women have equal rights with men."

> It goes without saying that they have the right to vote and use it. They worked loyally with us when we created our administration, and their enthusiasm for our great aim was a constant source of inspiration to us. After that it would have been blackest ingratitude on the part of the men to relegate them to the kitchen or the seraglio, even if called by some other name. [52]

Political equality did not detract from women's devotion to family life. "Don't imagine that our women have become worse housewives because they've been given the vote. My wife, for instance, never goes to meetings—political meetings—I mean." David explained, "While she was nursing the boy, she forgot about her inalienable rights. Before I married her, she belonged to the radical opposition—that's how I met her, as a political opponent. Now she confines her opposition to the home; but it's an entirely loyal opposition you must understand." To Loewenberg, Sarah was "an ideal of maternal and wifely happiness," and Miriam was a "delightful girl" who performed "duties no girl of the Loeffler set would have dreamed of." [53]

Sasha Eichenstamm, the daughter of the president of the New Society, never married, focusing instead on charitable activities. Through the character of Sasha, Herzl demonstrated how the New Society would be organized to provide an outlet to women who otherwise would have no useful role in society.

> She is an eminent oculist also, the head of our largest clinic. A grand woman. She has never married, but devotes all her life to the sick and the poor. She is a wonderful example of the part that spinsters and lonely women can play in a sensibly organized society. Half a century ago they were derided or felt to be a burden to their families. Today they are a blessing to others and lead happy lives. Our Welfare Department, for instance, is run exclusively by such women. [54]

Although Sasha was extremely accomplished, especially for a woman at that time, she exhibited all the qualities of Herzl's ideal Jewish woman: she dressed plainly, found her happiness in helping those in need, headed the greatest eye clinic in the world, and was modest about her accomplishments. She demonstrated the notion of the New Society, or the Jewish state, as serving in a sense as a "home" by taking care of all its citizens.

In spite of the equality of the sexes, the New Society still valued traditional roles for women. Even the female Muslim character, Fatma Bey, found contentment in her seclusion. Miriam and Sarah both defended Muslim customs with respect to women, depicting Fatma as "a most cultivated and charming young woman."

> "Don't imagine that Fatma feels unhappy or frustrated, though," added Sarah. "It's a very happy marriage indeed. They have charming children. But the wife does not step outside the bounds of her

peaceful seclusion. That's also a form of happiness which I certainly understand, in spite of being a member of the New Society. If my husband wished it, I shouldn't mind living like Fatma!"

Later, while leaving for a tour of the country, the group stopped to pick up Reshid Bey at his home. Fatma fluttered a handkerchief from an upper-story window. Once again, Miriam commented on her contented nature, and Loewenberg declared his admiration for "a woman who remains contentedly at home."[55]

While giving equal rights to women, the New Society maintained the distinction between men and women. For example the best male students studied in foreign lands in organized groups to learn foreign languages and customs. " 'The girls don't go on these trips,' said Miriam. 'It is our belief that a growing girl's place is at home with her mother, even though she must learn something to fit herself for a career and do her duty by the commonwealth.' "[56]

Women who devoted themselves to the New Society, to charitable causes, or to their families, served the New Society without sacrificing their femininity. In contrast, the bourgeois, materialistic women had absolutely no useful role. Herzl described these women just as he had in *The New Ghetto*, as "overly dressed heavily bejeweled women," except that in *Altneuland* they had become outcasts. For example, at the opera, Loewenberg sat next to "two overly dressed heavily bejeweled women," the Laschner women he had known in Vienna. Then he met up with Ernestine Loeffler, now Mrs. Weinberger. His idealized image of her quickly melted away.

> There she sat, down below, and at first he was subject to a strange illusion. Why, Ernestine looked exactly as she had done twenty years ago! The same delicate features, the same slender figure. But after a minute he realized that this young girl was not Ernestine, but her daughter. Mrs. Weinberger was the fat matron beside the girl, dressed too youthfully in gaudy colors, her features faded and bloated. She looked up at him, smiled invitingly and nodded delightedly when Friedrich bowed.[57]

Later, they came upon some Jews, "overdressed ladies, idling men. They sat under the palms, commenting on the passers-by, flirting, gossiping—just as they do all over the world." For some reason, this comforted Kingscourt, who said: "Why, here they are at last, the Jewesses with the jewels! I was feeling quite nostalgic for them! I thought: my dear Adalbert, perhaps we were not in the land of the Jews at all, but the whole thing was a hoax! And now I see it's true. Here are the ostrich-feather hats, the gaudy silks, the jeweled Israelite women." The Jewish professor Steineck did not take offense at Kingscourt's remarks, but on the contrary, he "laughed uproariously" and said:

> Of course we don't mind, Mr. Kingscourt. There was a time when we should have been offended, but not today. You understand? Once upon a time people thought the idlers, the moneyed snobs, the bejeweled Jewesses were representative of our people. Today everybody knows there are other Jews too. Go ahead and jeer at this mob as much as you like. I'll join you when it gets dark, my noble stranger![58]

The "new Jew" did not feel offended because he had acquired the pride that came with belonging to a nation. He even joined the non-Jew in deriding this type of Jew, although only if he could do so anonymously. Herzl's inclusion of these women highlights his low opinion of Viennese upper-middle-class Jewish women and their values, and his hope for a future in which these women would lose their influence and importance.

Herzl portrayed a last type of Jewish woman, the self-sacrificing and suffering Jewish mother, in the character of Mrs. Litwak. At her death, David delivered the following eulogy idealizing her qualities.

> She was my mother. She was love and suffering, both so deep that my eyes filled with tears when I looked at her.
> I shall not see her again. She was my mother.
> She was our house, our home—when we had neither house nor home.
> She supported us when we were ready to break down under our misery—for she was love.
> She taught us humility when better days had come—for she was suffering.
> In bad days and in good she was the honor of our house, and its pride.
> When we were so poor that we lay in the straw, we were rich in having her.
> She thought of us always—never of herself.

She was sick and suffering for a long time, but suffering did not
bow her down, it lifted her up.
She was my mother—and I shall not see her again—never.
I must bear it.[59]

The qualities of the Jewish mother extolled in David's speech—love,
suffering, support, humility, and self-sacrifice—mirror those described
by members of the mainstream Jewish community, such as Jellinek.
Not only Herzl's image of the Jewish mother, but his images of Jewish women in general, both positive and negative, had parallels in non-
Zionist writings. For example, the materialistic bejeweled Jewish
woman appeared in the writings of Darnau, Jellinek, and Güdemann.
Zionists however asserted that Jewish women would transform into
women who would be useful to society without sacrificing their femininity in a new nation. Although women had equal rights in Herzl's
New Society, they remained feminine.

Herzl acted upon his belief in the potential of Zionism to bring about
a transformation and improvement in Jewish women by taking practical steps to involve women in the Zionist Congresses and the Zionist
Movement. Fourteen women participated in the first Zionist Congress
in 1897.[60]

Prior to the second Zionist Congress in Basel (1898), Herzl drafted a
letter to all the women who had participated in the First Congress.

The Zionist Congress will take place on the 29th, 30th, and 31st
of August in Basel. In the face of the enthusiasm, which the previous
Congress awoke in the Jewish masses, every counter-agitation had
to end. We have two halls at our disposal: the Burgvogtei and the
music hall. Dear Madam, in the next days you shall receive identity
cards, working programs as well as all the details through our sec-
retaries' office.
With the expression of the highest esteem,
Theodor Herzl.[61]

At a special women's caucus held in 1898, prior to the Second Congress, women were not only seated as delegates but given full voting
rights. This was quite unusual for the time, when women had been
granted full suffrage only in New Zealand, Australia, and some states in
the United States.[62] Women's equality in Zionism, Priska Gmür percep-
tively points out, benefited men as well as women. In a small movement,

Basel Zionist Congress Attendees, 1903. Courtesy of the Leo Baeck Institute, New York.

with insignificant numbers, women boosted membership. In cultural Zionism, which placed value on the revival of Jewish tradition, "it was virtually impossible to bypass women in their capacity as the traditional 'guardian of the Jewish house.'"[63] In other words, by giving women rights, Zionists expected them to provide services to the movement.

This, however, opened the door for the kind of criticism found in some of Herzl's writings and those of other Zionists. At the Second Congress, Rozia Ellmann read a proclamation stating that women must devote themselves to Zionism and stand by their husbands.[64] Gmür interprets this as follows: "The ideal female Zionist thus appears as the true companion of the man on whose side she fights for the common Jewish cause, thus for an almost familial cause, as she maternally empathizes with the suffering and selflessly feels solidarity with them—a pattern of argumentation which is encountered over and over again in the voting of other women."[65] In this context, Zionist women founded their own associations, committees, and organizations to work on limited areas such as youth education in Jewish religion and culture, watching over Zionist ideals in the family—in short, being the guardians and transmitters of Jewish culture and tradition.

Like Herzl, other Viennese Zionists criticized contemporary Jewish women for not adequately serving Zionism. For example, on December 15, 1900, Leon Kellner (1859–1928), the Shakespearian scholar who was among the first followers of Herzlian Zionism, delivered a lecture entitled "Our Women" to the Zionist Women's Association in Vienna, in which he primarily spoke about the shortcomings of Jewish women, and the historical background responsible for these traits.[66] While women of all races had much in common, according to Kellner, the Jewish woman's love for jewels evolved historically. He used an evolutionary analogy to living organisms developing traits that lost their use over time, in order to describe modern Jewish women. They had adopted many qualities and bad habits from their "oriental home" that had since become superfluous. In the insecure circumstances of earlier times, Jews adapted to the disruptive lifestyle of reckoning with daily torment, settling down only to be driven away from a place. It was for this reason, he asserted, that the Jews bought their women costly jewelry, as a savings bank. "The preference for jewels has still to this day been maintained by the Jewish woman. Today, thank God, the premises for such an investment of capital are lacking. . . . Away with diamonds, the Jewish woman must learn to walk modestly."

Kellner discussed the excesses produced by emancipation and assimilation, mentioning names of two prominent salon women, Dorothea Mendelssohn and Rahel Levin. Gradually, Jews became aware that girls must be educated in more than just piano playing—in a vocation. He reproached the bourgeois Jewish mother, commenting that she had a pathological excessive love for her children, which oftentimes led her to neglect her husband. Comparing her to Glückel of Hameln, the only known Jewish female writer of the seventeenth century, he concluded, "It is truly moving how this modest Jewish woman, who could not write and dictated her memoirs, in her entire behavior, in all of her deeds, identified with her people; the love of Israel filled her entire life."[67]

Kellner maintained that modernity did not threaten Jewish men's national self-awareness as it did Jewish women's. The practice of religious duties continually reminded men of their Jewishness, but women, as the "guardians of the Nation," held the key to the Jewish future. The report of the lecture concluded:

Herr Prof. Kellner was not sparing of the Jewish woman of our time in his lecture; he sharply chastised her faults, and if one or another of the numerous audience members came to the lecture on "Our Women" with the intention of hearing her praises sung, she would have departed rather disappointedly. But all the more worthy of consideration were his words. Let the seeds sprout fruitfully, that lay in the abundance of useful stimulation and suggestions of the lecturer.[68]

Kellner's lecture emphasized Zionist women's passivity and their role as transmitters of Jewish values in the family and "guardians of the Nation." A sense of women's importance in serving the state by providing the anchor for family life permeates his generally negative indictment of bourgeois Jewish life.

Heinrich York-Steiner (1859–1935), the author of the stories "Maskir," "Talmud Kessuboth 110b," and "Der Talmudbauer" (The Talmudic Farmer, 1904), belonged to Herzl's early circle, and spoke regularly at Zionist women's organizations.[69] In "Der Talmudbauer," he told of the encounter of a young man brought up in a struggling religious family in Jerusalem and an enlightened Zionist woman in a settlement. Through his encounter with Miriam, Chaim was exposed to modern enlightened ideas and the notion that Talmudic laws found a form through nature and practical application. He "became more masculine" by working in the sun and fresh air, started to dress in modern attire, cut off his sidelocks, and shaved his beard. While in other York-Steiner stories, non-Zionist female Jewish characters met with tragic ends, Miriam was intelligent and independent, tolerant and open-minded, but secure in her faith. Like the characters in Herzl's *Altneuland*, the various types of Diaspora Jews changed in the new circumstances. Chaim and Miriam abandoned traditional norms of marriage, making their own decision to get married. To the objection that they could not get married because they both lacked money, Miriam answered, "We could never ask for something better, than to become an honest settler-couple on the home soil of the holy land. People will trust us and make money and land available to us."[70] The Zionist youth movement influenced York-Steiner, as evidenced in this story in the generational rebellion against traditional forms of marriage, arranged marriages, and financial considerations.

On April 6, 1901, York-Steiner led a "lively discussion" on how to educate children in Jewish religion. The participants concluded that the Jewish woman must first educate herself in Jewish belief, in order to properly educate her children. To do so, she had to become involved in charitable religious activities, such as establishing homes for the poor and Jewish nursing. A report in *Die Welt* described both Kellner's and York-Steiner's lectures as animated and pleasurable, and concluded with the following admonition to women.

> If our Jewish women pay attention to the warnings which were heard on both these evenings, if they immerse themselves in the nation, open their hearts to the poverty, that shows itself at every turn; if they observe and listen, when Jewish thought lives even underneath poor clothing: than they will also acquire that education of the heart, than they will find that national awareness, that strength of character, which makes it possible for them to remain Jewish mothers, in spite of the pressure of the circumstances of Jewish women.[71]

Charity, according to Zionist ideology, would not only lead to an improvement in the character of those women who participated as donors, but it would also enable the impoverished recipients to achieve their potential as Jewish women. This activity was to lead them to a greater national self-awareness and to Zionism.

Another article, excerpted from a novel by Robert Jaffee, suggested that poverty in Eastern Europe dulled the Jewish woman's positive qualities and that charity would return the "sweet, delightful melody of love" to the East European Jewish woman.[72] The Zionists in Vienna, like their non-Zionist coreligionists and their non-Jewish bourgeois contemporaries, understood charitable activity as an appropriate form of involvement and activism for women.

The Cultural Movement

Berthold Feiwel (1875–1937), born in Pohrlitz, Moravia, became involved in the Zionist movement early on through Herzl. In his student years he founded the *Jüdische Volksstimme* with Max Aickel and Robert Stricker. He later became one of the leading spirits, along with Martin Buber, of the oppositionist group, the "Democratic-Zionist Faction," which made its debut at the fifth Congress in 1901. It was composed of thirty-seven delegates, but its power exceeded its numbers, and it sometimes dominated the entire Congress.[73] Herzl entrusted Feiwel with the editorship of *Die Welt*; when he resigned due to illness, Martin Buber took over, but also resigned after a few months. Herzl praised their work and gave them full editorial freedom to express their ideas.[74] Nevertheless, he worried that the cultural movement threatened the unity of Zionism. Because of their concern with the creation of a national culture and their belief in the need to preserve Judaism by teaching Jewish values and Hebrew language to future generations, cultural Zionists often expressed concern over the role of Jewish women.[75]

In an article on the Jewish woman and family, Feiwel criticized bourgeois Jewish women.[76] He asserted that the best women were the least spoken of, and therefore Jewish women must have become thoroughly bad, because anti-Semites, who once spared Jewish women in their criticism, now targeted them. He held Jewish women accountable for the rising hostility in anti-Semitic criticism of women.

> The tone, in which the Jewish woman is spoken of today ever more frequently in newspapers and books, in theater and even by speakers in public gatherings, is widely distanced from the almost harmless irony of earlier times . . . The reproaches that are raised against the Jewish woman are severe: She is vain and superficial, dressy, arrogant, urgent, extravagant—but this is not much: She is also a bad despotic housewife, a bad spouse and mother, the bearer of loose and sinful marriage-, family- and society-morality. She offends morals and good taste.[77]

According to Feiwel, once anti-Semites had even candidly praised Jewish women, as women, mothers, and guardians of the family; he quoted an anti-Semitic leader as saying, "I am an anti-Semite, but no hater of Jewish women." This attitude toward Jewish women used to prevail. What changed? Rather than attribute the change to the growing aggression or the changing nature of anti-Semitism, he asserted that Jewish women had changed for the worse. "The times have changed for the worse, and the Jewish woman with them."

Using Nordau's terminology, Feiwel described the current state of Western European Jewish women as "degeneration." He warned that while anti-Semites exaggerated the situation and the danger that these women posed to non-Jewish society, they could actually threaten Judaism, by working for its disintegration. They threatened *Nationaljudentum* more than assimilated men, because domestic assimilation was harder to control and to correct than the large-scale and public anti-nationalist activities of men. The Jewish woman, Feiwel warned, not only herself became de-Judaized but also transformed the Jewish family through assimilation and destroyed the personalities of her husband, her sons, and most of all, her daughters.

Feiwel also argued that Jewish school alone could not give Jewish children a feeling for Judaism. The religious feeling could only come from the home. When Jewish mothers failed to teach their children to regard Judaism positively, even a good Jewish education at school would not help. His solution was to develop a Jewish consciousness in women through emotional influences. They needed to come back into touch with their "racial instincts" through religion, family, work, and contact with anti-Semitism. "Religion and family are the foundation on which to base her national consciousness. . . . [Also essential is] the participation of the wife in the livelihood of the husband and personal contact with anti-Semitism."

While remaining critical of the contemporary Jewish woman, Martin Buber placed slightly more emphasis on the positive, albeit romanticized, image of Jewish women of the past. Buber (1878–1965), a religious philosopher and native of Vienna, became involved in the Zionist movement as a result of his encounter with Herzl, joining the movement in 1898. Buber came to advocate cultural over political Zionism and to believe that "the cultural renaissance of Judaism rather than anti-Semitism must be made the fountain and driving force of Zionism." [78]

Buber defined the phrase "Zion of the Jewish woman" not as something that could only take place in the future when the Jews returned to their homeland, where the new Jewish woman could emerge, but as an "inner Zion of the soul." A transformation in the souls of Jewish women would bring about Zion. He particularly idealized Jewish women of the ghetto, who created a culture within the family, helped in the family business to enable their husbands to pursue study and spirituality, supported their husbands, and educated their children. The "degenerate" Jewish women of his day compared unfavorably to these ghetto women. He argued that during the ghetto period, persecution gave rise to internal strength. As persecution became more petty and perfidious, Jewish life disintegrated. Emancipation reinforced this trend by ending the isolation of ghetto life. Particularly susceptible to assimilation, women emulated the surrounding culture, paralyzing Judaism and its independent culture. This led to "degeneration" as Jewish women looked for fulfillment in luxury and ostentation, and became idle and snobbish.

Buber held the Jewish woman responsible for the downfall of her people, but also counted on her for its future regeneration. In *galut* (exile), he asserted, the Jewish home is the Jewish nation; hence the importance of Jewish women in the cultural rebirth of Zion. The Jewish woman needed to work alongside the man to disseminate the national idea. But because of her love and deep understanding, she could do even more than the man.[79] Buber's belief in the need for a spiritual, cultural rebirth prior to a political solution led him to emphasize the potential of Jewish women in working for Zionism. It was in the spiritual realm, after all, that women's perceived strengths could be most beneficial. He also asserted that women had greater intuition and talent than men when it came to economics. They could better understand the causes of Jewish poverty and therefore had better solutions. But their talents could come to full fruition only if Jewish women educated themselves to value, foster, and develop Judaism.

Like other Jewish leaders, Zionist and non-Zionist, Buber stressed, above all, the need for Jewish women to be good mothers and nurture their families. The new Jewish woman, he predicted, would not be ashamed but proud if her child looked Jewish. She would make sure that her children were physically healthy and "nip in the bud the primary affliction of modern Jews, the over-growth of the life of the nerves." The new Jewish woman would bring about a future generation of Jews balanced in mind and body, educated in Judaism and also in humanitarian wisdom. "The Jew of the future will be a complete Jew and a complete human being at the same time."[80] Buber concluded by saying that one word, "love," summarized the Jewish woman. She had love for the grand destiny of her people, the love to help the poor and oppressed Jews, and love for the dream of a future nation. This love was necessary to bring about the Zion of the soul, the creation of a Jewish culture, which would then make possible a territorial Zion.

Herzl's image of Jewish women set the tone for the general Zionist image of women. However, as time went on, the Zionist promise of equality for women fell further into the background, or at least changed its meaning. The ideal Zionist woman came to mirror the Sarah Litwak type, to the exclusion of the alternative types represented by the characters Miriam Litwak and Sasha Eichenstamm. Like the traditionalists, the Zionists emphasized the importance of the Jewish woman as housewife, mother, charity worker, and guardian of religious tradition and values. They also criticized contemporary Jewish women as materialistic, assimilated, ostentatious, and superficial.

Zionist leaders in Vienna envisioned that in exchange for equal rights, Jewish women would form the basis of new Jewish families which would serve the nation by providing a supportive, nurturing environment for the "new Jew," creating and shaping the citizens of the future, as well as fulfilling the social, cultural, and educational needs of the New Society. They emphasized the importance of the Jewish woman as housewife, mother, charity worker, and guardian of religious tradition and values. They criticized contemporary Jewish women as materialistic, assimilated, ostentatious, and superficial, asserting that they would be brought back to Judaism through Zionist national awareness. Jewish women of the ghetto, on the other hand, suffered from the physically and sexually stifling restrictions and unhealthy conditions of ghetto life, which gave rise to unnatural gender relationships, according to Zionist ideology. The Zionist movement sought to restore the spiritual dimension to the lives of western Jewish women and revitalize eastern Jewish women through more physical activity and fresh air.

Never delineated as specifically as the "new Jew," the "new Jewish woman" of Viennese Zionism emerges as a collection of varied, at times contradictory, images. According to most Zionist writings, Jewish women's lives would be transformed in the process of creating a Jewish state. As a result, future generations of Zionists would emerge in order to ensure the future of the Jewish people. Criticism of Jewish women for their lack of Jewish feeling, their level of assimilation, and most especially for their materialism and love of luxury, entered into almost all the Zionist works on women. The Jewish woman of the contemporary European world needed to be transformed from a bejeweled, assimilated, self-centered, degenerate Jewess into a virtuous, nurturing, charitable, feminine, and nationally minded Jewish mother. While Herzl's declaration that women should have equality in the Zionist movement may not seem to have had a positive impact on the perception of women's roles either in the movement or in the future state, it did encourage the participation of women through the formation of women's Zionist organizations, societies, and agencies. But it also led to the marked tendency of both men and women to focus on the passivity of women in the Zionist movement and attribute it to the bourgeois Jewish women's assimilation into their world and distance from their traditions.

The general perception of gender in fin de siècle Vienna influenced the image of the ideal Jewish woman in Zionism. Certain stereotypes of women, such as their affinity for social work, their preference for art and culture over politics and ideas, and their innate materialism, were absorbed from Viennese modern culture and incorporated into Zionist ideology. Zionist leaders used Jewish women as scapegoats, blaming them for assimilation, for the lack of support for the Zionist movement, and for the moral deficiencies of Diaspora Jewry. In spite of the statements regarding women's equality in a future Zionist state, the images of Jewish women that pervaded their ideology as a whole both idealized traditional Jewish women and regarded the modern women's movement as antithetical to Judaism and Zionism. In these respects Viennese Zionists' understanding of Jewish women paralleled that of Vienna's Jewish community leaders.

Another similarity with the spiritual leaders of the Viennese Jewish community lay in their common notion of the importance of mediation and cooperation between the Jewries of the east and west. Many Viennese and Austrian Zionists believed that while the western Jews could provide the economic wherewithal and the knowledge of modern science and technology necessary to build the Jewish homeland, the eastern Jews held the crucial link to Jewish tradition and ritual. These two groups needed to join forces in order to effectively solve the Jewish question. Likewise, the Jewish women of the east and west could contribute in different but complimentary ways to the Zionist movement in general as well as to the question of women's role in the Zionist movement.

In contrast to the views of the Viennese organized Jewish community, Viennese Zionists found the solution to the problems facing Diaspora Jews in general and Jewish women in particular in working for Jewish national renewal. The New Society would create an order in which certain "unnatural" gender characteristics of the ghetto would be rectified, while undesirable aspects of bourgeois family life would be transcended. Reversing the image of the traditional relationship between the sexes in the East European ghetto, Zionists believed that Jewish men would become manly by working the land, while Jewish women would become more feminine. Hence, Zionists' connection to traditional Judaism was paradoxical. On the one hand, they emphasized Jewish identity and awareness, as well as Jewish spirituality and culture, as prerequisites for Jewish national renewal, especially for women. They criticized modern Jewish women for their apathy toward tradition and their lack of knowledge and feeling for Judaism. On the other hand, they viewed the traditional Jewish relationship of the sexes as an unnatural product of Diaspora life, which needed to be corrected.

Ironically, the resulting Zionist ideals of masculinity and femininity were not rooted in Jewish culture, but incorporated from European bourgeois culture. Feeling the need to assert their masculinity, in contrast to the image of the feminine Jewish male, Viennese Zionists in the end relegated Jewish women to a more passive and depoliticized role.

The role of women in Zionism suffered from a basic contradiction between the notion that the Jewish state would resolve the issue of gender inequality by granting women an equal status in the new society and on the other hand the argument that women had a unique contribution to make to Zionism because of their female nature. This contradiction also shaped the participation and attitudes of Zionist women as they sought to stake out a place for themselves in the growing movement, and through their involvement negotiated their own identities as Jews and women. Although the latter idea often predominated over the former, the concept of difference never completely eclipsed that of equality. Moreover, the need for women's active involvement in the work of building the Jewish state, as well as the influence of the women's movement, continually challenged the limitation of women's roles to the domestic sphere.

5 ≫ Medicine and Psychoanalysis

Writing about the sexual development of girls in 1923, Sigmund Freud (1856–1939), the father of psychoanalysis, asserted that "unfortunately we can describe this state of things [the development of sexuality] only as it affects the male child; the corresponding processes in the little girl are not known to us."[1] He also wrote the following in 1926: "The sexual life of adult women is a 'dark continent' for psychology. But we have learnt that girls feel deeply their lack of a sexual organ that is equal in value to the male one; they regard themselves on that account as inferior, and this 'envy for the penis' is the origin of a whole number of characteristic genuine reactions."[2] Although Freud's ideas about sexuality and women changed over time and in many ways were revolutionary, he clearly failed in reaching an understanding of female sexuality, never moving beyond the notion of femininity as failed masculinity.

Sander Gilman points out the parallel between this portrayal of women as unknowable and associated with darkness and Freud's image of the Jew. Gilman focuses on the construction of Jewish masculinity in his interpretation of notions of gender and race held by Freud and other Jews.[3] Building on his work, the analysis presented here will further explore the Jewish women in Freud's circle and the descriptions and images of Jewish women found in the writings of Jews in psychoanalysis and medicine in order to shed more light on the construction of Jewish femininity.

Despite Freud's lack of understanding of femininity, psychoanalysis attracted Viennese Jewish women as both patients and practitioners. Through their involvement in the psychoanalytic movement and in Freud's circle, they dealt with the pressures of life as Jewish women in Vienna at the fin de siècle, such as gender-based and anti-Semitic stereotypes, limitations on women's education and careers, the sexualized stereotypes of Jews, the attraction of feminism, and uncertainty about their Jewish identity. Similarly, Jewish men in the fields of psychoanalysis as well as psychology and medicine focused attention on issues of gender and Jewish identity in their work. Among the Jewish practitioners and patients of psychoanalysis and medicine, gender played a key role in shaping their identity as Jews, and as a result, many incorporated and/or responded to the sexualized stereotypes of Jews, women, and Jewish women. These stereotypes took hold in Viennese society, culture, and politics, as well as in medicine and in the University. We will begin with an examination of the distinctive variety of anti-Semitism that prevailed in Austria around the fin de siècle and the notions of Jewish sexuality associated with it.

Austrian Anti-Semitism and Jewish Sexuality

Anti-Semitism in Austria influenced the lives and identities of Viennese Jewish women and men in the medical and psychoanalytic fields. The role played by nationalism—i.e., the multi-ethnic character of the Habsburg monarchy, the role of the Catholic Church, and the composition and size of the Jewish population—all contributed to the unique nature and intensity of Austrian anti-Semitism.[4] Robert Wistrich has written that "the multi-ethnic Habsburg Empire was the cradle of the most successful modern political movement based on anti-Semitism to emerge anywhere in nineteenth century Europe."[5] Austrian anti-Semitism had a multi-ethnic character, the Jewish identification with the "historic" nations, such as the Germans, Magyars, and Poles, exacerbating the antagonism of the oppressed nationalities, such as the Slovaks, Serbo-Croats, Ukrainians, and Romanians.[6] The evolution of anti-Semitism within the dominant nations, embodied in the Austrian Pan-German Movement and the Christian Social Party, endangered the Jews even more, at least until the fall of the Habsburg monarchy.[7]

Carl Schorske describes the Pan-German leader Georg von Schönerer (1842–1921) and the Christian Social leader and mayor of Vienna from 1897 Karl Lueger (1844–1910) in his classic essay "Politics in a New Key: An Austrian Trio."[8] Looking at the "two leading virtuosi of the new key"—that is, a more abrasive and more creative approach to politics compared to rational liberalism—Schorske points out their similarities and differences. "Both men began as liberals, both criticized liberalism initially from a social and democratic viewpoint, and both ended as apostates, espousing explicitly anti-liberal creeds. Both used anti-Semitism to mobilize the same unstable elements in the population: artisans and students."[9] However, while Schönerer passionately opposed the liberal bourgeoisie and was fiercely anti-Semitic, Lueger was more of an opportunist, a Viennese politician loyal to the Habsburg monarchy and not attracted to German nationalism. "Even in his anti-Semitism Lueger lacked the rancor, conviction, or consistency of Schönerer . . . Lueger therefore tolerated the most vicious anti-

Semitism among his lieutenants, but, more manipulator and machine-builder than ideologue, he himself employed it rather than enjoyed it." [10] Lueger used anti-Semitism as a political weapon. In spite of the overt racism on the part of some members of his party, he ultimately retreated from extreme racial anti-Semitism.

Although historians generally agree with this assessment, some have challenged Schorske's views on Lueger and have pointed out that regardless of the conviction behind Lueger's anti-Semitism, it caused a great deal of damage to the position and security of Viennese Jews, or have argued that it is impossible to ascertain Lueger's actual views on anti-Semitism. The overlapping nature of the followers of Lueger and Schönerer supports that the two movements shared some common ground. Richard Geehr remarks, "Lueger ensured the continuation and intensification of anti-Semitic politics throughout his mayoralty—and beyond." [11] Steven Beller concludes, "Indeed the Christian Socials' anti-Semitism was an extreme threat to the liberal ideal precisely because it could seem 'harmless' and yet at the same time sacrifice the autonomy of the individual to the whim of others." [12] It was in this atmosphere that Adolf Hitler, as a young student in Vienna, first became introduced to anti-Semitic politics. Hitler, who spent the years between 1907 and 1913 in Vienna, was "a child of fin de siècle Vienna in his anti-Semitic politics," in Wistrich's words. [13]

The prominence and centrality of sexualized images of Jews and the linking of Jews and women also characterized Austrian anti-Semitism, although it took hold elsewhere as well, as shown by Sander Gilman for Europe in general, Nancy Harrowitz for Italy, and Shulamit Volkov for Germany (and Austria.) [14] Austrian anti-Semites accused Jews of possessing over-abundant sexual drives, posited an overlapping of male and female qualities among Jews, and condemned Jews' supposed victimization of women (Christian and Jewish), and involvement in prostitution, and the allegedly materialistic motivation of their marital arrangements. That stereotypes of Jews as effeminate contradicted stereotypes of Jews as overly masculine and sexually aggressive did not bother Austrian anti-Semites. Furthermore, anti-Semites linked Jews to venereal diseases, especially syphilis, and to a generally corrupt sexual morality, as seen in the discussion of August Rohling and Joseph Samuel Bloch in Chapter 2. According to these stereotypes, the physical difference of the male Jew, namely circumcision, caused the Jews' sexual abnormalities, either by increasing or decreasing sexual desire. Another prevalent image of Jewish sexuality involved a tendency toward masturbation. On the other hand, the Jews' family life and values were often idealized. The sexualized image of the Jew was a mixed bag full of inconsistencies and contradictions.

Jewish sexuality became a target of attack, as is typical in discourses about "Others." Due to the strength of clericalism in Vienna, these stereotypes found an important breeding ground in the capital city.[15] The Jews were viewed as a subversive element, according to Catholic tradition. Despite the anti-clerical trend in the second half of the nineteenth century, traditional cultural principles of the Catholic Church still appealed to the Viennese artisans.[16] The nineteenth century also witnessed the birth of a new racial anti-Semitism expressed in scientific language. This granted long-standing stereotypes about the Jews a new legitimacy in the language of science. The science of race and sex, which flourished in Vienna, insisted on a clear distinction between male and female and viewed transgression of this boundary as deviance or illness. It regarded Jews as exemplary of the failure to conform to gender roles, because Jewish women supposedly dominated effeminate Jewish men.[17]

The sexual component of Viennese anti-Semitism undoubtedly had an impact on the young Adolf Hitler. In a well-known quote, Hitler recalled his impression of Viennese Jews and their sexuality. "In no other city of Western Europe could the relationship between Jewry and prostitution and even now the white slave traffic, be studied better than in Vienna . . . An icy shudder ran down my spine when seeing for the first time the Jew as an evil, shameless and calculating manager of this shocking vice, the outcome of the scum of the big city."[18] The Viennese anti-Semitic press encouraged Hitler's fantasies blaming the Jews for everything from the stock market collapse to prostitution. The *Deutsches Volksblatt*, a racist newspaper edited by Ernst Vergani (1848–1915), contained pornography and emphasized sexual images of the Jews. It contained stories of Jewish lechers assaulting Christian girls and Jewish madams who ran bordellos and used their own daughters as prostitutes.[19] The parish priest Joseph Deckert (1846–1901) tirelessly proclaimed that Jews murdered Christian children for ritual purposes.

In addition to the *Deutsches Volksblatt*, Hitler also became a reader of the extremist anti-Semitic pamphlet, *Ostara*, in which the editor, Adolf Josef Lanz (Lanz von Liebenfels) (1874–1954), described a conflict between the blond, blue-eyed "Asings" or "Heldings" with ape-like creatures he called the "Aefflings" or "Scraettlings." According to this philosophy, man had degenerated from the heroic being, made in God's image, through interbreeding. The solution was "the extirpation of the animal-man and the propagation of the higher man." The ape-men, who were clearly understood to be Jews, were destroying the entire race by sexual interbreeding. "Lurid drawings of blond women caught in the embraces of dark, hairy men filled the quotient of morbid erotica that appealed to the Viennese. This super-potent ape-man drew the Aryan woman to him and despoiled her."[20]

There was also a long tradition of anti-Semitic stereotypes of Jews in images, i.e., caricatures, in Vienna. Anti-Semitic comic papers, which aimed to wage a satirical war against the Jews, emerged in the nineteenth century. The oldest anti-Semitic comic paper (*Witzblatt*), the Viennese *Kikeriki* founded in 1862 as an anti-clerical paper, became an organ for the Christian Social Party at the time of the party's ascendancy.[21] In 1891, the chief editor of *Kikeriki* was Theodor Herdlicka (pseud. Theodor Taube) (1840–1904). An example of the level of humor in *Kikeriki* was the "Kohn-Lexicon," which paired words with "Kohn" in the root to caricatures of Jews, such as Concert (Kohn zehrt) with a caricatured drawing of a Jew eating, or Concurrirt (Kohn kurirt) with a caricature of a Jewish doctor.[22]

Many authors, including George Mosse and Sander Gilman, have demonstrated how sexuality came to play a crucial part in stereotypes of others.[23] Playing on the fears and anxieties of the population, racists presented others as a threat to bourgeois respectability. The medicalization of the stereotype of Jews portrayed them as racially prone to mental illnesses such as nervousness and neurasthenia due to inbreeding, and hysteria. Furthermore, the Jews were believed to carry and transmit venereal disease, and to use sex as a means to pollute the Aryan race. According to Mosse, "sexuality was not just one more attribute of the racist stereotype, but by its attack upon respectability threatened the very foundations of bourgeois society."[24]

Various groups defined as others by a society and culture are often linked to one another. A tendency to link Jews and women emerged in late nineteenth century Vienna. For example, scientific discourse argued that both Jews and women possessed physical and mental disabilities. Neurasthenia, a nervous disorder thought to afflict primarily Jewish men, had "womanly" symptoms, such as depression, moodiness, unreasonable fear, nervousness, and hyper-sensibility. Jean-Martin Charcot (1825–1893), the Paris physician and one of Freud's teachers, and Richard von Krafft-Ebing (1840–1902), the Viennese sexologist, held that Jews were prone to mental illnesses such as nervousness and neurasthenia because of an inbred weakness of their nervous system and an uncontrollable drive for acquisitions.[25] According to these physicians, women's nervous systems were weaker than men's. They also claimed that women and Jews shared a predisposition to hysteria because of an inability to cope with city life, sexual excesses, incestuous inbreeding, and susceptibility to venereal disease.[26]

In Vienna, the Jews' position in the medical community suffered from these emerging racial stereotypes. In 1875, Theodor Billroth (1829–1894), an eminent medical professor and surgeon, argued that Jews from Hungary and Galicia should not be accepted at the Viennese medical school.[27] He claimed that they lacked talent for the natural sciences, and that their influx into the medical school threatened its high standards. This made for a problematic environment for Jews in the medical school, who began to face verbal and physical attacks. In 1884, the Jewish doctor Carl Koller (1858–1944), during an argument with a surgeon over a technical matter, was called a *Saujud* (Jewish swine). Koller hit the man in the face and the surgeon challenged Koller to a duel (which Koller won).[28]

While the sexualized images of the Jew influenced the discourse of Viennese rabbis, Jewish leaders, and Zionists, Jewish women in psychoanalysis and images of Jewish women in psychoanalytic and medical texts more directly corresponded to the context of Viennese anti-Semitism. As Jewish masculinity came increasingly under attack, Jews in psychoanalysis and medicine responded in a variety of ways. Some tried to universalize the Jewish stereotype into a general theory of human development, thereby obscuring the distinction between Jews and non-Jews. Others attributed aspects of the Jewish stereotype to the cultural and social conditions of the Jews instead of seeing them as racially determined. A third group inverted negative stereotypes into positive ones and asserted Jews' superior health and sexuality. Finally, some Jews accepted the negative stereotypes of Jewish sexuality and became Jewish self-haters. Each of these responses translated differently with regard to the Jewish woman. Jews in Viennese medicine and psychoanalysis concentrated more on the image of the male Jew than the female Jew. As a result, they frequently blurred distinctions between male and female Jews, and between Jewish and non-Jewish women. For example, in the work of Freud, gender overrides race, and women and Jewish women are equated. He applied the characteristics of Jewish women to all women and based his descriptions and theories of the female sex on Jewish women. Therefore, the woman for Freud equals the Jewish woman.

In contrast to this, medical texts written by Viennese Jews did not usually distinguish between male and female Jews. In Viennese medicine, the category of race took precedence over the category of gender. They discussed the Jews without distinguishing between male and female Jews. When they did single out Jewish women, they understood them in terms of gender stereotypes. Racist notions of Jewish sexuality also played a role in leading some Jewish women to psychoanalysis as either practitioners or patients (or in some cases both) in fin de siècle Vienna.

Psychoanalysis: Jewish Women as Practitioners

The quest for a national or ethnic identity in the face of assimilation and anti-Semitism, alongside the need to find a way to reconcile bourgeois views of femininity with their awakening feminist desire to assert themselves, led some Jewish women to become psychoanalysts and/ or seek psychoanalytic treatment for their ailments. The movement, founded by and primarily consisting of Jews, afforded Jewish women the opportunity for solidarity with fellow Jews. Like Zionism, psychoanalysis provided a framework for negotiating female identity and confronting gender and racial stereotypes.

The Jewish women in Freud's psychoanalytic circle belonged to a generation which grew up surrounded by anti-Semitism and limitations due to gender, and found in psychoanalysis a refuge, a world where being a Jewish woman was not a hindrance to their success. They remained faithful to Freud's theories of sexuality, although they also further examined areas such as motherhood and female sexuality. Although their analytical theories usually remained within the prescribed boundaries of femininity, in their personal and professional lives they transgressed those boundaries. Among the women in Freud's circle, Jewish women such as Sabina Spielrein (1885–1941), Helene Rosenbach Deutsch (1884–1982), and Anna Freud (1895–1982) became central contributors. Other Jewish women in psychoanalysis included Else Pappenheim (b. 1911), Marie Glas Langer (1910–1987), Margaret Schoenberger Mahler (1897–1985), Charlotte Malachowski Bühler (1893–1974), Judith Silberpfennig Kestenberg (1910–1988), and Jolanda Jacobi.

In her study of Jewish university women in Central Europe, Harriet Pass Freidenreich points out that "approximately one-quarter of the

Jewish women physicians under consideration eventually specialized in some aspect of mental health."[29] She attributes this to the low professional status of mental health as a relatively new field making it more accessible to women. She also mentions the motivation of either avoiding or coping with their mental or personal problems. Additionally, as Jews, Jewish women found themselves more welcome and encountered less resistance in the psychoanalytic circle because it was primarily composed of other Jews.

Sabina Spielrein grew up in Russia, where girls were allowed to attend *Gymnasium*, and she had obtained a *Gymnasium* degree which allowed her to attend University. In her diary, she described her attachment to religion and longing for a Jewish girl friend.

> Until the age of 13 I was extremely religious; in spite of numerous contradictions I perceived, in spite of my father's derision, I dared not give up the idea of God. Relinquishing God proved extremely difficult for me. What resulted was a void. I kept my "guardian spirit." When I dreamed in my loneliness of a girl friend, I always pictured her as being a Jewish girl, who would be the best student in our class after me. And such a girl actually turned up. At first she was my "pontifex maximus," as my father liked to tease me. I was sure she was smarter and a much, much nobler person than I, and I loved her with all the intensity of childish love. That lasted a while (one year). Then I became somewhat disappointed in her and chose a Christian girl as my best friend.[30]

In 1904, she went to Zurich to receive psychoanalytic treatment in the Burghoelzli clinic at the age of nineteen. Her symptoms included a preoccupation with defecation, especially during mealtimes, masochistic fantasies about her father's hand, and displays of disgust, sticking out her tongue at anyone who reproached her. She was treated by Carl Jung (1875–1961), who also became her colleague and lover. A Christian, Jung confessed to her that he loved Jewish women and that he wanted to love a dark Jewish girl. "So in him, too, the urge to remain faithful to his religion and culture, as well as the drive to explore other possibilities through a new race, the drive to liberate himself from the paternal edicts through an unbelieving Jewess."[31]

Her parents also brought her to Zurich with the idea that she could attend medical school there when her symptoms cleared. In 1905 she enrolled at the University of Zurich.[32] After a falling out with Jung,

Spielrein moved to Vienna and worked closely with Freud. She was the second woman to apply for membership in the Vienna Psychoanalytic Society in 1911.[33] The first woman to apply for membership, Margarete Hilferding (1871–1942), squeaked through in 1910 after a spirited debate over whether women could be members. Spielrein married Paul Scheftel, a Russian Jewish doctor, in 1912, and had two daughters. Jung's affair with Spielrein and her growing affinity for Freudian interpretations may have contributed to the growing animosity between Freud and Jung, but she also served as a link between the two. Spielrein emigrated to Moscow in 1923, where she engaged in many activities. In 1941 she and her two daughters were taken to a synagogue and shot during the Nazi occupation.[34]

Helene Rosenbach Deutsch attended a school in Zurich, where Swiss ideas of women's education influenced her. She broke off her relationship with Herman Lieberman in 1910 following her pregnancy and subsequent abortion.[35] Her lifelong interest in medicine led to her attendance at the University of Vienna medical school. Although some professors displayed prejudices against women, she recalled no special difficulties in medical school. However, she did recall facing discrimination as a Jew when looking for a room to rent in Vienna. When landladies asked her where she came from and heard the name of her Polish hometown, their friendly smiles disappeared. Their next question was invariable: "What religion are Poles from there?" Knowing what they meant she would answer, "mostly Jewish."[36]

In 1912, she married Felix Deutsch (1884–1964), a native Viennese Jewish doctor who specialized in internal medicine, and they had one son, Martin, in 1917. While in medical school she was given a copy of *The Interpretation of Dreams*, introducing her to psychoanalysis. She joined Freud's Psychoanalytic Society in 1918. Her career in psychoanalysis flourished in the 1920s, although she worried that her ambitions succeeded at the expense of her femininity. She regarded herself as having strong masculine aspirations, and felt that the gender roles in her marriage were reversed.[37]

Jewish women in Freud's circle, like Zionist women, chose to participate in a movement comprised mainly of Jews. Through their involvement in the movement, they could comfortably identify with Jewish ethnicity. In their contributions to psychoanalytic theory, Jewish women in Freud's circle for the most part accepted Freud's theory of sexuality. This stemmed partially from their veneration of Freud together with the influence of bourgeois cultural norms for women in Vienna.

Portrait of Helene Deutsch in hat. The Schlesinger Library,
Radcliffe Institute, Harvard University.

Spielrein contributed many ideas to psychoanalytic theory, such as
the connection between religious fantasies and schizophrenia and the
problem of sexual repression.[38] She increasingly shifted her attention
to the area of child psychology, incorporating the findings of develop-
mental psychology in her work on the development of speech in children.[39] Due to a footnote in Freud's *Beyond the Pleasure Principle*, she
falsely earned the reputation of founder of the death instinct. What she
actually argued was that sexuality brought with it themes such as dying in the arms of the beloved. In 1909 she wrote about the sexual drive
as a destructive drive and a creative force.

> This immortal saying [taken from *Faust*]: "Part of a power that
> would / Alone work evil, but engenders good." This demonic force,
> whose very essence is destruction (evil) and at the same time is the
> creative force, since out of the destruction (of two individuals) a new

one arises. That is in fact the sexual drive, which is by nature a destructive drive, an exterminating drive for the individual, and for that reason, in my opinion, must overcome such great resistance in everyone; but to prove this here would take too much of your time.[40]

Helene Rosenbach Deutsch became a specialist in the psychology of women, describing the "masculinity complex" as a normal stage of female sexual development. Intellectually ambitious women (such as herself) sacrificed their valuable feminine attributes for the sake of their careers. She generally accepted Freud's statements about femininity. In a well-known piece entitled "The Significance of Masochism in the Mental Life of Women" she stated, "I want to examine the genesis of 'femininity,' by which I mean the feminine, passive-masochistic disposition in the mental life of women." She also reaffirmed Freud's theory of the castration complex. "The woman's whole passive-feminine disposition, the entire genital desire familiar to us as the rape-phantasy, is finally explained if we accept the proposition that it originates in the castration complex. My view is that the Oedipus complex in girls is inaugurated by the castration complex." [41] However, by shifting her focus onto the study of female sexuality on its own terms, she left behind the discussion of what distinguished the sexes, looking at what each sex possessed on its own. She also rejected Freud's assertion that women were inherently more unreliable than men in a paper on the pathological lie in 1921. Therefore, she did cautiously move beyond Freud in her writings on women's psychology, which she based on her own experiences and those of her female patients, mostly from Vienna.

Freud's youngest daughter, Anna, also had a pattern of "masculinity complex." Rather than feeling inadequate in relation to the maternal role, her complex involved the renouncing of her love for her father and the abandonment of her feminine role in a romantic relationship. In her fantasies and daydreams she assumed male roles. "In her fantasy life and in her dreams, Anna Freud often identified with male story characters . . . this tendency later became one of the most important focuses of her analysis." [42] In contrast to her brothers Martin and Ernst, she did not become interested in Zionism. This was the case even though she worked closely with Siegfried Bernfeld, who organized a large Zionist youth rally in Vienna in 1918.

As a result of the tensions between feminism, Freudian theories of sexuality, bourgeois and Jewish notions of femininity, and their life experiences, Jewish women in psychoanalysis felt inner contradictions

Portrait of Helene Deutsch. The
Schlesinger Library, Radcliffe Institute, Harvard University.

about their own identity as Jewish women. This played itself out for
Spielrein in her attraction to the Other (Jung), which conflicted with
the urge to remain faithful to her religion. Even after her marriage, she
found it difficult to overcome the love for Jung. For Deutsch and Anna
Freud, the difficulty was in fulfilling what they perceived as feminine
roles.

The atmosphere in Vienna made life difficult for them as Jews and
as women. As women, they faced an audience eager to condemn them
for crossing gender boundaries. The effort to gain acceptance and
legitimacy demanded a certain amount of submission to prevailing
ideas. Firmly entrenched in their culture, these women had difficulty
transcending its notions of femininity and masculinity. While women's
rights and feminist ideology attracted them, loyalty to Freud's theory
of sexuality and the prevailing notions of acceptable roles for women
hindered the incorporation of feminism into the theories of Jewish female psychoanalysts in Vienna.

Psychoanalysis: Jewish Women as Patients

In psychoanalysis, the surrounding paranoia and fear of Jewish sexuality undoubtedly influenced the development and interpretation of
illnesses in Jewish women. Psychoanalytic literature does not contain
stereotypes of Jewish women per se, because of the tendency to focus
exclusively on the male Jew, when describing the sexuality and medical condition of "the Jew."[43] Additionally, Jews in psychiatry and psychoanalysis tended to disregard race when looking at Jewish women.
For example, the Jewishness of the two most famous case studies of

hysteria, Anna O. and Dora, was concealed. In other words, psycho-analysis gendered the Jew as always male.

Sander Gilman, who has dealt with these issues extensively and contributed greatly to the understanding of the role of race and gender in the work of many Jewish thinkers including Freud, asserts that Freud did not distinguish between male and female Jews. For example, in discussing the birth of Sabina Spielrein's child, he concludes that, according to Freud, "Jews, male and female, have a 'common mental construction' as 'dark' Jews."[44] However, given that Freud definitely differentiated female from male mental constructions, Freud would not see Jewish men and women as having the same mental construction. Rather, it seems that Freud actually conflated Jewish and non-Jewish women. In other words, Freud's woman is always Jewish.

The issue becomes even more complex when one begins to look at the literature on Freud's Jewish identity and his views on gender, in which the central question has been whether Judaism, nineteenth-century science, or some combination of the two determined Freud's views on women. Recently it has been suggested that Jewish views of gender and anti-Semitic stereotypes of the effeminate Jew influenced Freud's understanding of femininity. According to this argument, Freud displaced his negative self-image onto another vulnerable group, namely women, in order to reinforce his threatened masculinity.[45] Therefore Freud did not challenge the "Jewish stereotype" of women because he instead projected his fears of his own otherness onto women. Gilman challenges this argument, pointing out that Freud grew up in an assimilated, non-Orthodox environment and systematically rejected all religious values. He prefers to see Freud's construction of gender as a product of nineteenth-century medical and scientific theories of race.[46]

Another explanation for Freud's reluctance to distinguish between Jewish and non-Jewish women lies in Freud's efforts to universalize human experience. Freud's views on women and female sexuality developed and changed over time, as his overall theories evolved. In his letters to Wilhelm Fliess (1887–1904), a Berlin ear, nose, and throat specialist, Freud put forward the claim that neurasthenia and hysteria were disturbances of sexuality.[47] In *Studies on Hysteria* (1895), Freud and Josef Breuer (1842–1925) stressed that hysteria afflicted women almost exclusively. In "Fragment of an Analysis of a Case of Hysteria" or the case study of "Dora," written in 1905, Freud examined Dora's bisexuality through analyzing her dreams.

What is fascinating is that in all of this discussion of hysteria as a sexual affliction, Freud did not mention that hysteria afflicted Jewish women more than any other group. This is even more puzzling when we see the emphasis put on the connection between the male Jew and hysteria.[48]

As Freud's theory of female sexuality developed, he increasingly stressed the bisexuality of women, "penis envy," "feminine masochism," and the "masculinity complex."[49] According to Freud, some women failed to transfer their sexuality from the clitoris to the vagina, signaling that they continued to hope for a penis. These bisexual women did not make the transition in puberty to femininity. Some girls substituted a beating fantasy for masturbation, leading to "feminine masochism." Given that the stereotype of the Jewish male as feminine prevailed in Vienna, perhaps the "masculinity complex" of women was a counterpart to this stereotype. Although Freud universalized his theory of femininity to apply to all women, many of his female patients, including his daughter Anna Freud (1895–1982), Ida Bauer (Dora) (1883–1945), Bertha Pappenheim (Anna O., actually a patient of Josef Breuer's) (1859–1936), Emma Eckstein (1865–1924), Anna Hammerschlag Lichtheim, Ilona Weiss (Fraulein Elisabeth von R.), and Matilde Altmann Breuer (1846–1931), were Jewish.[50] Therefore both hysteria and the "masculinity complex" afflicted Jewish women.

Freud attributed these psychological disorders to their gender rather than to their "race" or religion. This corresponds to Freud's general effort and concern with making psychoanalysis a general movement. He knew that psychoanalysis was in danger of becoming a Jewish movement unless it attracted more non-Jewish ties. At the second Psychoanalytic Congress in 1910, Freud stated: "Most of you are Jews, and therefore you are incompetent to win friends for the new teaching. Jews must be content with the modest role of preparing the ground. It is absolutely essential that I should form ties in the world of general science . . . The Swiss will save us."[51] His initial resistance to the idea of a group mentality eventually gave way. In 1926, he wrote:

. . . the question may be raised whether the personality of the present writer as a Jew who has never sought to disguise the fact that he is a Jew may not have had a share in provoking the antipathy of his environment to psychoanalysis. . . . Nor is it perhaps entirely a matter of chance that the first advocate of psychoanalysis was a

Jew. To profess belief in this new theory called for a certain degree of readiness to accept a situation of solitary opposition—a situation with which no one is more familiar than a Jew.[52]

According to Gilman, Freud projected qualities of the male Jewish stereotype found in nineteenth-century racial theory onto the feminine. Gilman focuses on Freud's construction of masculinity, which determined the image of the female.[53] Freud transferred anti-Semitic images of the Jew as unknowable, mentally and physically ill, engaged in conspiracies, and dishonest to women. However, this does not account for Freud's view of femininity as failed masculinity, female bisexuality, and the feminine "masculinity complex." Although he avoided explicit references to "race," his masculine, hysterical, masochistic woman makes sense as quintessential Jewish woman, counterpart to the feminine Jewish male.

Why did Freud avoid explicitly discussing "race" as a factor in variations of feminine sexuality? Most likely he did so in his effort to universalize the experience of his patients in order to develop a general theory of human sexual development and to reject the racial stereotypes of Jews. Therefore, while most of his female patients were Jewish, he thought of their gender rather than their Jewishness as the determining factor in their psychological constitution. Protection of the identity of his patients, which was of utmost importance for Freud, may also have been a factor.

Freud's image of Jewish women can be further explored through his analyses of the female Jewish patients he analyzed and/or discussed. Bertha Pappenheim, born in Vienna to wealthy Orthodox Jewish parents, became a patient of Josef Breuer, Freud's older, more established colleague. Based on his analysis of Pappenheim, he contributed the case study of "Anna O." to their joint work, *Studies on Hysteria* (1895).[54] The case study described the illness of an attractive, imaginative young woman, who at the age of twenty-one, after nursing her dying father, developed paralysis, partial blindness, and a disruption in her language. In his case notes, Breuer referred to Anna O.'s lack of religious feeling, implying that as part of her illness she lost her identity as a Jew.[55] He also described how she developed a strategy of survival called the "talking cure"—articulating repressed memories leading to the disappearance of symptoms. Breuer abandoned her case after she went into imaginary childbirth and cast him in the role of father.

Portrait of Bertha Pappenheim, undated. Courtesy of the Leo Baeck Institute, New York.

During the next seven years she somehow overcame her illness, and she later emerged as a prominent German-Jewish feminist and social worker.[56]

Breuer's description of the case focused on the disruption of language. Anna O. lost her command of German and began to communicate with her family and her physician in English, a language in which she was neither fluent nor comfortable.[57] She also forgot Hebrew, the religious language of the Jews and of her father. When she tried to recite a prayer because she imagined that she was threatened by a snake, she could only think of an English children's rhyme. In his case notes, Breuer stressed that Anna O. was "completely without belief." He also mentioned that she seemed to lack any overt sexuality, avoiding his final encounter with her.[58] Freud, in his account of the case, recognized the sexual dimension of her illness. But as Gilman notes, "just as Breuer repressed the question of Anna O.'s sexuality, Freud represses the relationship between her illness and her rejection of her Jewish identity."[59] While the image of the Jewish woman (Anna O.) was, for Breuer, framed in terms of her Jewishness rather than her gender, for Freud the image was framed in terms of her gender to the exclusion of her Jewishness.

Another example of Freud's image of Jewish women can be found in his dream, Irma's injection in *Interpretation of Dreams* (1900). The figure Irma was based on many of his patients, who happened to be Jewish women.

A large hall—numerous guests, whom we were receiving.—Among them was Irma. I at once took her on one side, as though to answer her letter and to reproach her for not having accepted my "solution" yet. I said to her: "If you still get pains, it's really your own fault." She replied: "If you only knew what pains I've got now in my throat and stomach and abdomen—it's choking me"—I was alarmed and looked at her. She looked pale and puffy. I thought to myself that after all I must be missing some organic trouble. I took her to the window and looked down her throat, and she showed signs of recalcitrance, like women with artificial dentures. I thought to myself that there was really no need for her to do that.—She then opened her mouth properly and on the right I found a big white patch; at another place I saw extensive whitish grey scabs upon some remarkable curly structures which were evidently modeled on the turbinal bones of the nose.—I at once called in Dr. M., and he repeated the examination and confirmed it. . . . Dr. M. looked quite different from usual; he was very pale, he walked with a limp and his chin was clean shaven. . . . My friend Otto was now standing beside her as well, and my friend Leopold was percussing her through her bodice and saying: "She has a dull area low down on the left." He also indicated that a portion of the skin on the left shoulder was infiltrated. (I noticed this, just as he did, in spite of her dress.) . . . M. said: "There's no doubt it's an infection, but no matter; dysentery will supervene and the toxin will be eliminated." . . . We were directly aware, too, of the origin of her infection. Not long before, when she was feeling unwell, my friend Otto had given her an injection of a preparation of propyl, propyls . . . propionic acid . . . trimethylamine (and I saw before me the formula for this printed in heavy type). . . . Injections of that sort ought not to be made so thoughtlessly. . . . and probably the syringe had not been clean.[60]

On the surface, the dream focused on Freud's patient Irma, whom he had treated in 1895. The treatment succeeded only in part. He proposed a solution which she rejected, after which they decided to break off treatment for the summer. Following an encounter with a friend who had been staying with Irma and her family at their country resort, Freud wrote out Irma's case history. That night or morning, he had his dream.

In Freud's analysis of the dream, it emerges that Irma was actually a composite of several different women, including former patients, his oldest daughter, and his wife. Irma's symptoms in the dream differed from her actual symptoms. At one point her intimate woman friend, whom Freud had reason to believe was also a hysteric, replaced her. Later, he substituted a third figure, his own wife, who had bad teeth (recalcitrant), was bashful in his presence, and had pains in the abdomen.[61] The white patch reminded him of the illness of his eldest daughter, and of another female patient who had used cocaine on his recommendation and had developed an "extensive necrosis of the nasal mucous membrane."[62] It also reminded him of the tragic death of a patient, Mathilde, in whom Freud had produced a severe toxic state by prescribing what he thought was a harmless remedy, sulphonal. The patient, Freud noted, had the same name as his eldest daughter. At the end of the analysis, Freud wrote: "The phlebitis brought me back once more to my wife, who had suffered from thrombosis during one of her pregnancies; and now three similar situations came to my recollection involving my wife, Irma and the dead Mathilde. The identity of these situations had evidently enabled me to substitute the three figures for one another in the dream." [63]

Later, Freud returned to the notion of the "collective figure" as represented by Irma. "Irma became the representative of all these other figures which had been sacrificed to the work of condensation, since I passed over to *her*, point by point, everything that reminded me of *them*." [64]

According to Gilman, Irma was on one level one of Freud's favorite patients, Anna Lichtheim, the daughter of his religion teacher Samuel Hammerschlag, whom he had described as "an admirable girl" and after whom he named his youngest daughter. [65] On another level, Irma was Emma Eckstein, a patient almost killed by Wilhelm Fliess's surgical ineptitude (and the feminist sister of Therese Schlesinger-Eckstein). Acting on his theory linking the nose to the genitalia, Fliess operated on the nose to relieve sexual problems. In the case of Emma Eckstein, he left a wad of surgical dressing in her nasal cavity, which caused massive bleeding and infection. [66] Irma of Freud's dream could not only be seen as a composite character, but as a composite of the Jewish women of his life. Gilman writes, "According to Freud, the source of Irma's disease is thus in the sexuality of the Jewish female, the widowed Anna Lichtheim and Emma Eckstein." As the quintessential Jewish woman, Freud's Irma suffered from a variety of ailments.

The traits which Freud found in Jewish women—sexuality, disease, hysteria, vulnerability, and recalcitrance—could be seen as components of the nineteenth-century medical stereotype of the Jew or the woman. When we turn to the case of Dora (Ida Bauer), a young Jewish woman whom Freud treated for hysteria, other traits emerge. Moreover, he established a link between hysteria and bisexuality. Freud wrote: "The jealous emotions of a woman were linked in the unconscious with a jealousy such as might have been felt by a man. These masculine or, more properly speaking, *gynaecophilic* currents of feeling are to be regarded as typical of the unconscious erotic life of hysterical girls." [67] Elsewhere, he wrote:

In general, the hysterical attack, like every form of hysteria, in women recalls to action a form of sexual activity which existed during childhood, and had at that time, a pronounced masculine character. One may often observe that it is just those girls who in the years before puberty showed a boyish character and inclinations who tend to become hysterical at puberty. In a whole series of cases the hysterical neurosis is nothing but an excessive over accentuation of the typical wave of repression through which the masculine type of sexuality is removed and the woman emerges.[68]

This new emphasis creates a problem for the thesis that Freud transferred the stereotype of the Jewish male onto the woman. The Jewish male was seen as feminine in the nineteenth century; Freud saw the Jewish woman, in this case Dora, as masculine.[69]

The case of Dora has commanded a great deal of subsequent interest, and recently her Jewish background has been examined.[70] The principal characters in the study were all Jewish: Dora (Ida Bauer), her compulsive mother (Kaethe Bauer), her philandering, syphilitic father (Philipp Bauer), his mistress, Frau K., and her husband, Herr K. (Hans Zellenka), whose proposition of Dora led to a crisis in her illness. Both parents were from Bohemia, and the children grew up in Bohemia, Vienna, and Merano in the Austrian Tyrol. Her father was a prosperous factory owner, and her parents did not practice Judaism.[71] Dora's older brother Otto, with whom she shared a close relationship, later became the leader of Austrian Social Democracy.[72] Dora was brought to Freud for treatment in 1900 at the age of eighteen for hysterical symptoms which included migraines, a nervous cough, loss of voice, a periodic limp, a vaginal catarrh or discharge, depression, fatigue, lack of concentration, suicidal thoughts, and a fainting spell.

Freud's case study and all the subsequent analyses and critiques of the case demonstrate the circumstances, familial and social, which brought about her symptoms. Hannah Decker convincingly argues that in Dora's treatment, which lasted only a few months and ended unsuccessfully, each party had different goals. Dora's father hoped that Freud would not only cure his daughter, but convince her to accept his relationship with the K.s and become pleasant around the house. Dora wanted to convince Freud that Herr K.'s seduction actually took place and was not merely a fantasy, and hoped that Freud would intervene on her behalf to persuade her father to break off his relationship with the K.s. Freud, himself, wanted not only to cure the patient, but also to find evidence which would support his emerging theories about the interpretation of dreams, the deleterious effects of masturbation, bisexuality, and the instinctual bases of infantile and childhood sexuality.[73] In his efforts to verify his theories, Freud bombarded Dora with a series of sexual interpretations of her illness. These ranged from finding the source of her cough in her fantasizing about Frau K. performing fellatio on her father to his insistence that masturbation was the cause of her illness. Freud overlooked the counter-transference that occurred during his treatment of Dora, as well as the fact that he identified with her father and with Frau K. finding his patient sexually attractive.[74] Freud also failed to recognize anti-Semitism as a factor in her illness. "There is no hint that Freud and Dora talked about her feelings about being Jewish." That Dora felt Judaism to be a burden is corroborated by her conversion to Protestantism four and a half years after she quit psychoanalysis. She converted together with her husband and son two months after his birth.[75]

Gilman refers to the case as "the classic example of the transmutation of images of gender and race (masculinity and 'Jewishness') into the deracinated image of the feminine."[76] In addition to the omission of Dora's racial identity, he emphasizes the diseased nature of the father (syphilis), the male Jew, and its connection to the daughter's hysteria.[77] In his rereading of Dora's first recurrent dream, which involved a jewel case [*Schmuckkasten*] which Freud interpreted as the female genitals, he points out that *Schmock* referred to the circumcised male penis in Viennese urban dialect borrowed from Yiddish, concluding that this is another example of Freud's suppression of references to male Jewish sexuality. In his reinterpretation of the case, Gilman places male Jewishness at the center. "Ida Bauer's act of seeing her father is the act of seeing the (male) Jew. Central to the definition of the Jew—here to be understood always as the "male" Jew—is the image of the male Jew's circumcised penis as impaired, damaged, or incomplete and therefore threatening."[78] This interpretation leaves out the female Jew, who was after all the subject of the case study. While Freud's suppression of Jewish aspects of the case is important, the definition of the male Jew alone cannot explain every aspect of Freud's analysis of Dora. Born in 1882, Ida Bauer would have felt vulnerable as a female Jew. The social background of anti-Semitism and misogyny must have contributed to her illness.

The imperial splendor of fin-de-siècle Vienna was for her a hostile world. As a girl and a woman, she was enveloped by the prevalent misogyny, which, through much of contemporary science and art as well as social conventions, denigrated femaleness. In a medical atmosphere unfriendly to hysterical sufferers, she was considered scheming and devious. Before she came to Freud she had already endured a series of painful and ineffective electrical and hydropathic treatments.

In an economically and politically transitional society at odds with itself, Dora was also maligned as a Jew. Vienna's virulent anti-Semitism made her feel both inferior and frustrated.[79]

Dora's illness can be seen as a reaction to these feelings of inferiority and frustration. Through it she asserted herself amid the pressures which faced her.

During Freud's analysis of Dora, he discovered that she had an intimate relationship with Frau K. They had shared a bedroom when she stayed with the K.s, and "she had been the wife's confidante and adviser in all the difficulties of her married life."

> When Dora talked about Frau K., she used to praise her "adorable white body" in accents more appropriate to a lover than to a defeated rival. Another time she told me, more in sorrow than in anger, that she was convinced the presents her father had brought her had been chosen by Frau K., for she recognized her taste. . . . Indeed, I can say in general that I never heard her speak a harsh or angry word against the lady, although from the point of view of her supervalent thought she should have regarded her as the prime author of her misfortunes.[80]

Freud concluded that Dora's concern over her father's relations with Frau K. was "designed not only for the purpose of suppressing her love for Herr K., which had once been conscious, but also to conceal her love for Frau K., which was in a deeper sense unconscious."[81] The confusion of gender roles played out differently for Jewish men and women. The Jewish man was seen as feminine, according to the nineteenth-century stereotype (which Freud rejected but Carl Jung embraced). Freud instead adopted the masculinity (or homosexuality) of the hysterical (Jewish) woman.

As Freud's theory of femininity developed over time, the notions of bisexuality, narcissism, masochism, and masculinity complex became more central. In *Three Essays on the Theory of Sexuality* (1905), he presented the idea that women could assume mental sexual characteristics of the masculine type, while men could not have the feminine type.[82] In

"A Child Is Being Beaten" (1919), based in part on the training analysis of his daughter Anna, he analyzed the recurrent fantasy of four female patients. They fantasized that a father figure beat a child, then beat her, and finally beat either her in a male guise or a group of male children. Thus part of the fantasy was the assumption of a male guise. This was a case of "feminine masochism" in which the women fantasized themselves as men being turned into females. "The precondition for the masochistic fantasy in these cases was a denial of anatomical femininity or the continued longing for a penis that Freud called the 'masculinity complex.'"[83] He also wrote a case study of a homosexual woman in which he linked her love of an older woman to the disappointment of her mother's new pregnancy when she was sixteen.[84] In the 1920s, he began to question his conviction that females and males undergo analogous developments, i.e., the Oedipus complex, and to examine how his prejudice for male cases had influenced his views on women.[85] His last works on femininity, "Female Sexuality" (1931) and "Femininity" (1932), were composed in response to growing dissent among his followers on the topic of female sexuality. He reviewed his work on the topic, continuing to stress female bisexuality.

Young-Bruehl makes a connection between the shift in Freud's theory of femininity and the female patients with whom he was dealing at different points of his career.

> [Freud] was probably also influenced by the fact that his female patient population was changing. After the First World War, he analyzed women, including his own daughter, who were set on intellectual careers or on training to be psychoanalysts. These were not hysterics. Most came for what are known as "character analyses," not for relief from debilitating psychoneuroses, and most were, in Freud's terms, examples of the feminine "masculinity complex." Their bisexuality, so sustaining to their creativity and formative to their characters, may well partly explain why Freud's analysand trainees were not critical of his female psychology—the criticism came from outside his circle, and outside the reach of the transferences he received.[86]

While the nature of the analysis of female Jews shifted away from hysteria toward character analyses, the underlying current of bisexuality persisted.

Freud's Disciples Confront Sexual Stereotypes of Jews

Unlike Freud himself, some of his Viennese Jewish colleagues and disciples exhibited a tendency to confront the anti-Semitic image of the Jew. For example, rather than repressing the painful stereotype of Jewish sexuality, Otto Rank (1884–1939) reinterpreted it as a virtue. Initially critical of Judaism, Rank formally left the Jewish confession in 1903.[87] Internalizing anti-Semitic stereotypes of the Jews, he wrote that observant Jews go to synagogue out of boredom, and reduce it to a place of business. The women, he wrote, go to show off their dresses, or what is beneath them. He also changed his surname from the Jewish-sounding Rosenfeld to "Rank" as a way of distancing himself from Judaism.

From 1905–1906, Rank became one of Freud's closest disciples. In connection to his ties with Freud and the psychoanalytic movement, he reconciled himself with Judaism and developed the theory that the Jews had maintained a direct relation to nature and to primitive sexuality, leading to their creativity. In his 1905 essay on the "Essence of Judaism," he compared Jews to women as both had preserved themselves from civilized morality.[88] He wrote that the Jews were the women among the people and needed to join themselves to the masculine life-source in order to become productive. He argued that the anti-Semitism of the most important artists of the nineteenth century was "nothing more than an expression of the denial of sexuality."[89] He regarded hostility against the Jews as a symptom of a highly repressive culture. Assimilation caused the Jews to repress their sexuality and become neurotic. The Jews, according to Rank, were forging the way for regeneration by looking for a radical cure of neurosis. Judaism was the foundation of regeneration for Rank.

Fritz Wittels (1880–1950), who traveled in two circles, psychoanalysis and the literary circle of Karl Kraus, argued in *Der Taufjude* (1904) that conversion signified a neurosis and dishonesty, although he made an exception for Jewish women, children, and sick people, who converted out of belief.[90] He also referred to the Jewish Salon women in Berlin, Dorothea Mendelssohn, Henriette Herz, and Rahel, but wrote that he must not dwell on the past, which would lead to a completely different judgment about converts.[91] He regarded female converts as less hypocritical than male converts.

During the period 1907–1908, his writings combined the ideas of Kraus and Freud. He expressed a strong disapproval for educated women and the feminist movement. In 1907, he wrote that hysteria was responsible for women's desire to study medicine, and their struggle for equal rights.[92] In 1908, he presented a paper to the Psychoanalytic Society in which he condemned "our accursed present-day culture in which women bemoan the fact that they did not come in to the world as men; they try to become men [via the] feminist movement."[93] He later, in his memoirs, distanced himself from these views and wrote that the article against women doctors was "a 'masculine protest' dictated by fear."[94]

In 1909, he published *Die sexuelle Not*, which appealed for uninhibited sexual gratification.[95] Jung wrote of the book, "I have not read a book on the problem of sexuality that so harshly and so mercilessly tears to pieces our present day morality."[96] The book also contained an account of childhood based on his harsh personal experience, as well as attacks on sexual hypocrisy and monogamous and arranged marriages. Kraus saw the book as a "travesty of his own ideas, a reduction of erotic insights to propaganda for sexual permissiveness."[97] Freud commented:

> Wittels' book, which presents proposals for reform, stems from two different sources—from, so to say, a paternal and a maternal source. The first one, represented by the *Fackel*, goes part of the way with us in its assertion that suppression of sexuality is the root of all evil. But we go further, and say: we liberate sexuality through our treatment, but not in order that man may from now on be dominated by sexuality, but in order to make a suppression possible—a rejection of the instincts under the guidance of a higher agency. The *Fackel* stands for "living out" one's instinctual desires to the point of satiating them [*ausleben*]; we distinguish, however, between a pathological process of repression and one that is to be regarded as normal.[98]

Timms points out that Kraus did not advocate sexual hedonism, and that the title page slogan of *Die sexuelle Not*, "Human beings must live out their sexuality, otherwise they become crippled," was not the program of Kraus's *Die Fackel*. He also suggests that both Freud and Kraus believed that Wittels's work was derivative.[99]

In reversing the negative image of unbridled sexual gratification as a symptom of disease into a positive cure for disease, arguing that the person who represses sexuality by adhering to civilized morality becomes crippled, he came to the same conclusion as Rank. Just as in

Der Taufjude, he found fault with hypocrisy and perjury. The Jews should be satisfied with who they really are, and therefore should remain healthy by remaining Jews, and living out their sexuality.

Alfred Adler (1870–1937), another of Freud's adherents who later broke with him, dealt with the stereotype of Jewish sexuality by deemphasizing its importance in understanding the psyche. Adler, who converted to Protestantism as a young man in order to "escape from Judaism," wished to remove the sexual or Jewish element from psychoanalysis. He stressed the role of will-power, self-assertion, and the search for security, creating a new school of Individual Psychology.[100] Having been ill as a child, he argued that children with inferior physiques compensate for weaknesses by exaggerating strengths. He regarded sex as one of several weapons by which children express a will to power.[101] Like Wittels, he distrusted feminism, denouncing it as the masculine protest of some women who tried to compensate for feeling inferior to men. The image of Jewish sexuality was seen as a virtue by some psychoanalysts and an embarrassment by others.

Medical Literature

Viennese Jewish physicians, scientists, and sexologists also confronted sexual stereotypes of Jewish men and women. The belief in a Jewish tendency for certain illnesses prevailed, with many non-Jewish psychiatrists and physicians attempting to prove it scientifically. These physicians accepted and incorporated notions about the Jews from nineteenth-century racial science. For example, Alexander Pilcz (1871–1954), a non-Jewish psychiatrist in the Department of Psychiatry at the University of Vienna and author of one of the period's standard handbooks of racial psychiatry, wrote prolifically about Jewish illness.[102] In a 1906 study of comparative race-psychiatry, he based his analysis on 2,886 cases, which he examined according to illness, race, and gender.[103] He created a series of charts and lists in order to show which races were more prone to certain disturbances. He divided the charts according to gender as well. In the accompanying discussion, he gave an unusual indication of the differing perception of male and female Jews with regard to the predisposition for certain mental disturbances, at the same time comparing both groups to other "races."

According to his results the most common disturbances for Jewish men were, in order, progressive paralysis (the final stage of neurosyphilis), dementia praecox (schizophrenia), paranoia, and periodic psychosis (manic-depressive disorder), while for Jewish women they were dementia praecox, paranoia, progressive paralysis and periodic insanity (tied), and melancholy. In the next list, he organized the data to show the order of racial groups' susceptibility for each specific disturbance, again according to gender. While for men, the Jews were most likely to be afflicted with three illnesses, dementia praecox, paranoia, and periodic insanity, and were second in line for two others, progressive paralysis and amentia (mental deficiency), Jewish women were first for only two illnesses, dementia praecox and periodic insanity, and were last in all the other categories.

This and other studies of racial psychiatry began with the assumption that certain races had a predisposition for certain forms of mental illness. The fact that he analyzed the genders separately further implies that he regarded gender as being as important as race in this connection. He treated Jewish males and Jewish females as completely separate categories, as he did with Hungarian or German males and females.

In spite of these results, Pilcz tended to blur the distinction between Jewish men and women in his analysis. For example, in his discussion of paranoia, he tried to account for the discrepancy between numbers of Jewish male and female sufferers.

> Of the men the Jews have the largest share, while the Jewish women rank in last place here. Now otherwise we see very consistently, that the Jews predominate in hereditary-degenerative forms, so that this last named exception requires an explanation. Perhaps I may find one such [explanation] in the following. We find among the Jewish women a completely exorbitant high percentage for dementia praecox. When, as everybody knows, the demarcation of paranoia as opposed to the so called paranoid dementia more frequently must remain more or less arbitrary, might perhaps the deficit of Jewish female cases of paranoia lie in the surplus of Jewish female cases of dementia praecox? Then it would certainly follow, that for Jewish women paranoia is especially quick, that it develops adversely and arrives swiftly into the terminal stage.[104]

Through his explanation, Pilcz reversed what initially appeared as an indicator of Jewish women's health into a weakness by arguing that the deficit of Jewish female cases of paranoia was due to the fact that the disease progressed so quickly in them that it was usually classified as a more serious illness.

According to Pilcz, dementia praecox was most common among the Jews, male and female. For female patients of Jewish and northern Slavic ancestry, he asserted, dementia praecox was the most frequent form of psychological illness. Even where the Jews, especially female Jews, did not show a predilection for certain diseases according to his own findings, he did not question the truth of the stereotype but rather tried to explain his data in ways that upheld the image of the mentally ill Jew. For example, in his discussion of hysteria, Pilcz wrote:

> Whoever knows the especially strong predisposition of the Jewish race for hysteria (a fact which was already mentioned by Charcot and numerous other authors), will be astonished by the relatively low percentages of these charts for Jewish mental patients. It depends indeed exclusively on external factors. Hysterical mental disturbances would here include chiefly the psychoses, etc., which were presently in need of institutions, not the neurosis in itself with its habitual mental condition.[105]

In an earlier work on the mental disturbances of the Jews, Pilcz had reached the conclusion that Jews were less prone to alcoholism than non-Jews, about equally prone to disorders resulting from external factors such as infections, poisoning, etc., much more prone to youthful imbecility, the dementia after acute psychoses, and progressive paralysis, and were disproportionately strongly disposed to psychoses of a hereditary-degenerative basis.[106] He cited many other works which came to similar conclusions, attributing to Jewish men and women a strong disposition to psychoses of the hereditary-degenerative type. He concluded that one should not speak of a "Jewish psychosis" but of "Jewish psychoses." At this point, he more or less abandoned the distinction between male and female Jews. He noted that Georg Buschan found that even in Palestine, Jews suffered from mental illness.[107] He concluded that "since the heightened disposition is also to be found in women, it cannot be the exhausting mental life, the *struggle for life* [in English], the damage of 'civilization,' that can explain the prevalence of the Jewish insane."[108] The fact that in his findings, Jewish women were significantly less prone to mental disturbances than Jewish men never received sufficient analysis.

Even more prominent than Pilcz in Viennese psychiatry was Richard von Krafft-Ebing (1840–1902). In contrast to Freud, Krafft-Ebing wrote about sex as a vice and looked for physical causes for mental illness.[109] In his second large work, *Lehrbuch der Psychiatrie*, which appeared in 1879 and was used extensively and translated into a number of languages, he linked the Jews to insanity and sexuality.

> Statistics have been collected with great care to show the percentage of insanity in the various religious sects, and it has been shown that among the Jews and certain sects the percentage is decidedly higher. This fact stands in relation with religion only in so far as it constitutes a hindrance to marriage among those professing it; the more when its adherents are small in number, and there is consequent insufficient crossing of the race and increased inbreeding.[110]

He linked the Jews' insanity to the religious prohibition of intermarriage. Thus, he conceives the Jewish tendency for mental illness and abnormal sexuality in relation to both race (interbreeding) and religion. He saw religious inclination as a symptom of abnormal character or disease, and asserted that abnormal sexuality was not infrequently hidden beneath the veil of religious enthusiasm.[111]

In Krafft-Ebing's *Psychopathia Sexualis* (1886), he paid special attention to the sexual sphere and created the first systematic classification of sexual abnormalities. He named and described perversions such as sadism, masochism, and fetishism, and saw them as resulting from degeneration.[112] In the opening chapter, which described the history of sexuality from primitive man to the Christians, he wrote that the Jews, along with the Egyptians, the Greeks, and the Teutons, were at an intermediate stage, showing "a high appreciation of virginity, chastity, modesty, and sexual fidelity." Christianity was at the highest level because it "raised the union of the sexes to a sublime position by making women socially the equal of man and by elevating the bond of love to a moral and religious institution."[113] Thus, Krafft-Ebing incorporated the anti-Semitic view that Jews are predisposed to certain mental illnesses and are more overtly sexual than Christians.

Medical texts also debated physical and anatomical differences of the Jews. In 1893, the Viennese anatomist Oskar Hovorka (1866–1930) wrote about the inability to prove a special "Jewish type" of nose, in spite of the popular conception to the contrary and the caricatures of "Jewish noses" as crooked and hawk-like seen daily in comic papers.[114] The notion of a Semitic or Jewish nose did not account for the lack of purity of the Jewish race.[115] According to Hovorka, the anthropologist Felix von Luschan proved that the Jews no longer constituted a pure race, but a mixed people. Luschan suggested that the source of the characteristically Jewish bent noses was Armenian. While Hovorka did not believe that Luschan had succeeded in proving the Armenian origin of the bent nose, he did accept the notion that "the bent nose, which we often find among Jews, was attributed not at all to a Semitic influence, but otherwise to an admixture of non-Semitic races."[116]

However, when Hovorka conducted a close investigation of the Jewish nose, he found that it was not as uniform as one might have thought at first glance. First from a study of Jewish patients at the Rothschild Hospital, and then from research on Jewish skulls, he found that Jews had all types of noses, bent, straight, and up-turned. He found that Jewish women had a higher incidence of up-turned noses than Jewish men, as did women in the general population. Thus he concluded that Jews showed a similar pattern in this respect to non-Jews. In spite of his results and his clear statements that no evidence supported the existence of a Jewish type of nose, he still tacitly accepted that the Jews had a higher tendency to bent noses than did non-Jews. He asserted that a lay person, even at a distance, would be able to recognize a Jewish nose. In this respect, Hovorka, like Pilcz, disregarded his own scientific results in favor of accepting a popular stereotype of the Jews.

Forced to contend with this anti-Jewish tendency among the non-Jews in their field, the many Jews who entered medicine in nineteenth-century Vienna followed several different courses of action.[117] Some Jews chose to convert in order to facilitate their careers, while others succeeded while maintaining their loyalties to Judaism. Still others made an effort to respond to the medical stereotypes of the Jews, either by challenging them, or by attributing their symptoms to social rather than racial causes. However, none of them concentrated on the topic of Jewish women or examined the question of how they may or may not have differed from Jewish men. There are only scattered and passing references to female Jews to be found in their writings.

Moritz Benedikt (1835–1920), an important neurologist and professor at the University of Vienna, argued against the notion of the Jewish racial predisposition to mental illness. While accepting the charge that Jews had a tendency for nervousness, he attributed it to social pressures. He wrote that "other nations could find an outlet for their passions and emotions in outward actions; the Jews found an outlet for them usually at the expense of health, and so became more and more neurotic." He attributed the incidence of hysteria and other illnesses among Jewish men and women to the ill-treatment and cruelty to which Jews had been subjected, coupled with the pressures of acculturation. Jewish women, he asserted, became "eccentric . . . Very many of them became, by reason of superficial learning, actually perverse."[118]

Benedikt held on faster to gender-based stereotypes. He did not hesitate to assert that hysteria, which he defined as "a heightened disturbance and shock to the nervous system," was more common in the female sex because of "the strains and irritations from its special organs and also the incongruity of sexual satisfaction which is so common in the female sex."[119] He viewed women in general as excessively emotional, which could result in rigid views, such as extreme nationalism. In one incident which he recounted in his memoirs, two women whom he had befriended reacted with hostility when he suggested to them that some people may place religious feelings above nationalism.[120]

In a lecture delivered to the association "Zion" of Mariahilf-Neubau in 1895, the Jewish general practitioner in Vienna and supporter of Herzl, Martin Engländer, focused specifically on the illnesses of Western Jews in contrast to those of Eastern Jews.[121] He noted that most of the authors who wrote about the diseases of the Jews were themselves not Jewish. As an exception, he discussed Max Mandelstamm (1839–1912), the leading Russian Zionist and eye specialist, who provided Theodor Herzl's model for "Dr. Eichenstamm" in *Altneuland*.[122] In a speech before the fourth Zionist Congress in London entitled "The Physical Improvement of the Jews," Mandelstamm examined the physical state and diseases of Russian Jews. He expressed the opinion that the "decrepit, pitifully weak physical constitution of the ghetto Jews is the exclusive product of their disconsolate socio-economic position, so I need not consider the Jews of Western lands, who are not overall worse off economically than their Aryan countrymen."[123]

Engländer agreed that Western European Jews were not at an economic disadvantage; however, he felt that their physical condition still warranted special consideration. He summarized what had previously been written about the physical condition of the Jews, by Mandelstamm and by non-Jews such as Krafft-Ebing, Erb, Kraepelin, Eichhorst, and others, in order to provide an overview of the physical relationship of the Jews of the East and the West. He began with a disparaging description of the situation of the ghetto Jews, the unhygienic and crowded conditions in which they lived, attributing their suffering to the cruelty of the Russian regime. "Where else on the Earth is there a people who still are robbed of their freedom of movement like a yard dog, locked up in huts, handled with kicks and the whip?—Justice and human dignity, how deep has the whip perverted them!"[124]

Aiming at a scientific analysis of the physical condition of the Eastern Jews, Engländer asserted that heredity and mode of life had physical consequences. First, he said, the average skull circumference of the Jews was larger, while the breast circumference was smaller than that of non-Jews.[125] This resulted in the susceptibility to certain diseases, such as tuberculosis and eye diseases. He also argued that early marriages put Jewish women at risk for certain illnesses. "According to the reports of women's doctors the female sex also has its special suffering to endure. In these respects compulsory relationships are however less to blame than is the institution of early marriages—at the ages of 14, 15, and 16."[126]

He went on to discuss the strengths of the Eastern Jews as well, including their treatment of women. Because they avoided alcohol and lived chaste lives, they did not exacerbate their misery with alcoholism and syphilis. He also praised their domestic virtues, their tender and concerned treatment of women and children, their protection of women in childbed from heavy work, their laws of hygiene in marital relations, and their care for the sick, as moments which formed "hygienic resistance."[127] In order for the Eastern Jews to transform their decrepit bodies, they needed to engage in physical work, and move in fresh air, etc., activities which Russian law prohibited.

Engländer asserted that the Western Jews, while no longer subjected to the restrictions of the ghetto and no longer exhibiting signs of physical degeneration, still showed a striking frequency of certain illnesses and a notable level of degeneration. He explained that following their emancipation, the Western Jews entered the competitive world of the marketplace in disproportionate numbers. This new life took its toll on their nerves, which led to a rise in nervous disorders, psychoses, and suicides. Because of the years of persecution, he claimed, the Jewish brain was more vulnerable to these pressures than the non-Jewish brain.

Engländer accepted the commonly held view that the Jews had weaker central nervous systems than non-Jews. He believed this to be responsible for their high frequency of nervous disorders and perhaps even for their higher risks for certain physical ailments, such as diabetes and glaucoma. However, he did not attribute this to Jewish inbreeding, as Krafft-Ebing and Erb had done. He pointed out that

Jewish law forbade incest. While marriages between more distant relatives permitted by Jewish law could have caused problems, clearly Krafft-Ebing and Erb meant something else. They meant inbreeding in the racial sense, a phenomenon which had not been scientifically confirmed. Engländer objected, arguing that historians of the Jews recognized that they had mixed with other nations over the years, and scientists plainly disputed the existence of a typical Jewish race. Furthermore, he argued that Americans, the neurasthenics par excellence, were a mixed race. Therefore, he advised his audience, "You can accordingly, Ladies and Gentlemen, freely marry your daughters with Jewish sons and the reverse, only look, if you have the welfare of your grandchild in mind, more for the physical quality of the family and for a calm, secure existence of the couple, than for wealth and social rank at all cost." [128] In his discussion of other diseases which afflicted the Jews, he continued to emphasize the external factors, attributing them to the nerve-racking struggle of competition for material and spiritual existence. He concluded that the Jews needed land, air, and light for physical regeneration. [129] In this sense, Engländer is similar to the Jewish Italian criminologist Cesare Lombroso (1835–1909). Lombroso, in his work *Anti-Semitism and the Jews in the Light of Modern Science* (1893), accepted the notion of a Jewish tendency toward certain mental illnesses, and furthermore linked both Jews and women to the criminal and to prostitution, but rejected racial explanations, attributing it instead to persecution. [130]

In addressing the issue of the racial qualities of the Jewish people, the Austrian physician Ignaz Zollschan (1877–1948) argued that the Jews did in fact comprise a pure race. Born in Erlach, Lower Austria, Zollschan studied medicine at the University of Vienna but achieved his greatest recognition as an anthropologist, and later as a vocal opponent of the Nazis. [131] In his 1910 book, he argued that the Jew was a member of a *Kulturvolk* which possessed an intellectual and spiritual tradition at least as great as that of the Germans. [132] Zollschan vehemently denied that the Jews had mixed with other populations during the two and a half thousand years of exile. [133] He attributed certain physical characteristics, such as small chests, weak musculature, pale coloration, and a melancholic look, to circumstances and environment. He also argued that Jewish ritual laws and sexual-hygiene practices demonstrated that Judaism had the capacity for regeneration from within.

Zollschan also accepted the argument that the Jews were more prone to mental illness than the non-Jews, but not for the reasons commonly given. "The Jew, who possesses a delicate and sensitively organized nervous system, which reacts with greater sensibility to stimulus than the nerves of a robust peasant, is therefore not far from a Neurasthenic."[134] He attributed the higher rate of mental illness not to inbreeding, but to a higher rate of progressive paralysis (syphilis), resulting from their long isolation from this infection. "The syphilitic infection first began as a result of assimilation, and became epidemic among the Jews."[135] This view reinforced his anti-assimilationist stance and his position against mixed marriages and in favor of the preservation of Jewish racial purity. As a Zionist, he believed that the only solution for the unhealthy state of modern Jewry was the dissolution of the Diaspora and the establishment of a Jewish national homeland.[136]

Despite the originality of Zollschan's theory regarding the Jewish race problem, his views on women did not deviate significantly from those of his contemporaries. For example, in accounting for his use of a table on female racial attributes, he remarked, "Because of course ordinarily for the woman the racial character stands out more sharply, in contrast to the man for whom individuality is more pronounced, this table is very suitable for a comparative examination of the races."[137]

For Viennese Jewish physicians, gender did not play a large role in their defense of the Jews in the face of medical stereotypes. This is not surprising, considering that they faced an anti-Semitic environment and first and foremost desired to reject the notion of Jewish racial inferiority. Despite their critical stance with regard to stereotypes of race, they had a tendency to embrace stereotypes of gender. When the topic of Jewish women came up, their views were predictable and in line with those of their contemporaries. Jewish women had become degenerate and prone to certain illnesses due to the influences of assimilation and the inherently weak nature of women in general. On the other hand, while they criticized some aspects of ghetto life, they praised and idealized the position of women in traditional Judaism. They only criticized the early age of marriages in traditional domestic life as responsible for Jewish women's tendency for certain diseases. Primarily, they believed that foreign influences of modern decadent European culture caused Jewish women to succumb to mental and physical illnesses.

Jewish Self-Hatred

A final group of Jews responded to the Viennese anti-Semitic stereotype by accepting it fully. The phenomenon of Jewish self-hatred has received a great deal of scholarly attention, beginning with Theodor Lessing in 1930 and continuing to the present.[138] Jewish self-hatred as a general phenomenon and the philosophical theories of Otto Weininger, the quintessential Viennese self-hating Jew, are extremely complex topics which have received extensive treatment. For this reason, the discussion presented here will focus specifically on the image of the Jewish woman according to Weininger and his contemporary, Arthur Trebitsch, a topic which has not yet been explored and is directly relevant to the other material in this chapter.

Otto Weininger (1880–1903) is known for having linked Jews and women in his immensely popular work, *Sex and Character* (1903), and for his subsequent suicide on October 4, 1903, at the age of twenty-three. Like many other figures of his time, Weininger feared the feminine element inside himself, and also the so-called feminization of Viennese culture in the form of excessive ornamentation and decadence, dichotomy of soul and body, materialism, and in general simplistic thought. All that was negative was "feminized." Thus Weininger, who also feared the Jewish element inside himself and the Judaization of Viennese culture and society, saw the Jew as excessively feminine. As such, his views coincided with the dominant ideology which prevailed in Vienna during his lifetime. His work was a best-seller and established him as a "serious contributor to the discourse about the relationship between race and gender at the beginning of the century."[139] Weininger aimed in the work to draw an analogy between the male-female scale (borrowed from Schopenhauer) and the Aryan-Jew scale. Anyone could possess these traits to varying degrees; race and gender were frames of mind which could be altered.

The idea of bisexuality transformed Weininger's work, leading him to the theory that all individuals were made up of a mixture of masculine and feminine substance. At the same time, he broke with the tradition of experimental psychology of Ernst Mach and Richard Avenarius, which dominated in Vienna, and turned increasingly toward a more philosophical approach. His view of women grew out of his interpretation of the philosophy of Immanuel Kant. He viewed masculinity and femininity as two opposite poles, positive and negative. Masculinity was Being, while femininity was non-Being. He defined the woman in terms of sexuality, and she existed only for men. According to this view, women needed to renounce their sexuality in order to become human.[140] Weininger applied this theory of masculinity and femininity to the Jews, identifying Judaism with femininity.

He linked the sexuality of Jews and women in terms of three distinct characteristics: (1) femininity, (2) sense of community/lack of individuality, and (3) preoccupation with sex. Judaism, according to Weininger, was saturated with femininity. "It would not be difficult to make a case for the view that the Jew is more saturated with femininity than the Aryan, to such an extent that the most manly Jew is more feminine than the least manly Aryan."[141]

Jews and women both thought of themselves as groups rather than as individuals, according to Weininger. "Like women, Jews tend to adhere together, but they do not associate as free independent individuals mutually respecting each other's individuality."[142] He also believed that Jews and women did not interest themselves in the fates of other Jews or women, but defended the race or sex as a whole. The Jews lacked barriers between individuals and were "at the opposite pole" from aristocrats, for whom the preservation of limits between individuals was the leading idea. He also claimed that the family loomed large for Jews and women. "The family, in the biological sense, is feminine and maternal in its origin, and has no relation to the State or to society. The fusion, the continuity of the members of the family, reaches its highest point amongst the Jews."[143] Jews and women were "habitual match-makers" and Jews rarely married for love. Jews and women lacked humor, the antithesis of eroticism.

According to Weininger, women found a center in men, but Jews had no center at all. The Jew believed in nothing and took nothing seriously. In essence, Weininger believed that the Jew was more "feminine" than the woman. He feared that Jews and women would gain control and destroy humanity. "Judaism, at the present day, has reached its highest point since the time of Herod. Judaism is the spirit of modern life. Sexuality is accepted, and contemporary ethics sing the praises of pairing . . . It is the Jew and the woman who are the apostles of pairing to bring guilt on humanity."[144]

According to John Hoberman, Weininger suppressed the distinction between Jewish males and females.[145] He defines a syndrome called the "Jewish male predicament" to which Weininger conforms by unloading a set of anxieties about being Jewish and male onto an abstraction he called "Jewry" or "the Jew." This basically amounts to the perceived inability of the Jewish male to fulfill a masculine role and to experience masculinity.[146] For the Jewish woman there was no such conflict between being female and Jewish. Therefore the Jewish woman should be subject to the same criticisms as the woman in general, for Weininger.

Nevertheless, Weininger's contempt for Jewish women went even beyond that for the non-Jewish female. Non-Jewish women had the benefit of masculine men as a balancing force against their femininity. He asserted, "Amongst Christians even the daughters stand a little further apart from the family circle than happens with Jewesses, and more frequently take up some calling which isolates them and gives them independent interests."[147] The Jewish woman was the quintessential wife because she did not need to put on an appearance of depth in order to attract the feminine Jewish man.

> The fact that no woman in the world represents the idea of the wife so completely as the Jewess (and not only in the eyes of Jews) still further supports the comparison between Jews and women. In the case of the Aryans, the metaphysical qualities of the male are part of his sexual attraction for the woman, as so, in a fashion, she puts on an appearance of these. The Jew, on the other hand, has no transcendental quality, and in the shaping and molding of the wife leaves the natural tendencies of the female nature a more unhampered sphere; and the Jewish woman, accordingly, plays the part required of her, as house-mother or odalisque, as Cybele or Cyprian, in the fullest way.[148]

Weininger's criticism of the Jewish woman may have been fueled in part by his resentment of the more positive portrayal of Jewish women in the racial folklore of the era.[149]

Weininger's ideas influenced Arthur Trebitsch (1880–1927), a Viennese Jew who shared his antipathy for Jews and women. He completely identified with Weininger. He suffered from paranoia and believed that he was the victim of a Jewish conspiracy. In 1919, he suffered a massive paranoid episode. "He felt himself pierced by electromagnetic rays beamed at him by this Jewish conspiracy and fled from house to house in Berlin seeking refuge from these eternally persecuting Jews."[150] He wrote literature as well as cultural-historical and philosophical works. Inspired by Weininger, he demonized women in his literary works. Female characters lacked souls, were immoral, and lied. Sexuality and instincts ruled them like animals. In one of his novellas, *Der Herr Professor*, the hero was destroyed by two women, a Jewish woman "with the wild lust of her race" and a Bohemian girl "with the violent wildness of her nation."[151] In his major work, *Geist und Judentum* (1919), he argued that the Jews' psyche was pathologically unique because it was rooted in the world of the Messiah. He posited that the Jews mis-used language because of their sexual nature. For the Jews, sex was divorced from love.

Trebitsch believed that the Jews invented masturbation and homo-sexuality, mechanically sexual acts lacking any relationship or love between the sexual partners.[152] He claimed that the eroticism of the Jews was rooted and immortalized in the Old Testament, which con-tained an apparent contradiction.

> On the one hand the rigid commandment of fertility and the family sense, but on the other hand the deep perversion of sexual life, not out of overflowing fantasy, but out of a special disconnectedness to the primary experience of love, an empty and secondary view and grasp of sexual procedure, or better still the sexual functional possi-bilities . . . So in fact the Jew is the progenitor of masturbation (there was a man named Onan, etc.) and sodomy and similarly frivolous and fundamentally unimaginative reactions to an all too early un-covered sexual function.[153]

He argued that the essence of the Jewish spirit remained unchanged over thousands of years because "the strict commandment did not turn against sinfulness and unchastity, but only against the senseless mis-use or better said against the useless waste of fertility useful for pro-ductive functions." Hence the Jewish view of the relationship between the sexes was determined by utilitarian rather than emotional consid-erations. The "love" and devotion of the Jews to their wives originated more in habituation to their lives' companions, than in true love.[154] Ac-cording to Trebitsch, the eroticism of the Jews persisted despite so-ciological transformations, such as emancipation and assimilation. It became expressed in different ways. For example, he argued, it was a Jew (Arthur Schnitzler) who discovered the female type, the "Susse Mädel" in literature.[155]

Jewish self-haters like Weininger and Trebitsch took many of the ideas expressed in the medical writings about Jews to an extreme. The prevalence of notions of a Jewish racial predisposition to sexuality and the linkage between Jews and women in fin de siècle Vienna, combined with their own troubled psyches, led them not only to embrace these ideas but to further propagate them.

Conclusion

The climate of rising anti-Semitism in Vienna, with its heavy sexual emphasis, led Viennese Jews in the fields of medicine, psychology, and psychoanalysis to address Jewish sexuality in their works. To varying extents they challenged the racial basis of negative stereotypes of the male Jew, while embracing negative stereotypes of women and Jewish women.

Although Freud suppressed the Jewishness of the women in his case studies, making it difficult to distinguish Freud's image of the Jewish woman from his image of women in general, his increasing focus on the masculinity complex indicates that the image of femininity based on the masculine Jewish woman complimented the stereotype of the effeminate Jewish male. The fact that many of Freud's female patients were Jewish also supports this conclusion. Freud's understanding of the Jewish woman, therefore, was indeed influenced by the Viennese cultural context. In response to the prevailing views of Jewish sexuality, Freud's disciples, Rank, Wittels, and Adler, were ambivalent toward Judaism, although Rank and Wittels ultimately reconciled themselves with Judaism and argued in favor of the free expression of sexuality as a sign of health. In contrast, Adler distanced himself from Judaism and tried to de-emphasize the sexual element of psychoanalysis. Wittels and Adler both initially found the feminist movement and other attempts on the part of women to attain equal rights and education to be symptoms of hysteria. Rank had a more favorable attitude toward women, seeing them as having preserved their natural sexuality in the face of civilized morality, like the Jews. He also shifted the focus of Freud's Oedipal theory toward the mother, creating a less male-centered view of human development. Nevertheless, in his early work he criticized Jewish women as materialistic and promiscuous.

Viennese Jewish psychiatrists and medical practitioners, such as Moritz Benedikt, Martin Engländer, and Ignaz Zollschan, addressed the arguments found in Viennese medicine about the Jewish predisposition for certain illnesses. In this context, most of their work did not distinguish between male and female Jews, but generally challenged the view of Jewish racial inferiority and inbreeding. While Benedikt accepted that Jews were more neurotic, he attributed it to the history of oppression rather than to race or inbreeding. Still, he singled out Jewish women as often becoming eccentric and perverse, and while rejecting racial stereotypes, he embraced stereotypes of gender.

Engländer similarly attributed the nervous disorders of Jews to historical and socio-economic factors. He believed that Jewish women were susceptible to certain diseases due to the custom of early marriages, but also saw other traditional Jewish customs as favorable for women. Zollschan attributed the supposed Jewish tendency toward mental illness to an external rather than a racial influence. He argued that after a long isolation, the sudden exposure to syphilis was detrimental to their health. He blamed Jewish mental illness on assimilation, the opposite of the Viennese view, which attributed Jewish mental illness to inbreeding. Like his contemporaries, though, he incorporated gender stereotypes in his views of Jewish women. The challenging of negative stereotypes of the Jewish "race" was accompanied by the absorption of negative stereotypes of women, including Jewish women.

Influenced by the Viennese cultural context, which drew parallels between Jews and femininity, Weininger and Trebitsch feared feminization of culture and transgression of proper gender boundaries embodied in feminism, and the Jewish influence which had been unleashed by Jewish emancipation and assimilation. Recognizing that his own anxieties and crises of identity were intimately connected to his animosity toward women and Jews, Weininger ultimately turned against himself. Rather than using gender stereotypes alone to describe the Jewish woman, as was the case for Jews in Viennese medicine and psychoanalysis, he created a stereotype of Jewish women which reaffirmed the general discourse of gender and race in Vienna. Embracing the stereotype of the effeminate Jewish male, he concluded that the Jewish woman personified the negative qualities of women because she had no masculine counterpart to balance her femininity.

Jews in psychoanalysis and medicine experienced new possibilities in their professional lives, coupled with intense hostility on the part of non-Jewish society. Various individuals developed different methods of coping with this predicament. While most tried to challenge the prevailing stereotypes of Jews, some incorporated these as well. In these fields, sexuality and gender became central to their understanding of what it meant to be Jewish. The preoccupation with sexuality in Jewish psychoanalysis and medicine was analogous to the preoccupation with the Jewish woman in the works of the communal leaders and Zionists, in that it was characteristically Viennese.

6 *Literature and Culture*

The flourishing of Viennese culture at the turn of the century has been the subject of many works, and the Jews' role in this phenomenon has commanded a great deal of attention as well.[1] Despite the extensive treatment of these topics, the role of the Jewish woman in Viennese culture has not been adequately addressed. This final chapter will discuss the representations of Jewish women and their participation in Viennese literature, theater, journalism, and art. Viennese Jewish women found an arena for their creativity in literature and culture on the one hand, while they were often portrayed with stereotypes by Jewish male writers on the other hand. The Jewish female character played a central role in much of the literature produced in fin de siècle Vienna by Jews and non-Jews, in ghetto tales, and in the writings of the *Jung Wien* circle. As in the areas explored in the previous chapters, images of Jewish women in literature and culture shaped the extent and nature of their contributions to culture.

Jewish Women as Writers

By becoming writers and participating in the arts, Jewish women rejected bourgeois notions of femininity which did not consider writing an appropriate occupation for women. A large number of Austrian Jewish women pursued careers in art, music, theater, and writing.[2] Young Jewish women often took art or music lessons or wrote stories as a hobby. Bertha Pappenheim, for example, published a book of short stories in 1890 and a play about women's rights in 1899, under a male pseudonym.[3] Jewish women also became actresses, concert singers, painters, art historians, and photographers, and actively patronized the arts.[4] Although the contributions of Jewish men to Viennese culture have received much more attention, Jewish women's role in culture was notable. Cultural creativity provided another outlet for Jewish women to navigate their way through modernity.

In contrast to the Zionist or psychoanalytic movements, the course taken by these women did not provide an obvious avenue for them to identify as Jews. In fact, in a sense, by embracing Austro-German culture as women they distanced themselves from the Jewish community. Rarely did these women pursue Jewish topics in their work. The Jewish community for its part at times expressed disdain for women writers, possibly providing a disincentive for Jewish women to become writers. For example, an article condemning modern Jewish women writers, whose works "strayed in impropriety," appeared in *Die Neuzeit* in 1902. "They give the impression of wanting to solve the high moral problems of marriage in narrative tones and with false solemnity put on airs as reformers of the world."[5]

Like Jewish women in the university and politics, Jewish female writers in Vienna often came from assimilated backgrounds. For example, the poet Betty Paoli (Elizabeth Glück) was born Jewish but was buried in a Catholic cemetery.[6] Veza Canetti considered herself a socialist, but knew that others considered her a Jew. She wrote in Vienna for the *Arbeiter Zeitung* under three pseudonyms, because of latent anti-Semitism which prevented publishing so many stories from a Jewish woman.[7] One of the most prolific and popular Jewish female writers, Vicki Baum, author of *Grand Hotel*, never explicitly wrote about Jewish themes. Dagmar Lorenz suggests that she perceived that discussing the Jews' special interests would not have been well received, and therefore she only hinted at the Jewish identity of some characters.[8] In her memoirs, which dealt extensively with her early years in Vienna, she did not mention her Jewish background.[9] While some chose to pursue their art in feminine ways, by writing for female audiences or by restricting their cultural activities to a hobby rather than a profession, others incorporated feminist ideology into their work.

Ida Punitzer Barber (1842–1931), a prominent advocate of the women's movement who came to Vienna in 1880 from Berlin, where she had dedicated herself to girls' education, provides an exception to the general trend of maintaining a distance from Judaism. Not only did she raise the question of the role of women and the impact of feminism in her work, but she also chose to write about Jewish themes. In 1872, she began writing stories about Jewish life. She also participated in the establishment of many organizations, including the *Vereines d. Schriftstellerinnen und Künstlerinnen* (Society for Women Writers and Artists) in 1886. She wrote many prize-winning novels and enjoyed a large readership.[10] In her stories, she portrayed different types of Jewish female characters, and conveyed the message that women find happiness through their own lives rather than through men.

In her story "Toledo," the two daughters of the widowed free-thinker Simon Lewy, Rosa and Paula, represented different Jewish female types.[11] The idealistic sister, Rosa, married for love, while the practical sister, Paula, married for money. Rosa married Toledo, a young scholar and preacher, but despite their mutual love they endured great hardship. At first his free-thinking and reform philosophy brought him success, but when he began publishing his ideas, traditional Orthodox Jews of Prague opposed him and brought them to financial ruin. Rosa decided that she must work, although her upbringing and education had not prepared her for this. She became more practical and less idealistic as a result, and encouraged her sister to marry a rich man. While Paula gradually grew to love her husband, Rosa now faced the prospect of separation from Toledo. When he decided to go to New York in search of a receptive audience for his ideas, Rosa was determined to manage on her own.

> She, the delicate woman still in the blossom of her youth, who, though filled with independence from her home, was externally accustomed to the protection of her spouse, to whom she clung like ivy on the stump of an oak tree. She could not imagine the possibility of a long separation. And how did this weakness fit in with her ideas about the emancipation of woman? In her theories, she gave the woman full equality with the man, and now, where practice was concerned, she too still had petty prejudices to overcome.[12]

She opened a boarding school for girls, which earned an excellent reputation, and found her work rewarding. Finally the time came for Rosa to join her husband in New York. On the journey, her youngest daughter became ill and died. Then Rosa became ill from grief and also died. After her death Toledo began to question his faith and also became ill. Ironically, this misfortune became Paula's salvation. She had recently become widowed, and so she took it upon herself to care for the children and Toledo. "Mild and radiant, she was active in newly created circles, and she found new happiness, which was not granted her in marriage, in the care of the young orphans."[13]

Two themes underlie Barber's story; first, material wealth does not bring happiness, and second, deep and lasting happiness could come to a woman only through her independence. Although both women in the story created their own happiness, they did so within the boundaries of traditional feminine roles, such as the education of the children and caring for the sick.

Similar in its message was a piece by Barber which appeared in *Die Neuzeit* describing women who prayed at her synagogue on Yom Kippur (the Day of Atonement).[14] They came to the temple, adorned with expensive gowns, gems, and pearls, yet they were not necessarily happy in spite of their wealth. "There was the free-religious Frau F. next to her the pretty-intellectual professor's widow, then the Orthodox wife of a rich merchant, who out of piety not once allowed herself to wear her own hair; they all stood in the same prayers to the same God, Whom they worshipped in such different ways." She described the behavior of the "praying women" with irony. For example, she portrayed a beautiful once-famous singer who converted to Judaism out of love for her husband—or for his money. The woman rustled through the aisles with her burdensome silk dress, loudly took her seat, and surveyed the praying men, casting an affectionate look toward her husband. Once she sat down and found her place in her lilac-velvet-bound prayer book, she began an intimate discussion with her neighbor. "What a radiant fire disseminated from the diamonds of both these ladies. I believe that the worries of one hundred poor families could have been taken away with the proceeds!"

However, all the glamour of the gems did not make these women happy, she observed. One pretty young woman, the wife of a stockbroker, appeared far more beautiful and bejeweled than the other women. Nevertheless, the tears in her eyes showed great pain, "which neither riches nor external attractiveness could banish." "One knows all too well, how she was forced to marry, to sacrifice her beauty and youth to a rich stock broker, while her heart belonged to a brilliant artist." Her husband wanted only to show her off on walks, at balls, and in the theater. Another woman mourned the death of her only son. Next to her sat a pretty young woman, happily married, except that her marriage remained childless.

According to Barber, women had an "active susceptibility for religious solemnity," and took part in the main prayer (the Shema) with all their emotions. Women had different ways of serving God. Older uneducated women, who did not understand Hebrew, spent the entire day in the synagogue in their own religious ecstasy. Another woman spent only an hour in services but gave thirty meal tickets to be distributed to the poor. Barber concluded her sketch with a familiar reminder of the religious importance of the Jewish woman as the transmitter of Judaism.

Israel's women were in every time the guardians of family life and with this domestic happiness: in this lies her cultural historical merit which is not to be underestimated. She steps before God full of devotion and transmits the tranquility, which gathered in her chest, the higher dedication, which she believed was received in prayer to God, to her home, her husband, her children, in genuine piety, like magic, which illuminates the prose of everyday life with poetic breath, even if she does not uphold dogma.

For Barber, Jewish women had a greater inner piety than men, even when they abandoned strict adherence to the law. While she insisted on independence as a source for women's happiness, she nevertheless incorporated prevailing notions of femininity into her literary work.

Images of the Jewish Woman in Literature and Culture

All the Viennese literary genres, including journalism, feuilletons, ghetto stories, travel literature, plays, novellas and novels, depicted Jewish women. Jewish themes attracted non-Jewish Austrian writers, such as Friedrich Kaiser (1814–1874), Ludwig Anzengruber (1839–1889), Marie von Ebner-Eschenbach (1830–1916), Robert Hamerling (1830–1899), Ferdinand von Saar (1833–1906), and Leopold von Sacher-Masoch (1836–1895). On the other hand, prominent male Jewish writers of the period, such as Peter Altenberg (1859–1919), Arthur Schnitzler (1862–1931), Felix Dörmann (1870–1928), Felix Salten (1869–1945), Karl Kraus (1874–1936), Richard Beer-Hofmann (1866–1945), Stefan Zweig (1881–1942), and Joseph Roth (1894–1939), included female Jewish characters in their works less frequently.

Earlier Jewish writers, such as Leopold Kompert (1822–1888), Karl Emil Franzos (1848–1904), Eduard Kulke (1831–1897), and Ludwig August Frankl (1810–1894), drew on their experiences of emancipation in describing the transformation of Jewish society. Some later less prominent writers, such as Max Grünfeld (1856–1933), Heinrich York-Steiner (1859–1935), and Hermann Menkes (1863–1931), carried on the tradition of writing stories about the conflict of tradition and modernity. Female Jewish characters played key roles in these stories.

While Jewish writers tended to view the western Jewish woman as ideological, intellectual, and materialistic, the eastern Jewish woman was portrayed as exotic, dark, and "oriental." More than in other areas of Jewish scholarship, a tendency to romanticize the Jewish woman influenced the images of them in literature. As a result, contradictory images emerged. For example, while some writers portrayed the Jewish woman as the instigator of assimilation, others saw her as clinging to obsolete vestiges of religious practice which had long since been abandoned by Jewish men. As more spiritual beings, female characters had a greater tendency to fall at the extremes rather than linger in an indifferent fog of apathy and confusion about their identities. They were either the anticipators of change or the reminders of a past world.

Ghetto Tales

Ghetto tales (*Ghettogeschichte*), most popular between 1850 and 1880, often focused on the conflict between tradition and modernity. The writers of these stories fell between two extremes: a rejection of traditional Judaism in favor of European culture, and a nostalgic, idealized view of the tradition, with reluctant recognition of western supremacy. Jewish female characters played a special role in these stories as an integral part of their plots and messages.[15] The problematic of Jewish traditional culture and its lack of regard for women led many female characters to look beyond the traditional world for fulfillment. As victims of oriental Jewish customs, such as arranged marriages and the cutting of the bride's hair on the wedding day, they were naturally attracted to modern ideas.

Born in Bohemia, Leopold Kompert was the first major writer of ghetto fiction in German.[16] Arriving in Vienna at the age of sixteen, he became active in Viennese civic life, an official of the *Kultusgemeinde* (Jewish community organization), and a member during the 1850s of the primarily Jewish journalist club, *Condordia*. Along with Simon Szanto (1819–1882), with whom he edited *Die Neuzeit*, and Adolf Jellinek, he supported the trend toward religious liberalism in Vienna.[17]

Kompert published several collections of ghetto stories based on his childhood life in Bohemia. The themes of Jewish marriage and intermarriage were central in many of these stories. He commented to Adolf Neustadt, "in most of my female characters there lives a trait, which is taken from the spirit of my mother."[18] They suffered because they did not find a role in traditional Judaism. In a fragment from his posthumous works, "Auf der Beschau" (At the Inspection), seventeen-year-old Golde Mandelzweig's teacher tells her that Judaism lacked the female. It was a religion for men, and held the female sex in contempt.[19] Somewhat ambivalent toward the question of intermarriage, Kompert advocated respect and loyalty for tradition while sympathetically portraying Jewish characters that fell in love with Christians.

The story "Kinder des Randars" (The Randar's Children) revolved around a village Jew and his family.[20] The Randar, his daughter, Hannele, and his son, Moschele (later Moritz), interacted with Honza, who was studying to be a priest, and the Jerusalem-bound "schnorrer" (beggar) Mendel Wilna. Like Kompert's mother, the Randar's wife enlisted the help of the powerful Count in order to convince her husband to send Moschele to secondary school. Hannele fell in love with Honza, a classmate of Moschele's who later became his bitter enemy. When the Randar imprisoned Honza's father for burning down the barn, Honza vindictively sought Hannele's conversion.

At the climax of the story, when the Randar tried to find a husband for the already twenty-four-year-old Hannele, she ran off to the priest to become a Christian. All of her conversations with Honza sunk in when she faced the proposition of a traditional *shidduch* (arranged marriage). Moritz prevented her conversion at the last minute with the argument, "Do you want to bring sorrow to your father, Hannele? Did he not always love you more than me? What should he do now, if his most loved child treats him so?"[21] In conclusion, Hannele's fate was tragic. The priest cursed her, and the rift with her father could not be mended. When she returned he would not speak to her. In a short time he died from the shock of Hannele's near-apostasy, and she remained unmarried.

Earlier in the story, immediately preceding the chapter entitled "Hannele," Moritz expressed Hannele's dilemma as a Jewish woman.

> What our religion lacks is the female. Strictly speaking women have no position in it at all! Miriam, Deborah and Judith should stand higher in it, and be vividly outstanding. I am not thinking of Mary! But I am always astonished, how Moses, who had such high elucidations of female essence in his mother and sister, had such little consideration for it. He should have appointed Priestesses, as he had made Priests and Levites. Then a part of that inflexibility, which only now is beginning to soften, would have fallen away. Women understand how to moderate everywhere; they would have drawn the difficult material to themselves and made it physically softer. Thus Judaism is only a religion for men.[22]

Hence the moral of the story; Hannele wandered in foreign ways because Judaism failed to offer her anything. The message of Kompert's female characters clearly reflected his belief in the need for religious liberalism and reform.

More unequivocally than Kompert, Karl Emil Franzos disparaged Jewish religious life in Eastern Europe in his ghetto stories. He characterized the ghetto as an oriental, superstitious, "half-Asian" culture. In his representation of women, he stressed their victimization due to the superstitious and irrational culture of the ghetto.[23] Therefore, it is not surprising that he portrayed female characters as more enlightened and eager to assimilate than male characters.

Born in Czortkow (on the Russo-Galician border) in 1848, Franzos was baffled by the ethnic conflicts of Eastern Galicia. His father told him: "You are, by nationality, not a Pole, a Ruthenian or a Jew. You are a German. Your religion—you are a Jew."[24] He went on to study law in German-speaking Austria. He encountered anti-Semitism and fell in love with a Christian girl who rejected him. When denied a judgeship for which he was qualified, he turned to journalism and drama. He worked for Vienna's great daily paper, the *Neue Freie Presse*, contributing extraordinarily popular stories of East European Jewry.[25]

In his most celebrated work, *The Jews of Barnow* (1877), Franzos described the lives of Jews in the fictional town of Barnow. Characters and themes, such as the treatment of love and marriage, ran through the series of novellas. He saw Jewish marriages as business contracts in which love played no part. For example, in the story "Nameless Graves," the idea that "Lea with the long hair" could choose to marry Ruben "because I like him" was incomprehensible to the ghetto-dwellers. "It was an unheard of reason for a Podolian Jewess to give: so no one believed that it could be the real reason."[26]

In the end, Lea was buried in a nameless grave, according to the custom for sinners. Her story demonstrated the sad consequences of "fanatical Eastern Judaism" on the life of a gentle, modest Jewish girl.

> Lea was vain, but she was thoroughly good and modest. Jewish women are, as a rule, kind, charitable, and sympathetic with others; but Lea was even more so than the generality—so the poor used to bless her and revere her. The girl's great weakness was that she was in love with her own beauty, and especially with that of her splendid hair.[27]

When she married, she secretly kept her long hair. After losing two babies, and becoming pregnant for the third time, she insisted on fasting on Yom Kippur. She fainted and in the efforts to revive her, her "scheitel" (wig) became displaced, making her hair visible. This scandalized the town and the rabbi put Ruben in "cherem" (excommunicated him). When a healthy baby boy was born to the unfortunate couple, masked men broke into their home and cut off her hair, and both mother and child died from their fright.

Other of Franzos's female characters reacted to the prospect or reality of a loveless traditional Jewish marriage by falling in love with non-Jewish characters. Love between a Jew and a non-Jew became a common theme of many of his stories, for example in "Chane." He described Chane, later Christine, as an oriental beauty. "Her figure is straight and slender, and though her carriage is proud, she is extremely graceful. Her features are finely cut, and her dreamy dark eyes are unfathomably deep. But her most striking beauty is her rich olive complexion. Her appearance conjures up Zuleima and Zuleika, and the enchanted beauties of the East." [28] Chane's marriage to Nathan Silberstein was arranged according to Jewish custom, and though the couple grew to like one another, they were not in love. "They knew nothing of love except that Christians, previous to marriage, fell in love; and what concern had a Jew in Christian usages." [29]

Nathan recognized that he loved Chane only when she and the Christian district judge fell in love. He decided that he must allow her to marry the Christian man whom she loved. Nathan blamed the practice of arranging marriages without consulting the couple for his misfortune. "But oh, is a wife like other property, as I have always thought? Is she no more than any other chattel, such as an ornament or a house? Has she not a will like every other human being? And has that will ever been consulted? . . . That was the sin, and now we are suffering from its consequences." [30] Chane benefited from Nathan's gentleness, finding happiness in her new life. But the story had a tragic element as well, in that her father never forgave her. "My daughter Chane was a beautiful Jewess; but I do not know the heathen (goy) Frau Christine." [31]

"The Shylock of Barnow" told the tragic tale of the beautiful daughter of Moses Freudenthal. The narrator recounted the events which led up to the daughter's downfall. How were the people who produced the Song of Songs, the "eternal hymn of love," or the story of Ruth, "the most beautiful idyll of femininity," reduced to such benighted social conditions?[32] Freudenthal was condemned because he opposed his daughters' attempts to attain a German education.

Franzos pursued this theme further in the novel *Judith Trachtenberg* (1891), set in Eastern Galicia during the reactionary period before the 1848 revolutions.[33] The main character, Judith, grew up in an environment open to German culture in an acculturated family. Her father, Nathaniel, was clearly an allusion to Lessing's *Nathan der Weise* (Nathan the Wise).[34] As a result of her contact with the upper ranks of gentile society, Judith met and fell in love with the Polish aristocrat, Graf Agenor Baranowski. Florian Krobb describes the tensions which complicated their relationship. "The unfolding love story sharply highlights the limits of assimilation, the rejection which the individual faces in Galician gentile society, the unfortunate role that the authorities play in this assimilatory experiment, and the thresholds to cross before a fruitful symbiosis can be reached."[35] The circumstances of their relationship and marriage prevented her from attaining happiness. She lost her religious identity, but at the same time she never completely gained acceptance in non-Jewish society.

Judith's attempts at assimilation failed. She and her husband were forced to leave the country after their marriage, and she had to deny her Jewish identity. "I am not even sure of my own name anymore," she declared, as she had adopted a meaningless Christian name with her fake baptism. "One needs a language to pray in; I have forgotten my old language and I do not know the new one." The cost of assimilation, loss of home and identity, proved to be too great, and in the end she committed suicide. The novel suggested the need for cultural, educational, and political reform, which would allow Jewish assimilation without sacrificing Jewish identity. She was buried in a Jewish cemetery with the inscription "Judith Gräfin Baranowska, the daughter of Nathan ben Menasse of the Jewish people. She died in darkness, but day will dawn at last." Only after her death was the heroine able to fulfill her life's struggle: acceptance into non-Jewish society while maintaining her religious identity.[36]

Why did Franzos choose a female protagonist in this novel, in contrast to his other novels, *Moschko of Parma* and *Der Pojaz*? *Judith Trachtenberg* was unique in that Franzos directed his criticism at the obstacles to assimilation posed by the Habsburg State, rather than those limitations which the eastern Jews imposed on themselves. Here, he portrayed the Jews as enlightened and accepting. The protagonists of his other novels, Moschko and Sender, were rejected by the Jewish community because they failed to conform to the traditional Jewish ideal of manhood, i.e., studying Torah. Moschko proved inept at learning the Hebrew letters, but excelled physically "like a Christian child." Sender became an outcast because he learned German and pursued a career as an actor. Judith's attempt at assimilation, however, was not hindered but rather encouraged by her father. Her assimilation, which consisted of learning German and falling in love with a non-Jew, did not challenge Jewish femininity in the same way that Moschko's or Sender's activities defied Jewish masculinity. The Jewish woman's assimilation did not raise opposition from the Jewish community in comparison to the Jewish man's assimilation.[37] Nevertheless, Judith's attempt at assimilation ultimately failed because of non-Jewish obstacles.

Ludwig August Frankl (1810–1894), secretary of the *Kultusgemeinde* and the *Israelitische Blindeninstitut* (Israelite Institute for the Blind), wrote *Nach Jerusalem* (translated as "The Jews in the East") based on his travels.[38] Although his writing described his experiences and observations during travel, it shared some similarities to the fictional depictions of life in the "ghettos" of Eastern Europe. He described the oriental customs of the eastern Jews as a western observer. His account of Jewish women in the East especially resembled the images from fictional accounts of Kompert and Franzos. He portrayed them as victims of oriental religious customs. For example, he remarked on their lack of hygiene.

> . . . in this, the first Eastern city which I had visited, I was led to the conclusion, which subsequent experience tended to confirm, that the Oriental has no sense of cleanliness, except so far as regards his own person . . . Some women and girls were sitting in one of the larger cells, and picking maize, so as to have it clean for the baking of the Passover bread. The attire of the women, the hair of the girls hanging down in twenty scattered tresses, and their hands anything but white, induced the belief that the maize was more likely to be dirtied than cleaned.[39]

In another instance, his description of an eastern Jewish woman evoked a sense of oriental exoticism, also similar to the images found in fiction.

> Among the women, there was one singularly, strikingly beautiful. While the rest were clinging to our clothes and shrieking for alms,

there stood a young woman at the door of her cell, who did not beg; her lofty figure was dressed in a bright-blue tattered robe, secured at the waist by a parti-colored girdle; her bust, which might have been cut out of marble, was imperfectly covered by a yellow silk chemise; a piece of yellow cloth, a small stripe of embroidered woollen, was worn over one of her shoulders. Her brownish hair was covered by a white veil, worn like a turban, with the ends, which were spangled in imitation of gold, hanging loosely on each side of the head. Her head belonged to that style of beauty which is marked by sublime repose. She looked as if a statue of this once noble palace had been overlooked, and still stood forth in all its original beauty, with only its drapery slightly injured by the lapse of time. She was the only beautiful woman that I saw in the East.[40]

He also used oriental imagery in his account of a "child-woman" only twelve years old. He concluded that they all started out beautiful, but Eastern customs ruined them. "How soon will this beautiful human blossom, plucked by the sad customs of the East before it has attained the size of a full-blown rose, wither!"[41]

Eduard Kulke (1831–1897), the Viennese writer and music critic, wrote stories about life in the Moravian ghetto.[42] He also focused on conflicts in Judaism, such as the rift between enlightened and Orthodox Jews, and love between Christians and Jews. However, while he clearly advocated for a certain level of religious reform, his characters maintained strong Jewish affiliations. In the story "Eigene Haare" (Her Own Hair), Jewish women played out both sides of the conflict between tradition and modernity. Rosa (Rochele) Freibürger came from a place where the new style, the "enlightenment," had taken root, and thus she wanted to wear her own hair after her marriage to Jossef Kressel.[43] On one side of the conflict stood Rosa and her twelve-year-old sister-in-law, Blümele, and on the other side stood Frau Kressel, her pious mother-in-law. The rigidity of traditional Judaism had become an integral part of Frau Kressel's personality and she, rather than her son (a very weak character), became the oppressor. She found the idea of a bride refusing to have her hair cut unfathomable.

Kulke portrayed Frau Kressel not merely as a pious woman, but as fanatical. Religious not from insight but from habit, she could not see any boundary between what was allowed and what was prohibited other than that to which she had become accustomed. The slander which was heard in the "Gasse" tormented her. "Am I something of a Prophet Elias? How should I have known that she would wear her own hair? If one had predicted to me, that my daughter-in-law, that my Jossef's wife will wear her own hair, I would have spit in his face, and now—now I must unfortunately thank God, if only the people in the 'Gasse' do not spit in my face." [44] Primarily concerned with how others spoke of and regarded her, she was superficial and insincere.

On the other hand, Kulke portrayed Rosa as a sincere, well-meaning woman who simply did not understand the reaction of her mother-in-law. She felt herself to be a good Jewish woman, and did not see wearing her own hair as a great sin.

> I know what they say; they say, it is nothing but vanity; they say, I pride myself in many respects on my red hair. God knows, that it is different. Vanity! Why do I need to be vain still today? I was not vain as a single girl, should I now be so as a married woman! What do I want then? Do I still want to please other men? Am I going out in search of conquests? God knows my heart. And my husband? I know that I still would please him more with foreign hair than with my own. Why should I be vain? [45]

Young Blümele was the only one who understood Rosa's true reason for not letting her hair be cut, "that I do not tolerate anything false on me." [46] Thus sincerity rather than vanity motivated her refusal to compromise. When Blümele on her wedding day also refused to let her hair be cut, Frau Kressel fainted from shock. Ultimately, she accepted her daughter's decision and forgave her daughter-in-law. The enlightened woman who quoted Schiller and wore her own hair prevailed over her stubborn traditional mother-in-law.

A Jewish woman was also the central character in Kulke's novella *Die schöne Hausiererin* (The Beautiful Peddler), which described the life and loves of a beautiful young Jewess. [47] She became known as "die schöne Hausiererin" because she worked with her mother, who had taken over her husband's business as a merchant after his death, with the innovation that she went to people's homes to do business. Jentele was not only the most beautiful Jewess, but the most beautiful woman among both Jews and Christians in the entire region, and she knew it. She answered her mother with superiority: "If you want to say, what does the *Rittmeister* want from me? He is even a Count and is married and has a beautiful wife, and nevertheless I please him more . . . Still more beautiful than beautiful—answered the girl—did he not say this to me? I do not dare risk passing by him again."[48] When her mother suggested that she was conceited, she answered with a shrug of her shoulders, "I am not conceited, but if the entire world says, a person is *schiker* (drunk), he should go to bed and if everyone calls me: die Schöne Hausiererin, I am 'e wadde' (of course) certainly beautiful."[49]

A non-Jewish man, Sylvester Nedjelka, became attracted to her. This man loved her so desperately that he thought he could not live without her. If she married him, she would have to give up her Jewish identity, but if she refused and he did indeed commit suicide, she would be blamed for his death. After much discussion, she decided to meet with him face to face. During their meeting, he suggested that they move to a place where their union would be permitted. She reacted to the situation with extreme empathy and emotion. She cried, and allowed him to kiss and hold her, but insisted that she could not marry him because she could not abandon her family or her identity. She offered him her friendship, which he accepted. Moritz, her Jewish confidante, was portrayed in a very favorable light as educated, enlightened, worldly, and handsome, in contrast to Jentele's provincial non-Jewish suitor. The Jewish characters, Jentele, her mother, and Moritz, identified as Jews and successfully fulfilled their roles. Jentele, although conscious of her beauty and not ashamed to admit it, still remained a caring and compassionate figure. Kulke's female characters succeeded in modernizing without sacrificing their identity as Jews.

Ghetto Naturalism

While the above authors, born during the first half of the nineteenth century, emphasized the positive effects of assimilation on Jewish women, the next group of Jewish writers, born in the 1850s and 1860s, sympathized more with Jewish tradition. Max Grünfeld, born in Brünn, studied at the Beth Hamidrash and also at the University of Vienna. He was a religious teacher and wrote stories which described life in the ghetto.[50] His stories usually took place on a Jewish holiday, and focused on a character forced to choose between modernity and tradition. This character would at first decide to reject tradition, but would be warned in a dream of the importance of remaining loyal to Judaism. Finally, he would return to tradition, making a large sacrifice in order to remain a Jew. His enthusiasm for Jewish tradition sharply contrasted with the attitudes of earlier writers.

In an article on Jewish women in literature, Grünfeld gave an indication of his support for traditional Judaism.[51] He asserted that while the question of whether women should have the right to participate equally in all aspects of political and social life was debated in his day, women undeniably participated successfully in the literary realm. "The question which should now occupy us, whether women also participate in Jewish literature and science, will perhaps be denied with a doubtful shaking of the head."

Grünfeld wrote that while it may seem that the Talmudists had a low opinion of women, they spoke about honoring women long before the German poets. He claimed that the benediction thanking God for not making one a woman gave rise to a great deal of misunderstanding. The prohibition against teaching one's daughter Torah arose from the fear that a woman who occupied her time with learning would not be able to fulfill her calling as a housewife. Nevertheless, he asserted, examples of learned women abounded in Jewish tradition. He gave the example of Beruria, concluding: "Therefore we see the Talmudists also were fully aware of the scholarship of the woman. And if we read back in the history of our literature, we will find an astonishing number of women, who achieved real importance in the area of literature, the scientific as well as the belles-lettres."[52] He gave examples of Jewish women throughout the centuries who contributed to literature, from Glückel of Hameln to Grace Aguilar, comparing them to the women of the Bible. He concluded that Judaism had already in past centuries resolved some modern questions.

In his stories Grünfeld's female characters had stronger ties to Jewish tradition and used their influence to bring male characters back to Judaism. For example, in a story entitled "How Reb Ahron Missed an Important Historical Moment, a Simple Ghetto-Story from the Year 1848," Reb Ahron's wife Malkah served as the voice of tradition.[53] In the spirit of the ghetto woman stereotype, Malkah completely dominated her husband. She was his master; she was energetic, had a stronger, more courageous nature, and a truly religious disposition. Grünfeld made the reversal of gender roles explicit: "Such a strong-willed character was Malkah, Reb Ahron, as his nature already was so opposite, belonged more to the weaker sex."[54]

A young, energetic Jew, Reb Machel, tried to convince Reb Ahron to go to a Reichstag meeting to debate Jewish emancipation. As it happened, the meeting was scheduled on the Jewish Sabbath. "Shabbat, naturally after shul, we will go together to the Reichstag and listen, as they speak and negotiate." Reb Machel's enthusiasm intoxicated Reb Ahron. "Yes, he would gladly go with him, he wanted to see the Jewish deputies, Meisels and Mannheimer, Fischhof and Goldmark and Halpern. But there before his eyes rose the image of his Malkah, he saw her dressed with her Sabbath head covering; the thick siddur (prayer book) in her hand." [55] Malkah's image ignited his sense of manhood calling to him, "How, Reb Ahron, are you really worthy of attaining freedom, when you are a slave of your wife, . . . cast off your fetters, *show that you are a man*, worthy of the new time, in which you live" [56] (my emphasis). He then announced that he would go to the Reichstag.

Reb Ahron had a dream about the Reichstag meeting at which Malkah appeared. The dream made him realize that he wanted to maintain peace in his home, but feared appearing as a "slave of his wife" to Machel and the other Jews. Making a great sacrifice, he missed an important historical moment for the sake of peace in his home. Malkah's words convey the moral of the story. His absence at the meeting would soon be forgotten, but he proved himself a good husband and a pious Jew. To Reb Machel, she said, " 'We will do what the new time demands of us, as long as it is right before God and humanity, as long as the Almighty, blessed be his name, allows us to wander on this Earth. But we shall never forget that we are Jews and remain Jews.' Thus spoke the energetic Malkah, Reb Machel lowered his head almost ashamed." [57]

In another story, the death of his mother brought Josef Gläser, the enlightened son who went to University to study medicine and fell in love with a non-Jewish girl, back to Judaism. [58] Josef returned home for Passover with a new belief, that "religion is humanity." Herr Müllner, the marriage broker, was arranging a *shidduch* for Josef's childhood friend, Miriam Fränkel, who was in love with Josef. As Josef did not return her love, she became the victim of an arranged marriage to Mendel Kornitzer, an older gentleman who treated her well, but whom she did not love. Josef loved a poor Christian girl, Rosa Maresch. He knew his parents could accept her poverty. However,

> . . . that she was not our religion; how could he cause his parents the sorrow, not to bring him under the "chuppa." Did he want to renounce the faith of his fathers? Did he want to revolt against that which his ancestors revered as the Holiest, for which they bled and suffered? Before his eyes rose the image of his beloved mother, the

image of his despairing father, they did not blame him, they did not reproach him, in silent pain they looked at him as if wanting to say: Did this come from our blood, is this our son Josef, who is rebelling against the faith of the fathers, is this the fruit of the new time, which has freed us from the walls of the narrow and still so dear Gasse?[59]

Josef left the Gasse, but returned shortly when his mother became ill. On her deathbed, she demanded that he remain a Jew, and he gave her his promise. He wrote to Rosa Maresch, explaining his struggle between love and duty.

> If I presume, beloved girl, that you yourself will disregard the differ-ence of religions, our fathers will never do it. How should I demand this from my old father? I should disregard the death prayer of a mother, who so loved me? And what would your father say to you, if you went before him and said: I love a Jew, give him to me for a hus-band . . . In the battle between duty and love the enthusiastic duty is again victorious.[60]

After his father's death, Josef made his parents' home into a hospital and dedicated his life to helping his people. Rosa married a poor officer and had many children, but she received anonymous gifts from Josef. In each of Grünfeld's stories, the confused Jewish men are brought back to tradition by the Jewish women in their lives.

Heinrich York-Steiner, a Zionist political commentator and writer born in Hungary in 1859, helped found the Zionist weekly *Die Welt* in Vienna. He wrote many stories, such as *Der Talmudbauer* (The Talmudic Farmer) (1904), *Maskir*, and *Talmud Kessuboth 110b*, which described Orthodox Jewish life. In these stories, the Jewish female characters also influence the male characters, but toward modern ideas rather than traditional ones.

For example, *Der Talmudbauer* told of the encounter of a young man who was brought up in a struggling religious family in Jerusalem and an enlightened Zionist woman in a settlement.[61] Although the fa-ther, Reb Joine, believed in a life of prayer and learning for himself and his son Chaim, his son wanted to alleviate his family's suffering and hunger by working with his hands. Despite his wife's illness, Reb Joine strongly disapproved of Chaim's wishes and even opposed efforts to collect Chalukah, contributions from Jews in the Diaspora. Chaim be-came acquainted with the philanthropic Dr. Rapp when he brought a

poor, sick eight-year-old girl to the doctor who saved her life. Not be-
lieving that Chaim would be capable of hard physical labor, Dr. Rapp
suggested he become a farmer on a settlement.[62]

When Doctor Rapp brought Chaim to visit the sick child and her
mother, they met the mother's cousin, a female settler named Miriam.
He had never met a girl like her before. Her smiling, bold and daring
looks and the conversation between her and the doctor completely
startled him.

Dr. Rapp's eyes sparkled; he took both of the young girl's hands and
looked into her white countenance, in which her little up-turned nose
gave a roguish impression. She returned his look smiling.

> Chaim turned away ashamedly. He had never before seen a girl who
> did such daring things. Yes, yes, he had been told not without good
> reason in the *Bet Hamidrash* in Jerusalem, that they were impious
> outside in the settlements—and Dr. Rapp, from him he never would
> have thought such a thing, such a pious man. Had he forgotten that
> it was improper to look at an unfamiliar woman so—so—boldly?

Miriam intrigued Chaim. He wondered if she was a sinner, because
she smiled at unfamiliar men and intimately shook their hands. But she
did not look like a sinner. "There was nothing evil in her small lovely
face, and yet—why so intimate with a man, whom she saw for the first
time in her life?"[63]

As the condition of his mother worsened, he had no other choice
but to leave Jerusalem and his parents to work in a settlement. On his
last evening at home, his father took him aside and asked him never to
forget God's commandments. On his journey, he met many different
kinds of Jews who would accompany him to the settlement of Reho-
both. The experience of working as a farmer with other Jews, and living on the land according to Torah law, strongly impressed him. For
example, they followed the agricultural law of Orlah, not benefiting
from the fruit of the tree or vine for the first three years. The Sabbath,
the day of rest, took on new meaning for him after such demanding
physical labor.

Once on the Sabbath, news arrived that Arabs were attacking the
Jews on the settlement of Katra, where Miriam lived. Although it
turned out to be an exaggeration, the incident brought Miriam and
Chaim together. Very happy to see him, she warmly pressed his hand.
Miriam's family, the Kattowitzes, took him in. He discovered with as-

tonishment that Miriam understood and studied the Talmud. Chaim grew more amazed, curious, and confused, the more he learned about Miriam. In conjunction with her Talmudic erudition, she considered herself a rationalist. Miriam's father shocked Chaim when he revealed that she read Renan's *The Life of Jesus* in French. "Why was he horrified of Miriam, who understood foreign languages and read *The Life of Jesus*? All the same, she also knew how to read Hebrew books and to explain the Talmud.—She was simply an unusual girl. Was she generally like other girls? No, such a creation could not be bestowed twice upon the earth!" [64]

After a while, Miriam's view of the world began to seem more logical to Chaim. She taught him, through their discussions, that Talmudic laws found form and expression through nature and practical application, not in a vacuum. Chaim had "become more masculine" since Miriam first met him, as a result of working out in the sun and fresh air. Her father invited Chaim to be their Sabbath guest every week, as he enjoyed having another Talmudist around. (Kattowitz was the "Talmudbauer.") Chaim slowly transformed both his inner beliefs and his outer appearance. He grew more receptive to new ideas and started to dress in modern attire. He cut off his sidelocks and shaved his beard. He had become enlightened through his contact with Miriam.

When the time came for his return to Jerusalem, Kattowitz took him aside to speak to him privately. He suggested to Chaim that he remain in Katra and marry Lena, the daughter of their neighbor. When Chaim discussed this with Miriam, she broke down and cried. He knew he could not marry Miriam because both families lacked money. Miriam came up with a solution for their dilemma. "We could never ask for something better, than to become an honest settler-couple on the home soil of the holy land. People will trust us and make money and land available to us." "Charity again?" Chaim objected. "No, only a loan," answered Miriam. This solution satisfied everyone. The group made their way to Jerusalem to present the news to Reb Joine. To everyone's surprise, Reb Joine, who now had an eye disease, had become much more tolerant. The blind rabbi took his son's hand and said, "The voice is the voice of Jacob, but the hands are the hands of Essau." Chaim responded, "And here is Rachel, your future daughter." Reb Joine laid his hands on her head and said, "Be blessed as Sarah, Rebecca, Rachel and Leah, the ancestors of a great race (*Geschlecht*)."

The Kattowitz family pleased Reb Joine. "I am very content and convinced that you will remain a Jew in this house." And when Chaim told him that Miriam read foreign books and even *The Life of Jesus*, he called to her, "Miriam, Miriam! Did we do it? We, we Jews—did we crucify him?" She answered him, "No father, we did not do it, but the dark fervor of the Zealots incited the Romans against him." "Was I a Zealot?" he asked Chaim. And to God he said, "You have stricken my eyes with blindness, kindling a pure light on my soul." He concluded that he could not possibly have been a Zealot, "otherwise you, my son, would not have become a Jewish farmer."[65]

York-Steiner characterized Miriam as strong and intelligent. The other female character of note, Frau Malke, Chaim's mother, also showed the intelligence and independence to use Talmudic arguments with her husband. He portrayed the Jewish woman as the intellectual, if not the physical, equal to her male counterpart, and as more tolerant and open-minded toward modern ideas. She taught men to understand the value of studying and learning new ideas. She embraced new ideas without fear due to her greater security in her own faith. Therefore Miriam had the ability to remain pious and read *The Life of Jesus*. She also found a way to marry the man she loved, in spite of obstacles.

Elsewhere, York-Steiner's Jewish female characters did not fare as well. In his short story "Marhulka," a young Jewish girl became the victim of anti-Semitism.[66] A Czech servant named Anka raised the girl, gave her the name Marhulka, and loved her like her own child. Marhulka learned to speak Czech fluently, loved her surroundings, and had many Czech friends at school. The murder of a Christian girl and the resulting accusation of the Jews abruptly changed her peaceful existence. Suddenly all her friends hated her and she did not understand why. When she confronted her teacher, she discovered that even this apparently well-educated man believed in the Jews' guilt. She began to spend her time reading books and walking in the garden. During her time in the garden, she started a liaison with her neighbor, a handsome young non-Jew named Wlado. In her vulnerable state, she fell in love with him, although a fence always separated their meetings. She fell deeply in love with him and one night he promised to marry her. "That night he climbed over the fence."[67]

The next afternoon Wlado did not appear for their meeting. Her father, who went to Prague that day, returned in a state of extreme agitation and disbelief. Wlado had gone to Prague, boasting that he had avenged the murdered Christian girl (through violation of Marhulka). Her initial integration into non-Jewish society made the young Jewish girl vulnerable, and she became a tragic victim of anti-Semitism.

York-Steiner's story about the suicide of an assimilated Jewish doctor also ended in tragedy for the female protagonist.[68] The doctor's mother, Frau Jentele, widowed at a young age, completely dedicated her life to her son. The news that he committed suicide during a fit of jealousy over his wife devastated her. The refusal to grant his body a respectful Jewish burial because he had committed suicide, a travesty of Jewish law, compounded her grief. She learned that his body would be dissected before it was buried. An older doctor who participated in the procedure sympathized with her, but he could not accommodate her request to forgo the dissection. In responding to his younger colleague, who relished the opportunity to dissect the body, he described the mother in the following words:

> Otherwise a remarkable woman, this mother, is simple and uneducated, but responsible. Without complaints, without superfluous expressions, with natural confidence she sacrificed her entire existence to her child. She lived for only one thought and one feeling: her son—and all the joy and pain that a person is capable of feeling, was concentrated for her in motherly sentiment.[69]

Haunted by the belief that her son would never rest in his grave unless he had a proper burial, she finally found consolation with her own resources. She took from the morgue the pails of bloody liquid in which the doctors had washed their sponges, and spilled it into his grave, so that nothing would be lost to him. In this way, she ultimately fulfilled her motherly duty. A strong woman, she refused to abandon her maternal crusade to protect her only child. Ultimately she relied on her own resources, creative and physical, in order to find a solution for her son. She did this without rejecting Judaism, but finding a Jewish solution to her problem.

Born in Lemberg, Hermann Menkes worked in Vienna as an art critic, writer, and journalist for the *Neue Wiener Journal* from 1887–1902. In 1905, he became editor of the *Czernowitzer Tagblatt*. In an article in *Die Zeit* (Hermann Bahr's weekly) in 1897, he called for a new generation of Jewish writers to represent Jewish life as it really was, ghetto-naturalism, in order to educate the public about the essence of the Jews.[70]

In a sketch "Mutters Gebetbuch" (Mother's Prayer Book), Menkes described his own mother as a simple pious woman, comparing the course of her life to that of her prayer book.

Still now it [the prayer book] often lies open in her slender, weak, weary hands, which had often been clasped together in grief or gently stroked the feverish faces of children. Once these hands were young and delicate, and also the prayer book was brilliant, with gold and ivory on the cover, with white, shining and crisp pages and beautiful script. Now it aged along with Mother. The binding has loosened and become yellow, the pages are worn and no longer want to hold properly and throughout there are all sorts of marks of tears.[71]

Every major event of her life left its impression in the book. The children's birthdays and nicknames could be found in it, and on their birthdays she would read them a prayer before giving them a kiss and a present. The prayer book also accompanied her through the deaths of her parents, her husband, and one son, and she kept her husband's last letter tucked inside. Menkes, who described himself as a skeptic, could not look at certain pages of the old tattered book without shuddering.

The novella "Die Jüdin Leonora" (1912), set in the seventeenth century, told the story of a Jewish girl who lived a short tragic life during difficult times in the Jewish ghetto of Vienna.[72] She died at a young age in 1651, of so-called "unknown causes," but in truth she was murdered. Leonora suffered the death of her mother, her teacher, her first love, and her husband in succession. But she pulled herself together as best she could after each tragedy and continued on with her life. After the death of her husband, several of the Jewish men in the ghetto offered her their hand in marriage, but she declined them all.

At one and the same time, Menkes described her as somewhat masculine and yet a possessor of oriental beauty and charm. "Her business, which she conducted with masculine assurance, brought her in close relationships with Christian and aristocratic circles of the city, and here they took pleasure in the fine manners and tactful composure of the Jewess and in the strange charm of her genuine oriental beauty."[73] This brought her unwanted attention from some Christian men, but she defended her pride against these assaults. With this she also became estranged from her community.

Her beauty attracted one man in particular, Johan Amadeus von Sibelin, an anti-Semite who was also somewhat contemptuous toward women. He engaged in many light-hearted non-emotional affairs, and assumed Leonora was fair game for his pursuit. Upon entering the ghetto, soldiers asked for his identification. He started a fight with them, leading to his arrest. Unrest and fighting ensued, escalating to the point where Jewish homes burned down. Meanwhile, Johan Amadeus set out to conquer Leonora, but upon seeing her, her magic worked on him. He grasped her hands, looked at her in speechless humility, and then left as softly as he had come. Deeply consumed by his passion, he could not forget her as hard as he tried. For two years he avoided meeting her, until one chance encounter. He poured his heart out to her and she responded that it was too late. His love beyond control, he threw himself at her and kissed her. She hit him twice in the face and he let her go. The story ended with her realization that she also loved him and had to go find him. As she crossed the bridge she was shot. She looked up and saw her beloved and then another shot was fired and she died. Leonora was a victim of circumstances who was not at home in either world, and her life ended tragically.

In both the traditional ghetto tales and the "naturalist" ghetto tales, female Jewish characters were generally sympathetic. Traditional ghetto tale writers described the Jewish woman as beautiful in spite of stifling Jewish traditions and customs. They characterized women as more receptive to modern ideas than men, although the transition to modernity often entailed painful and tragic consequences. In the naturalist ghetto tales, there was a growing tendency to see the Jewish woman as the pillar of tradition in a world of change. She succeeded in accepting modern ideas and incorporating them into her world view without sacrificing her Jewish identity. Only women who forgot their identity as Jews by becoming too integrated met tragic fates.

Jung Wien

The image of the "western" assimilated Jewish woman differed from that of the Jewish woman of the East European ghetto. Viennese Jewish writers devoted minimal attention to representing already assimilated Jewish women. While Jews were prominent in the fields of Viennese literature and journalism at the turn of the century, much of their work focused on general themes, and even works with Jewish content and themes often did not include significant Jewish female characters. For example, the literary circle known as *Jung Wien* (Young Vienna), which consisted of Hermann Bahr (not Jewish) (1863–1934), Arthur Schnitzler (1862–1931), Felix Dörmann (1870–1928), Richard Beer-Hofmann (1866–1945), Leopold von Andrian (Jewish ancestry) (1875–1951), Hugo von Hofmannsthal (Jewish ancestry) (1874–1929),

Felix Salten (1869–1945), Peter Altenberg (1859–1919), and others concentrated on breaking with the past and finding new modes of expression (i.e., literary modernism), rather than depicting Jewish life.[74] *Jung Wien* writers gathered at the Cafe Griensteidl, and after its demolition in 1897, at the Cafe Central, where they exchanged ideas, information, and gossip. Karl Kraus (1874–1936), their outspoken opponent, also frequented the cafes.[75] The growing recognition that anti-Semitism threatened the Jews' future in Vienna and the resulting feelings of dissatisfaction, frustration, and isolation influenced the new literary movement. However, most of their writings had little to do directly with Judaism in general or Jewish women in particular.[76]

Michael Pollak has argued that the disappearance of the great literary salons and their replacement with cafes as gathering places for writers and artists in the late nineteenth century resulted in the loss of the female (actually the Jewish female) who played a maternal and protective role. According to Pollak, the last literary salon disappeared with the death of Josephine von Werthheimstein in 1894. In cafes, the men remained among themselves, creating small circles of friends to mitigate competition and compensate for the loss of consolation that had come from salon women.[77] At the same time, the feminist movement in Vienna took root, placing feminists in opposition to *Jung Wien* writers, whose theory of femininity consecrated the idea of masculine superiority. In fact, salons did continue into the twentieth century, including those run by Berta Zuckerkandl, Eugenie Schwarzwald, and Alma Mahler, and played a central role in the development of modern culture in Vienna.[78]

While women figured prominently, if not substantially, in the literature of the *Jung Wien* circle, only in Arthur Schnitzler's work were significant Jewish female characters to be found.[79] His most famous works, the three plays *Anatol* (1888–1891), *Liebelei* (1894), and *Reigen* or *La Ronde* (1898–1899), focused on the relationship between the sexes.[80] For this reason, Schnitzler, as well as some other prominent Jews such as Sigmund Freud; Felix Salten; the alleged writer of the pornographic novel *Josephine Mutzenbacher: Die Lebensgeschichte einer wienerischen Dirne* (Memoirs of a Viennese Whore); Karl Kraus; Peter Altenberg; and the poet Felix Dörmann, had the reputation of being obsessed with sexuality.[81] This contributed to the anti-Semitic stereotype of Jewish sexual perversity, despite the fact that Viennese non-Jews such as Richard von Krafft-Ebing, Leopold von Sacher-Masoch, and

Hermann Bahr also explored sexual themes in their works. *Die Reigen* was banned in Vienna and denounced as the embodiment of immorality by the clergy in many other cities and as "Jewish" pornography by German nationalists.[82] When first performed at the Kammerspiele Theater in Vienna in 1921, it created a theatrical scandal, with stink bombs and tussles in the theater followed by fist fights in Parliament and anti-Semitic street demonstrations. The police banned further performances.[83]

Schnitzler defined two types of women in his works. He contrasted the *süsse Mädel* (sweet girl), lower class and sexually free, uninhibited and natural, but unmarriageable, with the respectable, bourgeois daughter, who was protected from and raised in complete ignorance of sex. In addition to his literary interest in women, he also had some indirect connections with the feminist movement in Vienna.[84]

Jewish women figured prominently in Schnitzler's novel *Der Weg ins Frei* (The Road into the Open) (1908) and in his autobiographical work, *Jugend in Wien* (My Youth in Vienna). For example, he expressed his negative views of contemporary Jewish women in the following passage about his grandmother's relatives.

> Among the women and girls, beside those who because of their appearance and mannerisms can't deny their origin or don't want to, we find some who indulge in sport and fashion, and it is self-explanatory that snobbery—the world ailment of our times—found exceptionally favorable conditions for development during the epoch I touch upon fleetingly here.[85]

On the other hand, he countered this negative image in representing his grandmother, Amalia Markbreiterher, as "a capable housekeeper, a devoted and long-suffering wife to her difficult husband and a loving and beloved mother to her numerous children." Schnitzler's portrayal of the snobbish assimilated Jewess and the traditional Jewish housewife and mother resembles that of Theodor Herzl and other Zionists, as well as that of religious leaders, such as Adolf Jellinek.

Schnitzler also detailed many romantic involvements with Jewish women in his autobiography. His childhood love, Franziska Reich (Fännchen), the daughter of a commercial Jew, later married Jacob Lawner, with whom she had a son. After the death of her husband, she immersed herself in memories of her relationship with Schnitzler, following and collecting information on his intimate life. He recounted how at their eventual reunion, she exasperated him with non-stop speaking and Yiddish embellishments. She inspired his novel *Berthe Garlan*.[86]

Schnitzler recalled his relationship with Gisela Freistadt, a pretty Jewish girl from a humble middle-class family, at home literally and figuratively on the outskirts of the ghetto. He suggested that "Jewish parents, especially those in such lowly, almost needy circumstances, have no greater desire than to marry off their daughters as soon as possible." It did not surprise Schnitzler when she announced her engagement to a wine merchant from Löben.[87] On her wedding day she promised Schnitzler letters and "better things." Years later, the mother of several Löben children, she came to see him at his office, evidently ready and willing to keep the promise made on her wedding day. "But she had long ago ceased to please me. Her boring, banal way of speaking, which was not free of jargon, only served to further cool my ardor, and I withdrew into my medical profession so successfully that her visits soon ceased."[88]

Very few Jewish women from his past managed to escape Schnitzler's disparagement, although there were exceptions. For example, Charlotte Heit, daughter of a wealthy businessman, impressed Schnitzler as lively and sociable, intellectually attractive and clever. At eighteen, she fell in love with and hoped to marry him, but he told her that he planned never to marry. Furthermore, her mother rejected him as a potential husband. As a result, she temporarily fell into a melancholic condition, but soon recovered on her own strength. "She had been completely restored for some time when she gave her dear gentle hand, that same year, to an attractive and efficient young manufacturer and entered into a promising marriage, a promise which, according to all signs, was to be completely fulfilled."[89]

In *Der Weg ins Frei*, Schnitzler's complex novel depicting the cultural, political, and personal crises of fin de siècle Vienna, he introduced a wide variety of Jewish characters. Else Ehrenberg (daughter of the patriarchal industrialist Salomon Ehrenberg and social-climbing assimilationist Frau Ehrenberg), and the socialist agitator Therese Golowski were the most prominent female Jewish characters of the novel. Although they represented different types, he did not indicate a clear preference for one over the other. In fact, in a discussion at the Ehrenberg salon, Heinrich Bermann and Edmund Nuernberger explicitly compared and contrasted the two women.

"I was just thinking how easily it could have happened that Fraulein Else might have had to languish for two months in prison and that Fraulein Therese had given parties in an elegant salon as daughter of the house." . . .

"Herr Ehrenberg had good luck, Herr Golowski bad. . . . Perhaps that's the only difference."

"Well listen, Nuernberger," said Heinrich, "you can't completely deny the role of the individual in the world. . . . Else and Therese are of quite different natures." . . .

Nuernberger shrugged his shoulders. "Both are young ladies, quite gifted, quite pretty. . . . Everything else is like with most other young ladies—and with most other people—more or less circumstantial."[90]

Schnitzler suggested here that Therese and Else differed only superficially but that deeper down they shared the same struggles.

Else (inspired by Minnie Benedikt, youngest daughter of Moritz Benedikt) was inwardly restless. Her early artistic aspirations gave way to other impulses.

Sometimes she saw herself in the future as a grande dame, organizer of flower festivals, patroness of grand balls, collaborator for aristocratic charities; more often though, she saw herself enthroned among painters, musicians, and poets, at artistic salons, as a great cognoscente. Other times she would dream of a more adventurous life: sensational marriage to an American millionaire; elopement with a violin virtuoso or Spanish officer; demonic destruction of all men who came near her. Sometimes a quiet life in the country at the side of some capable estate owner seemed the most desirable to her; and then she would envision herself in a circle of many children, if possible with prematurely grey hair, a mild, resigned smile on her lips, sitting at a simply set table, and stroking the furrowed brow of her devoted husband.[91]

Else, completely natural in her salon hostess role, was portrayed as a feminine character. For example, she leaned on the piano "in her adolescent, girlish way."[92] She ultimately became engaged to the Englishman, James Wyner.

Therese, on the other hand, clearly devoted to the socialist cause, appeared simple, modest, and determined. She came to the Ehrenberg salon dressed in simple black, wearing her hair in an outmoded style. "Her lips were full and red; the eyes in the lively, pale face looked clear and hard." Her political engagement conflicted with her femininity. For example, when she replied that her calling left her little time for family relationships, she thrust her chin forward, "which made her appearance suddenly masculine and almost ugly."[93] She smoked cigars and functioned as "the boss" on her trip with her lover, Demeter. However, later in the novel Therese showed some of the same qualities as Else. She became distracted from her socialist calling by her love affair with Demeter Stanzides. She appeared more feminine to Georg von Wergenthin, the Catholic Baron, when he met her by chance on a vacation trip. She dressed in white, carried an open white parasol, and wore a straw hat with a red band. Again she thrust her chin forward when she spoke, "only without this motion making her face ugly this time like it did before."[94] When Georg saw her later that evening, he noted that she again wore white, only more elegant this time in embroidered English linen, with a string of coral around an open neck. When she was not delivering "loud heavy speeches," Georg found her attractive. The Jewish doctor, Berthold Stauber, said she would end up either on the scaffold or as a princess. Her feminine princess side allured Georg, while he found her activist side masculine and ugly.

Therese's brother Leo, a Zionist, repeatedly asserted "that she could not so completely forget her great task for days and weeks at a time if her compassion for the poor and suffering was really as deep as she imagined."[95] She had a propensity for speech making, but her acquaintances questioned the true motivation of her socialist activity, whether it was a desire for self-promotion or true concern for the poor. For example, the Jewish writer Heinrich Bermann wrote in a letter that he had gone with Therese to a political gathering in Brigittenau, where he listened to seven speeches on universal suffrage. "Each of the speakers—Therese among them—spoke as if there was nothing more personally urgent for them than the solution to this problem, and I believe that none of them suspected that in the depths of their souls the whole question was really a matter of profound indifference."[96]

Her friend Anna Rosner commented sarcastically, "the affair with Demeter is over. Her heart now beats only for the poor and suffering again—until further notice."[97] Anna described how Therese dressed as a poor woman and visited the warming houses, soup- and tea-kitchens, work-houses, and shelters for the homeless, concluding, "Naturally she wants to make a book out of it."[98]

Although her motivations were disparaged by her friends and acquaintances, Therese desired to play a meaningful role in the world and to believe in something. She freely expressed opinions about the issues of her times. In fact, in discussing her brother's persecution by an anti-Semitic first lieutenant, she stated her position on the Jewish question.

> It's well known that I'm in as little agreement with my brother as is possible in my political views; you know this better than anyone Georg; to me Jewish bankers are just as repulsive as the feudal estate owners, and orthodox rabbis just as repulsive as Catholic priests. But when someone feels superior to me because I have a different belief, or belong to another race, and in the consciousness of his advantage makes me feel this superiority, I would . . . I don't know what I would do to such a person. But in any case I'd understand if Leo flew in the face of this Herr Sefranek at the next provocation.[99]

In the end, Leo killed the anti-Semitic lieutenant in a duel and was arrested for murder. The investigation against him was later halted by imperial clemency and he was released from jail. Therese remained theoretically opposed to the release of her brother because of her opposition to the military world view and the concept of the duel. "If you had simply shot the rat to death, as was very well your right, without this disgusting dueling act, you would not have been released; you'd have sat for five or ten years for sure. But because you engaged in this grizzly, state-condoned gamble of life and death, because you bowed before the military world-view, you have been pardoned."[100]

Georg contemplated her future as he sat close to her for the last time. Would she find her dreams in "the dark delusion of the fulfillment of mankind, or the happy and lighthearted one of a new romantic adventure?" Before she left his wagon she said, "Yes, dear Georg, where does one turn . . . if one doesn't . . . have anything to offer to humanity? Do you know what I sometimes think? Maybe it's all just to get away from myself."[101]

Both Else and Therese identified more with their class than with their religion or gender. Else felt completely at home among the non-Jews whom she entertained at the salon, while Therese realized herself at the center of the Social Democratic Party. They shared an attraction to non-Jewish men. Compared to the male Jewish characters in the novel, they hardly concerned themselves with the Jewish question.

Like the aristocratic characters in the novel, the Jewish women represented a caste that had become irrelevant and obsolete.[102]

Schnitzler's contemporaries also wrote about women and sexuality, without giving much attention to Jewish women per se. Karl Kraus (1874–1936), the relentless critic and editor of the journal *Die Fackel* (The Torch), addressed feminist issues.[103] His attitudes toward women and feminism fit into his general outlook as an ardent moralist who criticized anything that appeared to abuse morality or language.[104] This translated into promotion of a more liberal attitude toward sex and advocating legal changes such as the legalization of contraception, abortion, and prostitution. In his early writings, he sympathized with the goals of the Austrian feminist movement, although later he rejected the idea of female emancipation as a threat to the distinction between the genders.[105] He reproached women who appeared to transgress the gender barrier, while defending female victims of the moral double standards of Viennese society.

When dealing with women who happened to be Jewish, Kraus understood their Jewishness as a factor in their plights. For example, in "The Witch Hunt at Löben," he defended Frau Hervay, the exotic foreign wife of a District Administrator, convicted of bigamy after her husband committed suicide. The anti-Semitic press emphasized her Jewish ancestry in its coverage of the case. Kraus turned the case around portraying Hervay as a victim of flawed education, rather than as his exotic wife. The public, in their zeal and nostalgia for the "time-honored institutions of branding, torturing and executing witches," was eager to blame his wife, and the press treated her as a "woman possessed," a "modern vampire," and a "Jew-woman of a devilish nature."[106]

On the other hand, Kraus targeted Alice Therese Schalek (1874–1956), the first female journalist in Austria and feuilleton editor for the *Neue Freie Presse*, as a symbol of the destruction of the barrier between femininity and masculinity.[107] In *Die Fackel* and in *The Last Days of Mankind*, he satirized Schalek, the only female reporter during the First World War.

From woman into journalist into feuilletonist into war correspondent—each change of role is a betrayal of that conception of womanliness which Kraus sought to uphold. In this case, satirical stylization is scarcely necessary. Merely by quoting verbatim from

Schalek's war feuilletons, Kraus is able to demonstrate the grotesqueness of a figure who inspects the front-line troops with the air of a commander-in-chief and describes the war as if it were a touristic spectacle. In the transformation of Alice Schalek Kraus sees the most monstrous exemplification of the tragic carnival. The betrayal of the traditional norms of femininity symbolizes that combination of hysteria and anaesthesia which grips mankind as a whole.[108]

In *The Last Days of Mankind*, Kraus used Schalek to link the themes of the press's culpability and the role of women in contributing to a civilization which embraced the war.[109]

Kraus's satire of Schalek also alluded to her Jewishness. For example, her nose appeared accentuated in caricatures, and he described her with the phrase "the enemy within."[110] According to Timms,

> there are continuous indications, often in coded form, that the "enemy within" is Jewish in origin. On the very page where this phrase occurs we are reminded that Alice Schalek has a long nose (an allusion to her Jewishness as well as to the "long face" she presumably makes when she finds herself snubbed). Her nose is also mocked in an earlier context, where the suggestion is that it is so long that it is likely to betray an Austrian military position to the enemy. These coded references with their humorous intention may seem harmless in themselves. But Kraus is here exploiting one of the stock devices of antisemitic caricature, to which he took grave exception when he found his own face portrayed with an accentuated "Jewish" nose.[111]

Schalek's Jewishness figured into Kraus's portrayal of her as a transgressor of the boundary between masculine and feminine, just as Frau Hervay's Jewishness influenced his characterization of her as a victim. He embraced the sexual Jewish woman, Frau Hervay, who conformed to his conception of womanly nature, while condemning the intellectual Jewish woman, Alice Schalek, as masculine and unnatural. Although heavily shaped by his general attack on hypocrisy, in the end his portrayal of Jewish women did not differ greatly from that of the writers, journalists, psychoanalysts, and Zionists whom he so vehemently opposed.

Alice Schalek, 1917. ÖNB/Wien.   *Alice Schalek, 1917. ÖNB/Wien.*

Theater and Art

In Vienna, the theater always occupied a central place in the culture, especially at the fin de siècle.[112] The Jewish woman appeared regularly on the Viennese stage during this period, with operas and plays such as Eugene Scribe's *Die Jüdin* (The Jewess), W. A. Wohlbrueck's *Die Templer und die Jüdin* (The Templar and the Jewess—loosely based on Walter Scott's *Ivanhoe*), Salomon Mosenthal's *Deborah*, Franz Grillparzer's *Esther* and *Die Jüdin von Toledo* (The Jewess from Toledo), and Friedrich Hebbel's *Judith* performed on a regular basis.[113] Plays with Jewish themes and female Jewish characters abounded, such as Karl Gutzkow's *Uriel Acosta*, Gotthold Ephraim Lessing's *Nathan der Weise* (Nathan the Wise), Otto Ludwig's *Die Makkabaer* (The Maccabees), Paul Lindau's *Ein Erfolg* (A Success), P. Suardon's *Freund Fritz* (Friend Fritz), Ludwig Anzengruber's *Der Meineidbauer* (The Perjurous Farmer), Friedrich Kaiser's *Neu-Jerusalem* (New Jerusalem), and Leopold Adler's *Das Buch Hiob* (The Book of Job). Elisabeth Frenzel lists twenty-eight plays with Jewish themes performed in Viennese theaters, remarking that the Jewish woman was a popular figure on the stage.[114]

Like many other domains in Vienna, the world of theater became tainted by anti-Semitism. In 1898 the Kaiserjubilaeums-Stadttheater, conceived as an "Aryan" anti-Semitic theater, opened with the support of Christian Social circles.[115] Furthermore, the anti-Semitic press charged that Jewish influence corrupted theater.[116] While the popularity of biblical themes, Jewish characters, and Jewish women on the Viennese stage seems incongruous with the desire to "Aryanize" theater, the attraction to these themes must be understood in the context of theater as a means of escape from politics and reality. For this reason, political, serious dramas found less favor with Viennese audiences than comedies and grand operas. Also, biblical dramas appealed to audiences for their universal messages rather than for their Jewish content. In some instances biblical dramas reflected negatively on Jews by portraying them as callous, petty, and impious on the one hand, and fanatical in their Temple worship on the other hand, thereby rendering them inconsistent and cowardly.[117]

The Jewish woman was an attractive figure on the Viennese stage despite anti-Semitism. Whether she functioned as a victim or as a villain, she almost invariably appeared exotic, alluring, and beautiful. To what extent was the female Jewish character unique in this respect? Rejecting Frenzel's assertion that the Jewish girl on the stage resembled other girls in similar situations, Florian Krobb asserts: "With this interpretation she entirely neglects the importance of the religious difference and with this contributes little to the understanding of the 'beautiful Jewesses.'"[118] Dangerous, clever, intelligent, and even masculine, female Jewish characters still held appeal for male audiences. The attraction to the "otherness" of the forbidden Jewish woman undoubtedly contributed to her popularity on the stage.

Sarah Loebenstein of Kaiser's *Neu-Jerusalem* (1867/68) exemplifies Jewish female characters.[119] In this play, Kaiser, a liberal non-Jewish author, attempted to resolve the prejudicial outlooks of Jews and Christians in the year of Jewish emancipation. He advocated Jewish assimilation but rejected conversion and intermarriage. The title had many connotations. Vienna had been called "New-Jerusalem" at the time of the Turkish siege when it became a Christian capital. Joseph II called the primarily Jewish town of Brody in Galicia "New-Jerusalem" when he visited it in 1787.

Overly nervous and eager to attain *Bildung*, Sarah Loebenstein typified the salon Jewess. "Her language is that of the distinguished heroines of Nestroy, always a little in danger of falling into absurdity."[120] She assimilated to a greater degree than her father, a Jewish banker, and fell in love with the Christian artisan Jakob. Both she and her father rejected the possibility of her conversion; however, it turned out that Jakob had converted to Christianity and was actually Jewish. Liberal and universal in her world view, she told her teacher Ephraim, who took credit for teaching her the importance of remaining true to her religion.

> Not your teaching. You taught me hate—for those of other religions—I respect those beliefs, and exactly for that reason I will not change my religion, because I must not despise myself. I know that there is only one God, who is the same for everyone, but is understood by no one. . . . How could a man believe in the endurance of my love, if I break faith with my own God? [121]

On a less serious level in the play, the simpleminded Christian Fanni fell in love with and married the merchant Leopold, a convert to Judaism who remained Christian in essence.

The Jewish writer, Solomon Mosenthal, portrayed the Jewish woman as a dangerous seductress in his popular play *Deborah* (1848).[122] He contrasted Deborah with the saint-like Christian Hanna. Deborah's beauty and sensuality made her irresistible to gentile men.[123] She used biblical imagery in her speeches, but also had a capacity for rage due to her Jewishness. The Christian woman, Hanna, conducted herself with tolerance and understanding, in contrast to the wild, undisciplined Deborah. Judaism was rendered the religion of hate, in contrast to Christianity, the religion of love.

Not only did the Jewish heroine embody a strong capacity for hate, but she also practiced witchcraft. Her prayers to the moon, her attempts to conjure up Joseph, the man she desired, and her curse against him and Hanna all suggested supernatural powers. The villagers feared her as a witch. An old woman warned, "Shall she bewitch your children so that they get the pox and ugly goiters." Joseph told Hanna: "Passion gripped me as painfully, as wildly, as if she had inspired it with prayer or magic." [124]

Other Jewish authors did little to respond to the stereotyped Jewesses of the Viennese stage. Ferdinand Bronner (1867–1948), Theodor Herzl, Jakob Julius David (1859–1906), Leo Stein (Rosenstein) (1861–1920), Richard Beer-Hofmann (1866–1945), and Arthur Schnitzler all wrote dramatic works, but none of them made a serious attempt to create diverse female Jewish characters for the stage. Therefore the pre-emancipation of eastern Jewish woman was destined to be seen

E. M. Lilien, The Song of Life. *From M. S. Levussove,* The New Art of an Ancient People: The Work of Ephraim Mose Lilien. *New York: B.W. Huebsch, 1906.*

as exotic, dangerous, and alluring, while the modern or western Jewish woman was seen as a salon woman who desired assimilation and *Bildung.*

Jews also contributed to the visual arts in turn of the century Vienna, but they achieved less distinction in this area than in other areas of culture. The Galician-born artist E. M. Lilien (1874–1925) designed the postcard for the Fifth Zionist Congress in 1901, and his black-and-white

Jugendstil drawings made him a leading Zionist artist.[125] The Jewish women in his drawings are dark, exotic, and beautiful, much like the descriptions found in literature.[126] Many of them have exquisite long hair, closed eyes, and seductive postures. Others have a determined look in their dark eyes, and wear exotic head-coverings and jewels. These visual images romanticize the Jewish woman, supplying a picture to complement the literary descriptions.

Conclusion

A combination of factors shaped images of Jewish women and their participation in Viennese literature and culture. The pressures of modernization led to conflicts over the role of Jewish women in the new circumstances. Thus, Jewish female characters embodied various solutions to the question of Jewish women's role in the modern world. In ghetto literature, Jewish women often led the way to enlightenment, but sometimes suffered from rejection by the traditional world. Although at times nostalgic for the past, Jews who wrote ghetto tales rejected certain religious practices. Regarding traditional Judaism, a male-dominated culture and religion, they naturally chose the Jewish woman as a protagonist (oftentimes a victim) who sought enlightenment and wanted to transcend primitive eastern customs. Later writers of ghetto tales found themselves somewhat disillusioned with emancipation and its effects on Jewish religious life. Critical of male Jewish characters who abandoned their roots, these writers portrayed Jewish women as the link to Judaism. Their presence in the lives of assimilated male Jews reminded them of the virtues of traditional Jewish life.

Prominent Jewish writers such as Schnitzler and Kraus created images of Jewish women which highlighted the inherent problems of Viennese society and culture. Schnitzler's Jewish female characters lacked true vocations. In his memoirs, the characterizations of Jewish women incorporated negative gender stereotypes. They were loquacious, flirtatious, snobbish, but afflicted with pain and suffering. The female Jewish characters in his novel, *Der Weg ins Frei*, identified with their social class in attempts to find a niche for themselves in the modern world, where Jewish women as such had become irrelevant. Schnitzler's female Jewish characters addressed the question of Jewish women's role in Viennese society, but failed to provide answers.

Kraus's representations of Jewish women reflected Viennese notions of gender and sexuality as well. He either portrayed them as victims of the contradictory Viennese code of morality, or condemned them as masculine intellectuals. The general notion of femininity in Viennese culture influenced the images of the Jewish woman in these circles. Similarly, stereotyped images of the beautiful, dangerous Jewess, or the materialistic Salon Jewess, prevailed on the Viennese stage.

In addition to addressing Jewish women's role in modern society, Jews in Viennese literary culture also demonstrated their own adjustment to modernity through their female Jewish characters. Like Viennese Jews in other fields, they incorporated general bourgeois gender stereotypes in their images of Jewish women. Thus, their artistic creations demonstrate the emergence of a newly created Jewish identity which synthesized elements from traditional Judaism with elements from bourgeois European culture. As Jews, they confronted challenges to their identity which came along with the desire to integrate. They created Jewish women who eased this transition by promoting enlightenment without abandoning Jewish identity, or provided a link to tradition in a changing world. As part of the general Viennese culture, their images of Jewish women took on many general characteristics of the stereotype of women.

The Jews' prominence in Viennese culture at the turn of the century has been attributed to certain aspects of Jewish culture, religion, and the history of persecution. These ingredients, when exposed to external influences, formed a potent mixture. The creation of Jewish female characters became a way of responding to a specific moment in the history of Viennese Jews. Jewish female characters provided a mechanism for coping with the dilemmas of modern Viennese Jews. The influx of eastern European Jews, the ambivalence toward assimilation and its effects on morality, and newly emerging notions of gender and sexuality, among other things, were deliberated and negotiated through these characters.

Conclusion

Since the publication of Carl Schorske's *Fin-de-Siècle Vienna: Politics and Culture*, historians have discussed and debated his thesis and have focused on his analysis of liberalism, the relationship of politics and culture, and his understanding of modern culture, for which the culture of fin de siècle Vienna is seen as paradigmatic.[1] Schorske proposes that accompanying the decline of liberalism, a new politics emerged in which the leaders "grasped a social-psychological reality which the liberal could not see. Each expressed in politics a rebellion against reason and law which soon became more widespread."[2] As this rebellion spread throughout Viennese politics, culture, and society, more segments of the population came under its influence. Part of this rebellion manifested itself in intense anti-Semitic politics.

Many works have been inspired by Schorske's masterpiece, mine among them. Focusing on Jewish women's contributions to Viennese culture and the perceptions of them in the context of the decline of liberalism and the development of modern culture and politics in Vienna, this book aims to show that Jewish women played a key role in fin de siècle Vienna, both in terms of their participation in the various spheres of activity, which they pursued with enthusiasm and which served them in their sometimes challenging position as Jewish women in a less than welcoming climate, and in terms of the imagined Jewish woman found in a wide array of works by Jewish (and non-Jewish) men.

Beyond demonstrating that Jewish women have not received enough attention in studies of fin de siècle Vienna, I have shown that examining their lives together with images of them contributes to the understanding of the overall cultural, social, and political climate of Vienna. Austrian high culture, according to Péter Hanák, was "dominated by the problems of existence and nonexistence, the finality of death, existential solitude, the place of the individual, and the secrets of love, in other worlds by Eros and Psyche, and the related embrace of Eros and Thanatos."[3] These problems wove their way into the cultural works by and about Jewish women as well, but by focusing specifically on Jewish women another dimension is added to the current understanding of fin de siècle Viennese culture and identity. The intersections of Jewish identity and female identity, the linkages of the woman and the Jew in the popular imagination, and the psychological implications of isolation, images of otherness, and discrimination on Jews, women, and Jewish women come to the fore. These factors played themselves out in Viennese Jewish women's identity, leading them to pursue all kinds of religious, cultural, intellectual, and political pursuits, including prayer, philanthropy, Zionism, psychoanalysis, socialism, university study, and writing through which they negotiated multiple loyalties.

Finally, while this book has focused primarily on two aspects of Jewish women's identity—Jewishness and gender—their identities also included other components which repeatedly played a role behind the scenes. As mentioned in the introduction, Marsha Rozenblit has suggested that Habsburg Jewry can be seen as having a tripartite identity. Their political loyalty to the Austrian Habsburg dynasty, their German (or other depending on where they lived) cultural identity, and their Jewish ethnic identity allowed them a certain latitude in making choices to be as Jewish as they chose. This tripartite identity distinguished Habsburg Jewry from the Jews of ethnically monolithic countries such as Germany and France.[4] Accordingly, German culture and Austrian political loyalty played an important role in the identity of Viennese Jews, male and female, and influenced their political, cultural, and other activities and contributions in addition to the images of Jewish women created by Jewish men.

The identity of Viennese Jewish women, the images of them, and their cultural contributions were shaped by the various cultural, ethnic, political, and gender loyalties and pulls, and therefore when gender is taken into account, one can speak of a quadripartite identity for Austrian Jewish women. While the thread of my argument has been the convergence of the Jewish and the female in the popular imagination and in fin de siècle Viennese culture and its impact on the identity and image of the Jewish woman, loyalty to Habsburg Austria and attraction to German culture played an important role for Jewish women as well as men. Viennese Jewish women incorporated notions of gender-appropriate roles from bourgeois German culture, immersed themselves in German literature and culture, and also displayed patriotism to Austria. Elisabeth Freundlich, for example, wrote that she "was also the mainstay of every patriotic festival, in which the great victories of our glorious Imperial and Royal Army were celebrated when the losses could be overlooked."[5]

This situation of multiple loyalties alongside the distinct cultural modernism of fin de siècle Vienna contributes to making it an ideal case study for examining the interaction between gender and Jewishness and its impact on the participation and images of Jewish women in culture and politics and on their identity as Jewish women. The conflation of the image of the Jew and the woman and the sexualized image of the Jew possibly found their most fertile soil in fin de siècle Vienna. Therefore, this reevaluation of fin de siècle Vienna takes the moment of the Jewish woman's identity in light of the linkage of the Jew and the woman as its focal and starting point. The development of Jewish and female identity in Viennese Jewish girlhood, their image and identity within the Jewish community, their involvement and depictions of them in politics and university study, their participation and representation in Zionism, psychoanalysis, and culture—all emanate from this point of convergence. I believe that still much more could be explored in light of this central point—the conflation of the feminine and the Jewish in fin de siècle Vienna as it played out in the lives and images of Viennese Jewish woman—and in that respect, I hope this work will inspire more studies along these lines.

Notes

Introduction

1. Recently, some works have focused on Jewish women in Vienna. Most notable is Elisabeth Malleier, *Jüdische Frauen in Wien, 1816–1938: Wohlfahrt—Mädchenbildung—Frauenarbeit* (Vienna: Mandelbaum, 2003). Also Marsha Rozenblit, "For Fatherland and Jewish People: Jewish Women in Austria during World War I," in Frans Coetzee and Marylin Shevin-Coetzee, eds., *Authority, Identity and the Social History of the Great War* (Providence: Berghahn Books, 1995), and Helga Embacher, "Aussenseiterinnen: bürgerlich, jüdisch, intellektuell—links," *L'homme: Zeitschrift für feministische Geschichtwissenschaft* 2 (1991).

2. Carl Schorske, *Fin-de-Siècle Vienna: Politics and Culture* (New York: Alfred A. Knopf, 1980).

3. Some recent examples of the continuing interest in fin de siècle Vienna include Janet Stewart, *Fashioning Vienna: Adolf Loos's Cultural Criticism* (London: Routledge, 2000), and Péter Hanák, *The Garden and the Workshop: Essays on the Cultural History of Vienna and Budapest* (Princeton: Princeton University Press, 1998). On Viennese Jewry, see Robert S. Wistrich, *The Jews of Vienna in the Age of Franz Joseph* (New York: Oxford University Press, 1989), Marsha Rozenblit, *The Jews of Vienna, 1867–1914: Assimilation and Identity* (Albany: State University of New York Press, 1983), Marsha Rozenblit, *Reconstructing a National Identity: The Jews of Habsburg Austria during World War I* (New York: Oxford University Press, 2001), and Steven Beller, *Vienna and the Jews, 1867–1938: A Cultural History* (Cambridge: Cambridge University Press, 1989).

4. Arthur Schnitzler, *Comedies of Words and Other Plays*, trans. and intro. Pierre Loving (Cincinnati: Stewart & Kidd Company, 1917), viii.

5. Schorske, *Fin-de-Siècle Vienna*, 7.

6. Marsha L. Rozenblit, "The Jews of Germany and Austria: A Comparative Perspective," in *Austrians and Jews in the Twentieth Century: From Franz Joseph to Waldheim*, ed. Robert S. Wistrich (New York: St. Martin's Press, 1992), 5.

7. Schorske's hypothesis of the failure of liberalism—that political frustrations on the part of Vienna's liberals led them to turn inwards and pursue cultural modernism and the "politics of fantasy"—and its impact on later works is described in a very important essay by Allan Janik, "Vienna 1900 Revisited: Paradigms and Problems," *Austrian History Yearbook* 28 (1997): 1–27. Janik mentions in passing the work done on Viennese women and Viennese Jews; however, he does not address the question of Jewish women. Janik's essay is reprinted in

Steven Beller, ed., *Rethinking Vienna 1900* (New York: Berghahn Books, 2001), which focuses on discussing and critiquing Schorske's thesis. It includes an article on the image of women in painting and an article on Jewish identity, but not one on Jewish women.

8. Allan Janik and Stephen Toulmin, *Wittgenstein's Vienna* (New York: Simon and Schuster, 1973), 93.

9. Berta Zuckerkandl is an example. See Emily Bilski and Emily Braun, *Jewish Women and Their Salons: The Power of Conversation* (New Haven: Yale University Press, 2005), 95.

10. Gerda Lerner, *The Creation of Feminist Consciousness* (New York: Oxford University Press, 1993).

11. Janik and Toulmin, *Wittgenstein's Vienna*, 47; William M. Johnston, *The Austrian Mind: An Intellectual and Social History, 1848–1938* (Berkeley and Los Angeles: University of California Press, 1972); Karlheinz Rossbacher, *Literatur und Liberalismus: Zur Kultur der Ringstrassenzeit in Wien* (Vienna: J&V, 1992), 319–320.

12. Jacques Le Rider, *Modernity and Crises of Identity: Culture and Society in Fin-de-Siècle Vienna*, trans. Rosemary Morris (New York: Continuum, 1993).

13. Rozenblit, *Reconstructing a National Identity*, 4.

Chapter 1

1. Käthe Leichter, *Käthe Leichter: Leben und Werk*, ed. Herbert Steiner, foreword by Hertha Firnberg (Vienna: Europa Verlag, 1973), 308. Her memoirs were written while she was imprisoned by the Gestapo in 1938. She was killed by the Nazis at Ravensbrück in 1944.

2. Minna Lachs, *Warum Schaust Du Zurück: Erinnerungen, 1907–1941* (Vienna, Munich, and Zurich: Europaverlag, 1986), 72–73.

3. Leichter, *Leben und Werk*, 238.

4. On Austrian anti-Semitism in general, see Peter Pulzer, *The Rise of Political Anti-Semitism in Germany and Austria*, rev. ed. (Cambridge: Harvard University Press, 1988); Bruce Pauley, *From Prejudice to Persecution: A History of Austrian Anti-Semitism* (Chapel Hill and London: University of North Carolina Press, 1992); I. A. Hellwing, *Der konfessionelle Antisemitismus im 19. Jahrhundert in Österreich* (Vienna: Herder, 1972); and John Bunzl and Bernd Merin, *Antisemitismus in Österreich: Sozialhistorische und soziologische Studien* (Innsbruck: Inn-Verlag, 1983). For the Christian Social Party and Karl Lueger, see John Boyer, *Political Radicalism in Late Imperial Vienna: Origins of the Christian Social Movement, 1848–1897* (Chicago: University of Chicago Press, 1981), and *Culture and Political Crisis in Vienna: Christian Socialism in Power, 1897–1918* (Chicago: University of Chicago Press, 1995); and Richard Geehr, *Karl Lueger: Mayor of Fin de siècle Vienna* (Detroit: Wayne State University Press, 1990). On the Pan-German Movement and Georg von Schönerer, see

Andrew G. Whiteside, *The Socialism of Fools: Georg Ritter von Schönerer and Austrian Pan-Germanism* (Berkeley and Los Angeles: University of California Press, 1975).

5. Lillian Bader, "One Life Is Not Enough: Autobiographical Vignettes," ME 784 Leo Baeck Institute, New York, 41–43. *Stern'sche Mädchen-Lehr-und Erziehungsanstalt* (Vienna: Emil Goldstein, 1929). On the Gymnasium and Viennese Jewry, see Marsha Rozenblit, *The Jews of Vienna, 1867–1914: Assimilation and Identity* (Albany: State University of New York Press, 1983), 99–125. Also see Gary B. Cohen, *Education and Middle-Class Society in Imperial Austria: 1848–1918* (West Lafayette: Purdue University Press, 1996), 73–75, and James Albisetti, "Female Education in German-Speaking Austria, Germany and Switzerland, 1866–1914," in *Austrian Women in the Nineteenth and Twentieth Centuries: Cross-Disciplinary Perspectives*, ed. David F. Good, Margarete Grandner, and Mary Jo Maynes (Providence: Berghahn Books, 1996), 43–45, on secondary educational opportunities for women. For a detailed overview of the development of education for girls, see Elisabeth Malleier, *Jüdische Frauen in Wien, 1816–1938: Wohlfahrt—Mädchenbildung—Frauenarbeit* (Vienna: Mandelbaum, 2003), 157–159; 186–194. For Jewish university women see Harriet Pass Freidenreich, *Female, Jewish and Educated: The Lives of Central European University Women* (Bloomington and Indianapolis: Indiana University Press, 2002).

6. Cohen, *Education and Middle-Class Society*, 73.

7. Alister Campbell (grandson of Toni Stopler), "Recorded Memories: Vienna, Berlin, New York," ME 390, Leo Baeck Institute, New York, 15.

8. Dora Amann, "Ferne Erinnerungen aus meiner Kindheit Jugend und Alter," ME 900, Leo Baeck Institute, New York, 34.

9. Ulrich R. Furst, "Windows to My Youth," ME 902, Leo Baeck Institute, New York, 3.

10. Ibid.

11. Esti Freud, "Vignettes of My Life," ME 149, Leo Baeck Institute, New York, 12. Esti Freud was the daughter-in-law of Sigmund Freud.

12. Lise Meitner to Frl. Hitzenberger, March 29/April 10, 1951 (Meitner Collection, Churchill College Archives Centre, Cambridge), and Lise Meitner, "Looking Back," *Bulletin of the Atomic Scientists* 20 (November 1964): 2–7. Both are cited in Ruth Lewin Sime, *Lise Meitner: A Life in Physics* (Berkeley and Los Angeles: University of California Press, 1996), 7.

13. Leichter, *Leben und Werk*, 305.

14. Max Grunwald, *Vienna* (Philadelphia: Jewish Publication Society, 1936), 338; Ottilie Bondy, *5. Jahrbericht des Vereins für erweiterte Frauenbildung in Wien*; Rosa Feigenbaum, "70. Geburtstag Ottilie Bondy," *Neuzeit*, July 26, 1902. Elisabeth Malleier, *Jüdische Frauen in der wiener bürgerlichen Frauenbewegung 1890–1938*, Ph.D. diss. (2001), 14–17.

15. Cohen, *Education and Middle-Class Society*, 75. According to Cohen, "women from disadvantaged minority groups like the Jews or from the families

of educated professionals and officials accounted for a large share of the pioneering female students in Austria's secondary schools and higher education."

16. Olly Schwarz, "Lebens-Erinnerungen," ME 590, Leo Baeck Institute, New York, 17–18.

17. Rozenblit, *The Jews of Vienna*, 118–122. Hans Deichmann, *Leben mit provisorischer Genehmigung: Leben, Werk und Exil von Dr. Eugenie Schwarzwald (1872–1940)* (Berlin and Vienna: Mühlheim, 1981).

18. Elisabeth Derow-Turnauer, "Women and the Musical Aesthetics of the Bourgeoisie," in *Vienna: Jews and the City of Music, 1870–1938*, ed. Leon Botstein and Werner Hanak, catalogue published in conjunction with the Yeshiva University Museum (Annandale-on-Hudson: Bard College and Wolke Verlag, 2004), 127.

19. Helga Embacher, "Aussenseiterinnen: bürgerlich, jüdisch, intellektuell—links," *L'homme: Zeitschrift für feministische Geschichtwissenschaft* 2 (1991): 64–65. Deichmann, *Leben*. Freidenreich, *Female, Jewish and Educated*, 11–12.

20. Hilde Spiel, "Jewish Women in Austrian Culture," in *The Jews of Austria: Essays on Their Life, History and Destruction*, ed. Josef Fraenkel (London: Vallentine, Mitchell, 1967), 109. On Spiel, see Jutta Dick and Marina Sassenberg, eds., *Jüdische Frauen im 19. und 20. Jahrhundert* (Reinbek bei Hamburg: Rowohlt, 1993), 350–352.

21. Derow-Turnauer, "Women and the Musical Aesthetics," 127, and Renate Göllner, *Kein Puppenheim* (Frankfurt/Main: Peter Lang, 1999).

22. Harriet Anderson, *Utopian Feminism: Women's Movements in Fin-de-Siècle Vienna* (New Haven and London: Yale University Press, 1992), 104–110.

23. Derow-Turnauer, "Women and the Musical Aesthetics," 128, and Hilde Spiel, *Die Hellen und die Finsteren Zeiten: Erinnerungen, 1911–1946* (Reinbek bei Hamburg: Rowohlt, 1991).

24. Embacher, "Aussenseiterinnen," 65.

25. Heinz Gstrein, *Jüdisches Wien* (Vienna: Herold, 1984), 94.

26. Campbell, "Recorded Memories," 16–17.

27. Rozenblit, *Jews of Vienna*, 120–123.

28. Stopler, "Recorded Memories," 3–4.

29. Ibid., 16.

30. Anny Robert, [Memoir], ME 899, Leo Baeck Institute, New York.

31. Bader, "One Life Is Not Enough," 25–26.

32. Elisabeth Freundlich, *The Traveling Years*, trans. and afterword by Elizabeth Pennebaker (Riverside, Calif.: Ariadne Press, 1999).

33. Marie Langer, *Von Wien bis Managua: Wege einer Psychoanalytikerin* (Freiburg: Kore, Verlag Traute Hensch, 1986), 28.

34. Ibid., 34–35.

35. Ibid., 45–46.

36. "The Reminiscences of Mimi Grossberg based on a tape-recorded interview by Mrs. Rose Stein, 1979," in Mimi Grossberg, *The Road to America:*

Mimi Grossberg, Her Times and Her Emigration (New York: Austrian Institute, 1986), 82.

37. Leichter, *Leben und Werk*, 305–306.

38. Ibid., 207.

39. Ibid., 308.

40. *Käthe Leichter: Leben und Werk*, ed. Herbert Steiner (Vienna: Europa Verlag, 1973), 23.

41. Leichter, *Leben und Werk*, 308.

42. Ibid., 309.

43. Ibid., 311.

44. Erna Segal, "You Shall Never Forget," ME 594, Leo Baeck Institute, New York.

45. Ibid., 6.

46. Ibid., 6–7.

47. Amann, "Ferne Erinnerungen," 18–19.

48. B. "Antisemitismus in der Schule," *Freies Blatt: Organ zur Abwehr des Antisemitismus* 2/53 (April 9, 1893): 1.

49. Lachs, *Erinnerungen*.

50. Ibid., 51, 71.

51. Ibid., 72.

52. Ibid., 75.

53. Sime, *Lise Meitner*, 4–6. According to Robert A. Kyle and Marc A. Shampo, she was baptized and raised as a Protestant, probably on the basis of her nephew's account. *JAMA* 245:20 (May 22/29, 1981), Lise Meitner Collection, AR 2729, Leo Baeck Institute, New York.

54. Sime, *Lise Meitner*, 6.

55. Ibid., 7.

56. Hans Helmut Christmann, *Frau und "Jüdin" an der Universität: Die Romanistin Elise Richter (Wien 1865–Theresienstadt 1943)* (Mainz: Akademie der Wissenschaften und der Literatur, 1980), 8.

57. Elise Richter, *Summe des Lebens* (Elise Richter Collection at Wienbibliothek im Rathaus), 76. The Matura-certificate (in the Elise Richter Collection) indicated "confessionslos." See Christmann, *Frau und Jüdin*, 8–9.

58. "Schule und Haus," *Die Wahrheit* 32 (August 15, 1913): 1–2.

59. Solomon B. Freehof, *Reform Jewish Practice and Its Rabbinic Background*, I and II (New York: Union of American Hebrew Congregations, 1964, 1944), 22–26.

60. W. Gunther Plaut, *The Rise of Reform Judaism: A Sourcebook of Its European Origins* (New York: World Union for Progressive Judaism, 1963), 171.

61. Michael Meyer, *Response to Modernity: A History of the Reform Movement in Judaism* (New York: Oxford University Press, 1988), 39.

62. Benjamin Maria Baader, *Gender, Judaism, and Bourgeois Culture in Germany, 1800–1870* (Bloomington: Indiana University Press, 2006), 148.

63. See, for example, Salomon Herxheimer, "Is Confirmation a 'Jewish' Ceremony?" in Plaut, *Rise of Reform*, 175–177. Recognizing that the Christian confirmation, as an integral part of baptism necessary for acceptance in the Church, did not apply to Judaism because Jews are Jewish by birth and descent, Herxheimer argued that the Jewish confirmation was intended as a pledge of the Jew to remain faithful to his faith. He gave examples from the Bible, Talmud, and Mishnah, in order to prove that vows of loyalty to specific laws and to Judaism as a whole were part of the Jewish tradition. He also justified the confirmation on the grounds that the traditional rabbi, Samuel Levi Eger (Egers) (1769–1842), of Brunswick, Germany, held confirmations for boys and girls beginning in 1831, and that a pious Jew includes a formal "confirmation" in his daily morning prayer, when he recites the Thirteen Articles of Faith by Maimonides.

64. Meyer, *Response*, 404 n. 112; Baader, *Gender*, 149.

65. Isaac Asher Francolm, "Simplicity, Not Pomp," in Plaut, *Rise of Reform*, 173–175.

66. See "For Total Equality (Report to the Breslau Conference, 1846)," in Plaut, *Rise of Reform*, 253–255. And David Philipson, "Age of Confirmation," in W. Gunther Plaut, *The Growth of Reform Judaism: American and European Sources until 1948* (New York: World Union for Progressive Judaism, 1965), 314–315.

67. Marion Kaplan, *The Making of the Jewish Middle Class: Women, Family, and Identity in Imperial Germany* (New York: Oxford University Press, 1991), 67.

68. Meyer, *Response*, 149–150. For more on Mannheimer's shift see Plaut, *Rise of Reform*, 42–44, and Robert S. Wistrich, *The Jews of Vienna in the Age of Franz Joseph* (New York: Oxford University Press, 1989), 98–105.

69. Meyer, *Response*, 145.

70. Gerson Wolf, *Geschichte der Israelitischen Cultusgemeinde in Wien (1820–1860)* (Vienna: Wilhelm Braumüller, 1861), 152.

71. Ibid.

72. Adolf Jellinek, "Die religiöse Erziehung des israelitischen Weibes (Wochenfest, 1864)" *Das Weib in Israel: Drei Reden* (Vienna: Herzfeld & Bauer, n.d.), 1–19.

73. Ibid., 19.

74. Salomon Wininger, *Grosse Jüdische National-Biographie, mit mehr als 8000 Lebensbeschreibungen namhafter jüdischer Männer und Frauen aller Zeiten und Länder.* Cernauti: Druck "Orient" (1925–1936), 349–350.

75. Meir Friedmann, "Mitwirkung von Frauen bei Gottesdienste," *Hebrew Union College Annual* 8 (1931): 511–523.

76. Ibid.

77. Ibid.

78. *Lehrplan und Instruktionen für den Konfirmations-Unterricht der weiblichen Jugend* (Vienna, 1896), Central Archives for the History of the Jewish People, Jerusalem, A/W 1634.

79. *Ibid.*

80. *Ibid.*

81. Fr. "Die Mädchenkonfirmation," *Die Wahrheit* 27 (July 11, 1913): 5–6.

82. Rabbi Löwy, "Die Mädchenkonfirmation," *Die Wahrheit* 29 (August 1, 1913): 5–6.

83. Amann, "Ferne Erinnerungen," 18.

84. "Müde bin Ich, geh zu Ruh,/ Schliesse meine Aüglein zu./ Vater lass die Augen dein,/ Über meinem Bette sein./ Alle, die mir sind verwandt,/ Gott lass ruh'n, in deine Hand." Robert, [Memoir], 27. ("I am tired go to rest/ Close my little eyes/ Father let your eyes/ Watch over my bed./ All that are related to me/ God let them rest in Your Hand.")

85. Gertrude Berliner, "From My Family: Fiction and Truth," ME 51, Leo Baeck Institute, New York, 5.

86. Ibid. 28.

87. Salka Viertel, *The Kindness of Strangers* (New York: Holt, Rinehart and Winston, 1969), 12.

88. Stella Klein-Löw, *Erinnerungen: Erlebtes und Gedachtes* (Vienna: Jugend und Volk, 1980), 13.

89. Ibid., 13.

90. Freud, "Vignettes," 7.

91. Toni Cassirer, "Aus meinem Leben mit Ernst Cassirer," ME 89, Leo Baeck Institute, New York, 4.

92. David Baumgardt, "Toni Cassirer," in ibid.

93. Viertel, *Kindness*, 8.

94. Ibid.

95. Ibid., 30.

96. Leichter, *Leben und Werk*; Gstrein, *Jüdisches Wien*, 94–95.

97. Leichter, *Leben und Werk*, 239.

98. Ibid., 240.

Chapter 2

1. Paula E. Hyman, *Gender and Assimilation in Modern Jewish History: The Roles and Representation of Women* (Seattle: University of Washington Press, 1995); Marion Kaplan, *The Making of the Jewish Middle Class: Women, Family, and Identity in Imperial Germany* (New York: Oxford University Press, 1991).

2. Hyman, *Gender and Assimilation*, chapter 2.

3. Jacob Freund, *Hanna: Gebet und Undachtsbuch für israelitische Frauen und Mädchen* (Breslau: Verlag von Wilh. Jacobsohn u. Comp, 1893), and Arnold Kiss, *Mirjam: Gebet und Andachtsbuch für Israelitische Frauen und Mädchen* (Budapest: Verlag von Schlesinger Jos, n.d.). These were brought to my attention by David Stern. These and others are discussed and analyzed in Bettina Kratz-Ritter, *Für "Fromme Zionstöchter" und "Gebildete Frauenzimmer": An-*

dachtsliteratur für deutsch-jüdische Frauen im 19. und frühen 20. Jahrhundert (Hildesheim: Georg Olms, 1995), and Benjamin Maria Baader, *Gender, Judaism, and Bourgeois Culture in Germany, 1800–1870* (Bloomington: Indiana University Press, 2006), 117–133.

4. Max Grunwald, *Beruria: Gebet- und Andachtsbuch für jüdische Frauen und Mädchen* (Vienna, 1907), 36–37.

5. Ibid., 90–91.

6. Ibid., 402.

7. Marsha Rozenblit, *The Jews of Vienna, 1867–1914: Assimilation and Identity* (Albany: State University of New York Press, 1983), 150.

8. Kaplan, *Making of the Jewish Middle Class*, 196–197.

9. Max Grunwald, *Vienna* (Philadelphia: Jewish Publication Society, 1936), 524–525.

10. According to Grunwald and Wolf, a Frauenverein was founded by Frau Nassau, mother of the well-known philanthropist Wolf Isak, in 1821. Despite the discrepancy in the dates, I believe this to be a reference to the same Israelitischer Frauen-(Wohltätigkeits)-Verein which was founded in 1815. Ibid., 386–387, 524; Gerson Wolf, *Geschichte der Israelitischen Cultusgemeinde in Wien (1820–1860)* (Vienna: Wilhelm Braumüller, 1861), 177–178.

11. Klaus Hödl, *Als Bettler in die Leopoldstadt: Galizische Juden auf dem Weg nach Wien* (Vienna: Böhlau Verlag, 1994), 224.

12. "Isr. Frauen-Wohltätigkeits-Verein in Wien," *Die Neuzeit* (1902), 65.

13. Grunwald, *Vienna*, 386–387.

14. Adolf Jellinek, "Rede zur Feier des funfzigjährigen Bestehens des israelitischen Frauen-Vereins in Wien (Am 1. Januar 1866)," *Das Weib in Israel. Drei Reden* (Vienna: Herzfeld & Bauer).

15. *100. Vereinsjahr. Jubilaeums- und Jahres-Bericht für das Jahr 1915 (Israelitischer Frauen-Wohltätigkeits-Verein)* (Vienna, 1916). Central Archives for the History of the Jewish People, Jerusalem, A/W 2232, 28, 20.

16. *Jahres-Bericht des Israelitischen Frauen-Vereines in Wien für das Jahr 1891* (Vienna, 1892). Central Archives for the History of the Jewish People, Jerusalem, A/W 2232, 24.

17. *Jahres-Bericht des Israelitischen Frauen-Vereines in Wien für das Jahr 1892* (Vienna, 1893). Central Archives for the History of the Jewish People, Jerusalem, A/W 2232, 25.

18. "Isr. Frauen-Wohltätigkeits-Verein in Wien," *Die Neuzeit* (1902), 65.

19. *Jahres-Bericht des Israelitischen Frauen-Wohltätigkeits-Vereines in Wien für das Jahr 1911* (Vienna, 1912). Central Archives for the History of the Jewish People, Jerusalem, A/W 2232, 27, 4–6.

20. *100 Vereinsjahr*, 14.

21. *Siebenunddreissigster Jahresbericht des Mädchen-Unterstützungs-Vereines* (Vienna, 1904). Central Archives for the History of the Jewish People, Jerusalem. A/W 2316.

22. "Der Mädchen-Unterstützungs-Verein in Wien," *Die Neuzeit* (February 8, 1889), Nr. 6.: 56; (February 22, 1889), Nr. 8: 75–76, 54.

23. *Zweiter Jahresbericht über das israelitische Mädchen-Waisenhaus in Wien im Jahre 1875* (Vienna, 1876). Leo Baeck Institute Archives, New York.

24. *Ibid.*, 7.

25. Clothilde Benedikt, "Rosa Zifferer-Schüler," *Österreichische Wochenschrift* 6 (Feb. 10, 1911): 90.

26. *Elfter Jahresbericht des "Frauenhort" Israelitischer Frauen-Wohltätigkeits-Verein im Bezirke Alsergrund in Wien* (Vienna, 1904). Leo Baeck Institute Archives, New York, 5–7.

27. Ibid., 7.

28. Benedikt, "Rosa Zifferer-Schüler," 90.

29. *Bericht des Brigittenauer Israelitischer Frauen-Wohltätigkeitsvereines in Wien über seine Tätigkeit im Vereinsjahre 1910.* Central Archives for the History of the Jewish People, Jerusalem, A/W 2373, 6.

30. "Frauenhort," 10; *Bericht des BIFWV 1910*, 8–11.

31. *Bericht des BIFWV 1910*, 10.

32. Rozenblit, *Jews of Vienna*, 78–79.

33. *Österreichische Wochenschrift* 17/16 (April 20, 1900); 28/9 (March 3, 1911); 29/7 (February 16, 1912).

34. *Jüdischer Frauen-Wohltätigkeits-Verein "Zuflucht"* (Vienna, 1902). Central Archives for the History of the Jewish People, Jerusalem, A/W 2266, 3.

35. *II. Jahres-Bericht des jüd. Frauen-Wohltätigkeits-Vereines "Zuflucht" in Wien 1902.* Central Archives for the History of the Jewish People, Jerusalem, A/W 2267.

36. *III. Jahres-Bericht des jüd. Frauen-Wohltätigkeits-Vereines "Zuflucht" in Wien 1903.* Central Archives for the History of the Jewish People, Jerusalem, A/W 2267, 2, 3.

37. *IV. Jahres-Bericht des jüd. Frauen-Wohltätigkeits-Vereines "Zuflucht" in Wien 1904.* Central Archives for the History of the Jewish People, Jerusalem, A/W 2267, 3, 4.

38. *V. Jahres-Bericht des jüd. Frauen-Wohltätigkeits-Vereines "Zuflucht" in Wien 1905.* Central Archives for the History of the Jewish People, Jerusalem, A/W 2267, 4, 3. *VII. Jahres-Bericht des jüd. Frauen-Wohltätigkeits-Vereines "Zuflucht" in Wien 1907.* Central Archives for the History of the Jewish People, Jerusalem, A/W 2267, 6, 4.

39. *IX. Jahres-Bericht des "Zuflucht" in Wien 1909.* Central Archives for the History of the Jewish People, Jerusalem, A/W 2267, 4.

40. *Zweiter Jahresbericht des Hietzinger Frauenwohltätigkeitsvereines* (Vienna, 1908). Central Archives for the History of the Jewish People, Jerusalem, A/W 2353, 2, 4.

41. *Jahresbericht des Hietzinger Frauenwohltätigkeitsvereines* (Vienna, 1907). Central Archives for the History of the Jewish People, Jerusalem. A/W 2353, 1, 7.

42. *Vierter Jahresbericht des Hietzinger Frauenwohltätigkeitsvereines* (Vienna, 1910). Central Archives for the History of the Jewish People, Jerusalem, A/W 2353, 3, 3.

43. *Hietzinger Frauenverein zum Schutze Armer, Verlassener Kinder. Neunter Jahresbericht* (Vienna, 1915). Central Archives for the History of the Jewish People, Jerusalem, A/W 2353, 6, 5.

44. *Achter Jahresbericht des Hietzinger Frauenwohltätigkeitsvereines* (Vienna, 1914). Central Archives for the History of the Jewish People, Jerusalem, A/W 2353, 5, 11.

45. *Vierter Jahresbericht des HFWV*, 4–7.

46. Rudolf Kraus, "Zentralisierung der Armenfürsorge" (Vienna, 1909), supplement to *Vierter Jahresbericht des HFWV*, 11–12.

47. *Statuten des Mädchen- u. Frauen-Vereines "Bikur Chaulim" in Wien.* Central Archives for the History of the Jewish People, Jerusalem, A/W 2236, 4, 3.

48. *VII. Jahresbericht des Mädchen- und Frauen-Vereines "Krankenbesuch": (Bikur Chaulim)* (Vienna, 1910). Central Archives for the History of the Jewish People, Jerusalem, A/W 2236, 2.

49. *II. Rechenschafts-Bericht des Mädchen- und Frauen-Vereines "Bikur Chaulim"* (Vienna, 1904). Central Archives for the History of the Jewish People, Jerusalem, A/W 2236, 1, 6.

50. *II. Rechenschafts-Bericht des "Bikur Chaulim,"* 6.

51. "J.," "Die Frauen in der Wiener Cultusgemeinde," *Die Neuzeit* (Dec. 14, 1888), Nr. 50, p. 1.

52. Dieter Josef Hecht, "Anitta Müller-Cohen (1890–1962): Sozialarbeiterin, Feministin, Politikerin, Zionistin und Journalistin; ein Beitrag zur jüdischen Frauengeschichte in Österreich 1914–1929," Ph.D. dissertation (Vienna, 2002).

53. Jacob Toury, *Die Jüdische Presse im Österreichischen Kaiserreich: 1802–1918* (Tübingen: J.C.B. Mohr, 1983), 73.

54. Michael Meyer, *Response to Modernity: A History of the Reform Movement in Judaism* (New York and Oxford: Oxford University Press, 1988), 193.

55. Robert Wistrich, "The Modernization of Viennese Jewry: The Impact of German Culture in a Multi-Ethnic State," in *Toward Modernity: The European Jewish Model*, ed. Jacob Katz (New Brunswick: Transaction Books, 1987), 54.

56. Mannheimer had come to Vienna as an ardent reformer, but he gradually became more traditional, and by 1830 he was eager to protect the status quo. For more on this shift see W. Gunther Plaut, *The Rise of Reform Judaism: A Sourcebook of Its European Origins* (New York: World Union for Progressive Judaism, 1963), 42–44, and Robert Wistrich, *The Jews of Vienna in the Age of Franz Joseph* (New York: Oxford University Press, 1989), 98–105.

57. Ismar Schorsch, "Moritz Güdemann: Rabbi, Historian and Apologist," *Leo Baeck Institute Yearbook* 11 (1966): 42–66, p. 46.

58. Wistrich, "Modernization," 50–51, and *Jews of Vienna*, ch. 4, 8.

59. Adolf Jellinek, "Orient und Occident," *Die Neuzeit* 21, 1883, 203. *Die Neuzeit* (1861–1904) was founded by Leopold Kompert and Simon Szanto. In 1882, Jellinek became the editor, and after his death in 1893, Moritz Lazarus became the editor.

60. Adolf Jellinek, *Die Psyche des Weibes* (Vienna, 1872).

61. Ibid., 12–14.

62. Ibid., 19–20.

63. Jellinek, *Der jüdische Stamm in nichtjüdischen Sprichwörtern*, 3 vols. (Vienna: Bermann & Altmann, 1882–1886) (1886), 31.

64. Adolf Jellinek, *Studien und Skizzen. Erster Theil. Der jüdische Stamm. Ethnografische Studie* (Vienna: Herzfeld & Bauer, 1869), 84–87.

65. Jellinek, *Stamm*, 89–90. Quoted and translated in Sander Gilman, *Freud, Race and Gender* (New Jersey: Princeton University Press, 1993), 43.

66. Ibid., 96–97.

67. Adolf Jellinek, "Juden und Weiber," *Die Neuzeit* 33 (1882): 277.

68. In this respect, his ideas are very similar to those of the contemporary scholar Daniel Boyarin, who makes the case that the ideal of masculinity according to traditional culture was the feminine, gentle, studious rabbi. Daniel Boyarin, *Unheroic Conduct: The Rise of Heterosexuality and the Invention of the Jewish Man* (Berkeley and Los Angeles: University of California Press, 1997).

69. George Mosse, *Nationalism and Sexuality: Middle Class Morality and Sexual Norms in Modern Europe* (Madison: University of Wisconsin Press, 1985), 16. "The clear and distinct roles assigned to men and women were basic— they will occupy us throughout our study."

70. Adolf Jellinek, "Die religiöse Erziehung des israelitischen Weibes (Wochenfest, 1864)," *Das Weib in Israel: Drei Reden* (Vienna: Herzfeld & Bauer, n.d.), 1–19.

71. Ibid., 7.

72. Ibid., 10.

73. Quotation is from Rabbi Eliezer. It refers to the belief that the merit of Torah study protected women from the effects of the ritual of "trial by ordeal." According to this ritual, a woman accused of adultery was forced to drink a bitter potion. If guilty "her belly shall distend and her thigh shall sag" (Num. 5:27), while if innocent, "she shall remain unharmed, and able to retain seed" (Num. 5:28). Ben Azzai advocates teaching one's daughter Torah in order to give her protection in case she ever faces the ordeal. R. Eliezer fears that such education gives her license for adultery. See Judith Romney Wegner, *Chattel or Person? The Status of Women in the Mishnah* (New York: Oxford University Press, 1988), 52–54, 161.

74. Jellinek, "Rede," 43–44.

75. Jellinek, *Stamm*, 69–80. This chapter, entitled "The Family Sense of the Jewish Tribe," was from a speech which depicted the Jewish family sense in biblical times, and also illustrated it through sayings and later legends.

76. Ibid., 71–74.

77. This chapter, entitled "Weibliche Arbeit," was written in 1863.

78. Ibid., 100. Probably a reference to Anna E. Dickinson, an American feminist who was prominent around that time.

79. Ibid., 101.

80. Ibid., 65–67.

81. Some other examples are A. Th. Hartmann, *Die Hebräerin am Putztische und als Braut*, 3 Volumes (Amsterdam, 1809–1810), and Stephan Darnau, "Die palästinensische Jüdin am Putztisch," Lecture at Österreichische-Israelitische Union, 21 February, 1909. Monatschrift der öst.-isr. Union XXI, 2: 16–29.

82. Jellinek, *Sprichwörtern*, 66–67.

83. In two articles which appeared in *Die Neuzeit* under the initial "J," Jellinek focused on the question of women and anti-Semitism. "J.," "Die Frauen und der Antisemitismus," *Die Neuzeit* 1 (1885): 7–8; and "J.," "Geistliche und weibliche Antisemiten," *Die Neuzeit* 5 (1886): 139–140. See Alison Rose, "Gender and Anti-Semitism: Christian Social Women and the Jewish Response in Turn-of-the-Century Vienna," *Austrian History Yearbook* 34 (2003): 173–189.

84. Wistrich, *Jews of Vienna*, 122.

85. The term *apologetic* had completely different connotations in the context of nineteenth-century Jewry than it has today. It was considered honorable to write apologetic works which defended Judaism from its detractors in the tradition of the disputations of the Middle Ages. For example, Güdemann argued in *Jüdische Apologetik* (Glogau: C. Fleming, 1906) that Jewish national history had no meaning other than to teach the non-Jewish world the lessons of universal brotherhood and the acceptance of God's kingdom by all humanity. See Moshe (Moritz) Güdemann, *HaYahadut HaLeumit*, foreword by Robert S. Wistrich, trans. by Miriam Dinur (Jerusalem: Dinur Center, 1995), 9.

86. Moritz Güdemann, *Das Leben des jüdischen Weibes. Sittengeschichtlich Skizze aus der mischnisch-talmudischen Epoche*. Separat-Abdruck aus Kobak's "Jeschurun," 5619 (Breslau: Sulzbach's Buchdruckerei, 1859), 2.

87. Ibid., 13–15.

88. Ibid., 16–18.

89. Ibid., 21.

90. Ibid., 26.

91. Schorsch, "Moritz Güdemann," p. 62.

92. Moritz Güdemann, *Geschichte des Erziehungswesens und der Cultur den Juden in Frankreich und Deutschland*, vol. I (Vienna: Alfred Holder, 1880), 229.

93. Ibid.

94. Ibid., 231.

95. Ibid., 237. He compared this to a contemporary statement by a Christian preacher to show that the Jews treated their wives better. However, he did not mention that some of the Jewish customs which he used to demonstrate the moral

superiority of the Jews, particularly that wives of martyrs should not remarry and that women who were abused by their husbands should be withdrawn from their husbands' dominion and granted means for subsistence, actually resulted from a Christian influence.

96. Ibid., 258.

97. Moritz Güdemann, *Geschichte des Erziehungswesens und der Cultur den Juden in Frankreich und Deutschland*, vol. II (Vienna: Alfred Holder, 1884), ch. VII.

98. Ibid., 213.

99. Ibid., 215.

100. Güdemann's conclusions differ from those of contemporary treatments such as Baskin's. According to Baskin, the "conflict between pious expectations and the realities of women's lives is paradigmatic of the ambiguities that must inform any study of Jewish women . . ." Judith Baskin, "Jewish Women in the Middle Ages," *Jewish Women in Historical Perspective* (Detroit: Wayne State University Press, 1991), 94. While Güdemann did make the distinction between reality and theory, he did not view the realities of Jewish lives as shortcomings. He saw them instead as useful and necessary ways to function in different situations. The Jews were praised by Güdemann for keeping in step with the morality of the day. However, in some cases outside influences on the Jews had a detrimental impact. Güdemann hints at this side as well, but it is not emphasized.

101. On Bloch, see Joseph S. Bloch, *My Reminiscences* (Vienna and Berlin: R. Löwit, 1923), Wistrich, *Jews of Vienna*, ch. 9, and Ian Reifowitz, *Imagining an Austrian Nation: Joseph Samuel Bloch and the Search for a Supraethnic Austrian Identity, 1846–1918* (Boulder: East European Monographs, 2003).

102. Wistrich, *Jews of Vienna*, 281.

103. Joseph S. Bloch, *Israel and the Nations*, trans. Leon Kellner and Henry Schneidermann (Berlin: Benjamin Harz Verlag, 1927).

104. Ibid., XXII.

105. August Rohling, *Der Talmudjude* (Munster: Adolph Russell's Verlag, 1876).

106. Bloch, *Israel*, XXIX.

107. Ibid., XXX.

108. Ibid., XXXII.

109. Ibid., XXXV.

110. Ibid., 288–289.

111. Ibid., 294.

112. Ibid., 295. Bloch cited Max Grunwald, *Österreichische Wochenschrift*, file 1908.

113. Edward J. Bristow, *Prostitution and Prejudice: The Jewish Fight against White Slavery, 1870–1939* (New York: Schocken Books, 1983).

114. Ibid., 75.

115. Ibid., 76.

116. Ibid., 80.

117. Bloch, *My Reminiscences*, 308.

118. Ibid., 309.

119. Ibid.

120. Bristow, *Prostitution*, 83.

121. Hans Tietze, *Die Juden Wiens: Geschichte-Wirtschaft-Kultur* (Vienna: Edition Atelier, 1987, 1933), 247–248.

122. Adolf Schwarz, *Der Frauen der Bibel (Drei Vorträge gehalten in der "Jüdischen Toynbee-Halle" in Wien)* (Vienna: Verlag von R. Loewit, 1903).

123. Leopold Goldhammer, "Die Ehe bei den Greichen, Römern und Juden: Eine culturhistorische Skizze," *Reichsbote* 1 (Vienna, 1894): 16, 9–11, 18, 10–12.

124. F[riedländer, Moritz], "Einiges über die Stellung des römischen und jüdischen Weibes im Altherthume," *Die Neuzeit* 22 (1882), 541–542, 550–551, 559–560.

125. Ibid., 551.

126. Ibid., 560.

127. Darnau, "Putztisch," 16–29, 10.

128. Ibid., 19–20.

129. Ibid., 22–26.

130. Naum Klugmann, *Die Frau im Talmud* (Vienna, 1898).

131. Ibid., 15–16.

132. See M. Löbel, "Die sociale Stellung der jüdischen Frau im Altertum. Vortrag, geh. am 8. Febr. 1896 in der OIU." *Mitteilungen der Österreichisch-Israelitischen Union* 8 1896; Heinrich Reich, "Die Frau im Talmud," *Reichsbote* 1 (1894) Nr. 1, p. 10, Nr. 2, p. 10, Nr. 3, 13–14, and J. Stern, "Die Frau im Talmud," *Monatschrift der Österreichisch-Israelitischen Union* 23 (1911), Nr. 2, 12–16.

133. Max Grunwald, *Die moderne Frauenbewegung und das Judenthum.* Lecture held in the OIU on March 11, 1903. Published as a manuscript (Vienna, 1903), 15.

134. Ibid., 24.

Chapter 3

1. Marion Kaplan, *The Making of the Jewish Middle Class: Women, Family, and Identity in Imperial Germany* (New York: Oxford University Press, 1991), 137.

2. Robert Wistrich, *The Jews of Vienna in the Age of Franz Joseph* (New York: Oxford University Press, 1989), 59.

3. Waltraud Heindl and Rudolf Wytek, "Die jüdischen Studentinnen an der Universität Wien, 1897–1938," in *Der Wiener Stadttempel, Die Wiener Juden* (Vienna: J & V, 1988), 139. Waltraud Heindl and Marina Tichy, "Durch Erkenntnis zu Freiheit und Glück . . ." *Frauen and der Universität Wien (ab 1897)* (Vienna: Schriftenreihe des Universitätsarchivs, V, 1990).

4. Heindl and Wytek, "Jüdischen Studentinnen," 139.

5. Ibid., 140.

6. Ibid., 143.

7. Ibid., 146.

8. Ibid.

9. Edith Prost, "Emigration und Exil österreichischer Wissenschaftler-innen," in *Vertriebene Vernunft I: Emigration und Exil österreichischer Wissenschaft, 1930–1940*, ed. Friedrich Stadler (Vienna: Jugend und Volk, 1989/90), 450.

10. James C. Albisetti, "Female Education in German-Speaking Austria, Germany and Switzerland, 1866–1914," in *Austrian Women in the Nineteenth and Twentieth Centuries: Cross-Disciplinary Perspectives*, ed. David F. Good, Margarete Grandner, and Mary Jo Maynes (Providence: Berghahn Books, 1996), 52.

11. Hans Helmut Christmann, *Frau und "Jüdin" an der Universität: Die Romanistin Elise Richter (Wien 1865–Theresienstadt 1943)* (Mainz: Akademie der Wissenschaften und der Literatur, 1980), 10, 14, 15.

12. R. A. Kyle and M. A. Shampo, "Lise Meitner," *Journal of the American Medical Association* 20, 2021 (May 22, 1981), and "Lise Meitner Dies," Lise Meitner Collection, AR 2729, Leo Baeck Institute Archives, New York. The first was Olga Steindler, who received her doctorate in 1903 and established the Handelsakademie für Mädchen with Olly Schwarz. Ruth Lewin Sime, *Lise Meitner: A Life in Physics* (Berkeley and Los Angeles: University of California Press, 1996), 398, n. 82.

13. MEITNER (Kyle and Shampo), Lise Meitner Collection; Prost, "Emigration," 447.

14. Wilhelm Frank, "Richard von Mises und Hilda Geiringer-Mises, Anmerkungen zu deren Lebenslauf," in *Vertriebene Vernunft II: Emigration und Exil österreichischer Wissenschaft, 1930–1940*, ed. Friedrich Stadler (Vienna, Munich: Jugend und Volk, 1989/90), 753.

15. Alister Campbell (grandson of Toni Stopler), "Recorded Memories: Vienna, Berlin, New York," ME 390, Leo Baeck Institute, New York, 17–22.

16. Ibid., 23.

17. Ibid., 24.

18. Lillian Bader, "One Life Is Not Enough: Autobiographical Vignettes," ME 784, Leo Baeck Institute, New York, 59.

19. Harriet Pass Freidenreich, "Jewish Identity and the 'New Woman': Central European Jewish University Women in the Early Twentieth Century," in *Gender and Judaism: The Transformation of Tradition*, ed. Tamar Rudavsky (New York: New York University Press, 1995), 113. Also Harriet Pass Freidenreich, *Female, Jewish, and Educated: The Lives of Central European University Women. The Modern Jewish Experience.* (Bloomington: Indiana University Press, 2002).

20. Freidenreich, "Jewish Identity," 114, 116.

21. Ibid., 118–119.

22. Albisetti, "Female Education," 44–53.

23. Kaplan, *Making of the Jewish Middle Class*, 209–214.

24. Harriet Anderson, *Utopian Feminism: Women's Movements in Fin-de-Siècle Vienna* (New Haven and London: Yale University Press, 1992), and "Feminism as a Vocation: Motives for Joining the Austrian Women's Movement," in *Vienna 1900: From Altenberg to Wittgenstein*, ed. Edward Timms and Ritchie Robertson (Edinburgh University Press, 1990); Erika Weinzierl, "Österreichische Frauenbewegungen um die Jahrhundertwende," in *Wien um 1900: Aufbruch in die Moderne*, ed. Peter Berner, Emil Brix, and Wolfgang Mantl (Vienna, Munich, Oldenbourg: Verlag für Geschichte und Politik, 1986).

25. Adelheid Popp, *The Autobiography of a Working Woman*, trans. E. C. Harvey (Westport, Conn.: Hyperion Press, 1983); Edith Prost, ed., *"Die Partei Hat Mich Nie Enttäuscht . . ." Österreichische Sozialdemokratinnen* (Vienna: Verlag für Gesellschaftskritik, 1989).

26. Marianne Hainisch, "Die Geschichte der Frauenbewegung in Öesterreich," (1901) in *Handbuch der Frauenbewegung*, vol. I, ed. Helene Lange and Gertrude Baumer (Weinheim: Beltz, 1980), 179.

27. Albisetti, "Female Education," 39–58.

28. Birgitta Bader-Zaar, "Women in Austrian Politics, 1890–1934: Goals and Visions," in *Austrian Women in the Nineteenth and Twentieth Centuries: Cross-Disciplinary Perspectives*, ed. David Good, Margarete Grandner, and Mary Jo Maynes (Providence: Berghahn Books, 1996), 59–85.

29. Gerda Neyer, "Women in the Austrian Parliament: Opportunities and Barriers," in *Austrian Women in the Nineteenth and Twentieth Centuries: Cross-Disciplinary Perspectives*, ed. David Good, Margarete Grandner, and Mary Jo Maynes (Providence: Berghahn Books, 1996), 91–114.

30. Anthony Tommasini, "Glorious, Yes, But Resisting Today's World: The Vienna Philharmonic Returns, Virtually a Male Bastion," *New York Times*, March 15, 1999, Arts section.

31. Marina Tichy, " 'Ich hatte immer Angst, unwissend zu sterben,' Therese Schlesinger: Bürgerin und Sozialistin," in *"Die Partei hat mich nie enttäuscht": Österreichische Sozialdemokratinnen*, ed. Edith Prost (Vienna: Verlag für Gesellschaftskritik, 1989), 135.

32. Ibid., 145.

33. Therese Schlesinger, "Ziele der Frauenbewegung (Vortrag)," *Volksstimme*, Nr. 227 (1896), 7, cited in Tichy, "Therese Schlesinger," 139–140.

34. Letter from Therese Schlesinger to Auguste Fickert 24.11.97, Handschriftensammlung, Wiener Stadt- und Landesarchiv, cited in Tichy, "Therese Schlesinger," 142.

35. Therese Schlesinger, "Mein Weg zur Sozialdemokratie," in *Gedenkbuch. 20 Jahre österreichische Arbeiterinnenbewegung*, edited by Adelheid Popp (Vienna, 1912), 139, cited in Tichy, "Therese Schlesinger," 138.

36. Therese Schlesinger, *Was wollen die Frauen in der Politik?* 2nd edition (Vienna, 1910), 26–27. Bader-Zaar, "Women in Austrian Politics," 65.

37. Charles Sowerwine, "Socialism, Feminism, and the Socialist Women's Movement from the French Revolution to World War II," in *Becoming Visible: Women in European History*, third ed., ed. Renate Bridenthal, Susan Mosher Stuard, and Merry E. Wiesner (Boston: Houghton Mifflin Company, 1998), 378–379.

38. Tichy, "Therese Schlesinger," 148–149.

39. Ibid., 135.

40. Anderson, *Utopian Feminism*, 56, 131.

41. Georg von Schönerer, *Alldeutsches Tagblatt* (January 1907). Peter Pulzer, *The Rise of Political Anti-Semitism in Germany and Austria* (New York: John Wiley & Sons, 1964), 222.

42. Karin J. Jušek, "The Limits of Female Desire: The Contributions of Austrian Feminists to the Sexual Debate in Fin-de-Siècle Vienna," in *Austrian Women in the Nineteenth and Twentieth Centuries: Cross-Disciplinary Perspectives*, ed. David Good, Margarete Grandner, and Mary Jo Maynes (Providence: Berghahn Books, 1996), 24–25.

43. Edward J. Bristow, *Prostitution and Prejudice: The Jewish Fight against White Slavery, 1870–1939* (New York: Schocken Books, 1983), 233.

44. Helga Thorson, "Confronting Anti-Semitism and Antifeminism in Turn of the Century Vienna: Grete Meisel-Hess and the Feminist Discourses on Hysteria," in *Jüdische Identitäten: Einblicke in die Bewusstseinslandschaft des österreichischen Judenthums*, ed. Klaus Hödl (Innsbruck: Studienverlag, 2000), 88–89.

45. Helga Embacher, "Aussenseiterinnen: bürgerlich, jüdisch, intellektuell—links," *L'homme: Zeitschrift für feministische Geschichtwissenschaft* 2 (1991): 71.

46. Prost, "Emigration," 456–457.

47. Marie Langer, *Von Wien bis Managua: Wege einer Psychoanalytikerin* (Freiburg: Kore, Verlag Traute Hensch, 1986), 31.

48. Paul Roazen, *Helene Deutsch: A Psychoanalyst's Life* (New Brunswick: Transaction Publishers, 1992), 62, 74, 88.

49. Bettina Hirsch, *Marianne: Ein Frauenleben an der Zeiten Wende* (A. Pichlers Witwe & Sohn, 1970), 18–23.

50. *Käthe Leichter: Leben und Werk*, ed. Herbert Steiner (Vienna: Europa Verlag, 1973), 296.

51. Ibid., 24.

52. Prost, "Emigration," 460.

53. Stella Klein-Löw, *Erinnerungen: Erlebtes und Gedachtes* (Vienna: Jugend und Volk, 1980) 40–43.

54. Embacher, "Aussenseiterinnen," 58.

55. Langer, *Von Wien*, 34.

56. Prost, "Emigration," 450, 452.

57. Ibid., 454–455.

58. Adolf Jellinek, "Weibliche Arbeit" (1863), *Studien und Skizzen. Erster Theil. Der jüdische Stamm. Ethnografische Studie* (Vienna: Herzfeld & Bauer, 1869), 100.

59. Adolf Schwarz, *Der Frauen der Bibel (Drei Vorträge gehalten in der "Jüdischen Toynbee-Halle" in Wien)* (Vienna: Verlag von R. Loewit, 1903), 30.

60. Max Grunwald, *Die moderne Frauenbewegung und das Judenthum*, lecture held in the OIU on March 11, 1903. Published as a manuscript (Vienna, 1903), 15.

61. Karl Kraus, *Die Fackel*, 345–346: 1–4, 426–430: 39. Edward Timms, *Karl Kraus: Apocalyptic Satirist, Culture and Catastrophe in Habsburg Vienna* (New Haven and London: Yale University Press, 1986), 68, 338–339.

62. Arthur Schnitzler, *The Road into the Open (Der Weg ins Frei)*, trans. Roger Byers (Berkeley and Los Angeles: University of California Press, 1992), 58, 279.

63. Prost, "Emigration," 467–468; Hilde Zaloscer, "Das dreimalige Exil," in *Vertriebene Vernunft* I, ed. Stadler, 544–572; Hilde Zaloscer, "Wissenschaftliche Arbeit ohne wissenschaftlichen Apparat," *Vertriebene Vernunft* II, ed. Stadler, 634–644.

64. "Jüdische Krankpflegerinnen," *Die Wahrheit* 11 (March 15, 1901), 3.

65. Emilie Exner, *Weibliche Pharmaceuten* (lecture held in Vereine Erwerbende Frauen) (Vienna: Verlag des Wiener Frauen-Erwerb-Vereines, 1902). Exner, Emilie, Wiener Stadt- und Landes-Archiv, Biographical Collection.

Chapter 4

1. Theodor Herzl, "Women and Zionism," *Zionist Writings: Essays and Addresses*, volume 2 (New York: Herzl Press, 1975), 159–164. Also Theodor Herzl, "Die Frauen und der Zionismus," in Leon Kellner, ed., *Theodor Herzl's Gesammelte Schriften* (Berlin, 1905), 195.

2. *Complete Diaries of Theodor Herzl*, trans. Harry Zohn, ed. Raphael Patai, 5 vols. (New York and London: Herzl Press and Thom Yoseloff, 1960), 1044.

3. Gertraud Diem-Wille, "Femininity and Professionalism: A Psychoanalytic Study of Ambition in Female Academics and Managers in Austria," in *Austrian Women in the Nineteenth and Twentieth Centuries: Cross-Disciplinary Perspectives*, ed. David F. Good, Margarete Grandner, and Mary Jo Maynes (Providence: Berghan Books, 1996), 157.

4. Michael Berkowitz, *Zionist Culture and West European Jewry before the First World War* (Cambridge: Cambridge University Press, 1993).

5. Elisabeth Malleier lists eight Zionist women's groups and seven Zionist girl's groups. Elisabeth Malleier, *Jüdische Frauen in Wien, 1816–1938* (Vienna: Mandelbaum, 2003), 72–73. For a different interpretation of Zionist women see

Mark Gelber, *Melancholy Pride: Nation, Race, and Gender in the German Literature of Cultural Zionism* (Tübingen: M. Niemeyer, 2000).

6. *Jüdische Zeitung* 18 (November 1908), 7.

7. *Die Welt* 5, nr. 20 (May 1901): 14; *Die Welt* 5, nr. 14 (April 1901): 31.

8. *Jüdische Zeitung* 28 (August 1907), 7.

9. Marta Baer-Issachar, "An unsere Frauen!" in *Der Zionismus und die Frauen* (1905?).

10. Edward Bristow, *Prostitution and Prejudice: The Jewish Fight against White Slavery, 1870–1939* (New York: Schocken Books, 1983), 260–261.

11. Baer-Issacher, "An unsere Frauen!"

12. Ibid.

13. Ibid.

14. Rosa Pomeranz, *Im Lande der Noth* (Breslau, 1901).

15. Rosa Pomeranz, "Die Frauen und der Zionismus," *Die Welt* 3:12 (1899): 7.

16. Rosa Pomeranz, *An die jüdischen Frauen: Ein Appell zur Umkehr* (Tarnopol: Verlag des Vereines "Ahawath-Zion," 1898), 19.

17. Ibid., 24.

18. Ibid., 25.

19. Rosa Pomeranz, "Die Bedeutung der zionistischen Idee im Leben der Jüdin," in *Der Zionismus und die Frauen* (1905?). This pamphlet was popular enough to be republished later in Yiddish along with a Yiddish version of Martin Buber's article (see discussion below), *Di yudishe froy un der Tsionizm* (Warsaw: Druckerei "Hazefira," 1918). Paula Hyman, *Gender and Assimilation in Modern Jewish History: The Roles and Representations of Women* (Seattle: University of Washington Press, 1995), 146.

20. "Rede des Fraulein Rosa Kollmann anlässlich der Debatte über 'Agitation,'" *Die Welt* 5:13 (1901), 11.

21. Rosa Feigenbaum, "Der Stellung der jüdischen Frau zum Zionismus," *Die Neuzeit* (1902): 29.

22. Hermine Schildberger, "Das Weib und der Zionismus," *Die Welt* 3:50 (1899): 4–5.

23. Ibid., 4.

24. Rozia Ellman, in *Stenographisches Protokoll der Verhandlungen des II. Zionisten-Kongresses gehalten zu Basel vom 28 bis 31 August 1898* (Vienna: "Erez Israel," 1898), 239ff., 48; Emma Gottheil, in *Stenographisches Protokoll der Verhandlungen des IV. Zionisten-Kongresses in London, 1900* (Vienna: "Erez Israel," 1900), 286, 181.

25. Miriam Schach, "Ein Bericht über zionistische Frauenarbeit," *Stenographisches Protokoll der Verhandlungen des X. Zionisten-Kongresses in Basell 1911* (Berlin: Jüdischer Verlag, 1911), 218–234. Michael Berkowitz, "Transcending 'Tzimmes and Sweetness': Recovering the History of Zionist Women in Central and Western Europe, 1897–1933," in *Active Voices: Women in Jewish Culture*, ed. Maurice Sacks (Urbana and Chicago: University of Illinois Press, 1995), 58.

26. Johanna Simon-Friedberg, "Gegenwartsaufgaben der jüdischen Frau (Vortrag, gehalten in Wien anlässlich des XI Kongresses)," *Die Welt* 18/4–5 (January 23, 30, 1914): 89.

27. Ibid., 91.

28. Ibid., 122.

29. Rahel Strauss, "Frauenarbeit in Palästina," *Jüdische Zeitung* 31 (July 31, 1908), 1.

30. For example, see David Biale, "Zionism as an Erotic Revolution," in *People of the Body: Jews and Judaism from an Embodied Perspective*, ed. Howard Eilberg-Schwartz (Albany: State University of New York Press, 1992), and Deborah Bernstein, ed., *Pioneers and Homemakers: Jewish Women in Pre-State Israel* (Albany: State University of New York Press, 1992); Rachel Elboim-Dror, "Gender in Utopianism: The Zionist Case," *History Workshop Journal* 37 (1994): 99–116; Matti Bunzl, "Theodor Herzl's Zionism as Gendered Discourse," in *Theodor Herzl and the Origins of Zionism, Austrian Studies* 8, ed. Ritchie Robertson and Edward Timms (Edinburgh: Edinburgh University Press, 1997), 74–86; Angelika Montel, "Women and Zionist Journalism: 'Frauen in der Welt der Männer,'" trans. Ritchie Robertson, in *Theodor Herzl and the Origins of Zionism, Austrian Studies* 8, ed. Ritchie Robertson and Edward Timms (Edinburgh: Edinburgh University Press, 1997), 87–95; Margalit Shilo, "The Double or Multiple Image of the New Hebrew Woman," *Nashim: A Journal of Jewish Women's Studies and Gender Issues* 1 (Winter 1998): 73–94; Claudia Prestel, "Zionist Rhetoric and Women's Equality (1897–1933): Myth and Reality," *San Jose Studies* 20/3 (1994): 4–28; and Billie Melman, "Re-Generation: Nation and the Construction of Gender in Peace and War—Palestinian Jews, 1900–1918," in *Borderlines: Genders and Identities in War and Peace, 1870–1930*, ed. Billie Melman (New York: Routledge, 1998), 121–140.

31. Biale, "Zionism as an Erotic Revolution," 283–284.

32. Berkowitz, "Transcending 'Tzimmes and Sweetness,'" 41; Berkowitz, *Zionist Culture and West European Jewry*.

33. Berkowitz, "Transcending 'Tzimmes and Sweetness,'" 44.

34. Otto Weininger, *Geschlecht und Charakter* (Munich, 1980). See also Jacques Le Rider, *Modernity and Crises of Identity: Culture and Society in Fin-de-Siècle Vienna*, trans. Rosemary Morris (New York: Continuum, 1993), esp. ch. 9.

35. Klaus Hödl, *Als Bettler in die Leopoldstadt: Galizische Juden auf dem Weg nach Wien* (Vienna: Böhlau Verlag, 1994), 208–209.

36. George Mosse, *Nationalism and Sexuality: Middle Class Morality and Sexual Norms in Modern Europe* (Madison: University of Wisconsin Press, 1985), 1–2.

37. Ibid., 97.

38. Pieter M. Judson, "The Gendered Politics of German Nationalism in Austria," in *Austrian Women in the Nineteenth and Twentieth Century: Cross-*

Disciplinary Perspectives, ed. David F. Good, Margarete Grandner, and Mary Jo Maynes (Providence: Berghahn Books, 1996), 3, 13–14.

39. Shilo, "New Hebrew Woman," 74.

40. David Biale, *Eros and the Jews: From Biblical Israel to Contemporary Israel* (New York: Basic Books, 1992), 178–179; see also Robert S. Wistrich, "Max Nordau: From Degeneration to 'Muscular Judaism,' " *Transversal: Zeitschrift für jüdischen Studien* 5/2 (2004); Max Nordau, *Max Nordau (1849–1923)*, edited by Delphine Bechtel, Dominique Bourel, and Jacques Le Rider (Paris, 1996); Christophe Schulte, *Psychopathologie des Fin de siècle: Der Kulturkritiker, Arzt und Zionist: Max Nordau* (Frankfurt a.M., 1997); Hans-Peter Söder, "Disease and Health as Contexts of Modernity: Max Nordau as a Critic of Fin-de-Siècle Modernism," *German Studies Review* (1991).

41. George L. Mosse, introduction to *Degeneration* by Max Nordau (New York: Howard Fertig, 1968), xxiv. Max Nordau, *Paradoxe* (Leipzig: Verlag von B. Elischer, 1886), 44–50, 93–96, 136, 230, 246–251. In these pages Nordau presented a very negative image of women in general. For example, he asserted that all women were basically the same, that the woman was not a personality, but a kind (46), so-called "original women" could be explained either as a disease, or as a spiritual reversal of gender, a person with a woman's body and a man's character, viewpoints, and tendencies (47). He also said that the woman had no true ambition and was an enemy of progress (49) and a spiritual robot (50). He said that there was only one form of female success, and that was to please men (93). Women were far more emotional than men (136) and had a more strongly developed sexual center (246).

42. Max Nordau, *Die Conventionellen Lügen der Kulturmenschheit* (Leipzig: B. Elischer Nachfolger, 1883), 262–263; part of this is cited in Michael Stanislawski, *Zionism and the Fin de Siècle: Cosmopolitanism and Nationalism from Nordau to Jabotinsky* (Berkeley: University of California Press, 2001), 27–28.

43. Stanislawski, *Zionism and the Fin de siècle*, 28–30.

44. Max Nordau, *Das Recht, zu Lieben: Ein Schauspiel in vier Aufzugen* (Berlin, 1893) and *Doktor Kohn: Bürgerliches Trauerspiel aus der Gegenwart* (Berlin: Ernst Hoffman, 1902).

45. Stanislawski, *Zionism and the Fin de Siècle*, 92, citing Max Nordau, "Muskeljudentum," in Max Nordau, *Zionistische Schriften* (Cologne: Jüdischer Verlag, 1909), 379–381. Zionists used the terms *ghetto Jew* or *ghetto mentality* and *galut Jew* or *galut mentality* interchangeably.

46. See Alex Bein, *Theodor Herzl: A Biography of the Founder of Modern Zionism*, trans. Maurice Samuel (New York: Atheneum, 1970), 62–65; Ernst Pawel, *The Labyrinth of Exile: A Life of Theodor Herzl* (London: Collins Harvill, 1990), 121–129; Steven Beller, *Herzl*, reprint edition (London: Peter Halban Publishers, Ltd., 2004); Peter Loewenberg, "Theodor Herzl: Nationalism and Politics," in *Decoding the Past: The Psychohistorical Approach* (Berkeley and Los Angeles:

University of California Press, 1985), 104–112; Stanislawski, *Zionism and the Fin de Siècle*, 4–5.

47. Theodor Herzl, "The New Ghetto," in *Theodor Herzl: A Portrait for This Age*, ed. Ludwig Lewisohn (Cleveland and New York: World Publishing Company, 1955), 157.

48. Ibid., 165.

49. Robert Wistrich, "Theodor Herzl: Zionist Icon, Myth-Maker and Social Utopian," in *The Shaping of Israeli Identity: Myth, Memory and Trauma*, ed. Robert Wistrich and David Ohana (London: Frank Cass, 1995), 14.

50. Arthur Hertzberg, *The Zionist Idea: A Historical Analysis and Reader* (New York: Atheneum, 1959), 49.

51. Theodor Herzl, *Altneuland, Old-New Land*, trans. Paula Arnold (Haifa: Haifa Publishing Company, 1960), 55.

52. Ibid., 57.

53. Ibid., 59, 66.

54. Ibid., 60.

55. Ibid., 75–76, 91.

56. Ibid., 174.

57. Ibid., 81–85.

58. Ibid., 131.

59. Ibid., 217.

60. Rachel Alcalay (Belgrade), Blanch Bahar (Paris), Ernestine Esther Ehrenpreis (Djakovar), Sara Gitelewitz (Marjapol), Klara Hirschensohn (Jassy), Dr. Wilhelmine Kornblueh (Freistadt), Bertha Markus (Meran), M. Reinus (Zurich), Klara Schapira (Heidelberg), Esther Schlaposchnikow (Charkow), Maria Sokolow (Warsaw), Rosa Sonneschein (New York), Hulda Tomaschewsky (Berlin), and Antonia Zimmern (Ashtore). Theodor Herzl and Alex Bein, *Briefe und Tagebücher*, vol. 3 (Berlin: Propyläen, 1983–1996), 668. Theodor Herzl, *Briefe und Tagebücher*, Volume 4, 668.

61. Herzl and Bein, *Briefe und Tagebücher*, 335 (1104).

62. Priska Gmür, " 'It Is Not up to Us Women to Solve Great Problems': The Duty of the Zionist Woman in the Context of the First Ten Congresses," in *The First Zionist Congress in 1897—Causes, Significance, Topicality*, ed. Heiko Haumann, trans. Wayne van Dalsum and Vivian Kramer (Basel: Karger, 1997), 292.

63. Ibid., 292–293.

64. Zionist Congress, *Stenographisches Protokoll der Verhandlungen des II. Zionisten-Congresses gehalten zu Basel vom 28. bis 31. August 1898* (Vienna: Buchdruckerei "Industrie," 1898), 239.

65. Gmür, " 'Not up to Us Women,' " 293–294.

66. "Zur zionistischen Frauenbewegung," *Die Welt* 4 (1900): 7–8.

67. "Frauenbewegung," 7. Glückel of Hameln was actually literate and she did not dictate, but wrote, her memoirs. See Glückel, *The Memoirs of Glückel of Hameln*, trans. Marvin Lowenthal (New York: Schocken Books, 1977).

68. Z. F., "Frauenbewegung," 8.

69. York-Steiner also addressed the Wiener zionistische Frauenverein in 1899, 1900, and 1901, and the Erste zionistische Frauenverein in 1909.

70. Heinrich York-Steiner, *Der Talmudbauer. Unterwegs. Erzählungen von H. York-Steiner* (Berlin: Jüdischer Verlag, 1904), 175.

71. Z. F., "Frauenbewegung," 7–8.

72. Robert Jaffee, "Das jüdische Weib," *Die Welt* 5:28 (July 12, 1901): 11–12.

73. Bein, *Theodor Herzl*, 372–373.

74. Pawel, *Labyrinth*, 452.

75. Michael Berkowitz deals with the topic of cultural Zionism and relates it to the question of women's role in *Zionist Culture*, 92–94.

76. Berthold Feiwel, "Die jüdische Familie. Die jüdische Frau," *Die Welt* 5:17 (April 26, 1901), 1–3.

77. Ibid., 1–2.

78. Wistrich, *Jews of Vienna*, 638–640.

79. Martin Buber, "Das Zion der jüdischen Frau," *Die Welt* 5/17 (April 26, 1901): 3–5.

80. Ibid., 5.

Chapter 5

1. Sigmund Freud, SE 19:142, cited in Sander Gilman, *Freud, Race and Gender* (Princeton: Princeton University Press, 1993), 36.

2. Freud, SE 20:212, cited in Gilman, *Freud, Race and Gender*, 38.

3. Gilman, *Freud, Race and Gender*, 36–48. Also *The Case of Sigmund Freud: Medicine and Identity at the Fin de Siècle* (Baltimore: Johns Hopkins University Press, 1993), and *The Jew's Body* (New York: Routledge, 1991).

4. P. G. J. Pulzer, *The Rise of Political Anti-Semitism in Germany and Austria*, revised edition (Cambridge, Mass.: Harvard University Press, 1988), 122–123.

5. Robert Wistrich, *The Jews of Vienna in the Age of Franz Joseph* (New York: Oxford University Press, 1989), 205.

6. Ibid., 208.

7. For more on Austrian anti-Semitism, see the following: Andrew G. Whiteside, *The Socialism of Fools: Georg Ritter von Schönerer and Austrian Pan-Germanism* (Berkeley and Los Angeles, 1975); John Boyer, *Political Radicalism in Late Imperial Vienna: Origins of the Christian Social Movement, 1848–1897* (Chicago: University of Chicago Press, 1981), and *Culture and Political Crisis in Vienna: Christian Socialism in Power, 1897–1918* (Chicago: University of Chicago Press, 1995); Bruce Pauley, *From Prejudice to Persecution: A History of Austrian Anti-Semitism* (Chapel Hill: University of North Carolina Press, 1992); John Bunzl and Bernd Marin, *Antisemitismus in Österreich: Sozialhistorische und soziologische Studien* (Innsbruck: Innsverlag, 1983); I. A. Hellwing, *Der konfessionelle Antisemitismus im 19. Jahrhundert in Österreich* (Vienna: Herder,

1972); Ivar Oxaal, Michael Pollak, and Gerhard Botz, eds., *Jews, Antisemitism and Culture in Vienna* (London: Routledge & Kegan Paul, 1987); and Jacob Katz, *From Prejudice to Destruction: Anti-Semitism, 1700–1933* (Cambridge: Harvard University Press, 1980), 223–229.

8. Carl E. Schorske, *Fin-de-Siècle Vienna: Politics and Culture* (New York: Vintage Books, 1981). Originally published as "Politics in a New Key: An Austrian Triptych," *Journal of Modern History* 39 (December 1967): 343–386.

9. Schorske, *Fin de Siècle Vienna*, 133.

10. Ibid., 145–146.

11. Richard Geehr, *Karl Lueger: Mayor of Fin de Siècle Vienna* (Detroit: Wayne State University Press, 1990), 16, 175–176. Geehr concludes: "Did Lueger himself believe his anti-Jewish remarks? We may never know" (175). I go into more depth on the topic of Lueger, focusing on Christian Social women, gender, and anti-Semitism, in my article "Gender and Anti-Semitism: Christian Social Women and the Jewish Response in Turn-of-the-Century Vienna," *Austrian History Yearbook* 34 (2003): 173–189.

12. Steven Beller, "Otto Weininger as Liberal?" in *Jews and Gender: Responses to Otto Weininger*, ed. Nancy A. Harrowitz and Barbara Hyams (Philadelphia: Temple University Press, 1995), 97.

13. Robert S. Wistrich, "Hitler and National Socialism: The Austrian Connection," in *Between Redemption and Perdition: Modern Antisemitism and Jewish Identity* (London: Routledge, 1990), 60.

14. Sander Gilman, *Jewish Self-Hatred: Anti-Semitism and the Hidden Language of the Jews* (Baltimore: Johns Hopkins University Press, 1986), 244–251; Shulamit Volkov, "Antisemitism as a Cultural Code—Reflections on the History and Historiography of Antisemitism in Imperial Germany," *Leo Baeck Institute Yearbook* 23 (1978): 31–35, and *Germans, Jews, and Antisemites: Trials in Emancipation* (New York: Cambridge University Press, 2006), 129–144; Nancy Harrowitz, *Antisemitism, Misogyny, and the Logic of Cultural Difference: Cesare Lonbroso and Matilde Serao* (Lincoln: University of Nebraska Press, 1994), 55–61. Also see Paula Hyman, *Gender and Assimilation in Modern Jewish History: The Roles and Representations of Women* (Seattle: University of Washington Press, 1995), 137–142.

15. Jacques Le Rider, *Modernity and Crises of Identity: Culture and Society in Fin-de-Siècle Vienna*, translated by Rosemary Morris (New York: Continuum Press, 1993); and Nike Wagner, *Geist und Geschlecht: Karl Kraus und die Erotik der Wiener Moderne* (Frankfurt: Suhrkamp, 1982).

16. John Boyer, *Political Radicalism*, 115.

17. George L. Mosse, *Nationalism and Sexuality: Middle Class Morality and Sexual Norms in Modern Europe* (Madison: University of Wisconsin Press, 1985), 36, 144.

18. Adolf Hitler, *Mein Kampf* (New York, 1939 ed.), 78. Edward Bristow, *Prostitution and Prejudice: The Jewish Fight against White Slavery, 1870–1939* (New York: Schocken Books, 1983), 84.

19. J. Sydney Jones, *Hitler in Vienna: 1907–1913* (New York: Stein and Day, 1983), 112. William A. Jenks, *Vienna and the Young Hitler* (New York: Octagon Books, 1976, c. 1960), 127–128.

20. Jones, *Hitler in Vienna*, 117.

21. Ruth Wodak, "Die sprachliche Inszenierung des Nationalsozialismus— einige soziolinguistische Überlegung," in *Zeitgeist wider den Zeitgeist: Eine Sequenz aus Österreichs Verirrung* (Vienna: Gisteldruck, 1988), 103.

22. "Kohn-Lexikon," *Kikerkei* (Vienna, around 1895). Reproduced in *Zeitgeist wider den Zeitgeist*, 76–77.

23. Mosse, *Nationalism and Sexuality*; Sander Gilman, *Difference and Pathology: Stereotypes of Sexuality, Race, and Madness* (Ithaca: Cornell University Press, 1985); *Jewish Self-Hatred*; *Inscribing the Other* (Lincoln and London: University of Nebraska Press, 1991); *The Jew's Body*; *Freud, Race and Gender*; and *The Case of Sigmund Freud*.

24. Mosse, *Nationalism and Sexuality*, 151.

25. Richard von Krafft-Ebing, *Nervosität und neurasthenische Zustande* (Vienna: Alfred Hoelder, 1895), 54, citing Wilhelm Erb, *Über die wachsende Nervosität unserer Zeit* (Heidelberg, 1893), 19.

26. Gilman, *Jew's Body*, 76–79.

27. Theodor Billroth, *Über das Lehren und Lernen der medizinischen Wissenschaften an den Universitäten der deutschen Nation* (Vienna, 1876); Wistrich, *Jews of Vienna*, 64, 551–552; Dennis Klein, *Jewish Origins of the Psychoanalytic Movement* (New York: Praeger, 1981); Gilman, *Jewish Self-Hatred*, 214–216.

28. Klein, *Jewish Origins*, 56.

29. Harriet Pass Freidenreich, *Female, Jewish and Educated: The Lives of Central European University Women* (Bloomington and Indianapolis: Indiana University Press, 2002), 85.

30. "The Diary of Sabina Spielrein (1909–1912)," trans. Krishna Winston, in *A Secret Symmetry: Sabina Spielrein between Jung and Freud*, ed. Aldo Carotenuto (New York: Pantheon Books, 1982), 23–24.

31. Ibid., 30.

32. John Kerr, *A Most Dangerous Method: The Story of Jung, Freud, and Sabina Spielrein* (New York: Vintage Books, 1993).

33. Ibid., 353.

34. Ibid., 478.

35. Paul Roazen, *Helene Deutsch: A Psychoanalyst's Life* (New Brunswick: Transaction Publishers, 1992), 74. Also Janet Sayers, *Mothers of Psychoanalysis: Helene Deutsch, Karen Horney, Anna Freud, Melanie Klein* (New York: W.W. Norton, 1991), 30.

36. Helene Deutsch, *Confrontations with Myself: An Epilogue* (New York: W.W. Norton, Inc., 1973), 19.

37. Roazen, *Helene Deutsch*, 189.

38. Kerr, *Dangerous Method*, 296–298, 319–325. The relevant papers are "On the Psychological Content of a Case of Schizophrenia (Dementia Praecox)," 1911, and "Destruction as a Cause of Coming into Being," 1912.

39. Kerr, *Dangerous Method*, 492–493.

40. Sabina Spielrein, Letter-drafts, 1909, cited in Kerr, *Dangerous Method*, 319.

41. Helene Deutsch, "Significance of Masochism," read at the Eleventh International Psychoanalytic Congress, Oxford, July 27, 1929.

42. Elisabeth Young-Bruehl, *Anna Freud: A Biography* (London: Papermac, 1992, 1988), 75.

43. "The very term 'Jew' is as much a category of gender, masculine, as it is of race." Gilman, *Freud, Race and Gender*, 8.

44. Ibid., 32–33. Bruno Bettelheim understood Freud's comments to be motivated by his frustration over Spielrein's continuing affection for Jung and her desire to have his child. Bruno Bettelheim, "A Secret Asymmetry," in *Freud's Vienna and Other Essays* (New York: Alfred A. Knopf, 1990), 78.

45. Estelle Roith, *The Riddle of Freud: Jewish Influences on His Theory of Female Sexuality* (New York: Tavistock Press, 1987); John Murray Cuddihy, *Ordeal of Civility: Freud, Marx, Levi-Strauss, and the Jewish Struggle with Modernity* (New York: Basic Books, 1974); Theodor Reik, *Jewish Wit* (New York: Gamut Press, 1962); Judith Van Herik, *Freud on Femininity and Faith* (Berkeley and Los Angeles: University of California Press, 1987). Otto Rank may have been the first to develop this theory. He said that Freud had projected onto women a Jewish mentality of the enslaved, the inferior, and the castrated. Otto Rank, *Beyond Psychology* (Camden, N.J., 1941). Cited in William M. Johnston, *The Austrian Mind: An Intellectual and Social History, 1848–1938* (Berkeley and Los Angeles: University of California Press, 1972), 260.

46. Gilman, *Freud, Race and Gender*, 7–8.

47. Sigmund Freud, *Freud on Women: A Reader*, ed. Elisabeth Young-Bruehl (New York and London: W.W. Norton, 1990), 4.

48. Even Gilman asserts that "it is the male Jew from the East, from the provinces, who is most at risk for hysteria," citing the bar chart of Professor H. Strauss of Berlin, which showed that male Jews suffered twice as often from hysteria as male non-Jews. Interestingly, he does not mention that the chart also clearly indicates that female Jews suffered the most. They were indeed off the chart! Gilman, *Jew's Body*, 63; *Freud, Race and Gender*, 116–120. For the bar chart, see fig. 6, 119. Taken from Hermann Strauss, "Erkrankungen durch Alkohol und Syphilis bei den Juden," *Zeitschrift für Demographie und Statistik der Juden* n.s. 4 (1927), 35. This is also discussed in Sander Gilman, *Hysteria beyond Freud* (Berkeley: University of California Press, 1993).

49. Freud initially believed that hysteria was caused by actual seductive experiences during childhood. He gradually abandoned this "seduction hypothesis" and concluded that seduction by the parent may have taken place only in

the child's fantasy life, and that hysteria resulted from multiple causes. Young-Bruehl, *Freud on Women*, 6–8.

50. In *Freud, Race and Gender*, Gilman writes that of Freud's ninety-two patients for whom records have been found, eighty-six were Catholic and five were Jewish, and one did not record a religious affiliation. Fifty-eight were men and thirty-four were women. Among the Jewish patients, one was a man and four were women. All were Eastern Jews from Hungary or Galicia (121–122). However, in *The Case of Sigmund Freud*, he writes that Freud felt intensely Jewish and lived his life in largely Jewish society. "His is the familiar history of the European Jewish intellectual. His friends were all Jews, his patients mostly so" (7).

51. Fritz Wittels, *Sigmund Freud: His Personality, His Teaching, and His School*, trans. Eden Paul and Ceder Paul (London: Allen & Unwin, 1924), 140. Cited in Gilman, *Freud, Race and Gender*, 31.

52. SE 19:222. Cited in Gilman, *Freud, Jews and Gender*, 35.

53. Gilman, *Freud, Race and Gender*, 37.

54. On Bertha Pappenheim, see the following: Ellen M. Jensen, *Streifzuge durch das Leben von Anna O./ Bertha Pappenheim*, (Frankfurt am Main: ZTV Verlag, 1984); Marion Kaplan, *The Jewish Feminist Movement in Germany* (Westport: Greenwood Press, 1979), ch. 2; Dora Edinger, *Bertha Pappenheim: Freud's Anna O.* (Highland Park, Ill.: Congregation Solel, 1968); Max Rosenbaum and Melvin Muroff, *Anna O.: Fourteen Contemporary Reinterpretations* (New York: Free Press, 1984); Naomi Shepherd, *A Price below Rubies: Jewish Women as Rebels and Radicals* (Cambridge, Mass.: Harvard University Press, 1993), ch. 6; and Thea Leitner, *Fürstin, Dame, Armes Weib* (Vienna: Überreuter, 1991), ch. 7.

55. Gilman, *Jewish Self-Hatred*, 259. Citing Albrecht Hirschmüller, *Physiologie und Psychoanalyse in Leben und Werk Josef Breuers. Jahrbuch der Psychoanalyse*, supp. 4 (Bern: Hans Huber, 1978).

56. Interpreters of Anna O. consider her feminism as a continuation of her illness or as proof that she was cured. Daniel Boyarin adopts the model of Hélène Cixous, interpreting hysteria as feminist resistance. He argues that Pappenheim, whom he refers to as his hero, was homosexual, a militant feminist, and a traditional Orthodox Jew. While previous interpreters argued that Pappenheim was fighting against traditional Judaism, Boyarin concludes that she was in favor of reconstructing Orthodox Judaism by enhancing women's access to Torah study. The factors leading to her hysteria, according to Boyarin, "had much more to do with Victorian Vienna than with traditional Judaism" (328). Daniel Boyarin, *Unheroic Conduct: The Rise of Heterosexuality and the Invention of the Jewish Man* (Berkeley and Los Angeles: University of California Press, 1997), chapter 8, 313–359.

57. Gilman, *Jewish Self-Hatred*, 260.

58. Ibid.

59. Ibid., 261.

60. Sigmund Freud, *The Interpretation of Dreams*, trans. and ed. James Strachey (New York: Avon Books, 1965), 139–140.

61. Ibid., 142–143.

62. Ibid., 144.

63. Ibid., 151.

64. Ibid., 327.

65. Wistrich, *Jews of Vienna*, 555.

66. Gilman, *The Case of Sigmund Freud*, 101.

67. Sigmund Freud, *Dora: An Analysis of a Case of Hysteria* (New York: Collier Books, 1963), 55.

68. Sigmund Freud, "General Remarks on Hysterical Attacks" (1909), in *ibid.*, 123–124.

69. George Mosse writes: "Jews were not as a rule accused of being homosexual themselves; instead, they were endowed by their enemies with an uncontrolled sexual drive directed against gentile women." *Nationalism and Sexuality*, 140.

70. Nancy C. Michael, *Elektra and Her Sisters: Three Female Characters in Schnitzler, Freud, and Hofmannsthal* (New York: Peter Lang Publishing, Inc., 2001); Mark Kanzer, M.D., and Jules Glenn, M.D., eds., *Freud and His Patients* (Northvale, N.J.: Jason Aronson, Inc., 1980, 1993); Steven Marcus, "Freud and Dora: Story, History, Case History," in *Representations: Essays on Literature and Society* (New York: Random House, 1972); Peter Loewenberg, "Austro-Marxism and Revolution: Otto Bauer, Freud's 'Dora' Case, and the Crisis of the First Austrian Republic," in *Decoding the Past: The Psychohistorical Approach* (University of California Press, 1985). See p. 203, n. 58, for other works on Dora. On the Jewish aspect of the case, see Loewenberg, who mentions that the Bauer family was Jewish, and discusses the problematic Jewish identity of Otto. Also Sander Gilman, *Jew's Body*, 81–103. And Hannah Decker examines Dora as a historical figure in her own right in *Freud, Dora, and Vienna 1900* (New York: Free Press, 1992), putting a great deal of emphasis on the Viennese-Jewish milieu in which Dora grew up.

71. A few vestiges of Jewish observance remained. Friday was Käthe's day of thorough cleaning, and Otto was ritually circumcised. However, the family exchanged Christmas gifts. Decker, *Freud, Dora, and Vienna*, 54–55.

72. Loewenberg, "Austro-Marxism." He argues that Otto's political role can be seen as "his analogue to 'Dora's' hysteria—it was his way of handling the family constellation in which he grew up." 188.

73. Decker, *Freud, Dora, and Vienna*, 95–98.

74. Ibid., 116–123.

75. Ibid., 126. Her conversion was not motivated by marriage or career advancement, but most likely by the desire to spare herself and her son from the humiliations of being a Jew in anti-Semitic Vienna. In spite of her conversion, she suffered great hardship and persecution in Vienna during the Nazi years until

she finally attained a visa to France and was brought to the United States by her son. In 1945, she died of colon cancer in New York. Ibid., 185–189.

76. Gilman, *Jew's Body*, 81.

77. Ibid., 84.

78. Ibid., 96.

79. Decker, *Freud, Dora, and Vienna*, 1–2.

80. Freud, *Dora*, 54.

81. Ibid., 55.

82. Young-Bruehl, *Freud on Women*, 31, 92. He later revised this belief in "The Psychogenesis of a Case of Homosexuality" (1920).

83. Ibid., *Freud on Women*, 35.

84. Ibid., 251.

85. For example, "The Dissolution of the Oedipus Complex" (1924); "Some Psychical Consequences of the Anatomical Distinction between the Sexes" (1925). Both are in ibid.

86. Young-Bruehl, *Freud on Women*, 35–36.

87. Klein, *Jewish Origins*, 110.

88. Otto Rank, "Das Wesen des Judentums" (The Essence of Judaism), in Dennis Klein, *Jewish Origins of the Psychoanalytic Movement* (Chicago: University of Chicago Press, 1985), Appendix C.

89. Ibid., 171.

90. Fritz Wittels, *Der Taufjude* (Vienna and Liepzig: M. Breitensteins Verlagsbuchhandlung, 1904), 37; Fritz Wittels, *Freud and the Child Woman: The Memoirs of Fritz Wittels*, ed. with preface by Edward Timms (New Haven: Yale University Press, 1995).

91. Wittels, *Taufjude*, 37.

92. *Minutes of the Vienna Psychoanalytic Society*, ed. Herman Nunberg and Ernst Federn, trans. M. Nunberg, 4 vols. (New York: International Universities Press, 1962–1975) I, 195–198. Cited in Decker, *Freud, Dora, and Vienna*, 202.

93. *Minutes of the Vienna Psychoanalytic Society*, I (Mar. 11, 1908), 347, 350–351. Cited in Decker, *Freud, Dora, and Vienna*, 203.

94. Wittels, *Freud and the Child Woman: The Memoirs of Fritz Wittels*, 51.

95. Fritz Wittels, *Die Sexuelle Not* (Vienna and Leipzig: C.W. Stern, 1909).

96. Klein, *Jewish Origins*, 138.

97. Edward Timms, *Karl Kraus: Apocalyptic Satirist* (New Haven and London: Yale University Press, 1986), 99.

98. *Minutes of the Vienna Psychoanalytic Society*, II, 89. Cited in Timms, *Karl Kraus*, 100.

99. Timms, *Karl Kraus*, 100. In his introduction to Wittels's memoirs, Timms explains that although he wrote that Wittels "was essentially a popularizer of other people's ideas," he later came to see Wittels as "a significant figure in his own right." *Freud and the Child Woman*, ix.

100. Wistrich, *Jews of Vienna*, 572.

101. Johnston, *The Austrian Mind*, 256.

102. Gilman, *Freud, Race and Gender*, 106.

103. Alexander Pilcz, *Beitrag zur vergleichenden Rassen-Psychiatrie* (Leipzig: Deuticke, 1906).

104. Ibid., 15–16.

105. Ibid., 18–19.

106. Ibid., 29.

107. Georg Buschan, "Einfluss der Rasse auf die Form und Jäufigkeit pathologischer Veränderungen," *Globus* 67 (1895): 21–24, 43–47, 60–63, 76–80.

108. Pilcz, *Beitrag*, 31.

109. Wistrich, *Jews of Vienna*, 564.

110. Richard von Krafft-Ebing, *Text-book of Insanity*, trans. Charles Gilbert Chaddock (Philadelphia: F.A. Davis Company, 1905), 143.

111. Ibid.

112. Erna Lesky, *The Vienna Medical School of the 19th Century*, trans. L. Williams and I. S. Levij (Baltimore and London: Johns Hopkins University Press, 1976), 346.

113. Richard von Krafft-Ebing, *Psychopathia Sexualis: A Medico-Forensic Study*, rev. trans. Harry E. Wedeck (New York: Putnam, 1956), 25.

114. Oskar Hovorka, *Die Äussere Nase: Eine Anatomisch-Anthropologische Studie* (Vienna: Alfred Hölder, 1893), 88–90.

115. Ibid., 88.

116. Ibid., 89.

117. For an overview on the Jews in Viennese medicine, science, technology, and manual work, see Max Grunwald, *Vienna* (Philadelphia: Jewish Publication Society of America, 1936), Appendix P, 518–523.

118. Gilman, *Freud, Race and Gender*, 120, citing Moritz Benedikt, "Der geisteskranke Jude," *Nord und Süd* 167 (1918): 266–270.

119. Moritz Benedikt, *Aus meinem Leben: Erinnerungen und Erörterungen* (Vienna: Verlagsbuchhandlung Carl Konegen, 1906), 132–133.

120. Ibid., 103.

121. Martin Engländer, *Die auffallend häufigen Krankheitserscheinungen der jüdischen Rasse* (Vienna: J.L. Pollak, 1902).

122. Theodor Herzl, *Altneuland, Old-New Land*, third edition, trans. Paula Arnold (Haifa: Haifa Publishing Co, 1964), 86.

123. Engländer, *Krankheitserscheinungen*, 6.

124. Ibid., 10.

125. Ibid., 12.

126. Ibid.

127. Ibid., 13.

128. Ibid., 25.

129. Ibid., 46.

130. Harrowitz, *Anti-Semitism, Misogyny and the Logic of Cultural Difference*, 55.

131. John M. Efron, *Defenders of the Race: Jewish Doctors and Race Science in Fin-de-Siècle Europe* (New Haven: Yale University Press, 1994), 154.

132. Ignaz Zollschan, *Das Rassenproblem unter besonderer Berücksichtigung der jüdischen Rassenfrage* (Vienna, Leipzig, 1912).

133. Ignaz Zollschan, "The Jewish Race Problem," *Jewish Review* 2 (1912): 400.

134. Zollschan, *Rassenproblem*, 269.

135. Ibid., 270.

136. Efron, *Defenders*, 164, Gilman, *Freud, Race and Gender*, 108-109.

137. Zollschan, *Rassenproblem*, 106.

138. Theodor Lessing, *Der jüdische Selbsthass* (Berlin: Zionistischer Bücher-Bund, 1930); Kurt Lewin, "Self-Hatred among Jews," *Resolving Social Conflicts* (New York: Harper Brothers, 1948), 186-200; Sander Gilman, *Jewish Self-Hatred*; Allan Janik, *Essays on Wittgenstein and Weininger*. Studien zur österreichischen Philosophie, 9 (Amsterdam: Rodopi, 1985); Jacques Le Rider, *Le Cas Otto Weininger: Racines de l'antifeminisme et l'antisemitisme* (Paris: Presses Universitaires de France, 1982); Le Rider and Norbert Leser, eds., *Otto Weininger: Werk und Wirkung* (Vienna: Österreichischer Bundesverlag, 1984); Robert Wistrich, *Jews of Vienna*, 513-536; Harrowitz and Hyams, eds., *Jews and Gender*.

139. Gilman, *Jew's Body*, 133.

140. Wistrich, *Jews of Vienna*, 520-523.

141. Otto Weininger, *Sex and Character* (New York: A.L. Burt, n.d.), 306.

142. Ibid., 308.

143. Ibid., 310.

144. Ibid., 329.

145. John M. Hoberman, "Otto Weininger and the Critique of Jewish Masculinity," in Harrowitz and Hyams, *Jews and Gender*, 141.

146. Ibid., 143.

147. Weininger, *Sex and Character*, 310-311.

148. Ibid., 319-320.

149. Hoberman, "Weininger," 141-142.

150. Gilman, *Jewish Self-Hatred*, 249.

151. "Der jüdische Selbsthass und Weiberverachtung: Otto Weininger und Arthur Trebitsch," in *Weininger*, ed. Le Rider and Leser, 130.

152. Gilman, *Jewish Self-Hatred*, 248-250; "Jüdische Selbsthass," 123-134.

153. Arthur Trebitsch, *Geist und Judentum: Eine grundlegende Untersuchung* (Vienna and Leipzig: Verlag Ed Sirach, 1919), 83-84.

154. Ibid., 85.

155. Ibid., 131.

Chapter 6

1. Carl Schorske, *Fin-de-Siècle Vienna: Politics and Culture* (New York: Vintage Books, 1981); Allan Janik and Stephen Toulmin, *Wittgenstein's Vienna* (New York: Simon and Schuster, 1973); Edward Timms and Ritchie Robertson, eds., *Vienna 1900: From Altenberg to Wittgenstein* (Edinburgh: Edinburgh University Press, 1990); Nike Wagner, *Geist und Geschlecht: Karl Kraus und die Erotik der Wiener Moderne* (Frankfurt a.m.: Suhrkamp, 1982); Jacques Le Rider, *Modernity and Crises of Identity: Culture and Society in Fin-de-Siècle Vienna*, trans. Rosemary Morris (Cambridge: Polity Press, 1993); Marsha Rozenblit, *The Jews of Vienna, 1867–1914: Assimilation and Identity* (Albany: State University of New York Press, 1983); Ivar Oxaal, Michael Pollak, and Gerhard Botz, eds., *Jews, Antisemitism and Culture in Vienna* (London/New York: Routledge & Kegan Paul, 1987); Steven Beller, *Vienna and the Jews, 1867–1938: A Cultural History* (Cambridge: Cambridge University Press, 1989); Robert Wistrich, *The Jews of Vienna in the Age of Franz Joseph* (Oxford, New York: Oxford University Press, 1989); Péter Hanák, *The Garden and the Workshop: Essays on the Cultural History of Vienna and Budapest* (Princeton: Princeton University Press, 1998); *Rethinking Vienna 1900*, ed. Steven Beller (New York: Berghahn Books, 2001).

2. Some examples of writers: Ida Barber (1842–1931), Vicki Baum (1888–1960), Emma Feibelsohn (1861–1900), Carola (Charlotte) Belmonte Groag (1851–1928), Berta Katcher (1860–1903), Charlotte von Gruenebaum (1849–1941), Else Tauber (1884–?), Bertha Zuckerkandl-Szeps (1864–1945), Lilly Körber (1897–1982), Gina Kaus (1894–1985), Veza Canetti (1897–1963), Rosa Barach (1841–1913), Marta Karlweis (1889–1965), Else Bernstein (1866–1949), Kaethe Braun-Präger (1888–1967), Mimi Grossberg (1905–1997), Elisabeth Freundlich (1907–2001), Alice Gurschner (1869–1944), Mela Hartwig (1893–1967), Anna Hirschler (1846–1889), Else Jerusalem (1877–1942), Alma Johanna König (1887–1942), Betty Paoli (1814–1894), Therese Rie (1879–1970), Alice Schalek (1874–1956), Helene Scheu-Riess (1880–1970), Fredrike Maria Zweig (1882–1971), and Marie Herzfeld (1857–1940).

3. Bertha Pappenheim [Paul Berthold], *In der Trödel-bude: Geschichten* (Lahr: Druck und Verlag von Moritz Schauenburg, 1890) and *Frauenrechte* (Dresden, 1899). Dagmar Lorenz, *Keepers of the Motherland: German Texts by Jewish Women Writers* (Lincoln: University of Nebraska Press, 1997), 47–65.

4. Katharina Frankl (1852–1918), Berta Hermann, Hermine Delia-Claar (1848–?), and her sister Regine, Stella Kadmon (1902–1989) in theater, Caroline von Gomperz Bettelheim (1845–1925), Rosa Czillag (1832–1892), Rosa and Theresa Schwarz, and Pauline Lucca (1841–1908), concert singers. Tina Blau (1845–1916) was a painter in the late nineteenth century, Olga Prager (1872–1930) a portrait painter, Hilde Zaloscer (1903–1999) an art historian, and Trude Fleischmann (1895–1990) a photographer.

5. E. M., "Moderne jüdische Schriftstellerin," *Die Neuzeit* (1902) 22: 236.

6. Max Grunwald, *Vienna* (Philadelphia: Jewish Publication Society of America, 1936), 283–284.

7. Helmet Göbel, Afterword to Veza Canetti, *Die Gelbe Strasse* (Carl Hanser Verlag, 1990), 178. Lorenz, *Keepers of the Motherland*, 102–111.

8. Lorenz, *Keepers of the Motherland*, 172–175.

9. Vicki Baum, *It Was All Quite Different: The Memoirs of Vicki Baum* (New York: Funk and Wagnalls Company, Inc., 1964). She discussed her religious beliefs and her father's murder by Nazis without making mention of Judaism. 12–13, 22–25, 100–101.

10. "Barber, Ida," in Salomon Wininger, *Grosse Jüdische National-Biographie mit mehr als 8000 Lebensbeschreibungen namhafter jüdischer Männer und Frauen aller Zeiten und Länder*. 7 Volumes. (Cernauti: Druck "Orient," 1925–1936), 242; and "Barber, Ida," Wiener Stadt- und Landesarchiv, Biographische Sammlung.

11. Ida Barber, *Genrebilder aus dem jüdischen Familienleben* (Prague, 1895).

12. Ibid., 28.

13. Ibid., 51.

14. Ida Barber, "Betende Frauen (Eine Tempelstudie)," *Die Neuzeit* (Sept. 10, 1888).

15. See Wilhelm Stoffers, *Juden und Ghetto in der deutschen Literatur bis zum Ausgang des Weltkrieges* (Graz: H. Stiansnys Sohne, 1939). Chapter 8, "The East, Vienna and the Austrian Mountain Lands before and after 1900."

16. Lothar Kahn, "Tradition and Modernity in the German Ghetto Novel," *Judaism* 28:1 (Winter 1979): 31–41, 32.

17. Max Grunwald, *Vienna* (Philadelphia: Jewish Publication Society of America, 1936), 327–328; Wistrich, *Jews of Vienna*, 121–122.

18. Thomas Winkelbauer, "Leopold Kompert und die böhmischen Landjuden," in *Conditio Judaica: Judentum, Antisemitismus und deutschsprachige Literatur vom 18. Jahrhundert bis zum Ersten Weltkrieg* II., eds. Hans Otto Horch, Horst Denkler (Tübingen: M. Niemeyer, 1988/9), 353.

19. Leopold Kompert, *Leopold Komperts Sämtliche werke* (Leipzig: M. Hesse, 1906) vol. 10, 115. Cited in Winkelbauer, 197.

20. A *Randar*, a common character in ghetto stories, was a wealthy Jewish innkeeper and estate lease owner who knew the village secrets and had some power over the *goyim*. Leopold Kompert, "Die Kinder des Randars," in *Aus dem Ghetto* (Leipzig, n.d.), 76–77. Kahn, "Tradition and Modernity," 31.

21. Kompert, "Kinder," 219.

22. Ibid., 197.

23. Kahn, "Tradition and Modernity," 40–41; Andrea Wodenegg, *Das Bild der Juden Osteuropas: Ein Beitrag zur komparatistischen Imagologie an Textbeispielen von Karl Emil Franzos und Leopold von Sacher-Masoch* (Frankfurt am Main, New York: Lang, 1987), ch. 7; Mark Gelber, "Ethnic Pluralism and Germanization in the Works of Karl Emil Franzos (1848–1904)," *German Quarterly*

56 (1983): 376–385; and Fred Sommer, *"Halb-Asien," German Nationalism and the Eastern European Works of Karl Emil Franzos* (Stuttgart: H.D. Heinz, 1984).

24. Kahn, "Tradition and Modernity," 37.

25. Wistrich, *Jews of Vienna*, 53.

26. Karl Emil Franzos, *The Jews of Barnow*, trans. M. W. Macdowell (New York: Arno Press, 1975), 325.

27. Ibid., 323.

28. Ibid., 76.

29. Ibid., 86.

30. Ibid., 111.

31. Ibid., 83.

32. Gelber, "Karl Emil Franzos," 382.

33. Karl Emil Franzos, *Judith Trachtenberg: A Novel*, trans. C. P. and C. T. Lewis (New York, 1891); Florian Krobb, "'Auf Fluch und Lüge baut sich kein Glück auf': Karl Emil Franzos's Novel *Judith Trachtenberg* and the Question of Jewish Assimilation," in *The Habsburg Legacy: National Identity in Historical Perspective*, ed. Edward Timms and Ritchie Robertson (Edinburgh: Edinburgh University Press, 1994); Florian Krobb, *'Die schöne Jüdin': Jüdische Frauengestalten in der deutschsprachigen Erzahlliteratur vom 17. Jahrhundert bis zum Ersten Weltkrieg* (Tübingen: Max Niemeyer Verlag, 1993), 207–208.

34. Krobb, "Auf Fluch," 85.

35. Ibid., 86.

36. Ibid., 90–91.

37. This was not the case for all Jewish women in Franzos's stories. For example, Lea in the story "Nameless Graves" and the daughter in "The Shylock of Barnow."

38. Ludwig August Frankl, *The Jews in the East*, trans. Rev. P. Beaton (London: Herst and Blackett, 1859).

39. Ibid., 102–103.

40. Ibid., 182–183.

41. Ibid., 280–281.

42. He also wrote other short stories and a tragedy called *Korah* which was supported by the reactionary though not anti-Semitic minister, Count Thun. He was the music critic of the *Fremdenblatt* and of the *Vaterland*. He defended Richard Wagner against the critic Edward Hanslick. Grunwald, *Vienna*, 323.

43. Eduard Kulke, "Eigene Haare," in *Erzählende Schriften* II (Leipzig: Deutsche Verlagsactiengesellschaft, 1906).

44. Ibid., 25–26.

45. Ibid., 28–29.

46. Ibid., 30.

47. Eduard Kulke, *Die schöne Hausierin. Erzählung* (Prague: B. Brandeis, 1895).

48. Ibid., 6.

49. Ibid., 7.

50. Salomon Wininger, *Grosse Jüdische National-Biographie*, vol. II, 537–538.

51. M. Grünfeld, "Die Frau und die jüdische Literatur," *Österreichische Wochenscrift* 1906, Nr. 23, 24, 372–373, 390–391.

52. Ibid., 372.

53. Max Grünfeld, "Wie Reb Ahron einen geschichtlich wichtigen Augenblick versäumt," in *Die Leute des Ghetto* (Prague, 1896).

54. Ibid., 40.

55. Ibid., 46.

56. Ibid., 47.

57. Ibid., 54.

58. Max Grünfeld, "Die Abtrünnigen, Eine Geschichte aus dem Leben der Gasse," *Leben und Lieben im Ghetto* (Prague: Brandeis, 1896).

59. Ibid., 49–50.

60. Ibid., 57.

61. Heinrich York-Steiner, *Der Talmudbauer. Unterwegs. Erzählungen von H. York Steiner* (Berlin: Jüdischer Verlag, 1904).

62. Ibid., 101.

63. Ibid., 111.

64. Ibid., 155.

65. Ibid., 175–176.

66. York-Steiner, "Marhulka," in *Der Talmudbauer*, 183–200.

67. Ibid., 197.

68. Heinrich York-Steiner, "Mater Dolorosa," in *Der Talmudbauer*, 203–229.

69. Ibid., 224.

70. Hermann Menkes, "Ghetto-Naturalismus," *Die Zeit* 12 (June 17, 1897): 40–41. See Gotthart Wunberg, *Das Junge Wien: Österreichische Literatur und Kunst Kritik, 1887–1902* (Tübingen: Niemeyer, 1976).

71. Hermann Menkes, "Mutters Gebetbuch," in *Die Jüdin Leonora und andere Novellen*, 15–19, 15.

72. Hermann Menkes, *Die Jüdin Leonora und andere Novellen* (Vienna, Leipzig: Interterritorialer Verlag "Renaissance," 1923).

73. Menkes, *Die Jüdin Leonora*, 29.

74. Schorske, *Fin-de-Siècle Vienna*.

75. Harold B. Segal, *The Vienna Coffeehouse Wits, 1890–1938* (West Lafayette, Indiana: Purdue University Press, 1993), 18–29, and William M. Johnston, *The Austrian Mind: An Intellectual and Social History, 1848–1938* (Berkeley and Los Angeles: University of California Press, 1972), 119–124.

76. The *Jung Wien* circle has received a great deal of scholarly attention. Therefore, this discussion will focus primarily on the images of Jewish women in their work, an aspect which has not been seriously treated. For more on *Jung*

Wien, see the following: Schorske, *Fin de Siècle Vienna*; Wistrich, *Jews of Vienna*; Karlheinz Rossbacher, *Literatur und Liberalismus: Zur Kultur der Ringstrassenzeit in Wien* (Vienna: J&V, 1992), 389–449; Wunberg, *Das Junge Wien*; Wagner, *Geist und Geschlecht*; Timms and Robertson, eds., *Vienna 1900*; Horch and Denkler, eds., *Conditio Judaica*, II.

77. Michael Pollak, *Viènne 1900: Une identité blessée* (Paris: Gallimard/Julliard, 1984), 163.

78. Leon Botstein, "Music, Femininity, and Jewish Identity: The Tradition and Legacy of the Salon," in *Jewish Women and Their Salons: The Power of Conversation*, ed. Emily D. Bilski and Emily Braun (New Haven: Yale University Press, 2005), 162.

79. Stoffers, 527–536; Florian Krobb, *Die schöne Jüdin*, 225–228; Renate Wagner, *Frauen um Schnitzler* (Vienna: Jugend und Volk, 1980).

80. Bruce Thompson, *Schnitzler's Vienna: Image of a Society* (London and New York: Routledge, 1990), 55.

81. Ibid., chapter 4. For Josephine Mutzenbacher, see Bernhard Doppler, ed., *Erotische Literatur: 1787–1958* (Vienna: Böhlau Verlag, 1990). On Kraus, see Wagner, *Geist und Geschlecht*; on Dörmann, see Larry Wolff, *Postcards from the End of the World: Child Abuse in Freud's Vienna* (New York: Atheneum, 1988), 24–29.

82. Wistrich, *Jews of Vienna*, 593.

83. Paul Hofmann, *The Viennese: Splendor, Twilight, and Exile* (New York: Anchor Books, 1989), 176.

84. Thompson, *Schnitzler's Vienna*, 68–78.

85. Arthur Schnitzler, *My Youth in Vienna*, foreword by Frederic Morton, trans. Catherine Hutter (New York: Holt, Rinehart and Winston, Inc., 1970), 12.

86. Renate Wagner, *Frauen um Schnitzler*, 11–18.

87. Schnitzler, *Youth*, 148.

88. Ibid., 150.

89. Ibid., 156.

90. Arthur Schnitzler, *The Road into the Open (Der Weg ins Frei)*, trans. Roger Byers (Berkeley and Los Angeles: University of California Press, 1992), 59–60.

91. Ibid., 13–14.

92. Ibid., 55.

93. Ibid., 57–58.

94. Ibid., 153.

95. Ibid., 85.

96. Ibid., 158–159.

97. Ibid., 189.

98. Ibid., 180.

99. Ibid., 168.

100. Ibid., 277.

101. Ibid., 279.

102. Ibid., 277.

103. For Kraus's views on women, see Edward Timms, *Karl Kraus: Apocalyptic Satirist, Culture and Catastrophe in Habsburg Vienna* (New Haven and London: Yale University Press, 1986), 63–93; Wagner, *Geist und Geschlecht*; Harriet Anderson, "Neues zu Karl Kraus und dem Allgemeinen Oesterreichischen Frauenverein," *Kraus Hefte* 41 (1987): 1–5.

104. Kraus's writings are extremely complex and have been treated elsewhere. See Timms, *Karl Kraus* (1986), and Edward Timms, *Karl Kraus, Apocalyptic Satirist: The Post-War Crisis and the Rise of the Swastika* (New Haven, London: Yale University Press, 2005). Also Wagner, *Geist und Geschlect*; Wistrich, *Jews of Vienna*, 497–516; Janik and Toulmin, *Wittgenstein's Vienna*, 67–91; Frank Field, *The Last Days of Mankind: Karl Kraus and His Vienna* (London: Macmillan, 1967); Johnston, *Austrian Mind*, 203–207. See bibliography in Timms for more. I will focus on his portrayal of Jewish women.

105. Timms, *Karl Kraus*, 63, 68.

106. Ibid., 64–67.

107. Edith Prost, "Vertriebene Frauen," in *Vertriebene Vernunft II*, 1079–1080; Harry Zohn, *"Ich bin ein Sohn der deutschen Sprache nur . . ." Jüdisches Erbe in der Österreichischen Literatur* (Vienna: Amalthea Verlag, 1986), 256; and Sigurd Paul Scheichl, "Die Schalek—Quelques observations sur le theme de la femme dans *Les Derniers jours de l'humanite*," *Austriaca: Cahiers Universitaires d'Information sur l'Autriche*, May/June 1986, n. 22, 73–81.

108. Timms, *Karl Kraus*, 328–329; *Fackel* n. 406–412, 15–19, and 426–430, 35–39.

109. Scheichl, "Die Schalek," 75.

110. Timms, *Karl Kraus*, 146, 338–339; *Fackel* n. 413–417, 36; 426–430, 39.

111. Timms, *Karl Kraus*, 339; *Fackel*, n. 426–430, 39, 413–417, 36, 374–375, 32.

112. See W. E. Yates, *Schnitzler, Hofmannsthal and the Austrian Theater* (New Haven and London: Yale University Press, 1992), 66–114.

113. I consulted the playbills which are included in the collection at the Wienbibliothek im Rathaus, for the K. K. Hof Burgtheater, and the K. K. Hof- Operntheater. From 1888 to 1901, Scribe's opera was produced 22 times, Mosenthal's opera 24 times, Wohlbrueck's opera 10 times, Hebbel's "Judith" 3 times, Grillparzer's Esther 12 times, Mosenthal's "Deborah" 7 times, and Grillparzer's "Jüdin" 27 times. From Minna Alth and Gertrude Obzyna, *Burgtheater 1776–1976: Aufführungen und Besetzungen von zweihundert Jahren* (Vienna: Überreuter, 1979). "Jüdin von Toledo" ran from 1889 to 1919 with a total of 75 productions; "Deborah" ran from 1864 to 1896 with 56 productions; "Esther" from 1868 to 1899 with 46 productions; and "Judith" from 1896 to 1903 with 4 productions.

114. Elisabeth Frenzel, *Judengestalten auf der deutschen Bühne. Ein notwendiger Querschnitt durch 700 Jahre Rollengeschichte* (Munich: Deutscher Volksverlag, 1942). Also see Horst Denkler, "Lauter Juden: Zum Rollenspektrum der

Juden-Figuren im populären Bühnendrama der Metternichschen Restaurationsperiode (1815–1848)," and Jürgen Hein, "Judenthematik im Wiener Volkstheater," in *Conditio Judaica: Judentum, Antisemitismus und deutschsprachige Literatur vom 18. Jahrhundert bis zum Ersten Weltkrieg* I., ed. Hans Otto Horch and Horst Denkler. (Tübingen: M. Niemeyer, 1988/9).

115. Yates, *Schnitzler and Hofmannsthal*, 75. Richard Geehr, *Adam Müller-Guttenbrunn and the Aryan Theater of Vienna: The Approach of Cultural Fascism* (Göppingen: A. Kummerle, 1973).

116. Yates, *Schnitzler and Hofmannsthal*, 76–77.

117. Frenzel, *Judengestalten*, 141.

118. Krobb, "Die schöne Jüdin," 6–7.

119. Friedrich Kaiser, *Neu-Jerusalem* (Vienna, 1869).

120. Rossbacher, *Literatur und Liberalismus*, 400–401.

121. Kaiser, *Neu-Jerusalem*, 49.

122. S. H. Mosenthal, *Deborah: Volks-Schauspiel in vier Aufzügen* (Leipzig: P. Reclam, 1900).

123. Charlene A. Lea, *Emancipation, Assimilation and Stereotype: The Image of the Jew in German and Austrian Drama, 1800–1850* (Bonn: Bouvier, 1978), 65.

124. Mosenthal, *Deborah*, 13, 30. Cited in Lea, *Emancipation*, 67.

125. E. M. Lilien, *Briefe an Seine Frau, 1905–1925*, ed. Otto M. Lilien and Eve Strauss (Königstein/Ts., 1985); Michael Berkowitz, "Art in Zionist Popular Culture and Jewish National Self-Consciousness, 1897–1914," in *Art and Its Uses: The Visual Image and Modern Jewish Society*, Studies in Contemporary Jewry VI, ed. Ezra Mendelsohn (New York, Oxford: Oxford University Press, 1990); M. Hirschfelder, "E. M. Lilien," *Ost und West* 7 (July 1901): 518–528; M. Hirschfelder, "Zwei Neue Lilien'sche Ex-Libres," *Ost und West* 11 (November 1901): 822–824; M. S. Levussove, *The New Art of an Ancient People: The Work of Ephraim Mose Lilien* (New York: B.W. Huebsch, 1906).

126. Reproductions in Lilien, *Briefe an Seine Frau*, 60–65, 152, 156, 160, 238–242.

Conclusion

1. Carl Schorske, *Fin-de-Siècle Vienna: Politics and Culture* (New York: Vintage Books, 1981).

2. Ibid., 120.

3. Péter Hanák, *The Garden and the Workshop: Essays on the Cultural History of Vienna and Budapest* (Princeton: Princeton University Press, 1998), xvi.

4. Marsha Rozenblit, *Reconstructing a National Identity: The Jews of Habsburg Austria during World War I* (New York: Oxford University Press, 2001).

5. Elisabeth Freundlich, *The Traveling Years*, trans. and afterword by Elizabeth Pennebaker (Riverside, Calif.: Ariadne Press, 1999), 28.

Bibliography

Primary Sources

Archival Collections

Archives of the Leo Baeck Institute, New York: Lise Meitner Collection AR 2729, Stella Kadmon Collection AR 4392, Mimi and Norbert Grossberg Collection AR 3815, Hilde Spiel Collection AR 1810, Miriam Beer Hofmann-Lens Collection AR 7258, Lillian M. Bader Collection AR 5455, and Gertrude Berliner Collection AR 1227; Memoir Collection—listed below; Austrian Heritage Collection AR 10378—Questionnaires St-T; Tauber, Oscar, Questionnaires A-Be, Alt, Franz Leopold, Questionnaires Bi-By; Buch, Fred; Photos Collection.

Austrian National Library Picture Archive (Österreichische Nationalbibliothek Bildarchiv), Vienna.

Austrian Resistance Archive (Dokumentations-Archiv des Österreichischen Widerstandes), Vienna: Oral History Collection, Photo of Käthe Leichter.

Central Archives for the History of the Jewish People, Jerusalem: A/W—Archiv der Israelitischen Kultusgemeinde, Wien.

Churchill College Archives Centre, Cambridge: Meitner Collection.

Schlesinger Library, Radcliffe Institute, Cambridge, Mass.: Helene Deutsch. Papers, 1900–1983.

Wienbibliothek im Rathaus (formerly Wiener Stadt- und Landesbibliothek), Vienna: playbills of Burgtheater and Burgoper, Nachlass Elise Richter.

Wiener Stadt- und Landesarchiv, Vienna: Biographical Collection, Death Registers.

Newspapers and Periodicals

Deutsches Volksblatt. Vienna, 1888–1890.

Deutsche Worte: Monatsheft. Leipzig, 1896–1902.

Die Fackel. Vienna, 1899–1914.

Dr. Bloch's Österreichische Wochenschrift. Central-Organ für die gesamten Interessen des Judentums. Vienna, 1884–1914.

Freies Blatt: Organ zur Abwehr. Des Antisemitismus Gleichheit. Vienna, 1887.

Globus. Hildburghausen, 1895.

Illustrierte Gemeinde Zeitung: Central-Organ für die Gesammt-Interessen der israel. Cultusgemeinden, Vienna, 1885–1886.

Jüdische Volksblatt. Vienna, 1899–1902.

Jüdische Volkszeitung. Vienna, 1894.

Jüdische Zeitung: National-jüdisches Organ. Vienna, 1907–1913.
Kikeriki: Humoristisches Volksblatt. Vienna, 1891.
Mitteilungen der Österreichisch-Israelitischen Union. Vienna, 1889–1900.
Monatschrift der Österreichisch-Israelitischen Union. Vienna, 1901–1914.
Neue Freie Press. Vienna, 1894.
Neue National-Zeitung. Vienna, 1907–1909.
Die Neuzeit: Wochenschrift für politische, religiöse, und Cultur-Interessen. Vienna, 1885–1914.
Ost und West. Berlin, 1901–1914.
Ostara. Vienna, 1911–1914.
Neue Jüdische Presse. Vienna, 1900.
Nord und Süd. Breslau, 1918.
Reichsbote: Zeitschrift für soziale, wissenschaftlische. Vienna, 1894.
Die Wahrheit: Unabhängige Zeitschrift für jüdische Interessen. Vienna, 1903–1914.
Die Welt. Zentralorgan der zionistischen Bewegung. Vienna, 1897–1914.
Wiener Jüdische Presse. Vienna, 1899.
Die Zeit. Berlin, 1897.

Letters, Memoirs, Interviews, Diaries

Amann, Dora. "Ferne Erinnerungen aus meiner Kindheit Jugend und Alter." ME 900. Leo Baeck Institute, New York.
Bader, Lillian. "One Life Is Not Enough: Autobiographical Vignettes." ME 784. Leo Baeck Institute, New York.
Baum, Vicki. *It Was All Quite Different: The Memoirs of Vicki Baum.* New York: Funk & Wagnalls, 1964.
Benedikt, Moritz. *Aus meinem Leben: Erinnerungen und Erörterungen.* Vienna: Verlagsbuchhandlung Carl Konegen, 1906.
Berliner, Gertrude. "From My Family: Fiction and Truth." ME 51. Leo Baeck Institute, New York.
Bloch, Joseph S. *My Reminiscences.* Vienna and Berlin: R. Löwit, 1923.
Campbell, Alister (Grandson of Toni Stopler). "Recorded Memories: Vienna, Berlin, New York." ME 390. Leo Baeck Institute, New York.
Cassirer, Toni. "Aus meinem Leben mit Ernst Cassirer." ME 89. Leo Baeck Institute, New York.
Deutsch, Helene. *Confrontations with Myself: An Epilogue.* New York: W.W. Norton, Inc., 1973.
Foster, Edith. *Reunion in Vienna.* Riverside, Calif.: Ariadne Press, 1991.
Freud, Esti. "Vignettes of My Life." ME 149. Leo Baeck Institute, New York.
Freud, Sigmund. *Letters of Sigmund Freud.* Selected and edited by Ernst L. Freud. New York, 1961.
Freundlich, Elisabeth. *The Traveling Years.* Translated and afterword by Elizabeth Pennebaker. Riverside, Calif.: Ariadne Press, 1999.

Furst, Ulrich R. "Windows to My Youth." ME 902. Leo Baeck Institute, New York.

Grossberg, Mimi. *The Road to America: Mimi Grossberg, Her Times and Her Emigration*. New York: Austrian Institute, 1986.

Herzl, Theodor. *Briefe und Tagebücher*. 7 vols. Berlin: Propyläen Verlag.

———. *Complete Diaries of Theodor Herzl*. 5 Vols. Translated by Harry Zohn. Edited by Raphael Patai. New York and London: Herzl Press and Thom Yoseloff, 1960.

Klein-Löw, Stella. *Erinnerungen: Erlebtes und Gedachtes*. Vienna: Jugend und Volk, 1980.

Lachs, Minna. *Warum Schaust Du Zurück: Erinnerungen, 1907–1941*. Vienna, Munich, and Zurich: Europaverlag, 1986.

Langer, Marie. *Von Wien bis Managua. Wege einer Psychoanalytikerin*. Freiburg: Kore, Verlag Traute Hensch, 1986.

Lazarsfeld, Sophie. *Wie die Frau den Mann erlebt: Fremde bekenntnisse und eigene Betrachtungen*. Leipzig and Vienna: Schneider & Co., 1931.

Leichter, Käthe. *Käthe Leichter: Leben und Werk*. Edited by Herbert Steiner. Foreword by Hertha Firnberg. Vienna: Europa Verlag, 1973.

Lerner, Gerda. *The Creation of Feminist Consciousness*. New York: Oxford University Press, 1993.

Lilien, E. M. *Briefe an Seine Frau, 1905–1925*. Edited by Otto M. Lilien and Eve Strauss. Königstein/Ts., 1985.

Lowe, Marianne. "Studying Psychology in Turbulent Times." ME 929. Leo Baeck Institute, New York.

Mahler, Margaret. *The Memoirs of Margaret S. Mahler. 1897–1985*. Compiled & ed. Paul E. Stepansky. New York: Free Press, 1988.

Meitner, Lise. Lise Meitner to Frl. Hitzenberger, March 29/April 10, 1951. Meitner Collection. Churchill College Archives Centre, Cambridge.

———. "Looking Back." *Bulletin of the Atomic Scientists* 20 (November 1964): 2–7.

Popp, Adelheid. *The Autobiography of a Working Woman*. Trans. E. C. Harvey. Westport, Conn.: Hyperion Press, 1983.

Puhm, Rosa. *Eine Trennung in Gorki*. Vienna: Verlag für Gesellschaftskritik, 1990.

———. *Weiter Weg nach Krasnogorsk: Schicksalbericht einer Frau*. Vienna and Munich: Molden, 1971.

Richter, Elise. *Summe des Lebens*. Elise Richter Collection at Wienbibliothek im Rathaus.

Robert, Anny. [Memoir] ME 899. Leo Baeck Institute, New York.

Schlesinger, Therese. "Mein Weg zur Sozialdemokratie." In *Gedenkbuch. 20 Jahre österreichische Arbeiterinnenbewegung*, edited by Adelheid Popp. Vienna, 1912.

Schnitzler, Arthur. *My Youth in Vienna*. Foreword by Frederic Morton. Trans. Catherine Hutter. New York: Holt, Rinehart and Winston, Inc., 1970.

Schwarz, Olly. "Lebens-Erinnerungen von Olly Schwarz." ME 590. Leo Baeck Institute, New York.

Segal, Erna. "You Shall Never Forget." ME 594. Leo Baeck Institute, New York.

Spiel, Hilde. *Die Hellen und die Finsterin Zeiten: Erinnerungen, 1911–1946.* Reinbek bei Hamburg: Rowohlt, 1991.

Spielrein, Sabina. "The Diary of Sabina Spielrein (1909–1912)." Translated by Krishna Winston. In Aldo Carotenuto. *A Secret Symmetry: Sabina Spielrein between Jung and Freud.* New York: Pantheon Books, 1982.

Viertel, Salka. *The Kindness of Strangers: A Theatrical Life.* New York: Holt, Rinehart and Winston, 1969.

Wittels, Fritz. *Freud and the Child Woman: The Memoirs of Fritz Wittels.* Edited with a preface by Edward Timms. New Haven: Yale University Press, 1995.

A Young Girl's Diary. Translated Eden and Ceder Paul. New York: Doubleday, 1991.

Zaloscer, Hilde. "Das dreimalige Exil." In *Vertriebene Vernunft I: Emigration und Exil österreichischer Wissenschaft, 1930–1940,* edited by Friedrich Stadler. Vienna: Jugend und Volk, 1989/90.

———. "Wissenschaftliche Arbeit ohne wissenschaftlichen Apparat." In *Vertrieben Vernunft II: Emigration und Exil österreichischer Wissenschaft,* edited by Friedrich Stadler. Vienna: Jugend und Volk, 1989/90.

Zuckerkandl, Berta Szeps. *My Life and History.* Translated by John Sommerfield. New York: A.A. Knopf, 1939.

Zweig, Fredrike. *Spiegelungen des Lebens.* Vienna: Hans Deutsch, 1964.

Zweig, Stefan. *The World of Yesterday.* New York: Viking Press, 1943.

Books, Pamphlets, and Articles

100. Vereinsjahr. Jubilaeums- und Jahres-Bericht für das Jahr 1915 (Israelitischer Frauen-Wohltätigkeits-Verein). Vienna, 1916. Central Archives for the History of the Jewish People, Jerusalem. A/W 2232.

Achter Jahresbericht des Hietzinger Frauenwohltätigkeitsvereines. Vienna, 1914. Central Archives for the History of the Jewish People, Jerusalem. A/W 2353, 5.

Adler, Samuel. "Ausschusbericht über die religiöse Verpflichtung der Frauen und deren Beteilung am Gottesdienst . . . Nebst einer hebräischen Abhandlung." *Protokolle und Aktenstücke der zweiten Rabbinerversammlung.* Frankfurt a/M, 1845: 334–348.

B. "Antisemitismus in der Schule." *Freies Blatt: Organ zur Abwehr. Des Antisemitismus* 2/53 (April 9, 1893).

Baer-Issachar, Marta. "An unsere Frauen!" In *Der Zionismus und die Frauen.* 1905?

Barber, Ida. "Betende Frauen (Eine Tempelstudie)." *Die Neuzeit*. September 10, 1888.

———. *Genrebilder aus dem jüdischen Familienleben*. Prague, 1895.

Benedikt, Clothilde. "Rosa Zifferer-Schüler." *Österreichische Wochenschrift* 6. February 10, 1911.

Benedikt, Moritz. "Der geisteskranke Jude." *Nord und Süd* 167 (1918): 266–270.

Bericht des Brigittenauer Israelitischer Frauen-Wohltätigkeitsvereines in Wien über seine Tätigkeit im Vereinsjahre 1910. Central Archives for the History of the Jewish People, Jerusalem. A/W 2273, 6.

Billroth, Theodor. *Über das Lehren und Lernen der medizinischen Wissenschaften an den Universitäten der deutschen Nation*. Vienna, 1876.

Bloch, Joseph S. *Israel and the Nations*. Trans. Leon Kellner and Harry Schneidermann. Berlin: Benjamin Harz Verlag, 1927.

Bondy, Ottilie. *5. Jahrbericht des Vereins für erweiterte Frauenbildung in Wien*.

Buber, Martin. "Das Zion der jüdischen Frau." *Die Welt* 5/17. April 26, 1901: 3–5.

Buschan, Georg. "Einfluss der Rasse auf die Form und Jäufigkeit pathologischer Veränderungen." *Globus* 67. 1895: 21–24, 43–47, 60–63, 76–80.

Canetti, Veza. *Die Gelbe Strasse*. Carl Hanser Verlag, 1990.

Darnau, Stephan. "Die palestinensische Jüdin am Putztisch." Lecture at Österreichische-Israelitische Union, February 21, 1909. *Monatschrift der österreichische-Israelitische Union* XXI: 16–29.

Deutsch, Helene. "Significance of Masochism." Read at the Eleventh International Psychoanalytic Congress. Oxford, July 27, 1929.

E. M. "Moderne jüdische Schriftstellerin." *Die Neuzeit*. 1902: 236.

Einladung zur Confirmation der Mädchen. 1892. Central Archives for the History of the Jewish People, Jerusalem.

Elfter Jahresbericht des "Frauenhort" Israelitischer Frauen-Wohltätigkeits-Verein im Bezirke Alsergrund in Wien. Vienna, 1904. Leo Baeck Institute, New York.

Ellman, Rozia. In *Stenographisches Protokoll der Verhandlungen des II. Zionisten-Kongresses gehalten zu Basel vom 28 bis 31 August 1898*. Vienna: Erez Israel, 1898.

Engländer, Martin. *Die auffallend häufigen Krankheitserscheinungen der jüdischen Rasse*. Vienna: J.L. Pollak, 1902.

Erb, Wilhelm. *Über die wachsende Nervosität unserer Zeit*. Heidelberg, 1893.

Exner, Emilie. *Weibliche Pharmaceuten*. Lecture held in Vereine Erwervende Frauen. Vienna: Verlag des Wiener Frauen-Erwerb-Vereines, 1902.

Feigenbaum, Rosa. "70. Geburtstag Ottilie Bondy." *Die Neuzeit*. July 26, 1902.

———. "Der Stellung der jüdischen Frau zum Zionismus." *Die Neuzeit*. 1902: 29–31.

Feiwel, Berthold. "Die jüdische Familie. Die jüdische Frau." *Die Welt* 5/17. April 26, 1901: 1–3.

"For Total Equality. (Report to the Breslau Conference, 1846)." In *The Rise of Reform Judaism: A Sourcebook of Its European Origins*, edited by W. Gunther Plaut. New York: World Union for Progressive Judaism, 1963.

Fr. "Die Mädchenkonfirmation." *Die Wahrheit* 27 (July 11, 1913): 5-6.

Francolm, Isaac Asher. "Simplicity, Not Pomp." In *The Rise of Reform Judaism: A Sourcebook of Its European Origins*, edited by W. Gunther Plaut. New York: World Union for Progressive Judaism, 1963.

Frank, Max. "Das Steuerwesen der Wiener Kultusgemeinde." *Ost und West* 10. August, September, 1910: 519-524.

Frankl, Ludwig August. *The Jews in the East*. Translated by the Rev. P. Beaton. London: Herst and Blackett, 1859.

Frankl, Moritz. "Die Stellung und Bedeutung der Frau im Judenthume. Vortrag in OIU, 6 Feb, 1892." *Mitt. der öst-isr. Union* 4/34. 1892: 2-8.

Franzos, Karl Emil. *The Jews of Barnow*. Trans. M. W. Macdowell. New York: Arno Press, 1975.

———. *Judith Trachtenberg: A Novel*. Trans. C. P. and C. T. Lewis. New York, 1891.

"Die Frau bei uns und—um uns." *Österreichische Wochenschrift* 12. December 20, 1895.

Freud, Sigmund. *Dora: An Analysis of a Case of Hysteria*. New York: Collier Books, 1963.

———. *Freud on Women: A Reader*. Edited by Elisabeth Young-Bruehl. New York and London: W.W. Norton, 1990.

———. *The Interpretation of Dreams*. Translated and edited by James Strachey. New York: Avon Books, 1965.

Freud, Sigmund, et al. *The Standard Edition of the Complete Psychological Works of Sigmund Freud*. London: Hogarth Press, 1900.

Freund, Jacob. *Hanna: Gebet und Undachtsbuch für israelitische Frauen und Mädchen*. Breslau: Verlag von Wilh. Jacobsohn u. Comp, 1893.

F[riedländer, Moritz]. "Einiges über die Stellung des römischen und jüdischen Weibes im Altherthume." *Die Neuzeit* 22. 1882: 541-542, 550-551, 559-560.

Friedmann, Meir. "Mitwirkung von Frauen beim Gottesdienste." *Hebrew Union College Annual* 8 (1931): 511-523.

———. "Das Passah-fest und die Frauen." *Österreichische Wochenschrift* 13 (1893): 234-236.

Fürth, Henriette. "Die jüdischen Frauen und ihre Aufgabe." *Österreichische Wochenschrift* 16. 1899: 257-258.

Geiger, Abraham. "Über die Stellung des weiblichen Geschlechtes in dem Judenthume unserer Zeit." *Wissenschaftliche Zeitschrift für jüdische Theologie* 3 (1837): 1-16.

Gerson, Adolf. *Die Scham*. Bonn: A. Marcus & E. Weber, 1919.

Glückel. *The Memoirs of Glückel of Hameln*. Translated by Marvin Lowenthal. New York: Schocken Books, 1977.

Goldhammer, Leopold. "Die Ehe bei den Greichen, Römern und Juden: Eine culturhistorische Skizze." *Reichsbote* 1 (Vienna, 1894). 16: 9–11, 18: 10–12.

———. "Das Weib bei Ariern und Semiten." (Stellungnahme gegen das Urteil über die jüdische Ehe und das jüdische Altertum bei Zmigrodzki, "Die Mutter bei den Voelkern des arischen Stammes.") *Österreichische Wochenschrift* 5 (1888): 616–619.

G[oldschmidt] H[enriette]. "Zur Frauenfrage." *Die Neuzeit* 18. 1878: 71–72, 79–80, 87–88.

Goslar, Hans. *Die Sexualethik der jüdischen Wiedergeburt. Ein Wort an unsere Jugend.* Berlin, 1919.

Gottheil, Emma. In *Stenographisches Protokoll der Verhandlungen des IV. Zionisten-Kongresses in London, 1900.* Vienna: Erez Israel, 1900.

Gottlieb, Heinrich. "Die moderne Frauenbewegung im Lichte des Judentums." *Österreichische Wochenschrift* 13. 1896: 174–175.

Grünfeld, Max. "Die Frau und die jüdische Literatur." *Österreichische Wochenschrift.* 1906: 372–373, 390–391.

———. *Leben und Lieben im Ghetto.* Prague: Brandeis, 1896.

———. *Die Leute des Ghetto.* Prague, 1896.

Grunwald, Max. *Beruria: Gebet- und Andachtsbuch für jüdische Frauen und Mädchen.* Vienna, 1907.

———. *Die modern Frauenbewegung und das Judenthum,* Lecture held in the OIU on March 11, 1903. Published as a manuscript. Vienna, 1903.

Güdemann, Moritz. *Geschichte des Erziehungswesens und der Cultur den Juden in Frankreich und Deutschland.* Volume I. Vienna: Alfred Holder, 1880.

———. *Geschichte des Erziehungswesens und der Cultur den Juden in Frankreich und Deutschland.* Volume II. Vienna: Alfred Holder, 1884.

———. *Jüdische Apologetik.* Glogau: C. Fleming, 1906.

———. *HaYahadut HaLeumit.* Foreword by Robert S. Wistrich. Translated by Miriam Dinur. Jerusalem: Dinur Center, 1995.

———. *Das Leben des jüdischen Weibes. Sittengeschichtlich Skizze aus der mischnisch-talmudischen Epoche.* Separat-Abdruck aus Kobak's "Jeschurun" 5619. Breslau: Sulzbach's Buchdruckerei, 1859.

Hainisch, Marianne. "Die Geschichte der Frauenbewegung in Österreich" (1901). In *Handbuch der Frauenbewegung.* Volume I, edited by Helene Lange and Gertrude Baumer. Weinheim: Beltz, 1980.

Hartmann, A. Th. *Die Hebräerin am Putztische und als Braut.* Amsterdam, 1809–1810.

Herxheimer, Salomon. "Is Confirmation a 'Jewish' Ceremony?" In W. Gunther Plaut. *The Rise of Reform Judaism: A Sourcebook of Its European Origins.* New York: World Union for Progressive Judaism, 1963.

Herzl, Theodor. *Altneuland, Old-New Land.* Third edition. Translated by Paula Arnold. Haifa: Haifa Publishing Company, 1964.

———. "Die Frauen und der Zionismus." In *Theodor Herzl's Gesammelte Schriften*, edited by Leon Kellner. Berlin, 1905.

———. "The New Ghetto." In *Theodor Herzl: A Portrait for This Age*, edited by Ludwig Lewisohn. Cleveland and New York: World Publishing Company, 1955.

———. "Women and Zionism." *Zionist Writings: Essays and Addresses*. Volume 2. New York: Herzl Press, 1975.

Herzl, Theodor, and Alex Bein. *Briefe und Tagebücher*. Berlin: Propyläen, 1983–1996.

Hietzinger Frauenverein zum Schutze Armer, Verlassener Kinder. Neunter Jahresbericht. Vienna, 1915. Central Archives for the History of the Jewish People, Jerusalem. A/W 2353, 6.

Hirsch, Samson Raphael. "The Jewish Woman." *Judaism Eternal: Selected Essays from the Writings of Rabbi Samson Raphael Hirsch*. Volume 2. Translated by Dayan Dr. I. Grunfeld. London: Soncino Press, 1956.

Hirschfelder, M. "E. M. Lilien." *Ost und West* 7. July 1901: 518–528.

———. "Zwei Neue Lilien'sche Ex-Libres." *Ost und West* 11. November 1901: 822–824.

Hitler, Adolf. *Mein Kampf*. New York, 1939.

Holdheim, Samuel. *Die religiose Stellung des weiblichen Geschlechts im talmudischen Judenthum*. Schwerin, 1846.

Horowitz, Anna. "Die Fragen der körperlichen, geistigen und wirtschaftlichen Hebung der Juden. Jüdische Frauenerwerbvereine. (Eine Zuschrift)" *Die Welt* 4/49. December 7, 1900: 9.

Hovorka, Oskar. *Die Äussere Nase: Eine Anatomisch-Anthropologische Studie*. Vienna: Alfred Hölder, 1893.

Husserl, Siegmund. "Die Israelitische Kultusgemeinde Wien." *Ost und West* 10. August, September, 1910: 493–520.

Instruktion für den Religionsunterricht an Maedchenlyzeen. 1913. Central Archives for the History of the Jewish People, Jerusalem.

Israelitischer Frauen-Wohltätigkeits-Verein, *100. Vereinsjahr. Jubilaeums- und Jahres-Bericht für das Jahr 1915*. Vienna, 1916. Central Archives for the History of the Jewish People, Jerusalem.

"Isr. Frauen-Wohltätigkeits-Verein in Wien." *Die Neuzeit*, 1902.

Jaffee, Robert. "Das jüdische Weib." *Die Welt* 5/28. July 12, 1901: 11–12.

Jahresbericht des Hietzinger Frauenwohltätigkeitsvereines. Vienna, 1907. Central Archives for the History of the Jewish People, Jerusalem. A/W 2353.

Jahres-Bericht des Israelitischen Frauen-Vereines in Wien für das Jahr 1889. Vienna, 1890. Central Archives for the History of the Jewish People, Jerusalem. A/W 2232.

Jahres-Bericht des Israelitischen Frauen-Vereines in Wien für das Jahr 1891. Vienna, 1892. Central Archives for the History of the Jewish People, Jerusalem. A/W 2232.

Jahres-Bericht des Israelitischen Frauen-Vereines in Wien für das Jahr 1892. Vienna, 1893. Central Archives for the History of the Jewish People, Jerusalem. A/W 2232.

Jahres-Bericht des Israelitischen Frauen-Wohltätigkeits-Vereines in Wien für das Jahr 1911. Vienna, 1912. Central Archives for the History of the Jewish People, Jerusalem. A/W 2232.

II. Jahres-Bericht des jüd. Frauen-Wohltätigkeits-Vereines "Zuflucht" in Wien 1902. Central Archives for the History of the Jewish People, Jerusalem. A/W 2267.

III. Jahres-Bericht des jüd. Frauen-Wohltätigkeits-Vereines "Zuflucht" in Wien 1903. Central Archives for the History of the Jewish People, Jerusalem. A/W 2267.

IV. Jahres-Bericht des jüd. Frauen-Wohltätigkeits-Vereines "Zuflucht" in Wien 1904. Central Archives for the History of the Jewish People, Jerusalem. A/W 2267.

V. Jahres-Bericht des jüd. Frauen-Wohltätigkeits-Vereines "Zuflucht" in Wien 1905. Central Archives for the History of the Jewish People, Jerusalem. A/W 2267.

VII. Jahres-Bericht des jüd. Frauen-Wohltätigkeits-Vereines "Zuflucht" in Wien 1907. Central Archives for the History of the Jewish People, Jerusalem. A/W 2267.

IX. Jahres-Bericht des jüd. Frauen-Wohltätigkeits-Vereines "Zuflucht" in Wien 1909. Central Archives for the History of the Jewish People, Jerusalem. A/W 2267.

VII. Jahresbericht des Mädchen- und Frauen-Vereines "Krankenbesuch:" (Bikur Chaulim). Vienna, 1910. Central Archives for the History of the Jewish People, Jerusalem. A/W 2236.

J[ellinek, Adolf]. "Die Frauen in der Wiener Cultusgemeinde." *Die Neuzeit.* December 14, 1888.

J[———]. "Die Frauen und der Antisemitismus." *Die Neuzeit* 1 (1885): 7–8.

J[———]. "Geistliche und weibliche Antisemiten." *Die Neuzeit* 5 (1886): 139–140.

———. "Juden und Weiber." *Die Neuzeit* 33. (1882): 277.

———. *Der jüdische Stamm in nichtjüdischen Sprichwörtern.* 3v. Vienna: Bermann & Altmann, 1882–1886.

[———]. "Kurze Anzeigen." *Der Orient* 12 (1851).

———. "Das Mutterherz (Huetten Fest, 1854)." *Das Weib in Israel: Drei Reden.* Vienna: Herzfeld & Bauer, n.d.

———. "Orient und Occident." *Die Neuzeit* 21 (1883): 203.

———. *Die Psyche des Weibes.* Vienna, 1872.

———. "Rede zur Feier des funfzigjährigen Bestehens des israelitischen Frauen-Vereins in Wien (Am 1. Januar 1866)." *Das Weib in Israel. Drei Reden.* Vienna: Herzfeld & Bauer, n.d.

———. "Die religiöse Erziehung des israelitischen Weibes (Wochenfest, 1864)." *Das Weib in Israel: Drei Reden.* Vienna: Herzfeld & Bauer, n.d.

———. *Studien und Skizzen. Erster Theil. Der jüdische Stamm. Ethnografische Studie.* Vienna: Herzfeld & Bauer, 1869.

Jüdischer Frauen-Wohltätigkeits-Verein "Zuflucht." Vienna, 1902. Central Archives for the History of the Jewish People, Jerusalem. A/W 2266.

II. *Jüdischer Frauen-Wohltätikeits-Verein "Zuflucht."* Vienna, 1902. Central Archives for the History of the Jewish People, Jerusalem. A/W 2266.

III. *Jüdischer Frauen-Wohltätikeits-Verein "Zuflucht."* Vienna, 1903. Central Archives for the History of the Jewish People, Jerusalem. A/W 2266.

IV. *Jüdischer Frauen-Wohltätikeits-Verein "Zuflucht."* Vienna, 1904. Central Archives for the History of the Jewish People, Jerusalem. A/W 2266.

V. *Jüdischer Frauen-Wohltätikeits-Verein "Zuflucht."* Vienna, 1905. Central Archives for the History of the Jewish People, Jerusalem. A/W 2266.

VII. *Jüdischer Frauen-Wohltätikeits-Verein "Zuflucht."* Vienna, 1907. Central Archives for the History of the Jewish People, Jerusalem. A/W 2266.

IX. *Jüdischer Frauen-Wohltätikeits-Verein "Zuflucht."* Vienna, 1902. Central Archives for the History of the Jewish People, Jerusalem. A/W 2266.

"Jüdische Krankenpflegerinnen." *Die Wahrheit* 11. March 15, 1901.

Kaiser, Friedrich. *Neu-Jerusalem.* Vienna, 1869.

Kaufmann, David, ed. *Memoiren der Glueckel von Hameln: 1645–1719.* Frankfurt a. M.: J. Kaufmann, 1896.

———. "Wie heben wir den religiösen Sinn unserer Mädchen und Frauen. Eine Antwort an Herrn Wilhelm von Guttman." *Österreichische Wochenschrift* (1893): 83–86, 100–102.

Kiss, Arnold. *Mirjam: Gebet und Andachtsbuch für Israelitische Frauen und Mädchen.* Budapest: Verlag von Schlesinger Jos, n.d.

Klugmann, Naum. *Die Frau im Talmud.* Vienna: J. Kaufmann, M. Waizner & Sohn, 1898.

Kollman, Rosa. "Rede des Fraulein Rosa Kollmann anlässlich der Debatte über 'Agitation'." *Die Welt* 5/13. 1901: 11.

Kommer, Jakob. "Die Fragen der körperlichen, geistigen und wirtschaftlichen Hebung der Juden. Jüdische Frauenerwerb-Verein." *Die Welt* 4/49. December 7, 1900: 9.

Kompert, Leopold. "Die Kinder des Randars." In *Aus dem Ghetto: Geschichten.* Leipzig: Grunow, 1848.

———. *Leopold Komperts Sämtliche werke.* Leipzig: M. Hesse, 1906.

Krafft-Ebing, Richard von. *Nervosität und neurasthenische Zustande.* Vienna: Alfred Hoelder, 1895.

———. *Psychopathia Sexualis: A Medico-Forensic Study.* Rev. trans. Harry E. Wedeck. New York: Putnam, 1956.

———. *Text-book of Insanity.* Trans. Charles Gilbert Chaddock. Philadelphia: F.A. Davis Company, 1905.

Kraus, Rudolf. "Zentralisierung der Armenfürsorge." Vienna, 1909. Supplement to *Vierter Jahresbericht des Hietzinger Frauenwohltätigkeitsvereines.* Vienna, 1910. Central Archives for the History of the Jewish People, Jerusalem. A/W 2353.

Kulke, Eduard. "Eigene Haare." In *Erzählende Schriften* II. Leipzig: Deutsche Verlagsactiengesellschaft, 1906.

———. *Die schöne Hausierin. Erzählung.* Prague: B. Brandeis, 1895.

Lehrplan für das Mädchenlyzeum des Schulvereins für Beamtentöchter. 1902. Central Archives for the History of the Jewish People, Jerusalem. A/W 1588.

Lehrplan für den israel. Religionsunterricht an der gymnasialen Mädchen-shule in Wien. 1902. Central Archives for the History of the Jewish People, Jerusalem. A/W 1588.

Lehrplan für den israel. Religionsunterricht an Mädchen-Lyceen in Wien. 1901. Central Archives for the History of the Jewish People, Jerusalem. A/W 1588.

Lehrplan für den israel. Religionsunterricht an Mädchen-Lyceen in Wien. 1913. Central Archives for the History of the Jewish People, Jerusalem. A/W 1588.

Lehrplan und Instruktionen für den Konfirmations-Unterricht der weiblichen Jugend. Vienna, 1896. Central Archives for the History of the Jewish People, Jerusalem. A/W 1634.

Leimdörfer, David. "Ein Wort zu unserer Frauenfrage." *Die Wahrheit* 26–27. July 20, 27, 1900.

Lessing, Theodor. *Der jüdische Selbsthass.* Berlin: Zionistischer Bücher-Bund, 1930.

———. *Weib, Frau, Dame: Ein Essay.* Munich: O. Gmelin, 1910.

Levussove, M. S. *The New Art of an Ancient People: The Work of Ephraim Mose Lilien.* New York: B.W. Huebsch, 1906.

"Lise Meitner Dies." Lise Meitner Collection. AR 2729. Leo Baeck Institute Archives, New York.

Löbel, M. "Die sociale Stellung der jüdischen Frau im Altertum. Vortrag, geh. am 8. Febr. 1896 in der OIU." *Mitt. der öst. isr. Union* 8. 1896.

Löwy, Rabbi. "Die Mädchenkonfirmation." *Die Wahrheit* 29 (August 1, 1913): 5–6.

"Der Mädchen-Unterstützungs-Verein in Wien." *Die Neuzeit.* February 8, 1889; February 22, 1889.

Menkes, Hermann. "Ghetto-Naturalismus." *Die Zeit* 12. June 17, 1897: 40–41.

———. *Die Jüdin Leonora und andere Novellen.* Vienna: Interterritorialer Verlag "Renaissance," 1923.

Minutes of the Vienna Psychoanalytic Society, edited by Herman Nunberg and Ernst Federn, translated by M. Nunberg, 4 vols. New York: International Universities Press, 1962–1975.

Mosenthal, S. H. *Deborah: Volks-Schauspiel in vier Aufzügen.* Leipzig: P. Reclam, 1900.

————. *Stories of Jewish Home Life*. Philadelphia: Jewish Publication Society of America, 1907.

Nordau, Max. *Die Conventionellen Lügen der Kulturmenschheit*. Leipzig: B. Elischer Nachfolger, 1883.

————. *Degeneration*. Intro. George Mosse. New York: Howard Fertig, 1968.

————. *Doktor Kohn: Bürgerliches Trauerspiel aus der Gegenwart*. Berlin: Ernst Hoffman, 1902.

————. *Max Nordau (1849–1923)*, edited by Delphine Bechtel, Dominique Bourel, and Jacques Le Rider (Paris, 1996).

————. "Muskeljudentum." In *Zionistische Schriften*. Cologne: Jüdischer Verlag, 1909.

————. *Paradoxe*. Leipzig: Verlag von B. Elischer, 1886.

————. *Das Recht, zu Lieben: Ein Schauspiel in vier Aufzugen*. Berlin, 1893.

Pappenheim, Bertha. [Paul Berthold]. *Frauenrechte*. Dresden, 1899.

————. *In der Trödel-bude: Geschichten*. Lahr: Druck und Verlag von Moritz Schauenburg, 1890.

Philipson, David. "Age of Confirmation." In W. Gunther Plaut. *The Growth of Reform Judaism: American and European Sources until 1948*. New York: World Union for Progressive Judaism, 1965.

Pilcz, Alexander. *Beitrag zur vergleichenden Rassen-Psychiatrie*. Leipzig: Deuticke, 1906.

Pomeranz, Rosa. "Die Bedeutung der zionistischen Idee im Leben der Jüdin." In *Der Zionismus und die Frauen*. 1905?

————. "Die Frauen und der Zionismus." *Die Welt* 3/12. 1899: 7.

————. *An die jüdischen Frauen: Ein Appell zur Umkehr*. Tarnopol: Verlag des Vereines "Ahawath-Zion," 1898.

————. *Im Lande der Noth*. Breslau, 1901.

Rank, Otto. *Beyond Psychology*. Camden, N.J., 1941.

————. "Das Wesen des Judentums" (The Essence of Judaism). In Dennis Klein. *Jewish Origins of the Psychoanalytic Movement*. Chicago: University of Chicago Press, 1985. Appendix C.

II. Rechenschaft-Bericht des Mädchen- und Frauen-Vereines "Bikur Chaulim." Vienna, 1904. Central Archives for the History of the Jewish People, Jerusalem. A/W 2236.

Reich, Heinrich. "Die Frau im Talmud." *Reichsbote* 1/1–3. 1894.

Reik, Theodor. *Jewish Wit*. New York: Gamut Press, 1962.

Retcliff, John. *Die Geheimnis des Judenfriedhofes in Prag*. Prague: Orbis, 1942.

Rohling, August. *Der Talmudjude*. Munster: Adolph Russell's Verlag, 1876.

"Rosa Kollman." *Die Welt* 5/13. 1901: 10–11.

Salten, Felix. *The Memoirs of Josephine Mutzenbacher*. Hollywood: Brandon House, 1967.

Schach, Miriam. "Ein Bericht über zionistische Frauenarbeit." *Stenographisches Protokoll der Verhandlungen des X. Zionisten-Kongresses in Basel.* 1911: 218–234.

Schildberger, Hermine. "Das Weib und der Zionismus." *Die Welt* 3/50. 1899: 4–5.

Schlesinger, Therese. *Die Frau im sozialdemokratischen Parteiprogramm.* Vienna, 1928.

———. *Was wollen die Frauen in der Politik?* 2nd edition. Vienna, 1910.

———. "Ziele der Frauenbewegung (Vortrag)." *Volksstimme* 227. June 14, 1896.

Schnitzler, Arthur. *Comedies of Words and Other Plays.* Translated and introduction by Pierre Loving. Cincinnati: Stewart & Kidd Company, 1917.

———. *The Road into the Open (Der Weg ins Frei).* Translated by Roger Byers. Berkeley and Los Angeles: University of California Press, 1992.

Schönerer, Georg von. *Alldeutsches Tagblatt.* January 1907.

"Schule und Haus." *Die Wahrheit* 32 (August 15, 1913): 1–2.

Schwarz, Adolf. *Der Frauen der Bibel* (Drei Vorträge gehalten in der "Jüdischen Toynbee-Halle" in Wien). Vienna: Verlag von R. Loewit, 1903.

Siebenunddreissigster Jahresbericht des Mädchen-Unterstützungs-Vereines. Vienna, 1904. Central Archives for the History of the Jewish People, Jerusalem. A/W 2316.

Simon-Friedberg, Johanna. "Gegenwartsaufgaben der jüdischen Frau (Vortrag, gehalten in Wien anlässlich des XI. Kongresses)." *Die Welt* 18/4–5. January 23, 30, 1914: 89–91, 119–122.

Spielrein, Sabina. "Destruction as a Cause of Coming into Being." 1912.

———. "On the Psychological Content of a Case of Schizophrenia (Dementia Praecox)." 1911.

Statuten des Mädchen- u. Frauen-Vereines "Bikur Chaulim" in Wien. Central Archives for the History of the Jewish People, Jerusalem. A/W 2236, 4.

Stein, E. P. "Frauenemanzipation und das biblische Weib." *Österreichische Wochenschrift* 15. 1898: 309–311.

Stenographisches Protokoll über die Sitzungen des Hauses der Abgeordneten des Österreichischen Reichsrat in den Jahren 1892 und 1893. IX. Session, VII. Volume. Vienna, 1893.

Stern, J. "Die Frau im Talmud." *Monatschr. der öst-isr. Union* 23/2. 1911: 12–16.

Stern'sche Mädchen-Lehr-und-Erziehungsanstalt. Vienna: Emil Goldstein, 1929.

Strauss, Hermann. "Erkrankungen durch Alkohol und Syphilis bei den Juden." *Zeitschrift für Demographie und Statistik der Juden* 4. 1927: 35.

Strauss, Rahel. "Frauenarbeit in Palästina." *Jüdische Zeitung* 31. July 31, 1908: 1.

Tänzer, Aron. "Die Stellung der Frau im Judenthume." *Die Neuzeit* 41. 1901, 310, 319–320, 329–330, 339–340, 349–350, 357–358.

Theimer, Kamilla. *Antisemitismus und Nationaljudentum*. 1908.

Tomaschewsky, Hulda. "Wie soll der Zionismus zur Frauenfrage Stellung nehmen." *Zion*. 1897.

Trebitsch, Arthur. *Geist und Judentum: Eine grundlegende Untersuchung*. Vienna and Leipzig: Verlag Ed Sirach, 1919.

Vierter Jahresbericht des Hietzinger Frauenwohltätigkeitsvereines. Vienna, 1910. Central Archives for the History of the Jewish People, Jerusalem. A/W 2353.

"Vom Jahrmarkt des Lebens: Fanatisirte Weiber." *Österreichische Wochenschrift* 12. December 6, 1895.

"Vortrag Kamilla Theimer." *Jüdische Zeitung* 14. April 3, 1908: 5.

Wachstein, Bernhard. *Literatur über die jüdische Frau. Mit einem Anhang: Literatur über die Ehe*. Vienna, 1931.

Weininger, Otto. *Geschlecht und Charakter*. Munich, 1980.

——. *Sex and Character*. New York: A.L. Burt, n.d.

Winkler, Paula. "Betrachtungen einer Philozionistin." *Die Welt* 5/36. 1901: 4–6.

——. "Die jüdische Frau." *Die Welt* 5/45. 1901: 2–4.

Wittels, Fritz. *Freud and the Child Woman: The Memoirs of Fritz Wittels*, edited with preface by Edward Timms. New Haven: Yale University Press, 1995.

——. *Die Sexuelle Not*. Vienna and Leipzig: C.W. Stern, 1909.

——. *Sigmund Freud: His Personality, His Teaching, and His School*. Translated by Eden Paul and Ceder Paul. London: Allen & Unwin, 1924.

——. *Der Taufjude*. Vienna and Leipzig: M. Breitensteins Verlagsbuchhandlung, 1904.

Wolf, Gerson. *Geschichte der Israelitischen Cultusgemeinde in Wien (1820–1860)*. Vienna: Wilhelm Braumüller, 1861.

York-Steiner, Heinrich. *Der Talmudbauer. Unterwegs. Erzählungen von H. York-Steiner*. Berlin: Jüdischer Verlag, 1904.

Z. F. "Zur zionistischen Frauenbewegung." *Die Welt* 5. January 18, 1901: 6–7.

Zionist Congress. *Stenographisches Protokoll der Verhandlungen des II. Zionisten-Congresses gehalten zu Basel vom 28. bis 31. August 1898*. Vienna: Buchdruckerei "Industrie," 1898.

Zollschan, Ignaz. "The Jewish Race Problem." *Jewish Review* 2 (1912).

——. *Das Rassenproblem unter besonderer Berücksichtigung der jüdischen Rassenfrage*. Vienna, Leipzig: Wilhelm Braumueller, 1912.

Zschokke, Hermann. *Das Weib im Alten Testamente*. Vienna: Verlag von Heinrich Kirsch, 1883.

"Zur zionistischen Frauenbewegung." *Die Welt* 4. 1900: 7–8.

"Zur zionistischen Frauenbewegung." *Die Welt* 5/19. May 10, 1901: 6–7.

Zweiter Jahresbericht des Hietzinger Frauenwohltätigkeitsvereines. Vienna, 1908. Central Archives for the History of the Jewish People, Jerusalem. A/W 2353.

Zweiter Jahresbericht über das israelitische Mädchen-Waisenhaus in Wien im Jahre 1875. Vienna, 1876. Leo Baeck Institute Archives, New York.

Secondary Sources

Abrahams, I. *Hebrew Ethical Wills*. Philadelphia: Jewish Publication Society of America, 1926.

Adelman, Howard. "Success and Failure in the Seventeenth-Century Ghetto of Venice: The Life and Thought of Leon Modena, 1571–1648." Ph.D. diss. Brandeis University, 1985.

Agus, Irving. *The Heroic Age of Franco-German Jewry*. New York: Yeshiva University Press, 1969.

Albisetti, James. "Female Education in German-Speaking Austria, Germany and Switzerland, 1866–1914." In *Austrian Women in the Nineteenth and Twentieth Centuries: Cross-Disciplinary Perspectives*, edited by David F. Good, Margarete Grandner, and Mary Jo Maynes. Providence: Berghahn Books, 1996.

Alth, Minna, and Gertrude Obzyna. *Burgtheater 1776–1976: Aufführungen und Besetzungen von zweihundert Jahren*. Vienna: Überreuter, 1979.

Anderson, Harriet. "Feminism as a Vocation: Motives for Joining the Austrian Women's Movement." In *Vienna 1900: From Altenberg to Wittgenstein*, edited by Edward Timms and Ritchie Robertson. Edinburgh: Edinburgh University Press, 1990.

———. "Neues zu Karl Kraus und dem Allgemeinen Österreichischen Frauenverein." *Kraus Hefte* 41. 1987: 1–5.

———. *Utopian Feminism: Women's Movements in Fin-de-Siècle Vienna*. New Haven and London: Yale University Press, 1992.

Andics, Hellmut. *Luegerzeit: Das Schwarze Wien bis 1918*. Vienna: Jugend und Volk, 1984.

Arens, Katherine. "Characterology: Weininger and Austrian Popular Science." In *Jews & Gender: Responses to Otto Weininger*, ed. Nancy A. Harrowitz and Barbara Hyams. Philadelphia: Temple University Press, 1995.

Aufbruch ins Jahrhundert der Frau?: Rosa Mayreder und der Feminismus in Wien um 1900. Exhibition Catalogue, Historisches Museum der Stadt Wien. Vienna, 1989.

Baader, Benjamin Maria. *Gender, Judaism, and Bourgeois Culture in Germany: 1800–1870*. Bloomington: Indiana University Press, 2006.

Bader-Zaar, Birgitta. "Women in Austrian Politics, 1890–1934: Goals and Visions." In *Austrian Women in the Nineteenth and Twentieth Centuries: Cross-Disciplinary Perspectives*. Ed. David F. Good, Margarete Grandner, and Mary Jo Maynes. Providence: Berghahn Books, 1996.

Baskin, Judith, ed. *Jewish Women in Historical Perspective*. Detroit: Wayne State University Press, 1991.

———. "Jewish Women in the Middle Ages." In *Jewish Women in Historical Perspective*, edited by Judith Baskin. Detroit: Wayne State University Press, 1991.

———, ed. *Women of the Word: Jewish Women and Jewish Writing.* Detroit: Wayne State University Press, 1994.

Bechtel, Delphine, Dominique Bourel, and Jacques Le Rider, eds. *Max Nordau (1849–1923).* Paris, 1996.

Bein, Alex. *Theodor Herzl: A Biography of the Founder of Modern Zionism.* Trans. Maurice Samuel. New York: Atheneum, 1970.

Beller, Steven, ed. *Rethinking Vienna 1900.* New York: Berghahn Books, 2001.

Beller, Steven. *Herzl.* Reprint edition. London: Peter Halban Publishers, Ltd., 2004.

———. "Otto Weininger as Liberal?" In *Jews and Gender: Responses to Otto Weininger,* edited by Nancy A. Harrowitz and Barbara Hyams. Philadelphia: Temple University Press, 1995.

———. *Vienna and the Jews, 1867–1938: A Cultural History.* Cambridge: Cambridge University Press, 1989.

Berkowitz, Michael. "Art in Zionist Popular Culture and Jewish National Self-Consciousness, 1897–1914." In *Art and Its Uses: The Visual Image and Modern Jewish Society.* Studies in Contemporary Jewry VI., edited by Ezra Mendelsohn. New York, Oxford: Oxford University Press, 1990.

———. "Transcending 'Tzimmes and Sweetness': Recovering the History of Zionist Women in Central and Western Europe, 1897–1933." In *Active Voices: Women in Jewish Culture,* edited by Maurice Sacks. Urbana and Chicago: University of Illinois Press, 1995.

———. *Zionist Culture and West European Jewry before the First World War.* Cambridge: Cambridge University Press, 1993.

Bernstein, Deborah, ed. *Pioneers and Homemakers: Jewish Women in Pre-State Israel.* Albany: State University of New York Press, 1992.

Bertin, Célia. *La Femme à Vienne au temps de Freud.* Paris: Librairie generale francaise, 1994.

Bettelheim, Bruno. "A Secret Asymmetry." In *Freud's Vienna and Other Essays.* New York: Alfred A. Knopf, 1990.

Biale, David. *Eros and the Jews: From Biblical Israel to Contemporary Israel.* New York: Basic Books, 1992.

———. "Masochism and Philosemitism: The Strange Case of Leopold von Sacher-Masoch." *Journal of Contemporary History* 17 (1982).

———. "Zionism as an Erotic Revolution." In *People of the Body: Jews and Judaism from an Embodied Perspective,* edited by Howard Eilberg-Schwartz. Albany: State University of New York Press, 1992.

Bilski, Emily D., and Emily Braun. *Jewish Women and Their Salons: The Power of Conversation.* New Haven: Yale University Press, 2005.

Bock, Gisela. "Racism and Sexism in Nazi Germany: Motherhood, Compulsory Sterilization and the State." In *When Biology Became Destiny: Women in Weimar and Nazi Germany,* edited by Renate Bridenthal, Atina Grossmann, and Marion Kaplan. New York: Monthly Review Press, 1984.

Bonfiglio, Thomas Paul. "Dreams of Interpretation: Psychoanalysis and the Literature of Vienna." In *Literature in Vienna at the Turn of the Centuries: Continuities and Discontinuities*, edited by Ernst Grabovszki and James Hardin. Rochester, N.Y.: Camden House, 2003.

Botstein, Leon, and Werner Hanak, eds. *Vienna: Jews and the City of Music, 1870–1938*. Catalogue published in conjunction with exhibition of the Jewish Museum Vienna in cooperation with the Yeshiva University Museum. Annandale-on-Hudson: Bard College and Wolke Verlag, 2004.

Botz, Gerhard, Ivar Oxaal, Michael Pollak, and Nina Scholz, eds. *Eine Zerstörte Kultur: Jüdisches Leben und Antisemitismus in Wien seit dem 19. Jahrhundert*. 2., neu bearbeitete und erweiterte Auflage. Vienna: Czernin Verlag, 2002.

Boyarin, Daniel. *Carnal Israel: Reading Sex in Talmudic Culture*. The New Historicism: Studies in Cultural Politics. Berkeley and Los Angeles: University of California Press, 1993.

———. *Unheroic Conduct: The Rise of Heterosexuality and the Invention of the Jewish Man*. Berkeley and Los Angeles: University of California Press, 1997.

Boyer, John W. *Culture and Political Crisis in Vienna: Christian Socialism in Power, 1897–1918*. Chicago: University of Chicago Press, 1995.

———. "Freud, Marriage and Late Viennese Liberalism: A Commentary from 1905." *Journal of Modern History* 50. March 1978.

———. *Political Radicalism in Late Imperial Vienna: Origins of the Christian Social Movement, 1848–1897*. Chicago: University of Chicago Press, 1981.

Braun, Christina von. "Antisemitismus und Misogynie: Vom Zusammenhang zweier Erscheinungen." In *Von einer Welt in die Andere: Jüdinnen im 19. und 20. Jahrhundert*, edited by Jutta Dick and Barbara Hahn. Vienna: Verlag Christian Brandstaetter.

———. "'Der Jude' und 'Das Weib': Zwei Stereotypen des 'Anderen' in der Moderne." *Metis* 2. 1992: 6–28.

Bristow, Edward. *Prostitution and Prejudice: The Jewish Fight against White Slavery, 1870–1939*. New York: Schocken Books, 1983.

Bunzl, John, and Bernd Marin. *Antisemitismus in Österreich: Sozialhistorische und soziologische Studien*. Innsbruck: Innsverlag, 1983.

Bunzl, Matti. "Theodor Herzl's Zionism as Gendered Discourse." In *Theodor Herzl and the Origins of Zionism*, Austrian Studies 8, edited by Ritchie Robertson and Edward Timms (Edinburgh: Edinburgh University Press, 1997): 74–86.

Carlebach, Julius. "Family Structure and the Position of Jewish Women." In *Revolution and Evolution: 1848 in German-Jewish History*, edited by Werner E. Mosse, Arnold Paucker, Reinhard Rurup. J.C.B. Mohr, 1981.

———. "The Forgotten Connection—Women and Jews in the Conflict between Enlightenment and Romanticism." *Leo Baeck Institute Yearbook* 24 (1979).

Carotenuto, Aldo. *A Secret Symmetry: Sabina Spielrein between Jung and Freud.* Trans. Arno Pomeranz, John Shepley, and Krishna Winston. New York: Pantheon, 1982.

Christmann, Hans Helmut. *Frau und "Jüdin" an der Universität: Die Romanistin Elise Richter (Wien 1865–Theresienstadt 1943).* Mainz: Akademie der Wissenschaften und der Literatur, 1980.

Cohen, Gary B. *Education and Middle-Class Society in Imperial Austria: 1848–1918.* West Lafayette: Purdue University Press, 1996.

Cohn, Norman. *Warrant for Genocide: The Myth of the Jewish World Conspiracy and the Protocols of the Elders of Zion.* London: Eyre and Spottiswoode, 1967.

Cuddihy, John Murray. *Ordeal of Civility: Freud, Marx, Levi-Strauss, and the Jewish Struggle with Modernity.* New York: Basic Books, 1974.

Decker, Hannah. *Freud, Dora, and Vienna 1900.* New York: Free Press, 1992.

Deichmann, Hans. *Leben mit provisorischer Genehmigung: Leben, Werk und Exil von Dr. Eugenie Schwarzwald (1872–1940).* Berlin and Vienna: Mühlheim, 1981.

Denkler, Horst. "Lauter Juden: Zum Rollenspektrum der Juden-Figuren im populären Bühnendrama der Metternichschen Restaurationsperiode (1815–1848)." In *Conditio Judaica: Judentum, Antisemitismus und deutschsprachige Literatur vom 18. Jahrhundert bis zum Ersten Weltkrieg* I., edited by Hans Otto Horch, Horst Denkler. Tübingen: M. Niemeyer, 1988/9.

Derow-Turnauer, Elisabeth. "Women and the Musical Aesthetics of the Bourgeoisie." In *Vienna: Jews and the City of Music, 1870–1938*, edited by Leon Botstein and Werner Hanak. Catalogue published in conjunction with exhibition of the Jewish Museum Vienna in cooperation with the Yeshiva University Museum. Annandale-on-Hudson: Bard College and Wolke Verlag, 2004.

Deutscher, Isaac. *The Non-Jewish Jew and Other Essays*, edited by Tamara Deutscher. New York: Hill and Wang, 1968.

Dick, Jutta, and Marina Sassenberg, eds. *Jüdische Frauen im 19. und 20. Jahrhundert.* Reimbek bei Hamburg: Rowohlt, 1993.

Diem-Wille, Gertraud. "Femininity and Professionalism: A Psychoanalytic Study of Ambition in Female Academics and Managers in Austria." In *Austrian Women in the Nineteenth and Twentieth Centuries: Cross-Disciplinary Perspectives*, edited by David F. Good, Margarete Grandner, and Mary Jo Maynes. Providence: Berghahn Books, 1996.

Dienst, Heide, and Edith Saurer, eds. *"Das Weib Existiert Nicht Für Sich": Geschleterbeziehungen in der bürgerlichen Gesellschaft.* Vienna: Verlag für Gesellschaftskritik, 1990.

Dishon, Judith. "Images of Women in Medieval Hebrew Literature." In *Women of the Word: Jewish Women and Jewish Writing*, edited by Judith Baskin. Detroit: Wayne State University Press, 1994.

Doppler, Bernhard, ed. *Erotische Literatur: 1787–1958*. Vienna: Böhlau Verlag, 1990.

Edinger, Dora. *Bertha Pappenheim: Freud's Anna O.* Highland Park, Ill.: Congregation Solel, 1968.

Efron, John. *Defenders of the Race: Jewish Doctors and Race Science in Fin-de-Siècle Europe*. New Haven: Yale University Press, 1994.

Eilberg-Schwartz, Howard. *God's Phallus and Other Problems for Men and Monotheism*. Boston: Beacon Press, 1994.

———, ed. *People of the Body: Jews and Judaism from an Embodied Perspective*. Albany: State University of New York Press, 1992.

Elboim-Dror, Rachel. "Gender in Utopianism: The Zionist Case." *History Workshop Journal* 37 (1994): 99–116.

Embacher, Helga. "Aussenseiterinnen: bürgerlich, jüdisch, intellektuell—links." *L'homme: Zeitschrift für feministische Geschichtwissenschaft* 2 (1991).

Endelman, Todd M. "Response." In *The State of Jewish Studies*, edited by Shaye J. D. Cohen and Edward L. Greenstein. Detroit: Wayne State University Press, 1990.

Field, Frank. *The Last Days of Mankind: Karl Kraus and His Vienna*. London: Macmillan, 1967.

Finney, Gail. *Women in Modern Drama: Freud, Feminism, and European Theater at the Turn of the Century*. Ithaca, N.Y.: Cornell University Press, 1989.

Fleck, Christian. "Marie Jahoda." In *Vertriebene Vernunft II: Emigration und Exil österreichischer Wissenschaft*, edited by Friedlich Standler. Vienna: Jugend und Volk, 1989/90.

Fraenkel, Josef. "The Chief Rabbi and the Visionary." In *The Jews of Austria: Essays on Their Life, History and Destruction*, edited by Josef Fraenkel. London: Vallentine, Mitchell, 1967.

———. "Moritz Güdemann and Theodor Herzl." *Leo Baeck Institute Yearbook* XI (1966): 67–82.

Frank, Wilhelm. "Richard von Mises und Hilde Geiringer-Mises, Anmerkungen zu deren Lebenslauf." In *Vertriebene Vernunft II: Emigration und Exil österreichischer Wissenschaft, 1930–1940*, edited by Friedrich Stadler. Vienna: Jugend und Volk, 1989/90.

Die Frau im Korsett: Wiener Frauenalltag zwischen Klischee und Wirklichkeit, 1848–1920. Exhibition Catalogue, Historisches Museum der Stadt Wien. Vienna, 1985.

Freehof, Solomon B. *Reform Jewish Practice and Its Rabbinic Background*, I and II. New York: Union of American Hebrew Congregations, 1964, 1944.

Frenzel, Elisabeth. *Judengestalten auf der deutschen Bühne: Ein notwendiger Querschnitt durch 700 Jahre Rollengeschichte*. Munich: Deutscher Volksverlag, 1942.

Freud, Martin. *Glory Reflected: Sigmund Freud—Man and Father*. London: Angus and Robertson, 1957.

Freidenreich, Harriet Pass. *Female, Jewish and Educated: The Lives of Central European University Women*. Bloomington and Indianapolis: Indiana University Press, 2002.

——. "Gender, Identity, and Community: Jewish University Women in Germany and Austria." In *In Search of Jewish Community: Jewish Identities in Germany and Austria, 1918–1933*, edited by Michael Brenner and Derek Penslar. Bloomington: University of Indiana Press, 1998.

——. "Jewish Identity and the 'New Woman': Central European Jewish University Women in the Early Twentieth Century." In *Gender and Judaism: The Transformation of Tradition*, edited by Tamar Rudavsky. New York: New York University Press, 1995.

——. *Jewish Politics in Vienna, 1918–1938*. Bloomingdale: Indiana University Press, 1991.

——. "Die jüdische 'Neue Frau' des frühen 20. Jahrhunderts." In *Deutsch-Jüdische Geschichte als Geschlechtergeschichte: Studien zum 19. und 20. Jahrhundert*, edited by Kirsten Heinsohn and Stephanie Schüler-Springorum. Göttingen: Wallstein Verlag, 2006.

Geehr, Richard. *Adam Müller-Guttenbrunn and the Aryan Theater of Vienna: The Approach of Cultural Fascism*. Göppingen: A. Kummerle, 1973.

——. *Karl Lueger: Mayor of Fin de Siècle Vienna*. Detroit: Wayne Sate University Press, 1990.

Gelber, Mark. "Ethnic Pluralism and Germanization in the Works of Karl Emil Franzos (1848–1904)." *German Quarterly* 56. 1983: 376–385.

——. *Melancholy Pride: Nation, Race, and Gender in the German Literature of Cultural Zionism*. Tübingen: M. Niemeyer, 2000.

Gillerman, Sharon. "The Crisis of the Jewish Family in Weimar Germany: Social Conditions and Cultural Representations." In *In Search of Jewish Community: Jewish Identities in Germany and Austria, 1918–1933*, edited by Michael Brenner and Derek Penslar. Bloomington: University of Indiana Press, 1998.

——. "Jüdische Körperpolitik: Mutterschaft und Eugenik in der Weimarer Republik." In *Deutsch-Jüdische Geschichte als Geschlechtergeschichte: Studien zum 19. und 20. Jahrhundert*, edited by Kirsten Heinsohn and Stephanie Schüler-Springorum. Göttingen: Wallstein Verlag, 2006.

Gilman, Sander. *The Case of Sigmund Freud: Medicine and Identity at the Fin de Siècle*. Baltimore and London: Johns Hopkins University Press, 1993.

——. *Difference and Pathology: Stereotypes of Sexuality, Race, and Madness*. Ithaca: Cornell University Press, 1985.

——. *Freud, Race and Gender*. Princeton, New Jersey: Princeton University Press, 1993.

——. *Hysteria beyond Freud*. Berkeley: University of California Press, 1993.

——. *Inscribing the Other*. Lincoln and London: University of Nebraska Press, 1991.

——. *Jewish Self-Hatred: Anti-Semitism and the Hidden Language of the Jews*. Baltimore: Johns Hopkins University Press, 1986.

——. *The Jew's Body*. New York and London: Routledge, 1991.

——. "Karl Kraus's Oscar Wilde: Race, Sex and Difference." In *Vienna 1900: From Altenberg to Wittgenstein*. Austrian Studies I, edited by Ritchie Robertson and Edward Timms (Edinburgh: University of Edinburgh Press, 1990).

——. "Otto Weininger and Sigmund Freud: Race and Gender in the Shaping of Psychoanalysis." In *Jews and Gender: Responses to Otto Weininger*, edited by Nancy A. Harrowitz and Barbara Hyam. Philadelphia: Temple University Press, 1995.

——. "Salome, Syphilis, Sarah Bernhardt and the 'Modern Jewess.'" *German Quarterly*. Spring 1993: 194–211.

Glatzer, Nahum. *The Judaic Tradition*. New York: Behrman House, 1969.

Gmür, Priska. "'It Is Not up to Us Women to Solve Great Problems': The Duty of the Zionist Woman in the Context of the First Ten Congresses." In *The First Zionist Congress in 1897—Causes, Significance, Topicality*, edited by Heiko Haumann. Translated by Wayne van Dalsum and Vivian Kramer. Basel: Karger, 1997.

Göllner, Renate. *Kein Puppenheim*. Frankfurt am Main: Peter Lang, 1999.

Good, David F., Margarete Grandner, and Mary Jo Maynes, eds. *Austrian Women in the Nineteenth and Twentieth Centuries: Cross-Disciplinary Perspectives*. Providence: Berghahn Books, 1996.

Grabovszki, Ernst, and James N. Hardin, eds. *Literature in Vienna at the Turn of the Centuries: Continuities and Discontinuities around 1900 and 2000*. Rochester, N.Y.: Camden House, 2003.

Grossman, Atina. "'Neue Frauen' im Exil: Deutsche Ärztinnen und die Emigration." In *Deutsch-Jüdische Geschichte als Geschlechtergeschichte: Studien zum 19. und 20. Jahrhundert*, edited by Kirsten Heinsohn and Stephanie Schüler-Springorum. Göttingen: Wallstein Verlag, 2006.

Grossman, Susan, and Rivka Haut, eds. *Daughters of the King: Women and the Synagogue*. Philadelphia: Jewish Publication Society, 1992.

Grunwald, Max. *Vienna*. Philadelphia: Jewish Publication Society, 1936.

Gstrein, Heinz. *Jüdisches Wien*. Vienna: Herold, 1984.

Hacken, Richard, ed. and trans. *Into the Sunset: Anthology of Nineteenth Century Austrian Prose*. Riverside, Calif.: Ariadne Press, 1999.

Halkin, Hillel. "Feminizing Jewish Studies," *Commentary*. February 1998.

Hanák, Péter. *The Garden and the Workshop: Essays on the Cultural History of Vienna and Budapest*. Princeton: Princeton University Press, 1998.

Harrowitz, Nancy A. *Antisemitism, Misogyny, and the Logic of Cultural Difference: Cesare Lombroso and Matilde Serao*. Lincoln & London: University of Nebraska Press, 1994.

Harrowitz, Nancy A., and Barbara Hyams, eds. *Jews and Gender: Responses to Otto Weininger*. Philadelphia: Temple University Press, 1995.

Hausen, Karin. "Family and Role Division: The Polarization of Sexual Stereotypes in the 19th Century." In *The German Family: Essays on the Social History of the Family in Nineteenth and Twentieth Century Germany*, edited by Richard Evans and Robert Lee. London/Totowa, N.J.: Croom Helm, 1981.

Healy, Maureen. "Becoming Austrian: Women, the State, and Citizenship in World War I." *Central European History* 35:1 (2002), 1–35.

———. *Vienna and the Fall of the Habsburg Empire: Total War and Everyday Life in World War I*. Cambridge: Cambridge University Press, 2004.

Hecht, Dieter Josef. "Anitta Müller-Cohen (1890–1962): Sozialarbeiterin, Feministin, Politikerin, Zionistin und Journalistin; ein Beitrag zur jüdischen Frauengeschichte in Österreich 1914–1929." Ph.D. dissertation (Vienna, 2002).

Hein, Juergen. "Judenthematik im Wiener Volkstheater." In Hans Otto Horch and Horst Denkler, eds. *Conditio Judaica: Judentum, Antisemitismus und deutschsprachige Literatur vom 18. Jahrhundert bis zum Ersten Weltkrieg* I. Tübingen: M. Niemeyer, 1988/9.

Heindl, Waltraud. "Die Studentinnen der Universität Wien. Zur Entwicklung des Frauenstudiums (ab 1897)." In *"Das Weib Existiert Nicht Für Sich": Geschleterbeziehungen in der bürgerlichen Gesellschaft*, edited by Heide Dienst and Edith Saurer. Vienna: Verlag für Gesellschaftskritik, 1990.

Heindl, Waltraud, and Marina Tichy. *Durch Erkenntnis zu Freiheit und Glück . . ." Frauen an der Universität Wien (ab 1897)*. Vienna: Schriftenreihe des Universitätsarchivs, V, 1990.

Heindl, Waltraud, and Rudolf Wytek. "Die jüdischen Studentinnen an der Universität Wien, 1897–1938." In *Der Wiener Stadttempel, Die Wiener Juden*. Vienna: J & V, 1988.

Heinsohn, Kirsten, and Stephanie Schüler-Springorum, eds. *Deutsch-Jüdische Geschichte als Geschlechtergeschichte: Studien zum 19. und 20. Jahrhundert*. Göttingen: Wallstein Verlag, 2006.

Hellwing, I. A. *Der konfessionelle Antisemitismus im 19. Jahrhundert in Österreich*. Vienna: Herder, 1972.

Helpersdorfer, Irmgard. "Die Wiener Frauenvereine und ihre Publikationsorgane, 1860–1920." In *Aufbruch ins Jahrhundert der Frau?: Rosa Mayreder und der Feminismus in Wien um 1900*. Exhibition Catalogue, Historisches Museum der Stadt Wien. Vienna, 1989.

Hertz, Deborah. *Jewish High Society in Old Regime Berlin*. New Haven: Yale University Press, 1989.

Hertzberg, Arthur. *The Zionist Idea: A Historical Analysis and Reader*. New York: Atheneum, 1959.

Herzog, Hillary Hope, and Todd. "'Wien bleibt Wien': Austrian Jewish Culture at Two Fins de Siècle." In *Literature in Vienna at the Turn of the Centuries:*

Continuities and Discontinuities, edited by Ernst Grabovszki and James Hardin. Rochester, N.Y.: Camden House, 2003.

Heschel, Susannah. "Configurations of Patriarchy, Judaism, and Nazism in German Feminist Thought." In *Gender and Judaism: The Transformation of Tradition*, edited by Tamar Rudavsky. New York: New York University Press, 1995.

Heschel, Susannah, ed. *On Being a Jewish Feminist: A Reader*. New York: Schocken Books, 1983.

Hirsch, Bettina. *Marianne: Ein Frauenleben an der Zeiten Wende*. A. Pichlers Witwe & Sohn, 1970.

Hirschmüller, Albrecht. *Physiologie und Psychoanalyse in Leben und Werk Josef Breuers. Jahrbuch der Psychoanalyse*. Supp. 4. Bern: Hans Huber, 1978.

Hoberman, John M. "Otto Weininger and the Critique of Jewish Masculinity." In *Jews and Gender: Responses to Otto Weininger*, edited by Nancy A. Harrowitz and Barbara Hyams. Philadelphia: Temple University Press, 1995.

Hödl, Klaus. *Als Bettler in die Leopoldstadt: Galizische Juden auf dem Weg nach Wien*. Vienna: Böhlau Verlag, 1994.

Hofmann, Paul. *The Viennese: Splendor, Twilight, and Exile*. New York: Anchor Books, 1989.

Howes, Justin, and Pauline Paucker. "German Jews and the Graphic Arts." *Leo Baeck Institute Yearbook*. 1989.

Hyams, Barbara. "Weininger and Nazi Ideology." In *Jews and Gender: Responses to Otto Weininger*, edited by Nancy A. Harrowitz and Barbara Hyams. Philadelphia: Temple University Press, 1995.

Hyman, Paula. "Feminist Studies and Modern Jewish History." In *Feminist Perspectives on Jewish Studies*, edited by Lynn Davidman and Shelly Tenenbaum. New Haven: Yale University Press, 1994.

———. *Gender and Assimilation in Modern Jewish History: The Roles and Representations of Women*. Seattle: University of Washington Press, 1995.

———. "The Ideological Transformation of Modern Jewish Historiography." In *The State of Jewish Studies*, edited by Shaye J. D. Cohen and Edward L. Greenstein. Detroit: Wayne State University Press, 1990.

———. "Immigrant Women and Consumer Protest: The New York City Kosher Meat Boycott of 1902." *American Jewish History* 70(1) (Sept. 1980): 91–105.

———. "The Modern Jewish Family: Myth and Reality." In *The Jewish Family: Metaphor and Memory*, edited by David Kraemer. New York: Oxford University Press, 1989.

Janik, Allan. *Essays on Wittgenstein and Weininger*. Studien zur österreichischen Philosophie, 9. Amsterdam: Rodopi, 1985.

———. "Vienna 1900 Revisited: Paradigms and Problems." *Austrian History Yearbook* 28 (1997): 1–27.

Janik, Allan, and Stephen Toulmin. *Wittgenstein's Vienna*. New York: Simon and Schuster, 1973.

Jenks, William A. *Vienna and the Young Hitler*. New York: Octagon Books, 1976, c. 1960.

Jensen, Ellen M. *Streifzuge durch das Leben von Anna O./ Bertha Pappenheim*. Frankfurt am Main: ZTV Verlag, 1984.

Johnston, William M. *The Austrian Mind: An Intellectual and Social History, 1848–1938*. Berkeley and Los Angeles: University of California Press, 1972.

Jones, J. Sydney. *Hitler in Vienna: 1907–1913*. New York: Stein and Day, 1983.

"Der jüdische Selbsthass und Weiberverachtung: Otto Weininger und Arthur Trebitsch." In *Otto Weininger: Werk und Wirkung*, edited by Jacques Le Rider and Norbert Leser. Vienna: Österreichischer Bundesverlag, 1984.

Judson, Pieter M. *Exclusive Revolutionaries: Liberal Politics, Social Experience, and National Identity in the Austrian Empire, 1848–1914*. Ann Arbor: University of Michigan Press, 1996.

———. "The Gendered Politics of German Nationalism in Austria." In *Austrian Women in the Nineteenth and Twentieth Centuries: Cross-Disciplinary Perspectives*, edited by David F. Good, Margarete Grandner, and Mary Jo Maynes. Providence: Berghahn Books, 1996.

Judson, Pieter M., and Marsha Rozenblit, eds. *Constructing Nationalities in East Central Europe*. Austrian Studies 6. New York: Berghan Books, 2005.

Jušek, Karin J. "The Limits of Female Desire: The Contributions of Austrian Feminists to the Sexual Debate in Fin-de-Siècle Vienna." In *Austrian Women in the Nineteenth and Twentieth Centuries: Cross-Disciplinary Perspectives*. Ed. David F. Good, Margarete Grandner, and Mary Jo Maynes. Providence: Berghahn Books, 1996.

———. "Sexual Morality and the Meaning of Prostitution in Fin de Siècle Vienna." In *From Sappho to De Sade: Moments in the History of Sexuality*, edited by Jan Bremmer. New York: Routledge, 1989.

Kahn, Lothar. "Tradition and Modernity in the German Ghetto Novel." *Judaism* 28/1. Winter 1979: 31–41.

Kanzer, Mark, M.D., and Jules Glenn, M.D., eds. *Freud and His Patients*. Northvale, N.J.: Jason Aronson, Inc., 1980, 1993.

Kaplan, Marion. *The Jewish Feminist Movement in Germany: The Campaigns of the Jüdischer Frauenbund, 1904–1938*. Westport, Conn.: Greenwood Press, 1979.

———. *The Making of the Jewish Middle Class: Women, Family, and Identity in Imperial Germany*. New York: Oxford University Press, 1991.

———. "Priestess and Hausfrau: Women and Tradition in the German-Jewish Family." In *The Jewish Family: Myths and Reality*, edited by Steven M. Cohn and Paula E. Hyman. New York: Holmes & Meier, 1986.

———. "Sisterhood under Siege: Feminism and Antisemitism in Germany, 1904–1938." In *When Biology Became Destiny: Women in Weimar and Nazi Germany*, edited by Renate Bridenthal, Atina Grossmann, and Marion Kaplan. New York: Monthly Review Press, 1984.

Katz, Jacob. "Family, Kinship and Marriage among Ashkenazim in the Sixteenth to Eighteenth Centuries." *Jewish Journal of Sociology*. 1959.

———. *From Prejudice to Destruction: Anti-Semitism, 1700–1933*. Cambridge, Mass.: Harvard University Press, 1980.

Kerr, John. *A Most Dangerous Method: The Story of Jung, Freud, and Sabina Spielrein*. New York: Vintage Books, 1993.

Kieval, Hillel J. *The Making of Czech Jewry: National Conflict and Jewish Society in Bohemia, 1870–1918*. New York: Oxford University Press, 1988.

Klein, Dennis. *Jewish Origins of the Psychoanalytic Movement*. New York: Praeger, 1981.

Kollmann, Monika. "Essayistinnen und Feuilletonistinnen der Wiener Jahrhundertwende: Eine Forschungslücke." In *Zeitungen im Wiener Fin de Siècle*, edited by Sigurd Paul Scheichl and Wolfgang Duchkowitsch. Vienna and Munich: Verlag für Geschichte und Politik and R. Oldenburg Verlag, 1997.

Köpl, Regina. "Adelheid Popp." In *"Die Partei Hat Mich Nie Enttäuscht . . ." Österreichische Sozialdemokratinnen*, edited by Edith Prost. Vienna: Verlag für Gesellschaftskritik, 1989.

Kratz-Ritter, Bettina. *Für "Fromme Zionstöchter" und "Gebildete Frauenzimmer": Andachtsliteratur für deutsch-jüdische Frauen im 19. und frühen 20. Jahrhundert*. Hildesheim: Georg Olms, 1995.

Krobb, Florian. "'Auf Fluch und Lüge baut sich kein Glück auf': Karl Emil Franzos's Novel *Judith Trachtenberg* and the Question of Jewish Assimilation." In *The Habsburg Legacy: National Identity in Historical Perspective*, edited by Edward Timms and Ritchie Robertson. Edinburgh: Edinburgh University Press, 1994.

———. *'Die schöne Jüdin': Jüdische Frauengestalten in der deutschsprachigen Erzahlliteratur vom 17. Jahrhundert bis zum Ersten Weltkrieg*. Tübingen: Max Niemeyer Verlag, 1993.

Kyle, R. A., and M. A. Shampo. "Lise Meitner." *Journal of the American Medical Association* 20, 2021 (May 22, 1981).

Lea, Charlene A. *Emancipation, Assimilation and Stereotype: The Image of the Jew in German and Austrian Drama, 1800–1850*. Bonn: Bouvier, 1978.

Leitner, Thea. *Fürstin, Dame, Armes Weib*. Vienna: Überreuter, 1991.

Le Rider, Jacques. *Le Cas Otto Weininger: Racines de l'antifeminisme et l'antisemitisme*. Paris: Presses Universitaires de France, 1982.

———. *Modernity and Crises of Identity: Culture and Society in Fin-de-Siècle Vienna*. Trans. Rosemary Morris. New York: Continuum, 1993.

———. *Modernité Viennoise et crises d'identité*. Paris: Presses Universitaires de France, 1990.

Le Rider, Jacques, and Norbert Leser, eds. *Otto Weininger: Werk und Wirkung*. Vienna: Österreichischer Bundesverlag, 1984.

Lesky, Erna. *The Vienna Medical School of the 19th Century*. Translated by L. Williams and I. S. Levij. Baltimore and London: Johns Hopkins University Press, 1976.

Levenson, Alan. "An Adventure in Otherness: Nahida Remy-Ruth Lazarus (1849–1928)." In *Gender and Judaism: The Transformation of Tradition*, edited by Tamar Rudavsky. New York: New York University Press, 1995.

———. "Theodor Herzl and Bertha von Suttner: Criticism, Collaboration and Utopianism." *Journal of Israeli History* 15/2. Summer 1994: 213–222.

Lewin, Kurt. "Self-Hatred among Jews." *Resolving Social Conflicts*. New York: Harper Brothers, 1948.

Loewenberg, Peter. "Austro-Marxism and Revolution: Otto Bauer, Freud's 'Dora' Case, and the Crisis of the First Austrian Republic." In *Decoding the Past: The Psychohistorical Approach*. Berkeley, Los Angeles and London: University of California Press, 1985.

———. "Theodor Herzl: Nationalism and Politics." In *Decoding the Past: The Psychohistorical Approach*. Berkeley, Los Angeles and London: University of California Press, 1985.

Lorenz, Dagmar C. G. "Austrian Women and the Public: Women's Writing at the Turn of the Centuries." In *Literature in Vienna at the Turn of the Centuries: Continuities and Discontinuities*. Rochester, N.Y.: Camden House, 2003.

———. *Keepers of the Motherland: German Texts by Jewish Women Writers*. Lincoln: University of Nebraska Press, 1997.

———. "Mass Culture and the City in the Works of German-Jewish Novelists: Claire Goll, Veza Canetti, Else Lasker-Schüler, and Gertrud Kolmar." In *Gender and Judaism: The Transformation of Tradition*, edited by Tamar Rudavsky. New York: New York University Press, 1995.

Malleier, Elisabeth. *Jüdische Frauen in der wiener bürgerlichen Frauenbewegung 1890–1938*. Ph.D. dissertation. 2001.

———. *Jüdische Frauen in Wien, 1816–1938: Wohlfahrt—Mädchenbildung—Frauenarbeit*. Vienna: Mandelbaum, 2003.

Mandl, Henriette. *Cabaret und Courage: Stella Kadmon-Eine Biographie*. Vienna: WUV Universitatsverlag, 1993.

Marcus, Steven. "Freud and Dora: Story, History, Case History." In *Representations: Essays on Literature and Society*. New York: Random House, 1972.

Mayer, Hans. *The Outsiders: A Study in Life and Letters*. Trans. Denis M. Sweet. Cambridge: MIT Press, 1984.

McCagg, Jr., William O. *A History of Habsburg Jews, 1670–1918*. Bloomington: Indiana University Press, 1989.

Melammed, Renee Levine. "Sephardi Women in the Medieval and Early Modern Periods." In *Jewish Women in Historical Perspective*, edited by Judith Baskin. Detroit: Wayne State University Press, 1991.

Melman, Billie. "Re-Generation: Nation and the Construction of Gender in Peace and War—Palestinian Jews, 1900–1918." In *Borderlines: Genders and*

Identities in War and Peace, 1870–1930, edited by Billie Melman. New York: Routledge, 1998.

Mendes-Flohr, Paul. "The Study of the Jewish Intellectual: A Methodological Prolegomenon." In *Divided Passions: Jewish Intellectuals and the Experience of Modernity*. Detroit: Wayne State University Press, 1991.

Meyer, Michael. *Jewish Identity in the Modern World*. Seattle: University of Washington Press, 1990.

———. *Response to Modernity: A History of the Reform Movement in Judaism*. New York: Oxford University Press, 1988.

Michael, Nancy C. *Elektra and Her Sisters: Three Female Characters in Schnitzler, Freud, and Hofmannsthal*. New York: Peter Lang Publishing, Inc., 2001.

Milton, Sybil. "Women and the Holocaust: The Case of German and German-Jewish Women." In *When Biology Became Destiny: Women in Weimar and Nazi Germany*, edited by Renate Bridenthal, Atina Grossmann, and Marion Kaplan. New York: Monthly Review Press, 1984.

Montel, Angelika. "Women and Zionist Journalism: 'Frauen in der Welt der Männer.'" Trans. Ritchi Robertson. In *Theodor Herzl and the Origins of Zionism. Austrian Studies* 8, edited by Ritchie Robertson and Edward Timms (Edinburgh: Edinburgh University Press, 1997).

Mosse, George L. Introduction to *Degeneration*, by Max Nordau. New York: Howard Fertig, 1968.

———. *Nationalism and Sexuality: Middle Class Morality and Sexual Norms in Modern Europe*. Madison: University of Wisconsin Press, 1985.

Natter, Tobias G., and Gerbert Frodle, eds. *Klimt's Women*. Cologne and Vienna: Österreichische Galerie Belvedere and DuMont Buchverlag, 2000.

Neyer, Gerda. "Women in the Austrian Parliament: Opportunities and Barriers." In *Austrian Women in the Nineteenth and Twentieth Centuries: Cross-Disciplinary Perspectives*. Ed. David F. Good, Margarete Grandner, and Mary Jo Maynes. Providence: Berghahn Books, 1996.

Oxaal, Ivar, Michael Pollak, and Gerhard Botz, eds. *Jews, Antisemitism and Culture in Vienna*. London: Routledge & Kegan Paul, 1987.

Patsch, Sylvia M. *Österreichische Schriftsteller im Exil in Grossbritannien*. Vienna, Munich: Verlag Christian Brandstätter, 1985.

Pauley, Bruce. *From Prejudice to Persecution: A History of Austrian Anti-Semitism*. Chapel Hill and London: University of North Carolina Press, 1992.

Pawel, Ernst. *The Labyrinth of Exile: A Life of Theodor Herzl*. London: Collins Harvill, 1990.

Plaut, W. Gunther. *The Rise of Reform Judaism: A Sourcebook of Its European Origins*. New York: World Union for Progressive Judaism, 1963.

Poliakov, Léon. *The History of Anti-Semitism. Volume Three: From Voltaire to Wagner*. Translated by Miriam Kochan. New York: Vanguard Press, Inc., 1975.

Pollak, Michael. *Vienne 1900: Une identité blessée*. Paris: Gallimard/Julliard, 1984.

Prestel, Claudia. "Die jüdische Familie in der Krise. Symptome und Debatten." In *Deutsch-Jüdische Geschichte als Geschlechtergeschichte: Studien zum 19. und 20. Jahrhundert*, edited by Kirsten Heinsohn and Stephanie Schüler-Springorum. Göttingen: Wallstein Verlag, 2006.

———. "'Youth in Need': Correctional Education and Family Breakdown in German Jewish Families." In *In Search of Jewish Community: Jewish Identities in Germany and Austria, 1918–1933*, edited by Michael Brenner and Derek Penslar. Bloomington: University of Indiana Press, 1998.

———. "Zionist Rhetoric and Women's Equality (1897–1933): Myth and Reality." In *San Jose Studies* 20/3 (1994): 4–28.

Prost, Edith. "Emigration und Exil österreichischer Wissenschaftlerinnen." In *Vertriebene Vernunft I: Emigration und Exil österrichischer Wissenschaft, 1930–1940*, edited by Friedrich Stadler. Vienna: Jugend und Volk, 1989/90.

———. *"Die Partei Hat Mich Nie Enttäuscht . . ." Österreichische Sozialdemokratinnen*. Vienna: Verlag für Gesellschaftskritik, 1989.

———. "Vertriebene Frauen." In *Vertriebene Vernunft II: Emigration und Exil österreichischer Wissenschaft*, edited by Friedrich Stadler. Vienna: Jugend und Volk, 1989/90.

Pulzer, Peter G. J. *The Rise of Political Anti-Semitism in Germany and Austria*. Rev. ed. Cambridge, Mass.: Harvard University Press, 1988.

Reifowitz, Ian. *Imagining an Austrian Nation: Joseph Samuel Bloch and the Search for a Supraethnic Austrian Identity, 1846–1918*. Boulder: East European Monographs, 2003.

Rife, Patricia Elisabeth. *Lise Meitner: The Life and Times of a Jewish Woman Physicist*. Ph.D. diss., Union Graduate School, 1983.

Roazen, Paul. *Helene Deutsch: A Psychoanalyst's Life*. New Brunswick: Transaction Publishers, 1992.

Roith, Estelle. *The Riddle of Freud: Jewish Influences on His Theory of Female Sexuality*. New York: Tavistock Press, 1987.

Rose, Alison. "Femininity, Feminism and Jewish Identity Redefined: Jewish Women in Viennese Zionism, Psychoanalysis and Culture." *Transversal: Zeitschrift des Centrums für Jüdische Studien* 2/2005.

———. "Gender and Anti-Semitism: Christian Social Women and the Jewish Response in Turn-of-the-Century Vienna." *Austrian History Yearbook* 34 (2003): 173–189.

———. "Imagining the 'New Jewish Family': Gender and Nation in Early Zionism." In *Families of a New World: Gender, Politics, and State Development in a Global Context*, edited by Lynne Haney and Lisa Pollard. New York: Routledge, 2003.

———. "The Jewish Woman as 'Other': The Development of Sexual Stereotypes in Vienna, 1890–1914." Ph.D. diss., Hebrew University of Jerusalem, 1997.

———. "The Manifestations of Shame: Mental Illness and the Jewish Woman in Turn of the Century Vienna." In *Jüdische Identitäten: Einblicke in die Bewusstseinslandschaft des österreichischen Judenthums*, edited by Klaus Hödl. Innsbruck: Studienverlag, 2000.

———. "Die 'Neue Jüdische Familie': Frauen, Geschlecht und Nation im zionistischen Denken." In *Deutsch-Jüdische Geschichte als Geschlechtergeschichte: Studien zum 19. und 20. Jahrhundert*, edited by Kirsten Heinsohn and Stephanie Schüler-Springorum. Göttingen: Wallstein Verlag, 2006.

Rosenbaum, Max, and Melvin Muroff. *Anna O.: Fourteen Contemporary Reinterpretations*. New York: Free Press, 1984.

Rosenmann, Moses. *Dr. Adolf Jellinek: Sein Leben und Schaffen*. Vienna: Jos. Schlesinger Verlag, 1931.

Rossbacher, Karlheinz. *Literatur und Liberalismus: Zur Kultur der Ringstrassenzeit in Wien*. Vienna: J&V, 1992.

Rozenblit, Marsha. "For Fatherland and Jewish People: Jewish Women in Austria during World War I." In *Authority, Identity and the Social History of the Great War*, edited by Frans Coetzee and Marylin Shevin-Coetzee. Providence: Berghahn Books, 1995.

———. "Jewish Ethnicity in a New Nation-State: The Crisis of Identity in the Austrian Republic." In *In Search of Jewish Community: Jewish Identities in Germany and Austria, 1918–1933*, edited by Michael Brenner and Derek Penslar. Bloomington: University of Indiana Press, 1998.

———. "Jewish Identity and the Modern Rabbi: The Cases of Isak Noa Mannheimer, Adolf Jellinek, and Moritz Güdemann in Nineteenth-Century Vienna." *Leo Baeck Institute Yearbook* 35 (1990).

———. "The Jews of Germany and Austria: A Comparative Perspective." In *Austrians and Jews in the Twentieth Century: From Franz Joseph to Waldheim*, edited by Robert S. Wistrich. New York: St. Martin's Press, 1992.

———. *The Jews of Vienna, 1867–1914: Assimilation and Identity*. Albany: State University of New York Press, 1983.

———. *Reconstructing a National Identity: The Jews of Habsburg Austria during World War I*. New York: Oxford University Press, 2001.

Rudolf, E. V. [Elmayer-Vestenbrugg, Rudolf von]. *Georg Ritter von Schönerer: Das Vater des politischen Antisemitismus*. Munich: Verlag Franz Eher Nachfolger, 1942.

Rürup, Reinhard. *Emanzipation und Antisemitismus: Studien zur "Judenfrage" der bürgerlichen Gesellschaft*. Göttingen: Vandenhoeck & Ruprecht, 1975.

Saurer, Edith. "Scham- und Schuldbewusstsein. Überlegungen zu einer möglichen Geschichte moralischer Gefühle unter besonderer Berücksichtigung geschlechtsspezifischer Aspekte." In *"Das Weib Existiert Nicht Für Sich": Geschleterbeziehungen in der bürgerlichen Gesellschaft*, edited by Heide Dienst and Edith Saurer. Vienna: Verlag für Gesellschaftskritik, 1990.

Sayers, Janet. *Mothers of Psychoanalysis: Helene Deutsch, Karen Horney, Anna Freud, Melanie Klein.* New York: W.W. Norton & Company, 1991.

Scheichl, Sigurd Paul. "Die Schalek—Quelques observations sur le theme de la femme dans *Les Derniers jours de l'humanite.*" *Austriaca: Cahiers Universitaires d'Information sur l'Autriche.* May/June 1986: 73–81.

Scheichl, Sigurd Paul, and Wolfgang Duchkowitsch, eds. *Zeitungen im Wiener Fin de Siècle.* Vienna and Munich: Verlag für Geschichte und Politik and R. Oldenburg Verlag, 1997.

Schorsch, Ismar. "Moritz Güdemann: Rabbi, Historian and Apologist." *Leo Baeck Institute Yearbook* 11 (1966): 42–66.

Schorske, Carl. *Fin-de-Siècle Vienna: Politics and Culture.* New York: Vintage Books, 1981.

Schulte, Christophe. *Psychopathologie des Fin de Siècle: Der Kulturkritiker, Arzt und Zionist: Max Nordau.* Frankfurt a.M., 1997.

Segal, Harold B. *The Vienna Coffeehouse Wits, 1890–1938.* West Lafayette, Indiana: Purdue University Press, 1993.

Shepherd, Naomi. *A Price below Rubies: Jewish Women as Rebels and Radicals.* Cambridge, Mass.: Harvard University Press, 1993.

Shilo, Margalit. "The Double or Multiple Image of the New Hebrew Woman." *Nashim: A Journal of Jewish Women's Studies and Gender Issues* 1 (Winter 1998): 73–94.

Showalter, Elaine. *Sexual Anarchy: Gender and Culture at the Fin de Siècle.* New York: Viking, 1990.

Sime, Ruth Lewin. *Lise Meitner: A Life in Physics.* Berkeley and Los Angeles: University of California Press, 1996.

Singer, Peter. *Pushing Time Away: My Grandfather and the Tragedy of Jewish Vienna.* New York: Ecco, 2004.

Söder, Hans-Peter. "Disease and Health as Contexts of Modernity: Max Nordau as a Critic of Fin-de-Siècle Modernism." *German Studies Review* (1991).

Sommer, Fred. *"Halb-Asien," German Nationalism and the Eastern European Works of Karl Emil Franzos.* Stuttgart: H.D. Heinz, 1984.

Sowerwine, Charles. "Socialism, Feminism, and the Socialist Women's Movement from the French Revolution to World War II." In *Becoming Visible: Women in European History.* Third Edition. Ed. Renate Bridenthal, Susan Mosher Stuard, and Merry E. Wiesner. Boston: Houghton Mifflin Company, 1998.

Spiel, Hilde. "Jewish Women in Austrian Culture." In *The Jews of Austria: Essays on Their Life, History and Destruction*, edited by Josef Fraenkel. London: Vallentine, Mitchell, 1967.

Stadler, Friedrich. *Vertriebene Vernunft I & II: Emigration und Exil österreichischer Wissenschaft, 1930–1940.* Vienna, Munich: Jugend und Volk, 1989/90.

Stanislawski, Michael. *Zionism and the Fin de Siècle: Cosmopolitanism and Nationalism from Nordau to Jabotinsky.* Berkeley: University of California Press, 2001.

Steiner, George. "Some Meta-Rabbis." In *Next Year in Jerusalem: Jews in the Twentieth Century*, edited by Douglas Villiers. London: Harrap, 1976.

Steines, Patricia. *Hunderttausend Steine: Grabstellen grosser Österreicher jüdischer Konfession auf dem Wiener Zentralfriedhof*. Vienna: Falter Verlag, 1993.

Stewart, Janet. *Fashioning Vienna: Adolf Loos's Cultural Criticism*. London: Routledge, 2000.

———. "The Written City: Vienna 1900 and 2000." In *Literature in Vienna at the Turn of the Centuries: Continuities and Discontinuities*, edited by Ernst Grabovszki and James Hardin. Rochester, N.Y.: Camden House, 2003.

Stoffers, Wilhelm. *Juden und Ghetto in der deutschen Literatur bis zum Ausgang des Weltkrieges*. Graz: H. Stiansys Sohne, 1939.

Svoboda, Silvia. "Die 'Dokumente der Frauen.'" In *Aufbruch ins Jahrhundert der Frau?: Rosa Mayreder und der Feminismus in Wien um 1900*. Exhibition Catalogue, Historisches Museum der Stadt Wien. Vienna, 1989.

Thompson, Bruce. *Schnitzler's Vienna: Image of a Society*. London and New York: Routledge, 1990.

Thorson, Helga. "Confronting Anti-Semitism and Antifeminism in Turn of the Century Vienna: Grete Meisel-Hess and the Feminist Discourses on Hysteria." In *Jüdische Identitäten: Einblicke in die Bewusstseinslandschaft des österreichischen Judenthums*, edited by Klaus Hödl. Innsbruck: Studienverlag, 2000.

Tichy, Marina. "'Ich hatte immer Angst, unwissend zu sterben': Therese Schlesinger: Bürgerin und Sozialistin." In *"Die Partei hat mich nie enttäuscht" Österreichische Sozialdemokratinnen*, edited by Edith Prost. Vienna: Verlag für Gesellschaftskritik, 1989.

Tietze, Hans. *Die Juden Wiens: Geschichte-Wirtschaft-Kultur*. Vienna: Edition Atelier, 1987, 1933.

Timms, Edward. "The Child-Woman: Kraus, Freud, Wittels, and Irma Karczewska." In *Vienna 1900: From Altenberg to Wittgenstein*, edited by Edward Timms and Ritchie Robertson. Edinburgh: Edinburgh University Press, 1990.

———. *Karl Kraus, Apocalyptic Satirist: Culture and Catastrophe in Habsburg Vienna*. New Haven and London: Yale University Press, 1986.

———. *Karl Kraus, Apocalyptic Satirist: The Post-War Crisis and the Rise of the Swastika*. New Haven and London: Yale University Press, 2005.

Timms, Edward, and Ritchie Robertson, eds. *Vienna 1900: From Altenberg to Wittgenstein*. Edinburgh: Edinburgh University Press, 1990.

Tommasini, Anthony. "Glorious, Yes, But Resisting Today's World: The Vienna Philharmonic Returns, Virtually a Male Bastion." *New York Times*. March 15, 1999. Arts Section.

Toury, Jacob. "Defense Activities of the Österreichisch-Israelitische Union before 1914." In *Living with Antisemitism: Modern Jewish Responses*, edited by Jehuda Reinharz. Hanover: University Press of New England, 1987.

———. *Die Jüdische Presse im Österreichischen Kaiserreich, 1802–1918*. Tübingen: J.C.B. Mohr, 1983.

———. "Troubled Beginnings: The Emergence of the Österreichisch-Israelitische Union." *Leo Baeck Institute Yearbook* 30 (1985): 457–475.

———. "Years of Strife: The Contest of the Österreichisch-Israelitische Union for the Leadership of Austrian Jewry." *Leo Baeck Institute Yearbook* 33 (1988): 179–199.

Van Herik, Judith. *Freud on Femininity and Faith*. Berkeley and Los Angeles: University of California Press, 1987.

Volkov, Shulamit. "Antisemitism as a Cultural Code—Reflections on the History and Historiography of Antisemitism in Imperial Germany." *Leo Baeck Institute Yearbook* 23 (1978).

———. "German Jews between Fulfillment and Disillusion: The Individual and the Community." In *In Search of Jewish Community: Jewish Identities in Germany and Austria, 1918–1933*, edited by Michael Brenner and Derek Penslar. Bloomington: University of Indiana Press, 1998.

———. *Germans, Jews, and Antisemites: Trials in Emancipation*. New York: Cambridge University Press, 2006.

Wagner, Nike. *Geist und Geschlecht: Karl Kraus und die Erotik der Wiener Moderne*. Frankfurt a.M.: Suhrkamp, 1982.

Wagner, Renate. *Frauen um Schnitzler*. Vienna: Jugend und Volk, 1980.

Wegner, Judith Romney. *Chattel or Person? The Status of Women in the Mishnah*. New York: Oxford University Press, 1988.

Weinzierl, Erika. *Emanzipation? Österreichische Frauen im 20. Jahrhundert*. Vienna: Jugend und Volk, 1975.

———. "Österreichische Frauenbewegungen um die Jahrhundertwende." In *Wien um 1900: Aufbruch in die Moderne*, edited by Peter Berner, Emil Brix, and Wolfgang Mantl. Vienna, Munich: Oldenbourg: Verlag für Geschichte und Politik, 1986.

Weissler, Chava. "The Traditional Piety of Ashkenazic Women." In *Jewish Spirituality from the 16th Century Revival to the Present*. Vol. II, edited by Arthur Green. New York: Crossroad, 1987.

Weitzmann, Walter R. "The Politics of the Viennese Jewish Community, 1890–1914." In *Jews, Antisemitism and Culture in Vienna*, edited by Ivar Oxaal, Michael Pollak, and Gerhard Botz. London: Routledge and Kegan Paul, 1987.

Whiteside, Andrew G. *The Socialism of Fools: Georg Ritter von Schönerer and Austrian Pan-Germanism*. Berkeley and Los Angeles: University of California Press, 1975.

Wininger, Salomon. *Grosse Jüdische National-Biographie, mit mehr als 8000 Lebensbeschreibungen namhafter jüdischer Männer und Frauen aller Zeiten und Länder*. 7 Volumes. Cernauti: Druck "Orient," 1925–1936.

Winkelbauer, Thomas. "Leopold Kompert und die böhmischen Landjuden." In *Conditio Judaica: Judentum, Antisemitismus und deutschsprachige Litera-*

tur vom 18. Jahrhundert bis zum Ersten Weltkrieg II., edited by Hans Otto Horch, Horst Denkler. Tübingen: M. Niemeyer, 1988/9.

Wisely, Andrew C. *Arthur Schnitzler and Twentieth Century Criticism.* Rochester, N.Y.: Camden House, 2004.

Wistrich, Robert S. "Austrian Social Democracy and the Problem of Galician Jewry, 1890–1914." *Leo Baeck Institute Yearbook* 26 (1981): 89–124.

———. "Hitler and National Socialism: The Austrian Connection." In *Between Redemption and Perdition: Modern Antisemitism and Jewish Identity.* London: Routledge, 1990.

———. *The Jews of Vienna in the Age of Franz Joseph.* New York: Oxford University Press, 1989.

———. "Max Nordau: From Degeneration to 'Muscular Judaism.'" *Transversal: Zeitschrift für jüdischen Studien* 5/2 (2004).

———. "The Modernization of Viennese Jewry: The Impact of German Culture in a Multi-Ethnic State." In *Toward Modernity: The European Jewish Model,* edited by Jacob Katz. New Brunswick: Transaction Books, 1987.

———. *Socialism and the Jews: The Dilemmas of Assimilation in Germany and Austria-Hungary.* London and Toronto: Litmann Library, 1982.

———. "Theodor Herzl: Zionist Icon, Myth-Maker and Social Utopian." In *The Shaping of Israeli Identity: Myth, Memory and Trauma,* edited by Robert Wistrich and David Ohana. London: Frank Cass, 1995.

Wistrich, Robert, ed. *Austrians and Jews in the Twentieth Century: From Franz Joseph to Waldheim.* New York: St. Martin's Press, Inc., 1992.

Wodak, Ruth. "Die sprachliche Inszenierung des Nationalsozialismus—einige soziolinguistische Überlegung." In *Zeitgeist wider den Zeitgeist: Eine Sequenz aus Österreichs Verirrung.* Vienna: Gisteldruck, 1988.

Wodenegg, Andrea. *Das Bild der Juden Osteuropas: Ein Beitrag zur komparatistischen Imagologie an Textbeispielen von Karl Emil Franzos und Leopold von Sacher-Masoch.* Frankfurt am Main, New York: Lang, 1987.

Wolff, Larry. *Postcards from the End of the World: Child Abuse in Freud's Vienna.* New York: Atheneum, 1988.

Wunberg, Gotthart. *Das Junge Wien: Österreichische Literatur und Kunst Kritik, 1887–1902.* Tübingen: Niemeyer, 1976.

Yates, W. E. *Schnitzler, Hofmannsthal and the Austrian Theater.* New Haven and London: Yale University Press, 1992.

Young-Bruehl, Elisabeth. *Anna Freud: A Biography.* London: Papermac, 1988, 1992.

Zohn, Harry. *"Ich bin ein Sohn der deutschen Sprache nur . . ." Jüdisches Erbe in der österreichischen Literatur.* Vienna: Amalthea Verlag, 1986.

Index

The letter *f* following a page number denotes a figure.

Ark of the Covenant, 114
Aryans, 78, 145, 177
Ascher, Franzi, 106
Asings, 144
assimilation, 1, 22, 36, 37, 39, 40, 43,
58, 59, 80, 84, 87, 93; advocated by
Kaiser in *Neu-Jerusalem*, 213–214,
215; associated with bourgeois
snobbery in Schnitzler's work,
205; blamed for higher Jewish rate
of neurosyphilis by Zollschan,
174; critiqued in Herzl's *Das Neue
Ghetto* and *Altneuland*, 125–126;
identified with "degeneration" in
Jewish women, 136; identified with
Women's Movement, 104; linked
to increased anti-Semitism against
Jewish women by Feiwel, 135–136;
linked to sexual repression, 164;
opposition by Rosa Pomeranz, 114;
relation to psychoanalysis, 147,
188, 190–191, 194; role in estrang-
ing women from Zionism, 119
Association Law of 1867, 97
atheism, 19
Austrian Communist Party (KPDÖ),
102–104
Austrian Republic, 97
Austrian Social Democracy, 160
Ave Maria, 19
Avenarius, Richard, 175

Baader, Benjamin Maria, 28
Bader, Lillian, 18, 92
Baer-Issachar, Marta (Martha Baer), 112
Bahr, Hermann, 203, 205
Barber, Ida, 106
Barber, Ida Punitzer, 182–185
bar mitzvah, 25, 28, 29, 31, 54
Bartsch, Hans, 21
Baskin, Judith, 235n100
Bauer, Ida (Dora), 153, 154, 159–162,
250n70

Bauer, Jacob, 59
Bauer, Otto, 101
Baum, Vicki, 182
Baumann, Ida, 100
Beamtentöchter-Lyzeum (Officials'
daughters' school), 20, 22
Beck, Amalie, 52
Beer-Hofmann, Naemah, 56f
Beer-Hofmann, Richard, 2, 185, 203,
214
Beller, Steven, 143
Ben Azzai, Simeon, 83
benediction "thanking God for not
making one a woman," 76–77, 195
Benedikt, Clothilde, 50
Benedikt, Minnie, 207
Benedikt, Moritz, 50, 170–171, 179
Berhrend, Charlotte, 49
Berkowitz, Michael, 121
Berlin, 29, 90
Berliner, Gertrude, 37
Bernays, Jacob, 68
Bernfeld, Siegfried, 151
Beruria, 68–69, 195
Beruria, 44–45, 57, 83
Beth Hamidrash, 73, 194
Bettelheim, Gottlieb, 50
Beyond the Pleasure Principle (Sig-
mund Freud), 150
Biale, David, 121
biblical dramas, 213
Biederman, J., 47
Biedermann, Charlotte, 47
Bielohlawek, Hermann, 22
Bikur Chaulim (visitation of the sick),
43, 54–55, 57
Bildung, 89, 213, 215
Billroth, Theodor, 146
bisexuality, female, 154, 159–160,
162–163, 175–176
Bloch, Joseph Samuel, 5, 46, 58, 59,
100, 143; examination of anti-
Semitism in *Israel and the Na-*

Freehof, Solomon B., 28
Freidenreich, Harriet Pass, 92–94,
147–148
Freies Blatt, 23
Freistadt, Gisela, 206
Frenssen, Gustav, 20
Frenzel, Elisabeth, 212, 213
Freud, Anna, 147, 151, 154
Freud, Esti, 12–13, 39
Freud, Sigmund, 1, 2, 100, 168; admission of first women into psychoanalytic practice by, 149; admission that anti-Semitism blocked the acceptance of psychoanalysis, 154–155; belief in "common mental construction" in male and female Jews, 153; changes in theory of femininity in later years, 162–163; "A Child Is Being Beaten" (1919), 163; concealment of Jewish identity of "Anna O" and "Dora," 152–153, 155, 250n70; conflation of Jewish and non-Jewish women patients, 153; desire to "universalize" human experience, 153, 154, 155; disciples of, 164–166; effect of anti-Semitic stereotypes on, 153, 155; effects of "scientific" medical and racial theories on, 153; equation of Jewish women with all women, 146–147; explores bisexuality of women, 154, 159–160; failure to recognize anti–Semitism as a factor in Jewish women's mental problems, 161; failure to understand female sexuality, 141; "Fragment of an Analysis of a Case of Hysteria" (1905), 153; *Interpretation of Dreams*, 149, 157–159; reputation as being obsessed with sexuality, 204; *Studies in Hysteria*, 155–157; *Three Essays on the Theory of Sexuality* (1905), 162–163

Freund Fritz (*Friend Fritz*, P. Suardon), 212
Freundlich, Elisabeth, 18, 106, 220
Friedländer, Moritz, 79, 81
Friedländer-Delia, Anna, 49
Friedmann, Meir (*Ish Shalom*), 31–32
Furst, Ulrich R., 12
Furtmüller, Aline Klatschko, 14, 101, 106

Galicia, 10, 14, 24, 37, 81, 88, 101, 102; ethnic conflict in, 188, 190, 213; Jewish life depicted in Pomeranz's *Im Land der Not*, 114; prejudice against Jewish medical students from, 146
galut (exile), 137
Gamaliel, Rabban, II, 69, 83
Geehr, Richard, 143
Geiringer-Mises, Hilda, 90
Geist und Judentum (Arthur Trebitsch), 177–178
gender, suppression of distinction, 146, 152
gender roles: Adolf Jellinek's attitudes toward, 65; idealization of women of the past versus modern women, 58–59, 80–81; negative stereotypes in Schnitzler's memoirs, 216; perceived violation of by intellectual Jewish women, 211; reinforcement by Austrian education system, 12; role of psychoanalysis as a method of confronting, 147; threat of women's movement to, 105–106; Zionist attitudes toward, 109–110, 113, 119–121, 138
gender stereotypes: effect on psychoanalysis, 141; in fin de siècle Viennese society, 138–139; among Viennese Jewish physicians, 174
German Association of Orientalists, 74–75

Geschichte des Erziehungswesen (Moritz Güdemann), 68–71

Ghettogeschichte (Ghetto tales), 186–203; characteristics of, 186; enlightenment versus traditional customs in, 216; portrayal of Jewish family life in Herzl's *Das Neue Ghetto*, 125; role of female protagonists in, 216; use of female characters to lead men back toward tradition, 216; work of Karl Emil Franzos, 188–190; work of Leopold Kompert, 186–188

ghetto mentality, 243n45

Gilman, Sander, 141, 145, 153, 155, 159, 161, 248n48, 249n50

glaucoma, 172

Glückel of Hameln, 132, 195, 244n67

Goetzl, Franziska, 47

Goldhammer, Leopold, 79, 80–81

Goldmann, Salka, 16, 106

Gomperz, Mina, 49

Gomperz, Theodor, 89

Gottheil, Emma, 118

Graetz, Heinrich, 34, 68

Grillparzer, Franz, 212, 259n113

Grossberg, Mimi, 19, 106

Grünfeld, Max, 185; cautionary tales in favor of tradition, 194–195; "How Reb Ahron Missed an Important Historical Moment," 195–196

Grunwald, Max, 44–45, 57, 84, 104

Güdemann, Moritz, 5, 48, 49–50, 57, 58, 59, 80; on education of Jewish girls, 68–69; *Geschichte des Erziehungswesen*, 67–69; historical approach to women's role in Judaism, 68, 235n100; on Jewish women's love of luxury and jewelry, 71–72; on learned Jewish women, 71–72; on marriage and children, 69; on modesty and marital relations, 71; as a scholar of Jewish history, 67–70; on social position of women in Mishnaic and Talmudic times, 69–70; stricter interpretation of Jewish law by, 67; study of Jewish education in France and Germany, 70–71; on women's prayer limited to the vernacular, 71; writings as apologetics, 234n85

Gutmann, Ida, 49

Gutmann, Sophie, 49

Gutmann, Wilhelm Ritter von, 31

Gutzkow, Karl, 212

Gymnasiale Mädchenschule, 13

Gymnasium, 12, 13, 20, 26, 89, 91, 102

Hainisch, Marianne Perger, 16, 96

hair, long: as act of defiance, 189; as expression of "enlightened" values, 192; in fiction of Eduard Kulke, 192–193

Hamerling, Robert, 185

Hanák, Péter, 219

Handelsakademie für Mädchen (Business Academy for Girls), 14

Hanukkah, 53, 55

Hebbel, Friedrich, 212

Hebrew: forgetting of language by "Anna O.," 157; in *Jüdenclassen*, 17–18, 22, 25; prayers in the women's *Beruria* prayer book, 45; study of, among girls in Palestine, 119; use in girls' confirmations, 32–34

Heilige Skarabäus, Der (Else Kotányi Jerusalem), 100

Heindl, Waltraud, 89

Heinemann, Jeremiah, 28

Heit, Charlotte, 206

Heldings, 144

Herdlicka, Theodor (Theodor Taube), 145

intermarriage, 80; prohibition of, linked to inbreeding and mental illness by Krafft-Ebing, 169; rejected by Kaiser in *Neu-Jerusalem*, 213; role in ghetto stories, 186–187, 189–190

International Communist Youth, 103

International Socialist Congress (1907), 99

Interpretation of Dreams, The (Sigmund Freud), 149, 157–159

ish/isha, 80

Israel and the Nations (Joseph Samuel Bloch) 73, 75–77

Israel in Floribus (J. Biederman), 47

Israelitische Blindeninstitut (Israelite Institute for the Blind), 191

Israelitische Kultusgemeinde Wien, (Vienna Jewish Community), 32, 34, 54, 55

Israelitische Mädchen-Waisenhaus in Wien (Israelite Home for Orphaned Girls), 46, 49, 57

Israelitischen Frauen-Wohltätigkeits-Verein des VIII. Bezirkes in Wien (Israelite Women's Charity Society of the 8th District in Vienna), 46, 52

Israelitischer Frauen-Wohltätigkeits-Verein (Israelite Women's Charity Society), 46, 47–48, 55, 57

Israelitischer Frauen-Wohltätigkeitsverein Floridsdorf (Israelite Women's Charity Society, Floridsdorf), 46

Israelitisch-theologischen Lehranstalt, 79

Italy, 71–72

Ivanhoe (Sir Walter Scott), 212

Jacobi, Jolanda, 147

Jaffee, Robert, 134

Jeitteles, Fanny, 46

Jellinek, Adolf, 5, 45, 47, 49, 57, 58, 68, 71, 72, 80, 104, 186; attitudes on assimilated versus traditional Jewish women, 65–66, 205; attitudes on girls' confirmations, 30–31; on centrality of ancestry in Jewish life, rather than land, 65; on "femininity" of Jewish race, 61–63; idealization of women of the past versus present-day women, 58–59, 63–64; on Jews as mediators between West and East, 60; *Der jüdische Stamm*, 64–65; portrayal of women as lacking originality and creativity, 61; praise of Jewish women's role in charity and philanthropy, 55; view of women influenced by Comte, 60–61; on women's work, 65

Jeniel, Nathan ben, 72

Jerusalem, Else Kotányi, 100, 106

Jewish charity organizations, 44–57

Jewish men: depicted as weak and "feminized" in the Diaspora, 122–123; portrayal as feminine and unindividualized by Weininger, 176

Jewish women: assimilationist versus religious, 65–66, 84, 136, 139, 186, 197, 203; attraction to psychoanalysis among, 141; common careers available to, 105–106; convalescent home for, 50–51; criticized by Zionists for lack of interest in their race, 112, 138, 139; critique of interest in jewelry and luxury among, 62, 65–66, 71, 72, 83, 132, 138; demonization of by Arthur Trebitsch, 177–178; depiction in drama, 212–215; depiction in literature and culture, 185–186; depiction in writings of Arthur

newspapers, 144; anti-Semitism and charges of Jewish involvement with, 143–144; *Josephine Mutzenbacher: Die Lebensgeschichte einer wienerischen Dirne* (*Memoirs of a Viennese Whore*, attrib. to Felix Salten), 204

Positive Historical School of Judaism, 68

Prague, 23, 75, 97, 100

prayer, 44–45

progressive paralysis (neurosyphilis), 166, 174

Prost, Edith, 89

prostitution, 95, 100; Bloch's Parliament speech on, 78–79; Schlesinger's anti-Semitic question on, 78; Schnitzler's *Die Reigen* condemned as, 205; subject of lectures by Marta Baer-Issachar, 112; subject of study by Joseph Samuel Bloch, 58

psychoanalysis: accessibility of field to Jewish women, 148; Jewish women as patients of, 152–162; Jewish women as practitioners of, 147–151; removal of Jewish and sexual elements by Alfred Adler, 166

Psychoanalytic Congress, Second (1910), 154

Psychoanalytic Society, 149, 165

Psychopathia Sexualis (Richard von Krafft-Ebing), 169

Quittner, Franz, 103

Quittner, Genia, 102–103

race, 153–155, 166–173, 249n50

Rahel, 164

"Kinder des Randars" ("The Randar's Children," Leopold Kompert), 187–188, 255n20

Rank, Otto, 164, 165, 179

Rav, 74

Realschulen, 12

reform, religious, 59, 192

reform versus orthodoxy, Viennese approach to, 10, 29–30, 59, 60

refugees, charity for, 56

Reich, Franziska, 205, 206

Reich, Wilhelm, 102

Reichsbote, Der, 80

Reichsrat, 78

Reichstag, 195

Reigen, Die (Arthur Schnitzler), 204, 205

religious fantasies, link to schizophrenia, 150

repression, sexual, 150

Richter, Elise, 26, 89, 90f

Richter, Helene, 26

Riel, Regina, 79

Right to Love, The (Max Nordau), 124

ritual murder, 75, 77, 144

Robert, Anny, 17–18

Rohling, August, 143; anti-Semitic interpretation of Talmud by, 73–74; libel suit against Bloch, 75; on mistreatment of Jewish women, 74; on ritual murder, 75; on Talmudic marriage and morality, 74; *Der Talmudjude*, 73–75

Ronde, La (Arthur Schnitzler), 204

Rosh Hashanah, 26

Roth, Joseph, 185

Rothschild, Bettina von, 48

Rothschild Hospital, 170

Rozenblit, Marsha, 2, 3, 16, 46, 220

Russia: health and diseases of Jews in, 171–172; oppression of Jews in, 23, 117, 148

Saar, Ferdinand von, 185

Sabbath observance, 44–45, 66, 72

Sacher-Masoch, Leopold von, 185, 204

sadism, 169
salons, 15, 16, 50; disappearance of,
204; in Fritz Wittels' *Der Taufjude*,
164; stereotype of the "salon Jewess," 217; twentieth century reviv-
als of, 204
Salten, Felix, 185, 204
Schach, Miriam, 118
Schalek, Alice Therese, 106; as first
female journalist in Austria, 104,
210; satirized by Karl Kraus, 104,
210–211; subject of "Jewish nose"
caricature, 211
Scheftel, Paul, 149
scheitel (wig), 189
Scheu-Riesz, Helene, 53
Schildberger, Herminie, 117–118
Schiller, Friedrich, 97, 193
schizophrenia, 150, 166–168
Schlesinger, Joseph, 78
Schlesinger, Viktor, 97
Schlesinger-Eckstein, Therese,
97–100, 99f, 159
Schmuckkasten (jewel-case), 161
Schneider, Franz, 78
Schnitzler, Arthur, 1, 2, 21, 178, 185;
Anatol, 204; attitudes toward
women, 205, 216; *Liebelei*, 204;
as member of *Jung Wien* circle,
203; negative portrayal of Therese
Golowski by, 105; portrayal of
romantic involvement with Jewish
women, 205–206, 216; *Reigen* or
La Ronde, 204; reputation as being
obsessed with sexuality, 204; sig-
nificant Jewish female characters
portrayed by, 204
Schoenberg, Arnold, 1, 2, 14
Schönerer, Georg Ritter von, 11,
78–79, 142–143
Schopenhauer, 62, 175
Schorske, Carl, 1, 2, 142–143, 219
Schutzdamen (patron women), 49, 54

Schwarz, Adolf, 79–81, 104
Schwarz, Emil, 14
Schwarz, Olly Frankl, 14
Schwarzwald, Eugenie Nussbaum,
14–16, 15f, 106, 204
Schwarzwald Mädchen Lyzeum, 12–16,
101
*Schwarzwaldschule Realgymna-
sium*, 19
Scott, Walter, 212
Scraettlings, 144
Scribe, Eugene, 212
Seder, 39, 40
Segal, Erna, 22–23
Seitenstettengasse synagogue, 29,
30, 60
self-hatred, 62, 146, 174–178, 253n138
Sex and Character (Otto Weininger),
175–176
sexology: racial stereotypes within,
146; sexual stereotypes of Jews
within, 166–173
sexuality: abnormal, linked to religious enthusiasm by Krafft-Ebing,
169; acceptance of Freudian
views on by Jewish women in
psychoanalysis, 149; control of
within the ideology of Zionism,
122; hedonism and gratification
advanced by Wittels, 165; Jewish,
affected by intermarriage prohibition and religion, 169; Nordau's
critique of bourgeois marriage
and sexuality, 123–124; removal
of, in psychology of Alfred Adler,
166; repression of, linked to
neurosis by Freud's disciples,
164–165; reputation of Jung Wien
writers for obsession with, 204;
role of anti-Semitism in creation of
Jewish sexual stereotypes, 142–147;
stereotype of Jewish sexual perversity, 204

Milton Keynes UK
Ingram Content Group UK Ltd.
UKHW040959120924
448236UK00001B/8